"LAST OF THE TITANS"

This is a photograph of the original portrait, painted by John Clay Parker, of Chairman F. Edward Hebert of the House Armed Services Committee, which hangs in the Carl Vinson Room of the Rayburn Building at the United States Capitol.

"Last of the Titans"

The Life and Times of Congressman F. Edward Hébert of Louisiana

See P 54

by

F. EDWARD HÉBERT
with
JOHN MCMILLAN

Preface by
BASCOM N. TIMMONS
Edited by
GLENN R. CONRAD

Published by

CENTER FOR LOUISIANA STUDIES
The University of Southwestern Louisiana
Lafayette, Louisiana
1976

Library of Congress Catalog Number 76–15774

Copyright 1976 by
The F. Edward Hébert Autobiography Trust
New Orleans, Louisiana
ALL RIGHTS RESERVED

FIRST EDITION

Manufactured in the United States of America by
Moran Industries, Inc., Baton Rouge, Louisiana

This autobiography is dedicated with gratitude, devotion, and affection

To Lea, My Mother;
To Gladys, My Wife;
To Dawn, My Daughter.

. . . Hébert is the prototype of a vanishing breed, the southern conservative Democrat who is powerful, as in "the powerful chairman of the House Armed Services Committee," which he has been since 1971. He is also powerful because he has been in Congress since 1941 and has squeezed out every perquisite and prerogative due him by virtue of his seniority. In 1974 it could be said that Hébert was the Last of the Titans. He was unbending in his rightist ideology, shrewd in combat, flamboyant in style and comfortable with power. Other men in the House of Representatives still had these traits, but Hébert was the only one who possessed all of them.

—Daniel Rapoport, *Inside the House*

(Permission to use this quote granted by Follett Publishing Company, publisher of *Inside the House* by Daniel Rapoport, Copyright 1975)

TABLE OF CONTENTS

INTRODUCTION

THERE ARE THREE THINGS I said I would never do. One, if I ever left the newspaper business, I would never tell anyone I was a newspaperman once myself. Two, I would never get into an argument with a newspaper because, having been on the newspaper end, I knew it had more paper and ink than the individual who attacked it. Three, writing a book or an autobiography was out of the question. Now look what has happened.

Once I left the newspaper business, I found myself discussing or telling stories about my days as a reporter before five minutes of conversation had elapsed. It was that very thing which burned me up when I covered some big shot and the first words out of his mouth were, "I was a newspaperman once myself." He had probably written a few stories for his high school paper and wouldn't know a front page if you waved it in front of him.

My second resolution fell within less than a year after I entered Congress when I found myself in a fight with a newspaper, and of all the papers in the world, my old employer, the *New Orleans States*. I got into the damndest fight and wrote a series of letters in response to stories and editorials the paper had published. But I proved my point. They had more paper and ink than I had—and the last word.

Finally, I come to the third thing I said I would never do—write a book or an autobiography. Strike three. Originally, this book was not intended to be an autobiography, but rather a biographical account of the exploits and experiences of my life based upon the facts. I personally favored a biography because I wanted the warts and wrinkles to remain, and a biographer can criticize easier than a person writing about himself.

I have attempted in writing this book to present, as well as I know how, my life and times from my recollections, the printed record, and the statements of other persons who have known me. Therefore, I hope this book presents an objective portrait, and not a flattering touch-up job. I think that would be self-serving and accomplish nothing. On the other hand, as a former reporter—there I go again saying I was a newspaperman once myself—I think the facts speak for themselves, allowing the reader to draw his own conclusions. I have tried my best to protect the living in these factual tales by not deliberately offending anyone. It is a human book, I hope; an effort to tell about a human being and those with whom he associated.

In an undertaking such as this, many persons make significant contributions, and I want to give due recognition to them.

In John McMillan, who cooperated with me in writing this book, I discovered an individual with the zeal, enthusiasm, and determination which was needed to bring this monumental task to fruition. No one contributed more as he dug up everything he could find about my life, printed and otherwise, and always factual. I am forever indebted to John McMillan for his unselfish devotion to this book. Without him, *"Last of the Titans"* would still be only an idea, and I would have at least kept my third pledge.

Glenn R. Conrad, who in 1970 wrote *Creed of a Congressman*, a book about my philosophy in Congress, edited this manuscript. While it is a lengthy volume, it is considerably shorter than the original manuscript, which indicates the task Glenn Conrad accomplished.

I find myself immensely pleased that Bascom N. Timmons, one of the greatest newspapermen to pound a typewriter on the Washington beat, agreed to do the Preface for this book. He knew me when I was a kid reporter, and we have been close friends for nearly sixty years. I am grateful and appreciative for his contribution to my autobiography.

My special thanks, too, to many other individuals who helped to make this autobiography possible:

To Gordon, my brother, who did such a wonderful job recalling the days of our early childhood;

To Dan Rapoport, whose characterization of me in his book, *Inside the House*, was the inspiration for the title of my autobiography;

To Virginea Burguières, who runs my district office, for her encouragement, advice, and assistance;

To Lou Gehrig Burnett, my press secretary, who was the head over the shoulder in this endeavor;

To Bonnie Nelson and Patricia Gormin for their editorial advice and assistance with the manuscript;

To Patricia L. Dakin for her expert typing and proofreading;

To Thomas Sancton for his invaluable transcripts of interviews;

To Dev O'Neill, Phil Guarisco, Tony Vidacovich, Wilfred D'Aquin, Ron Hall, Jim Guillot, and Carl Gustafson for their photographic contributions;

To Ann Gwyn, William Menaray, and Connie Griffith, able librarians, who helped in gathering and locating information at Tulane University;

To Alice Huy for her orderly maintenance of my records, files, and pictures;

To John Clay Parker, the superb artist, who twice has painted portraits of me, one of which appears in this book;

To Lester Lautenschlaeger who remembered so many interesting tales of our youth and college days;

To Bob Roesler, Mel and Nona Leavitt, Phil Kelleher, Clarence Doucet, Al Spindler, David Chandler, Warren Rogers, John Reddan, Don Lewis, Claude Witze, W. Waller Young, and Clark Mollenhoff, the Pulitzer prize-winning reporter, for their journalistic contributions;

To Mary Swann, my administrative assistant, who has been with me for many years; Alma Moore, my receptionist; and Nancy Fanning, members of my personal Washington staff;

To those persons who listened to my ramblings and stories about my two careers and who without exception said, "Why don't you write a book?"; and

To Gladys, my wife, and Dawn, my daughter, who urged me to write this book and without whom, of course, none of this would have ever happened.

I realize this is not a complete list and that it is impossible to remember the numerous people who aided along the way in so many various ways. To those I have not listed, I want them to know it is an inadvertent omission on my part, and my gratitude is there nevertheless.

This autobiography is simply written in reportorial style, the only way I know how to write. I hope I have done at least a fair job of chronicling some of the highlights of my life which I think may be of interest to those who read this book.

—F. EDWARD HÉBERT

EDITOR'S NOTE

PERHAPS NO OTHER individual dead or alive knew or knows more about F. Edward Hébert and his two careers than does Bascom N. Timmons, who for sixty one years covered the nation's business as head of one of the largest, independent news syndicates in Washington.

He knew F. Edward Hébert as a high school reporter, a city editor, and cooperated with him in breaking the Louisiana Scandals. He knew him when he came to Congress as a freshman, saw him climb the ladder of seniority and success and become chairman of the powerful House Armed Services Committee. And he knew him when he finally announced his retirement from public life.

The by-line of Bascom N. Timmons appeared on page one of American newspapers from coast to coast alongside the names of every famous journalist of this century. His syndicate appeared in the *Houston Chronicle*, the *New Orleans States-Item*, *Chicago Sun-Times*, *Boston Evening Transcript*, *Philadelphia Daily News*, New York *Morning Telegraph*, *Cleveland News*, *Columbus Evening Dispatch*, *Pittsburgh Sun-Telegraph*, *Milwaukee Sentinel*, *Nashville Tennessean*, Dallas *Daily Times-Herald*, *Fort Worth Star-Telegram*, *San Antonio Express*, *Tulsa Daily World*, *Shreveport Times*, and many other leading newspapers. He also contributed to *Collier's*, *Coronet*, and other national magazines.

This premier journalist has since 1912 personally known twelve Presidents—from William Howard Taft to Gerald R. Ford. He knew and wrote about scores of eminent members of the United States Senate and House of Representatives, Supreme Court, Presidential

xv

Cabinets, distinguished ambassadors, and the highest-ranking military figures.

Bascom N. Timmons covered fifteen Presidential inaugurations and twenty-nine quadrennial Presidential nominating conventions— fifteen Democratic and fourteen Republican. At the 1940 and 1944 Democratic National Conventions, he received complimentary votes for Vice President.

He is the author of three books: *Garner of Texas*; *Charles W. Dawes: Portrait of a Statesman*; and *Jesse H. Jones, The Man and the Statesman*.

Bascom N. Timmons remains one of the most influential members of the National Press Club of which he was president in 1932 and of the exclusive Gridiron Club.

In retirement since 1973, he has graciously consented to do the Preface for *Last of the Titans*, a gesture for which the publishers of this book on the life and times of F. Edward Hébert are duly grateful and appreciative.

THE EDITOR

PREFACE

Every age has its individualists; men who stand apart from their fellowman. In the political arena they are easily visible. During much of the twentieth century, the United States Congress has been dominated by these men, Titans, exceptionally strong-willed and forceful individuals who cornered and kept power. Never tentative, but rather grandiose in manner, expansive in expression, and defiant by nature, these Titans ignored convention and made their mark, for better or worse.

In the Senate, names which come readily to mind are Lyndon Baines Johnson, Everett McKinley Dirksen, Richard Russell, "Pat" Harrison, Alben Barkley, and Barry Goldwater. Harry Truman had to become President before he entered the pantheon. There were many others who wielded power and possessed legislative skill, but their personalties and predilections prevented them from assuming the title of Titan.

To anyone who follows politics or simply collects and savors bedazzling characters, the House of Representatives is a national archives. Several of its Speakers were embodiments of Titanism: "Uncle Joe" Cannon, the crusty Republican who could be said to have started the race of larger-than-life modern congressmen; "Nick" Longworth, the Republican majority leader who became an unquestioned power as Speaker; "Cactus Jack" Garner, who went on to the vice presidency and then characterized that powerless position as "not worth a pitcher of warm spit;" Sam Rayburn, who coined the dictum "to get along, go along," and he meant with him.

Other Titans of the House could be found running their powerful committees: Carl Vinson, who served fifty-one years and ran the Armed Services Committee with an iron fist; Mendel Rivers, who succeeded him in chairmanship, temperament, and ideology; Howard Smith, who ran the Rules Committee and made the rules what he said they were; and Wilbur Mills, who was the undisputed master of the almighty Ways and Means Committee until a peeler stripped him of his power.

Most of the Titans were Southerners or Midwesterners. All climbed to power by virtue of their ability to keep being reelected. But it was more than that; many congressmen achieve congressional longevity. The ones who became Titans—*a fortiori*—were a breed apart. Only a few men were tough enough, skilled enough, vivid enough, and determined enough to earn the title of Titan. And now most of them are gone the way of the mastodon and the passenger pigeon.

As the century moved into the 1970s, a number of factors emerged to dim the distinctions among Congressional leaders. Fearing to offend anyone and trying to please everyone, they blurred into out-of-focus stick characters, totally predictable and consistently boring. By the middle of the seventies, only one man in the House of Representatives still had all the Titan traits. He defied convention and ran headlong in revolt against restrictions upon his individualism. He was subject to foibles. He was often flawed. He was hit occasionally by hubris. But he was the Last of the Titans. This is the story of that man, F. Edward Hébert of Louisiana—his life and times in his own way.

—BASCOM N. TIMMONS

"LAST OF THE TITANS"

Prometheus was one of the
Titans, a gigantic race . . .

THOMAS BULFINCH,
The Age of Fable

CHAPTER I

HARBINGERS

I WAS TALKING TO Secretary of Defense Robert S. McNamara at the White House one night, trying to make him understand what human beings are, which is something hard for him to understand. I said, "Bob, I've got to tell you this: Last week I had lunch in New Orleans. There were four of us at my table. The names may not mean anything to you. One man was a former governor of Louisiana, Dick Leche. You may remember his name. Another was Abe Shushan, a very prominent businessman in New Orleans. The third was Seymour Weiss, who owns the Roosevelt Hotel, and who is a very, very dear friend of mine. We were a foursome. The three men sitting with me all went to jail in the Louisiana Scandals. I had a hand in sending them to the federal penitentiary as a result of stories I broke when I was city editor of the *New Orleans States*. They are not only my friends; they are heavy contributors to my campaigns. I have never lost their friendship."

This attitude, which I believe is a large part of my life style, can be evidenced running throughout what has been a long and varied career, a career which has placed me among the top four men in seniority in the U.S. House of Representatives and among the top twenty of approximately 9,000 representatives who have been elected to Congress in the history of the country.

These sentiments expressed to McNamara, I took from New Orleans to the highest levels of government. Whenever called upon, I can be a dogged investigator ferreting out crime and corruption, as my record as both a newspaperman and a congressman will attest.

But, like the Creoles and Cajuns who people South Louisiana, I have always been able to let bygones be bygones; to live and let live. Therefore, I have never found it contradictory to respect and admire, for example, people like Strom Thurmond and Bella Abzug, the president of the Chamber of Commerce of the New Orleans area and the president of the local longshoreman's union, Dwight D. Eisenhower and Lyndon B. Johnson, John F. Kennedy and Richard M. Nixon. In turn, I think that this attitude toward life has earned for me the friendship and respect of my colleagues, regardless of their political philosophy. It has certainly allowed me to avoid being caught in an ideological or philosophical box.

I guess that I came by this personality through heredity and environment. I was born to Felix J. and Lea Naquin Hébert on Columbus Day, October 12, 1901, in New Orleans. While my father had a significant influence on my life, it was the dominant figure of my mother who molded my character and shaped my life. Mother came from the moderately well-to-do and considerably well-respected Naquin family of Terrebonne Parish in the heart of Acadiana, the land settled by the French-speaking refugees who fled their homeland of Nova Scotia to escape British rule and carve out a new life in the bayou swamplands and coastal marshes of Louisiana.

Her first ancestor in Louisiana, Pierre Naquin, apparently arrived in the early 1800s. Mother's father was Emile J. Naquin who was born September 16, 1838. He was a sugar boiler, a position which was in considerable demand as it was an integral part of the sugarcane economy, the financial backbone of the area. On several occasions, Grandfather Naquin traveled to Cuba to work the sugarcane season there. In addition, he was a masonry contractor and served as a deputy sheriff in Houma, where he built a large home for his family on a street bearing his name. He was a Confederate officer in the Civil War and, before he died in 1905, fathered three sons and five daughters.

My journalistic background I inherited from both sides of the family. One of mother's uncles, Anatole Naquin, was the co-owner and editor of a newspaper in Thibodaux called the *Comet*. At age 37 he was killed in a fight with a writer for a rival newspaper, O. Facquet of the *Sentinel*. The two men had an exchange of words on a street corner and Anatole whacked Facquet on the side of his head with a cane, whereupon Facquet pulled a pistol and killed Anatole on the spot. His obituary said he had "ever borne a good name, being a dignified and worthy young man."

Mother taught school in Houma prior to coming to New Orleans for her marriage. A tall, statuesque woman who wore clothes exceptionally well, she had a most imposing presence. After her death, a friend wrote to me: "Your mother had a rare gift all women would like to possess: Upon entering a room she immediately became the center of all eyes. She had poise, a keen intellect, and was very gracious. She was also far ahead of her time, a truly remarkable woman."

It was 1900 when Lea Naquin married Felix J. Hébert who was six years her junior. Dad had been born in New Orleans, but reared in Houma, not far from Thibodaux. Most of his forebears had come to Louisiana from Nova Scotia, as had Mother's; however, his maternal grandfather, Charles de la Bretonne, a controversial journalistic gadfly, arrived in New Orleans from France about 1840. While the causes he espoused may have not paralleled those of his great-grandson, I think we certainly share some characteristics, characteristics which, as they occasionally do, skip several generations until they find a harmonious home.

De la Bretonne had studied engineering at the Ecole Polytechnique and the Ecole d'Application in Paris. Why he decided to leave France is unknown, as is the background in which he developed his journalistic skills. However, in 1849, he became associated with a music magazine in New Orleans, which was dedicated to "God and the Belles," both of whom I have come to embrace with more than passing interest.

In addition to his journalistic chores, De la Bretonne wrote a history of Louisiana life, *Le Soulier Rouge* (Red Shoe), similar to James Fenimore Cooper's *Leatherstocking Tales*, a novel *Les Amours d'Hélène ou Deux Coeurs Brises* (*The Love Affair of Helene or Two Broken Hearts*), and a textbook, *Précis d'Histoire Ancienne*. He also taught history, architecture and applied mechanics at New Orleans College.

He next became editor of a newly formed newspaper, *Le Sud*, whose first edition appeared July 4, 1873. This, however, proved to be a most unfortunate alliance for De la Bretonne. The country was going through the worst tremors of Reconstruction, and *Le Sud* was billing itself as the newspaper of conciliation. General P.G.T. Beauregard, the Confederate hero from New Orleans, could see that greedy politicians and unscrupulous spectators who called themselves Republicans were staying in power by manipulating the black vote. The general, with the help of others, sought to bring blacks into the Democratic party with the idea that the unity of black and white Southerners would be sufficient to bring about the downfall of the carpetbaggers and scalawags. *Le Sud* became a zealous propaganda sheet for unification, and De la Bretonne's methods unfortunately did more to bring about diversification than unification.

Another New Orleans paper, *Le Carillon*, published a number of articles quoting various scientists to the effect that from a mental and moral standpoint, the Negro race was inferior to the white race. *Le Sud*, the voice of unification, picked up the gauntlet. Under a by-line, "A Plain Student," *Le Sud* published a series of articles which some thought to be excessively obnoxious in their praise of black intelligence. In one article, it was pointed out that the "gap" between Africans and Europeans was not as profound as was generally considered inasmuch as the Spaniards and French of the South were "mulattoes and Negroes to some extent."

This little piece of intelligence did not sit well with the Creoles of New Orleans. Newspapers were full of editorials in which the purity of the French and Spanish blood was defended, and they accused De la Bretonne publicly of writing the articles. One Alfred Roman asserted that the allegations of impure French and Spanish blood were directed against the Creoles, and thus against him. He sought retribution in a duel. De la Bretonne accepted and puckishly selected Aristide Marie, a well-educated octoroon poet, as one of his seconds. Roman's witnesses were insulted and refused to discuss the matter of honor with a colored man. De la Bretonne, to still the outcry, selected two white men to represent him, and the duel was set for September of 1873. Swords were chosen as the weapons by which honor would be defended.

Unfortunately for Roman, De la Bretonne, having grown to maturity in Paris, was familiar with the use of the épée. He wounded Roman twice before the duel was halted. The outcry continued, however, and a short time later, De la Bretonne, estranged from New Orleans society, was compelled to leave the city. He died in 1876. He was a real loser, but he must have been a very courageous man to stand up for those things. He was always fighting the cause of the underdog.

The family apparently overcame the slings and arrows of outrageous fortune, for one of the journalist's sons went on to become a judge, and another sat on a local school board. A daughter married the proprietor of a plantation store, and one of their offspring married Lea Naquin.

While it could prove lucrative, a lifetime running the family's store was not for Felix Hébert. He had seen the streetcars traversing the city's major thoroughfares. To operate one of those big mechanical vehicles which transported people to and from their homes and businesses intrigued him. He went to New Orleans, impressed those who did the hiring with his neatness and good looks, and got the job.

Once situated, he returned to Houma where Lea Naquin, the woman he worshipped, was teaching school. He asked her to marry him, and she accepted. They solemnized their vows at St. John the Baptist Church in New Orleans in 1900, and set up housekeeping in a small, inexpensive dwelling at 1915 Canal Street where they began life as a contented, happy couple. Whenever Dad ate, he would turn a bottle of Lea and Perrin sauce toward him so he could gaze at his wife's name. The practice became a habit throughout his life.

Then, in 1901, I was born. Mother wanted to name me Gordon, but Dad said no; the Cajuns in the rural parishes might call me "Goddarn Hébert," which is not a bad joke or a farfetched notion, if one is familiar with the Cajun patois. As a compromise they decided on Felix Edward Hébert, and I was called Eddie. Two years later another son was born. This time Mother held out for her choice of names, and my brother was named Gordon Roy.

Dad earned the living and, for the most part, left the child rearing to Mother, a very dashing, very domineering woman, but Gordon and I worshipped Mother as much as Dad did. She ran us, and was strict as hell. It's a wonder we didn't turn out to be a couple of little fruits. She used to give us dolls, and she bought me a toy stove to play cook on. It was the damndest thing in the world. I don't know why. And, of course, she didn't like rough sports.

I guess Mother was set upon raising two gentlemen and thought such toys would civilize her boys. They didn't; and she resigned herself to rearing two hellions who played cowboys all over the neighborhood, baseball in the streets, and shot marbles in the dirt. I even used the old dirty knuckles trick to get out of piano lessons Mother had arranged at 50 cents per session. I told her I would not play piano. Sissies played the piano. Whenever the teacher would come, I'd rub my knuckles in the dirt like I'd been playing chinas. The teacher would be offended and wouldn't teach me. Mother kept a strap behind the door, and I spent more time getting spanked. But my mind was set; by God, sissies played the piano and I was no sissy. Well, I withstood the rigors of the belt as long as I could, but I was only ten years old and that strap had a way of convincing. Finally, the matriarch of the household had me playing duets with her, selections from operas and waltzes.

When I was five, shortly after President Theodore Roosevelt had patted me on the head during his visit to New Orleans, the family moved to the 1500 block of Canal Street, which was in the process of being paved. It was a great moment for the city, having the world's widest street made presentable. I remember the event vividly, including the time a skeleton of an Indian was found during the excavation. I remember the workmen took it back by our cistern to wash off the bones. There was no public water system in those days. We used a cistern to collect rainwater. It was filtered through a pumice stone to purify it. I can also remember the "honey carts" going through the streets, just stacked with barrels of sewage. They'd take it to the river and dump it in.

It was not long before the family moved across the street to 1514 Canal, an impressive two-story home which dominated the 1500 block. That was to be home during the rest of my childhood and adolescence. Known as the "Old Graffagnini Mansion," after the family who built the house, it afforded an excellent view of the 171-foot wide, recently paved street with its two lanes of traffic separated by a broad neutral ground. In our new home Mother took in roomers, but there was no board.

It was a terrifically big house. I can picture it still. Marble steps outside, and a huge staircase going up right in the center of the house. It had two great living rooms and in the rear was the dining room, the pantry, and the kitchen. The bedrooms were upstairs, and Gordon and I stayed in two at the back of the house.

Among the roomers was a teenage girl whose family had died and left her the wealthy owner of a large box factory; a typewriter salesman; and a young medical student at Tulane University. The tenant who made the biggest impression on me was Dr. Oscar Solomon, one of the pioneer oral surgeons in the United States. He had his office in two of the large rooms of the house. He was a big German with a huge mustache. I always thought he looked like Bismarck. I remember he used to call my mother ''mudder.''

Dr. Solomon was involved in politics and was a member of the Old Regulars, the machine which governed the city through its hold over the wards. Through his connections the good doctor was appointed physician to Parish Prison. I would go over there with him as a child and watch them count the prisoners.

The doctor and Dad would discuss politics at every opportunity, and it was through these discussions that I first became aware of my father's political position as a reformer. The arguments! Oh, my God! They were terrible. Dr. Solomon was strictly a machine man. My father was a terrifically honest man. Meticulous for honesty. It was only part of his own type of religion, however: be a good man! He was born a Catholic, but never practiced his religion. Yet, there again he revealed himself; Gordon and I had better go to church on Sunday or we caught hell.

Dad died from cancer in 1926 at the age of 48. With the urging of Monsignor Joseph Greco, later bishop at Alexandria, Louisiana, he finally agreed to receive the sacraments before he succumbed. Monsignor Greco told Dad, ''You know your mother would be awfully happy if you would take the sacraments,'' and he took them. That was the most wonderful present he ever gave his mother. He received communion and when he was to be confirmed, Archbishop John W. Shaw came to our house and confirmed him. Now that was unusual, but I doubt that going to church or taking communion made him a better man. He simply did that out of respect to the suggestion his mother would have wanted it.

While there can be no doubt that Mother had the strongest influence on me, my father was not without sway. He ran for the state House of Representatives from the Third Ward. Of course he was defeated. Third Ward? He ran against the Old Regulars. He hated the Old Regulars. To his way of thinking, if you were an Old Regular, you were a thief. Machine politics to him was terrible. I wonder what he thinks now, the Old Regulars have supported me since the first day I ran for Congress. Although Dad was defeated, he received more votes in the Third Ward than John M. Parker, the reform candidate for governor, and he was proud of that.

My father was the most honest man I have ever known in my life. He was a real reformer. He backed every reform ticket. He was right in with the "Goo-Goos," the Good Government League. Those were his ideals, and he had very high ideals.

The reform group he was associated with was headed by John P. Sullivan, the national exalted grand ruler of the Elks. Sullivan was one of the greatest orators of all times. He had that big body and that booming voice, one of the real great orators in the style of Daniel Webster, Henry Clay and John C. Calhoun. Of course he reformed what suited John Sullivan. He was with Huey Long when Huey went into office, but he later broke with him. John Sullivan's father-in-law was John Fitzpatrick, a former mayor of New Orleans and a fight referee. John Fitzpatrick refereed the Sullivan-Kilrane fight over in Mississippi.

I'd go over to the Elks home with my father, who was a big Elk. I'd sit there and talk to Captain Fitzpatrick. I met John Sullivan there. He got me to make my first public speech. I was fifteen years old. I would stand in the streetcars and make a pitch for people to buy war bonds during World War I. I'd stand in front of the car and tell the people,

"Your country needs your help," and all that kind of stuff. Then I'd get off and talk to the people riding the next car that came by. I had no inhibitions about the task. I liked the attention and believed in the product I was selling. I think my father, who drove one of those streetcars, was proud of his son.

Dad conducted his job like he did his life, with attention to duty and honesty. He'd start at four in the morning, keeping his watch in front of him so as to be on schedule. When I was learning to type in the seventh grade, he got me to type a time schedule on a card for him and he would set this up in front of him to make sure he was on time. I still have that watch and I'll never forget the part it played in his life. Gordon and I would take turns delivering coffee and sandwiches to Dad as the streetcar arrived at the nearest approach to our home.

Felix Hébert's honesty and diligence eventually paid off, for he was promoted to a supervisory capacity. Whenever young men from the rural parishes came to the city seeking work, Dad, remembering his own odyssey to the metropolis, would intercede for them. But his temperament was not suited for the job of supervisor. He could not stand the idea of hurting anyone. Once, he caught a conductor stealing but wouldn't turn him in. He couldn't do that. He never could do anything like that. Instead he gave up the job and went back to being a motorman.

Dad survived a streetcar strike, which was mainly over safety and working conditions—the enclosing of the cab in which the motormen sat and the placing of fenders on the cars. But when the union went out a second time, he did not go back, although he kept paying his union dues. Old union men always continued to pay their dues, and when he died we got insurance from the union. It helped bury him.

During that second strike, my father took a job as city laundry inspector, and his principles carried over to that position. He would drive a little Ford provided by the city. Did any of his family ride in that Ford? Not a chance in the world. It was "city property," and was to be used only when he was on duty, inspecting. As a new inspector he proved to be a surprise to some of the city's laundry owners. On one of his first days he walked into a laundry and the proprietor handed him a slip of paper while pushing some money toward him. "I didn't come here to collect money," my father replied. "I came to inspect your laundry."

"What do you mean?" the proprietor asked. "It's been this way for. . . ."

"It's not that way anymore," Dad cut him off.

On one occasion a Chinese laundryman owed the city a sum of money, and Dad made the collection. That night at home, he discovered he had overcharged the man one dollar. He immediately got up from his chair and drove to the man's home to return the dollar. That was the basic difference between Dad and me. I would have invested that dollar, made a couple of bucks on it and then paid the guy back.

My father got all of one hundred and twenty-five dollars a month for that job. That was my father, a good man who never harmed anyone.

My mother also had an incalculable effect on my life. When I went to Congress I wrote her every day regardless of the circumstances or the locale. I've never hidden my love for my mother. On Mother's Day, 1948, I taped a radio address, ostensibly to my constituents, but actually it was directed to Mother. I quoted Lincoln and Adams referring to their mothers, cited actions by Roosevelt and Truman regarding their mothers, and, in this 1948 address, I continued with a passage which would get support from a modern-day women's lobby not necessarily noted for its rapport with me: "From the beginning of time itself, the symbol of 'Mother' has withstood the ravages of the ages, and has held out hope, even to those men and to those nations—because, after all, nations are but combinations of men— who have floundered in the abyss of despair."

Despite this sentimental paean of a mature man, I did on occasion displease her. I guess I possessed too much energy and too great a love of the good life to become a "momma's boy." Therefore, I could tease her and I could deceive her, even though I truly loved her. On my tenth birthday, for example, I told Mother that it was a school holiday on account of it being Columbus Day. Naturally, there was no holiday. We had to go to school that day, but Mother took my word that it was a holiday. There was a problem, however; I wasn't going to be able to get back into school without a note from Mother. I was in a hell of a fix. So, I got Gordon to play school with me. I was the teacher and Gordon was in my class, and I said, "Gordon, you have been absent. You go to your mother and get a note and tell your mother to ask the teacher to please excuse you because she kept you home. You bring that note back to me if you want to get in class." Mother was busy talking to someone and was pleased that we were playing so nicely. We were nice children; I was playing with my brother, teaching him school. Mother wrote, "Please excuse my children for being absent." I grabbed that damn note and took it to school the next day and got back in.

When Gordon and I set off to school, we were always neatly dressed. Mother sewed all of our clothes. In our first years at school she dressed us in the style that was *à la rigueur* for the well-dressed young man of the day—Little Lord Fauntleroy. Of course such clothes had an effect opposite to that desired by our mother. We did not remain neat and proper, for we would not forego the rough games at recess. Moreover, the other kids would tease us, and this, of course, we could not abide, and ended up on the ground grappling with our tormentors. It was a classic case of male hormones overcoming the will of the parent, like the preacher's son who proves his manhood by becoming the wildest kid in school.

Mother thought it was horrible that her boys were teased because they were neatly dressed, and she wrote a note to the principal about it. Word of her note leaked out, and the result was more fights. Mother was intelligent enough to eventually realize that the two boys she had on her hands were not candidates for Miss Amanda's Finishing School for Effete Gentlemen. While still maintaining an interest in her sons, she loosened the reins. She had to. She had no choice.

In 1945, during my fifth year in Congress, I took three congressional colleagues home to visit. After dinner, Mother, then a 73-year-old grande dame of the Old South, whispered to me that she thought I had such nice friends.

"Yes," I replied, "they're nice fellows—for Republicans."

"I don't want you to talk that way, even in fun," she replied with a seriousness which was understandable, considering she had grown to adulthood during Reconstruction. But when I told her I was not joking, she asked, "Eddie, you don't mean to tell me you talk to Republicans?"

I was never blind to Mother's character, and I found it interesting. Mother was domineering as hell. I can just imagine her as a schoolteacher. I'll bet she had discipline in that class like nobody had discipline. She was also attractive. They tell me the men used to go to church in Houma to see Miss Lea take up the collection, to see what kind of new clothes she would be wearing. Miss Lea would prance up the aisle and every eye would be on her. She could really wear clothes.

A close friend from my college and newspaper days, Alma Richards, who with her husband, ran the Broadway Pharmacy, a hangout for Tulane students and alumni, told me once: "Eddie, your sense of humor comes from your mother. She had that twinkle you have. She also had the most beautiful head of white curly hair. She knew you, Eddie. She was aware you weren't just out saying your prayers."

In all of this discussion about the family I should point out that one of my prime concerns is the pronunciation of my surname. It is, of course, pronounced, "A-Bear," but on first glance most people pronounce it "Hee-burt." Maybe they don't see the accent. At any rate, when Lionel Hébert, one of the famous golfing brothers from Lafayette, Louisiana, won the PGA championship, I sent him a wire: "You have done more for the name Hébert in 18 holes of golf than I have in 18 years in Congress."

Few people know that I was preceded in Congress by another Felix Edward Hebert, a senator from Rhode Island who was Herbert Hoover's floor leader. Known as Felix, he pronounced his name "Hee-burt," and spoke French fluently. When I (called Eddie by my friends) was elected to Congress I affected the accent over the "e" to make certain of the French pronunciation, "A-Bear." I insist on the accent and the French pronunciation, but I can't speak a damn word of French.

CHAPTER II

D. O. '24

MY PARENTS DECIDED I should have a private Catholic education, and in 1908 I entered St. Joseph Parochial School. I remained there for two years and then my parents transferred me to a public school, McDonogh 17, named after the miserly recluse, John McDonogh, who had surprised the city by leaving his considerable fortune to the school children of New Orleans.

At McDonogh, my teacher was Miss Felicie Pollet, an attractive 16-year-old Cajun girl fresh out of the bayou country. It was her first class, and she was my first crush. She was the prettiest thing I had ever seen in my life. Saucer eyes, a real buxom French gal. She wore a white shirtwaist and blue serge skirts.

I was a hellion. But I also knew I was her pet, there was no doubt about it. One day I threw a harmonica at her. I didn't want to hit her; I really threw it at her desk. It scared the hell out of her and she cried and called my mother. She said she couldn't do anything with me and all that sort of stuff. But Miss Pollet got over it, for she gave me the lead in the third-grade play, *Little Redwing*. They put me in a little Indian outfit with a little shirt, feathers in a headband, and I carried a hatchet. It was the damndest thing you ever saw in your life.

The affection between student and teacher blossomed, and when—to solve some administrative details at the school—the principal transferred some students, including me, to another class, I refused to go. For a week I did not return to school. Monday morning of the second week I came in about ten. I had gone to school with Mother, and she told the principal, "Eddie should be in Miss Pollet's room. That is where he belongs.'' The principal agreed. But it had taken considerable maneuvering on my part.

It was while I was in Miss Pollet's third-grade class that an incident occurred which has had a marked effect on my life, although I have seldom acknowledged the fact. Still, it is impossible to ignore its importance and the subliminal motivation it has produced. I was playing at the home of my cousin, Sidney Rideau, where I often spent weekends. I was not to spend the night because it was the middle of the week; I was to go home. But I crossed the street and used the telephone at the old Faust Hotel to ask my mother if I could stay. She said yes, and I went back to Sid's.

Sidney and a neighborhood friend, Louis Werner, and I had been playing with a .22 caliber rifle which belonged to Sidney's father. Sidney's mother had taken it away, forbidding us to touch it. But when I returned with the news that I could spend the night, we decided to sneak the gun out of the pantry where my aunt had locked it. We climbed through a window in the pantry and retrieved the rifle and three bullets. We took it in the backyard, and before I realized what had happened, I had almost killed my cousin. I was going to shoot a tin can, and the thing went off. It had a hair trigger, and he ducked out of the way just in time. My shot had hit the can. I handed the rifle to Louis as I ran to examine my marksmanship. I turned around, saw a bird on a chimney of a house next door, and said, "I'll bet you can't hit that bird."

Louis said, "I bet I can hit that bird!" But it was me! He shot me. He didn't mean to, of course, it was just that hair trigger.

The bullet struck my temple near the left eye. It was like a prick, but no pain. I threw my hand over my eye and ran to the house yelling, "I'm shot!" My uncle was home. He was a tough guy, and he said he was going to take me to the hospital. I said, "You're not gonna take me to the hospital. You call my mother, and when my mother comes, I'll go." But my uncle called an ambulance. It took about five men to put me in that ambulance. I was hitting them, kicking them, scratching them, everything in the world. I'll never forget that ride. I sat in the back and looked out.

By the time we got to the hospital, Mother, Dad and Gordon were there. Gordon had been to a Canal Street theater watching one of the old fight films. I remember asking him how he liked the fight as they took me into Charity Hospital. The doctors decided not to take the bullet out of my head. The optic nerve had been cut, and they decided no good would be served by removing the bullet. The eye was intact except for the optic nerve. The eye functioned except I couldn't see out of it.

In two weeks I was out of the hospital, and I came to accept the loss of my left eye as a fact of life. My teacher, Miss Pollet, kept expecting me to suffer from headaches, but I never had any ill effects from it at all. No headaches, nothing like that, and I accepted it the same way I accept it now. That is, it didn't concern me.

Mother, however, would not accept the fact that I had permanently lost sight in one eye. She always had the great idea that one day I'd miraculously see again. She and St. Lucy (the patron saint of the sightless) used to go together. Every quack doctor who'd come to town, she'd want me to go see him. One day a Brother Isaiah came to town. He was supposed to be curing people with the waters of the Mississippi. She wanted to take me down there and let him put his hands on me. All that foolishness. I wouldn't go; I told her it was foolish.

After the loss of the eye, organized sports were out for me and I had to seek accomplishment in other areas. I had a talent for talking; I only had to channel it into a constructive endeavor. In the seventh grade I found someone to guide me in the person of Sister Mary Joseph. But I still had a summer ahead of me after finishing the sixth grade at McDonogh before facing that disciplinarian.

I was invited to visit mother's sister, Alice Naquin Gagne, in New Rochelle, New York. She was the wife of Sidney Gagne, a state representative from Terrebonne Parish who had been a participant in the fight to rid Louisiana of the notorious lottery. The couple had one son, Nolan, a handsome, talented and precocious child. A verbal prodigy, Nolan was on the local stage at age five. His father died when he was seven, and his mother made her son the focal point of her life. She took him to New Orleans where she placed him in the care of the Jesuit fathers for several years. Under their tutelage ''his talent for elocution and acting became noticeable, and in school plays he always won praise for his work,'' as one Terrebonne newspaper put it.

By the time he was eleven, his mother had him acting in Chicago vaudeville, ''but this class of acting did not suit his taste and soon after he left for New York where he secured a position with a leading Broadway company which was then playing *Rags to Riches*, in which he took the lead role,'' the paper said.

You know that was bold; my aunt walking into New York City and putting that boy on the stage. She was a real stage mother. She was going to make a star out of him. She was a very industrious woman and developed a hair dressing to which she gave her name, Madam Gagne. She also taught knitting and things like that.

Somewhere between New Orleans and New York, Gagne had become Gane, which was Nolan's stage name. While he was starring in *Rags to Riches* his mother also enrolled him in Jesuit College in New York. There he won that institution's gold medal for elocution. Meanwhile he went on to star in a number of other Broadway productions, among them, *Billy the Kid, The Great Divide, Ninety and Nine, Forty-five minutes from Broadway,* and *Madame X.*

He created the role of Raymond Florio in *Madame X.* That is probably one of the greatest juvenile parts ever written for the American stage. Almost everyone knows the story—the absinthe-addicted woman, and the climax of the play comes when this boy defends this woman not knowing she's his mother. It is a great dramatic role.

Nolan Gane was a terrifically handsome man. Perhaps sensing he was photogenic, Nolan transferred his talents from the stage to film. It was 1914 and the cinema was in its infancy; New Rochelle was its cradle. Madame Gagne and her son took up residence at 74 Main Street there.

I remember going up there in 1914. It was the year the war broke out, the year before *The Birth of a Nation*. D. W. Griffith was making *Birth of a Nation* during this time, but the first big spectacular on the screen was *Cabrina*. It was about some Roman hero. Up until that time there were only two reelers. There was no Hollywood then.

In New Rochelle, the big motion picture company was Thanhouser Company, and they had a subsidiary, a smaller company called

Princess Company. Well, Nolan was the juvenile lead, but he also wrote screenplays. He wrote, directed, and acted. He wrote the first dog picture, *Shep*. It was the forerunner of Rin Tin Tin and the Lassie films.

I accompanied my aunt to New Rochelle by train. I remember everytime the train stopped I would get off and put my feet on the ground and write in my notebook that I'd been to that city. All I did was step off the train. I'll never forget seeing the Washington Monument from the window of the train. That impressed me.

New Rochelle of 1914 was a sleepy little town, but the flickers brought excitement to the community. I used to hang around the studio. James Cruze was there, the top banana at the studio, the leading man. He was married to Marguerite Snow. He later became famous as the director of *The Covered Wagon*. I had the run of the studio and would come and go as I pleased.

The Fairbanks twins, who later became *Ziegfeld Follies* stars, were there. At that time they were just about my age. One day the Fairbanks twins were walking down the street and I was fooling around in Nolan's Hudson automobile. It was the damndest thing you've ever seen in your life. Rumble seat. It was really something, and I was in the car, playing with it, goggle-eyed, looking at the speedometer and the other instruments. The twins came by and got in. We were parked in front of the house on top of a hill. Being the little brat that I was, I was going to show off, and I released the brake and we went down that hill. I couldn't steer the car so I just held on until we hit the sidewalk. Nolan had to come and retrieve his car.

Having been in *Little Redwing*, show business was naturally nothing new to me when I arrived in New Rochelle. Indeed, I had also written, directed, and acted in my own production on a stage Gordon and I had built. We erected the stage in our backyard, actually built a stage. It was against the side of a fence. I got some planks and built this stage with wings and dressing rooms. We got an old sheet and made a curtain out of it that would roll up and down.

I wrote a play, "The True Friend of the Western Cowboy," a three-act play. I got Gordon to play in it, and some kids in the neighborhood took parts. I had the lead. I'll never forget the plot. An

Indian stole a boy from his father, the Western Cowboy. Then at the end, the Indian returned the child. My closing line was: "You are a true friend of the Western Cowboy."

I guess that was the ham coming out in me. It was coming out and at the time I didn't even know there was ham in me; but I guess I've been a ham since I was a little kid. I love performing, and that's what being in Congress is all about, in a sense. Washington is your stage; the whole damn world is your audience. And a congressman, if he's candid, is really a ham actor.

I made my first dollar in New Rochelle. Thanhouser was making a series of films to follow up the success of *Million Dollar Mystery*. One was *The Undertow of Fate*, starring James Cruze and Marguerite Snow. They needed four altar boys for a wedding scene. I got the part. I got one dollar as an extra. I still have that dollar. I have it framed in my Washington office.

I was also in another picture, *Her Big Brother*, and almost drowned. We were in a swimming scene. A bunch of kids swimming off a platform. I went down twice. One of the grips pulled me out.

At the end of August, I returned to New Orleans to attend St. Joseph School. It was the last time I saw my cousin, Nolan Gane, alive. The following February he died. He was directing a picture in the snow and caught cold, which developed into pneumonia and he died. He was twenty-three years old, and having outgrown juvenile roles, Nolan was at the height of his directing career. He would have had a tremendous career with his talent and good looks. The women sure chased him. He'd stumble over them. I remember one night in New Rochelle we came home and some broad was waiting in the darkness for him. Boy, my aunt gave her hell.

Nolan, in addition to being my cousin, was also my godfather. His body was brought from New Rochelle to lie in state in New Orleans at the Hébert home. I remember when they brought him to my house on Canal Street. It was on Mardi Gras. Then they took him to Houma for the burial. The newsreel cameramen filmed it. It was a big event in those days. The papers were full of stories about the young actor and director who was laid to rest at a time when his future was "aglow with the fire of hope and reward."

When I returned to New Orleans in 1914, Mother enrolled Gordon and me in St. Joseph's. Sister Mary Joseph, who taught us in the sixth, seventh and eighth grades, had promised Mother that if I attended St. Joseph's she would get me a scholarship to Jesuit High School, then known as Jesuit College.

It was at St. Joseph School that I engaged in two undertakings which would figure prominently in my future. One turned out to be partially successful; the other was a complete success. The first effort was my initial journalistic adventure. I tried to put out a newspaper at St. Joseph's. I wouldn't say I made up the pages, because I didn't know the term "make up." But the outline, how I laid it out and all, I couldn't do a better job now than I did then. The trouble was I couldn't find the nine dollars needed to print the paper. I went over to a printer and got a price and all, but I just couldn't get the nine bucks. I wrote and laid out the paper because I wanted to do it, just to create something.

Sister Mary Joseph was always able to keep her young charges in line. She was a sturdy, medium-sized Canadian, who was a member of the Daughters of Charity. Her brother was a Jesuit priest who had been an army chaplain under General John J. Pershing when the general was leading his troops into Mexico after Pancho Villa. Militarism must have run in her family for Sister Mary Joseph, whom we called "T-May Joe," developed what was considered the finest uniformed cadet corps in the city, complete with drum and fife bugle corps. I can only characterize her as stern and demanding, but a woman who nevertheless held the affection of her students.

I was Sister Mary Joseph's pet. As far as she was concerned, I could do no wrong, but Gordon could do no right. She would say, "Gordon Hébert, before you're twenty-one you're going to die on the gallows." When Gordon got to be twenty-one, he remarked, "I wish I knew where Sister Mary Joseph was, I'd tell her I'm twenty-one and I'm not dead yet."

Anyway, it was the good sister who launched me on my career as an elocutionist. She was one of the most terrific women in the world. She molded me. I particularly remember her dedication in coaching me to a practically flawless performance of Ella Wheeler Wilcox's

How Salvator Won. That is as dramatic a recitation as anyone could want to undertake. It opens with the classic line: "I am just a jockey but I rode out as proud as any monarch who ever sat on a throne." The piece describes a horse race. You've got that horse going and you are riding and looking around and another horse is gaining on you, and finally, when you get down to the wire, you are exhausted, but it closes, "And Salvator, Salvator, Salvator won!"

That's great stuff for a seventh-grader to recite. Then, in the eighth grade, I recited Cardinal Wolsey's farewell address. "Farewell! a long farewell, to all my greatness!" And one of the big punch lines is: "Cromwell, I charge thee, fling away ambition: By that sin fell the angels; how can man then, the image of his Maker, hope to win by it?" Now that's heavy Shakespeare. "Had I but served my God with half the zeal I served my king, he would not in mine age have left me naked to mine enemies."

Those are beautiful lines. Beautiful lines. There's the ham coming out in me again. I like the dramatic. I love it. I love poetry. I love Shakespeare. I loved these recitations. I love words. I bask in them. Sometimes I feel that I can play an audience like a violinist plays a violin. Some guys can hit a ball; some guys can sing. I happen to be able to talk. That's all. I have been able to talk since I was a kid. I can make myself understood. I can communicate. I will never forget at Jesuit one day I had written a piece and I used the phrase "an injustice to justice." What in the world could be more stupid than a phrase like that? This priest tried to correct me. I told him he knew what I meant and that anybody who heard the piece would know what it meant. I had created a phrase and I wouldn't change it. I've always loved the music of Shakespearean prose. It is wonderful. I love to present it.

Perhaps Sister Mary Joseph recognized this ability in me for she had her heart set on me going to Cape Girardeau to become a priest in the Vincentian order. But I had other ideas, and when she realized the futility of her efforts to make me celibate, she arranged for the scholarship to Jesuit.

I was graduated first in my class from St. Joseph's, and my best friend, Gernon Brown, was second. We both entered Jesuit in the fall of 1916. We had become good friends in school and we both liked oratory. But I got a jump on Gernon by becoming an usher at the Tulane Theater where I could observe some of the greats of the day perform.

I went down and got myself a job from Colonel Thomas C. Campbell. He had quite a career as one of the great showmen around New Orleans. He built the Tulane and the Crescent theaters. Later, I recounted the colonel's career when I ghosted his memoirs.

I got fifty cents a performance for being an usher. I would get off from school every Wednesday afternoon to usher at the matinee. The interesting thing is the caliber of boys who ushered. My cousin, Sidney Rideau, was there; and Tommy Ryan, who later won the Medal of Honor for heroism in the Japanese earthquake, and became an admiral; another was Billy Porteous who became a prominent attorney; and John Burns, who became the United States Marshal of San Juan.

The old colonel called us his army. He would line us up at the end of the week and pay each of us three dollars and fifty cents. We worked seven performances for fifty cents a performance.

There were great stars in those days—John Drew, for example. I enjoyed talent like that. It helped me, too. I'd remember what they did and how they did it. I'd try to use their technique.

Ever since "The True Friend of the Western Cowboy," curtain lines, or the dramatic closing, have held a fascination for me. One which has always lingered is from *The Garden of Allah*, and comes at a most dramatic moment. When the fallen monk stands erect and raises his eyes toward heaven and exclaims: "Mea culpa, mea culpa, mea maxima culpa!"; and the curtain drops.

Another great line I remember was when Mrs. Leslie Carter was starring in *The Shanghai Gesture*. She had an unforgettable line: "My name is Mother Goddam, and my trade is flesh."

These classic lines which mesmerized me were not just words learned by rote. I understood what I heard, what I read, and what I recited. Moreover, I have been an avid reader since childhood. As a child I hated everything in the North. The religion of maturity is the religion one is born into. Nine out of ten people don't know any better. They're taught that. And naturally those of us in the South were influenced by what we were taught. As I said, I hated everything about the North. Then I read *The Sins of the Father* and changed my opinion—*The Leopard's Spots*, . . . all of Thomas Dixon's novels.

I came to understand that Lincoln was a great man, a great man. I think the Dixon novels are all good. They are not among the great literary classics of the world, far from that, but those novels really painted a vivid picture. They gave me an insight into other people's thinking, too. I now began to understand certain things. I also was greatly impressed by *The Birth of a Nation*. It was a great movie.

I think one of the finest books written about the South is *By the Dim Lamps* which deals with Reconstruction days in Louisiana. It was by Nathan Schachner, the man who wrote the story of Aaron Burr, who is probably one of the most misunderstood men in American history. Nevertheless, I have been greatly influenced by what I read, and by what I have heard.

I read every Horatio Alger book on the market. At the time, I thought they were the greatest pieces of literature I'd ever read in my life, but wasn't that a lot of foolishness. They're good reading for a child and can mold a youngster's mind. I like to see children read this type of literature because it stimulates them and implants the old idea of rags to riches, the idea they can succeed; that they don't have to lean on anybody else.

In the fall of 1916, just as I was turning fifteen, I entered Jesuit High School and, in time, came under the influence of Father James A. Greeley, S.J., a terrific man. He could sing and play the piano like nobody's business. He knew every girl that every guy in the class went with. He knew all about them. I thought he was the finest teacher we had.

At Jesuit, I continued to develop skills which would serve me well. Gernon Brown, who was to become a famous athletic coach at Jesuit, and I were both selected to join the Gold Medal Debating Team. We were the only two freshmen in the history of Jesuit to be on the Gold Medal Team. I'll never forget our first debate. We were great when we gave our fifteen-minute opening speech. Talk about two smart kids. We knew each paragraph, every period, every semicolon, every comma. But when the seniors debating against us, Harold Gaudin, who became president of Loyola University of the South, and John Zimmerman, who became a very prominent man in New Orleans, started the rebuttals, did we ever get cut to pieces! We were out of the running, those seniors cut the living hell out of us.

Nevertheless, I was the only student in the history of the school to be on the Gold Medal Debating Team four years, a feat which can be classified as a rather dubious honor. I had to go four years to win my gold medal. If I had won it earlier, I wouldn't have had to debate four years for it.

Gernon was admittedly the best elocutionist, the finest actor Jesuit ever produced; and I was recognized as the best debater. So what happens? He beats me at debating and I beat him in elocution. The elocution contests at Jesuit were arranged in categories: one for freshmen and sophomores, and another for juniors and seniors. If a student won as a freshman or as a junior, he was not allowed to compete as a sophomore or senior, and I won in both elocution categories in my first attempt.

But I took my debates seriously. I would debate more with myself after the debate was ended than I would on that stage. I would rehash the things I could have done. The things I didn't do. The things I should have done. I found myself listening to and studying good speakers. Studying their presentation. I heard some great Jesuit missionaries, and these men always intrigued me. The rabbi who used to be in New Orleans, Louis Binstock—I still use a technique I heard Binstock utter years ago. I think it is very effective. It is a repetitive phrase. Just say the most perfect phrase and repeat it; but use different adjectives each time. I think this is one of the most effective things that can be done in public speaking.

I remember as a reporter I covered a debate between St. Clair Adams, one of New Orleans' most famous attorneys, and Clarence Darrow, the great criminal lawyer. It was just like a high school debate. That is how they impressed me. They seemed so illogical in what they were doing. Binstock was much better, and I still use his technique.

One technique which did little good for me occurred when I was a senior, debating a freshman. I was flip. Here was this young kid and I was filling in for someone who didn't show up to debate him. I was throwing everything at him. He made some statement and I told him to prove it. I told him to show me the documentation. Of course I knew he didn't have the proof with him. I was outmaneuvering him. Then the damn priest stopped the debate and told the kid to go to his classroom and get his book. He put the pin in my balloon. The priest knew all along that I was pulling a fast one.

For the most part, however, I had my way at Jesuit, but not always. I faced disappointment, for example, when I was refused the lead in the play *Richelieu* by Edward Bulwer-Lytton. I was promised the role of Cardinal Richelieu, but Gernon got it after I was promised I would be able to play it. I got mad when they wouldn't give me the role and I said I wasn't going to be in the play and I wasn't going to debate either. It was my last year. Then I got a letter from Father Greeley, chewing me out. He said, "All right, don't debate. Twenty years from now they'll wonder who played Richelieu, if anybody remembers we put it on, and you won't have a debating medal. You go on and accept the role of the king, Louis XIII, and debate, and twenty years from now you'll have your debating medal." I took his advice. I've got the medal.

Throughout my speaking career, one piece in particular stands out in my mind as the most effective. The real winner was *The Progress of Madness*. It is a wild piece, a real bellringer. "He is not mad who kneels before thee." The actors go nuts on the stage, they seem to pull their hair out, they move all over the place.

When Gordon entered Jesuit, I insisted that he debate and act, despite the fact that he did not particularly care for it. Father Greeley wrote a piece for my brother called "The Tell Tale Heart" and I coached him. He didn't win. Then I gave him *The Progress of Madness*. I would practically beat his brains out coaching him. A football coach cussing out his players had nothing on me. I'd say, "Don't you have any brains? Listen to the way I'm saying it." But then all he would do was ape me. I mean he was not an elocutionist. All he did was to ape what I was telling him to do. I'd lock the door. Wouldn't let him out of the room. He couldn't get away from me.

He'd get mad and whine about it. Mother would say, "Eddie, you ought to be ashamed of yourself, the way you're treating your brother." I'd tell her, "I'm going to make him think. I'm going to make him win." And damn it, I made him win. He got the medal. Gordon said that after he won the medal, *The Progress of Madness* was barred from competition. "Anybody could win with it if I won with it," he explained.

One of the debates for which I was named best orator took place on June 16, 1916. The subject was: "Resolved: That Military Instruction in High School Should be a Compulsory Part of Education." Fifteen years old at the time, I debated, appropriately enough, the affirmative. Forty-nine years and eleven months later I would stand alongside General Wallace M. Greene, Jr., commandant of the United States Marine Corps, on the grounds of Jesuit High School as the first Junior Reserve Officers Training Corps in the nation was activated.

In the 1916 debate I argued my point, and then concluded: "What shall future America be, gentlemen? Her fate is in your hands. Shall we be defenseless America, a weak and harmless nation, or shall we be defensive America, the fear and dread of all nations?" Those few words pretty well sum up my position in the House of Representatives. While my thinking may have become more refined, the basis for it remains the same. When I was asked how my alma mater was selected to become the first school in the nation to get a Junior ROTC Marine program, I grinned broadly and said, "Say, that is a coincidence, isn't it?"

I guided the defense budget through Congress for years before I became chairman. With that undertaking came the responsibility of providing the funds to keep the United States in a position to defend itself. Whenever I heard complaints that the defense budget was too large, and I often did, I responded, "If I went to the floor of Congress with a minus budget, I'd get criticized for not being more minus."

My constituents apparently approve of my position for I have been elected to office more times than any man in the history of Louisiana—eighteen times. I think the first step toward that string of election successes was taken at Jesuit.

I am the only man in the history of Jesuit who was elected manager of the football team for three years. I was the only boy at the school who ever managed all the athletic teams: football, baseball, basketball, swimming, track, everything. I like elections. You've got the trauma of the wait. To see whether you're going to make it or not. I remember when I was first elected football manager, I was in the chapel praying while the voting was going on.

I was elected president of my third-year class, my junior class, and I was president the first half of my graduating year. I was president of the altar society for three years, and I was secretary-treasurer of the Philatelic Society. When I was a freshman, I was a cheerleader. I got into the action and would represent Jesuit in the prep league.

I even rang the angelus. That's the bell that rang at noon. I'd leave class about five minutes ahead of time so I could get down there to ring it. In truth, however, I did it just to get out of class. I also rang the bell to assemble class. I did everything but study. I would get cards and stamp them so kids could get back into class. If one had been sent to see the vice president for doing something wrong, the only way he could get back into class was with a stamp on his card. I'd give them to the guys who'd been sent down there. I had everything going.

Because I couldn't participate in sports as a result of my partial blindness, I turned my energies into boosting the teams. I even named Jesuit the Blue Jays. Our school colors were blue and white, so I picked "Blue Jay."

I organized the staff of the Blue Jay annual, the yearbook. The class of '20 put it out. We made money. We had overseas caps with the year on it for our class, and we had pins and our own stationery—all paid for with the money we made on the Blue Jay.

When the team played a game, I would make speeches at noon from the back steps of the church. Rah-rah stuff, tell them to play a good game, all that kind of stuff. We had our rallies out in the yard. It was all concrete except for the sacristy steps. They were black marble. That's where I would lead the rallies. I organized these pep meetings. I would get those guys so high they thought they were on a ladder. They were ready to kill when I finished. We'd whoop 'em up.

They were ready to go out and kill everybody. It's sort of demagogic, but it worked.

I even got the Jesuit football team a training field—at the baseball stadium used by the New Orleans Pelicans of the old Southern Association. The team and the ball park were owned by Alexander Julius Heinemann, who would become my very close friend. The team got the field gratis.

Through the use of Heinemann Park, I became acquainted with a young sports reporter for the *Times-Picayune*, Allen Dowling, whom I would meet on occasion at the ball park. At that time, football, particularly the high school variety, did not receive the sports coverage lavished upon it today. I wanted to change that. Dowling commented later, "Hébert, being always basically a promoter, basically someone seeking to achieve, to do the best he could do for the people he represented, became sort of a steady caller at the *Times-Picayune* office."

One day I went to Allen's office and announced, "I think I'm going to have quite a story for you in a few days." About a week later I returned and told Allen, "The Jesuit High School football team is going to do something that has never been done before; we are going to play two major games in three days and we're going to win both of them!"

Dowling told me later, "Of course it was a good story, and I wrote it to the best of my ability. It just happened that the next morning Bill Keefe, the sports editor, was a little short of news that ordinarily would have been given top reading. So the story of the Jesuit team, which planned to perform the iron-man stunt, made the lead story and it carried a top streamer across the sports page." After the article appeared, I phoned Allen to report that we had searched the paper for his story, that we scanned the sports page without finding it. Finally, we realized we had the top space in the *Times-Picayune* and we just didn't believe it—it was too sensational.

Unfortunately, Jesuit did not play the games, but in gratitude, I took up a collection of nickels and dimes from my schoolmates and purchased a box of cigars for Dowling. Hell, I didn't know he couldn't stand the damn things. He was a cigarette smoker.

However, the story on the Jesuit team sparked an idea. I knew the paper didn't have a prep sports reporter. I went to Bill Keefe and got myself a job covering prep sports. I wanted to get my team some action. I started all the great prep rivalries. When I went to work at the *Times-Picayune* in 1918, there weren't two hundred people at a prep game. I promoted the great rivalry between Jesuit and Warren Easton. When I got through we had five thousand people at Heinemann Park for that game.

I made five dollars a column and I was named assistant sports editor. I'd been writing all my life. I can't tell you when I started writing, and I knew sports. I wrote about three columns a week.

When I was graduated from Jesuit, under my picture in the school yearbook was inscribed my class prophecy: "Choose any office in the land and it shall be thine."

Throughout my years at Jesuit, I enjoyed the "action." I was having a hell of a good time, and I knew it. My memories of my days at Jesuit have remained fond ones, and in appreciation Gordon and I have established awards in memory of our parents. Additionally, I have established the F. Edward Hébert Award, presented each year to the outstanding Jesuit alumnus.

Upon graduation my friends and teachers at Jesuit expected me to enter Loyola University of the South when the college term began in the fall of 1920, but by then I was working nights at the *Times-Picayune* sports department. Loyola, in those days, was strictly a night school. Also, I was interested in joining a fraternity, but Loyola had none, that is, not until I organized one, Sigma Alpha Kappa, as a colony to the fraternity I joined at Tulane, Delta Sigma Phi. I wrote the ritual and everything for them.

Shortly after I entered Tulane University, Morris Duffy, a friend who had been graduated from Jesuit ahead of me, encouraged me to pledge Delta Sigma Phi. Duffy, it turned out, had motives other than just the pleasure of my company. I thought I had left my debating days behind me when I left the Jesuit fathers. However, on the day of Tulane's annual Glendy Burke Society Debating Tournament, Duffy found out to his amazement that I had not entered. He had assumed I would debate as a matter of course. When he found me, walking across the campus, Duffy was furious. "What in the hell do you mean by not entering the tournament?" he demanded.

"Aw, the hell with the debate. I'm tired of debating," I told him. Anyway, I had found that cruising the campus in my new green skull cap, talking to friends, and flirting with girls was a more enjoyable pastime.

"Why do you think I had the Delta Sigs extend you an invitation?" Duffy snapped, getting down to the nitty-gritty. "We expect something in return. What do you think you're good for? What do you think you got a pledge pin for? You better think it over, Hébert."

He really bawled the hell out of me. I told him, "Okay, you want me to enter, go put me in. I'll compete."

So that night I showed up for the debate. I brought a big book with me to make it look like I had prepared for the debate. Hell, I didn't know the subject until I got there. When I walked up to the rostrum, I threw that big book down and I went to town. I'd open the book, look at it; I used every trick in the trade.

When the verdict was in I was the winner—the first freshman in the history of Tulane University to win the debating championship. I then joined the debating team at the urging of my fraternity and that year Tulane defeated the University of Texas for the first time in seventeen years. With that victory under my belt, I was ready for the University of the South at Sewanee, a school which Tulane had not defeated in eight years. Selected to make the trip to Tennessee with me was Walter Barnett, who later became a prominent New Orleans attorney. Dr. John McBryde, the debating coach, and I had a difference of opinion over the philosophy of debate. McBryde was a wonderful old man, but we could never get along. I had been trained by the Jesuits, and I was going to present it like I had been trained. He wanted me to present my debate like a formal English essay, and I wouldn't, so we were fighting all the time. If anything is different, it is the spoken word compared to the written word. And he couldn't understand that.

Thus, prior to the Sewanee trip, McBryde and I were having our usual disagreement over the presentation of the debate. To satisfy the old man I wrote the speech, but when I got on that damn train, I tore the paper up. Poor Barnett nearly died. He said, "Are you crazy?

Have you lost your mind?'' He thought this was the most horrible thing that ever happened. I told him, "Don't worry. Just let me handle it myself. I'm away from school. I'm not on campus. I'll handle it.''

We beat our opponents two to one. Broke their streak of eight years. Unfortunately, however, the next year the University of Texas recouped, and stopped my winning streak.

At Tulane, I was busy with everything except my studies. I organized the White Elephants, an honorary freshman interfraternity council, and was chosen secretary of the Panhellenic Council. I eventually became president of the Chi Chapter of Delta Sigma Phi, and in 1938 was awarded a medal given annually to the member who has done the most for the national organization.

I also found time to put out the first sports page in the Tulane newspaper, the *Hullabaloo*. In those days the students owned the paper. At least three of them did—the editor, the managing editor, and the business manager. Usually by the end of the year the business manager had bought the other two out and was the sole owner. That trio wanted me to get in. I said I'd join the staff, but on one condition—that they cut me in. They did and gave me thirty dollars a month and two-fifths of the take. When I got in, things changed. Instead of the business manager owning the paper, I owned it with him. I became the sports editor. I'd let anybody write stories. I'd write the editorials, that's about all. I'd let them do the work and I got the money. Hell, they'd see their by-lines and it'd make them happy. At the same time I was running the sports page of the *Hullabaloo*, I was assistant sports editor of the *Times-Picayune* and campus correspondent for the *New Orleans States*.

When I entered Tulane, I had some vague notion of going to law school. At that time one year of undergraduate study was required to enter law school, thus I matriculated in the College of Arts and Sciences. I was elected president of my class. I ran against Hughes Walmsley, brother of T. Semmes Walmsley, who became mayor of New Orleans, and a fellow named Tom Arrington from Shreveport. Tom and I later became very good friends and fraternity brothers.

But the three of us, two city boys, and Tom, from the country, were running for president. When it came time to vote, Tom wanted to hold up the election because he wanted to go to the dormitory and get his votes. You don't think I was going to let him go get his votes out of the dormitory? Hell, I wasn't about to. Hughes wasn't either. I had the votes then. I wasn't going to fool around. And I became president of my freshman class.

While all of this points to the fact that I was an achiever, I think it is only fair to say that I was not especially noted for my scholarship. There were elections, fraternities, sports, journalism, dates. Studies could interfere with these pursuits if one were not careful, but I was most careful. I had a ball from the day I entered the university until the day I left. I didn't pass enough subjects to remain on the campus under ordinary conditions. I quit the math course three times in one semester—two weeks after each new math course started. Burning the candle at both ends, however, almost used up my wick.

When it came time to qualify for initiation into Delta Sigma Phi, I got caught in the switches. Of the five subjects, a student was allowed only one failing mark. I already had flunked math, so I had to pass the remaining four. I came up with three 70s and a 60. But I still had an ace up my sleeve. I went to see Dr. Edward Bechtel, the dean of the College of Arts and Sciences, a wonderful old gentleman. As I look back, I guess he had to be to put up with me. I showed him my notes and argued that to get a 60 in history with such good notes a student would have to be a dummy. He gave me the passing grade.

But I never did pass the required number of subjects the whole four years I was on campus despite the rule that if you failed you were asked to leave school. I took care of that situation by entering law school on probation. I started off by being elected president of the first-year law class, but as usual I continued to have a good time with my extracurricular activities which included my political campus buildup, which would be finalized when I became football manager.

When final examination time came I knew damned well I was trapped. I knew I wouldn't be able to pass the examinations, so I dropped out of law school. There were no rules against that or against returning the next year, which I did.

The 1922–23 term was, for me anyway, a wonderful year, socially, not scholastically. The professor of torts had my number and he knew it. When the finals came I appeared before the faculty to explain my absences. Mr. Walter Dalzell, the torts professor, said, "Mr. Hébert, you say you were sick on May 16?"

"Yes,sir," I replied righteously.

"Well, Mr. Hébert, I've got a copy of the *Times-Picayune* which indicates you covered a ball game on May 16 at Heinemann Park and reported it under your by-line."

After this procedure was repeated several times, I halted the charade and pulled my old resignation trick again in order to become the Tulane Green Wave football team manager the following year. I had been elected assistant football manager that year through my "political buildup," which led me into the inner circle of the campus political clique. It was a group of representatives from various fraternities which would meet to decide who they would support for campus office. I had them pledged to elect me assistant football manager, which they did. Then the next year I would succeed to manager and get my football letter, which is what I really wanted from Tulane.

Just in time to prevent me from having to reenter law school, Tulane instituted a school of journalism that was to open in the fall of 1923. Although I had been reporting on a major metropolitan daily since high school, I entered the department so that I could last out the football season. I got to be team manager, but before the first game I was tried for "treason." The coach, Clark Shaughnessy, was in favor of the trial. He was also in favor of immediate execution.

It all happened the night before the opening game. I was at my desk in the sports department of the *Times-Picayune* when the phone rang. It was Dr. Melvin Johnson White, faculty director of athletics at Tulane.

"I have some bad news for you, Eddie," Dr. White told me. "Cy Miske is not eligible to play." Miske had been the star end on the Green Wave team in 1922. He had, Dr. White reported, neglected to inform the Tulane athletic department that his name was not Miske, but Minsky. He also did not tell them about the little matter of his having played four years at Syracuse University before continuing his career at Tulane.

I printed the story. What else could I do? I was manager of the team, but I also was a reporter, the assistant sports editor, and I had been given an official announcement by the faculty athletic director. I couldn't do anything to change the facts or the decision. Others, however, did not quite see it that way. The next morning, after the paper came out, I was met at the door of the Tulane gymnasium by Dr. Wilbur Smith, the athletic director.

"Have you seen Shaughnessy?" he asked me.

Clark Shaughnessy was a great coach. He later went on to coach at the University of Chicago and Stanford University, where he was credited with developing the T-formation for his quarterback, Frankie Albert, and in the process, becoming the father of modern football. Assisting Shaughnessy was Bernie Bierman, who gained fame as a coach in his own right.

"No, I haven't seen Shaughnessy," I told Smith.

"Don't, he'll kill you," Dr. Smith warned.

When he found me, Shaughnessy brought me before the team and charged me with being a "traitor." But he made a concession to democracy, and decided to let me be tried before execution. The jury was the football squad which was captained by Harry "Little Eva" Talbot, now a prominent New Orleans attorney and one of my closest friends.

What a hell of a Gilbert and Sullivan operetta that was. The team was the jury and Claude "Monk" Simons, the trainer and the father of the famous All-American, "Little Monk" Simons, who's now in the Football Hall of Fame, was my "attorney." I was acquitted immediately and Shaughnessy restored me to full standing.

Things had to improve from that point, and they did. Before the season was over, Shaughnessy declared me to be the greatest manager he ever had. It happened when I recovered lost equipment after we played Vanderbilt and were on the way to Knoxville to play Tennessee. I remember Estes Kefauver was on that team. The equipment had been lost en route but I ferreted it out just in time for the game.

When the season ended, I left Tulane, with my football letter, but minus a degree. I became assistant sports editor of the *New Orleans States* on a full-time basis. While I did not graduate, I considered my time at Tulane well spent. Nobody could remain on a university campus for four years and not have the university rub off on him unless he was a dummy, and Dr. Bechtel admitted in my freshman year that I was no dummy. Besides, anybody can study and pass, but it takes a smart operator to flunk everything and stay on campus four years.

I was gone from the campus, but not forgotten. Forty-seven years later, Tulane awarded U.S. Representative Hale Boggs, U.S. Senator Allen J. Ellender, and myself its first distinguished service medals. The university staged a brilliant pageant in Washington at which we were honored. The lobby was lined with visual displays of our lives and the banquet hall was jammed with distinguished guests who came to offer congratulations. Two other Tulane graduates, Howard K. Smith, the ABC News commentator, and Bill Monroe, one-time NBC News Washington editor and now moderator of television's famed "Meet the Press," were the masters of ceremonies.

When it came time for the award, Dr. Herbert Longenecker, the president of Tulane University, made laudatory remarks, citing my contributions to the school, including my efforts in acquiring a five-hundred-acre site for the university which had once housed the old Naval Ammunition Depot in Belle Chasse, Louisiana. There, he said, Tulane has developed expansive science laboratories and "the marvels they produce all will be a tribute to the congressman, for all will be products of the F. Edward Hébert Center of Tulane University."

After all the laudatory remarks I could not resist the temptation to set the record straight. I stepped up to the podium to reply, and said: "I didn't graduate from Tulane. I only hold the degree of D.O. '24, Drop Out Magnum Cum Lousy." I added, "I was trying my damndest to stay in school and they were trying to kick me out."

Dr. Longenecker, however, never did like me admitting I was a dropout from Tulane. "Eddie," he whispered after I had concluded my remarks, "you shouldn't say that you are a dropout, it doesn't sound good." But I had to have my say as usual.

"Herbert," I replied, "let's face the facts of life. Suppose I had gone to Tulane and really studied. Now, anybody can study and repeat what he memorized. I would have gotten a degree in law and would have probably become an ambulance chaser. I would not have gone to work on the newspaper, I would not have broken the Louisiana Scandals, and I would not have gone to Congress where I got on the Armed Services Committee and in a position to manipulate the transfer without cost of more than 500 acres of land, worth more than $2 million, to Tulane for a campus in Plaquemines Parish. It's as simple as that."

With that, Dr. Longenecker interrupted: "Eddie, you know you've got something there."

"I know I do," I replied, "and Tulane's got those 500 acres which, in time, will become a beautiful campus."

Then we, and the banquet hall, were startled as the band struck up "Hail to the Chief." We looked around and saw President Richard M. Nixon emerge from backstage as the Secret Service fanned out into the audience. Secretary of Defense Melvin R. Laird was right behind him. Both had arrived to honor the three congressmen from Tulane, two graduates and one that even Dr. Longenecker now admitted had done all right by Tulane with his "degree" of "D. O. '24, Drop Out Magnum Cum Lousy."

CHAPTER III

ACTRESSES, ATHLETES, AND ACTION

As a reporter someone once said it would not be farfetched to call me the Herbert Bayard Swope of New Orleans. Well, while there were some similarities, my style was tempered by the rollicking, boisterous, freewheeling southern metropolis of New Orleans, which deserves the name "The City That Care Forgot." There my beat included show business, sports, hard news, politics, and features.

In most respects, New Orleans journalism of the 1920s and 30s was much closer to the Chicago style than that of New York or Washington. Ben Hecht and Charles MacArthur would have been more at home in the Crescent City than would Swope. On the other hand, Damon Runyon could have adjusted.

Gambling and prostitution flourished. Police were on the take. Most government jobs were held by patronage. Sports, show business, and misfortune (if not tragedy) occupied the attention of the readers of the city's newspapers.

It was in this atmosphere that I joined the sports department of the *New Orleans States* after leaving Tulane. In New Orleans, the only professional sports team was the baseball Pelicans of the Southern Association. I had established a friendship with the owner of the Pelicans, Alexander Julius Heinemann, while I was promoting the Jesuit Blue Jays. That friendship provided me with the entrée into the inner circles of the team and the sporting establishment of the city. It also provided me with extra money, for Heinemann commissioned me to prepare the Pelicans' sports brochures.

A closeness developed between us, one young and struggling, the other old and economically secure. Each admired something in the other. It became a daily routine for me to drive to the ball park at Tulane and Carrollton after work, pick Heinemann up, and drive him to the New Orleans Athletic Club where the minor league baseball magnate dined nightly.

Heinemann, quietly, was a philanthropist to local charity. He also protected the well-being of his ballplayers, allowing them to tear up contracts if they desired to play elsewhere, and often giving them traveling expenses as well. Still, Heine invoked criticism from the fans and relished being booed as he walked up and down the jammed aisles of Heinemann Park with straw hat, half-smoked cigar, open vest, and red suspenders.

The Heinemann Park press box was a gathering place for local gamblers on their day off. They would sit around making bets while listening to the play-by-play coming in on the sports wire. They'd bet on each pitch, whether it was a ball or strike. They'd bet on anything. You'd say, "Jesus, it's gonna rain." They'd say, "Three to two it don't." They'd lay anything, any side, anything you wanted to lay. You'd say, "Well, the sun's coming out now." "Five to one it don't." They'd take anything.

As a sports writer, I was in good company during that era of Southern journalism. Ralph McGill started as a sports writer. Ed Danforth, Morgan Blake, Zipp Newmann. Morgan Blake was a very famous sports editor out of Atlanta. The Crackers, the Atlanta baseball team, used to train at Bay St. Louis, Mississippi. Morgan would come down and get himself loaded. I mean loaded. I covered for him more times than anybody I ever knew. File his copy—"By Morgan Blake"—and Morgan is drunk. Morgan later became a big preacher up in Atlanta. He talked some convicts into surrendering after a riot in jail. He became a real preacher.

One of the most lasting associations I developed as a sports writer was with Eddie Morgan, who became my life-long friend. Extremely wealthy and possessing an unlimited lust for life in all its aspects, Morgan went from Heinemann's Pelicans to star for the Cleveland Indians. He was the greatest natural athlete I have ever known.

In his first year at Cleveland, playing under manager Roger Peckinpaugh, Morgan hit .318 while alternating between outfield and first base. In his best years, 1930 and 1931, he batted .350 and .351 while establishing the Indians' home run record for a single season. One year he was third in the American League batting race. His competition included such stalwarts as Babe Ruth, Lou Gehrig, Jimmy Foxx, and Al Simmons.

I shared an uptown New Orleans residence with Morgan and Abe Bannett for several years, during which the women were chasing Morgan all the time.

Ballplayers, aviators, and reporters would make our house their second home. It was from this house that what began as a traditionally gay Mardi Gras celebration ended as one of the worst events in my life. Anyone who has been there knows that the New Orleans population goes slightly beserk during the carnival season, which climaxes on Mardi Gras, or Fat Tuesday, forty days before Easter. In a last-ditch effort to store up the good life prior to that forty-day Lenten season, masses of people congregate in the city's streets, on balconies above them, and in bars everywhere to revel in the closest thing to a bacchanalian orgy. Naturally there is some trouble on occasion, but the city prides itself as being the only metropolis in the country where such an outpouring of diverse types can mingle without massive disruptions. Many persons belong to carnival organizations, called krewes, which parade with elaborate floats, tossing trinkets and doubloons to the crowds straining for the favors. Other krewes spend less exhorbitant sums for floats and inventively decorate trucks in which they navigate the city's main thoroughfares, imbibing spirits and dispensing cheer.

Permission to parade is more restricted today than it was in the 1920s and 30s. Then, practically anyone who could afford to rent a truck could parade, and that is what my buddies and I did. We had this truck, and at the time Eddie Morgan was the batting hero of Cleveland and naturally a famous guy. Billy Banker, who was known as the ''Blond Blizzard,'' a great All-American halfback at Tulane, was on the truck. So was Tiny Lawrence, a big football player, bigger than Primo Carnera in size, and Louie Pizzano, the brother of Jack Pizzano, who was a great athlete at Tulane, a fellow named Harold

Dietlein, and George Fisher. There were about a dozen of us on the truck. We also had a Negro jazz band with us and all the home-brew and bootleg liquor we could pile on board. It was Prohibition. When we left, the chief of police and George Reyer, a captain who later became police chief, were standing on the street. Reyer saw us leave and I heard him say, "No good is going to come of this, Chief."

Well, we rode off and didn't bother anybody. But later we ran out of booze and headed down to the French Quarter where we were going to get some bootleg gin. In the meantime we picked up four or five sailors from the U.S.S. *Texas*. The battleship *Texas* was in town, and we were riding through the streets when these sailors jumped on the truck with us. We got down to the Quarter and a bunch of Negroes were having a parade on St. Philip Street. Before we knew what happened a fight had started. I have always believed those sailors started the fight.

It was just a phalanx of blacks on one side and us on the other. Tiny Lawrence was so big and everything, he was just standing there knocking people down as fast as they could come to him. He was the only one who was doing any good. Everybody else was getting the hell kicked out of them. Morgan got cut across the hand with a knife. Another of our fellows backed up against a house to brace himself and some Negro woman opened a window on the second floor and dropped a chair on his head. It was really going on hot and heavy around there.

But we were getting beat, so we were trying to retreat and get the hell out of there. I started to get Lawrence to tell him, "Come on, they're kicking hell out of us, let's go." Just as I got to him there was a sound like the clap of hands. I looked up and Tiny fell right at my feet. The bullet had hit him right in the middle of the forehead. The blood just gushed out. My first thought was, "This is just like the moving pictures." Just about that time, Morgan came up and said, "Let's get out of here. We don't know him," meaning Tiny. He'd completely lost his mind. One of the sailors went into hysterics, and we had to get him out of there and quiet him down. Realizing there was nothing to be done for our dead friend, I gathered the others together and left the area.

Later on George Fisher and I went over to the place where I was living. The first thing I did was to call the editors of the papers and ask them to play the whole story down, not to give it too much play. How stupid could I have been.

About two hours later Charlie Campbell, the city editor of *The Morning Tribune,* called and told me that someone had recognized Morgan, Banker, and myself, and we'd better give ourselves up because the police were looking for us. So we went down to the Third Precinct Station. George Reyer met us and we were talking to him, giving him the details.

While we were there this Negro whore came in dressed up in a funny costume for Mardi Gras. George looked at her and asked, "Daisy, what are you doing here?"

She said, "Cap'n, I been in jail more times since I been out of the red light district than when I was in the district. They done brought me in again."

Reyer said, "Come here, Daisy," and he took her in a back room. About ten minutes later he came out—he had the name of the guy who killed Lawrence. He gave Daisy a half buck and told her to go buy some gin and forget about being booked.

Needless to say, the papers the next day did exactly what I asked them to do. They played it down—with an eight column headline across the top of page one.

A few years later, when Morgan reached the peak of his form with the Cleveland Indians, he provided me with the big sports story scoop of the day. Morgan was a rugged individualist who cared little for the tinsel-weighted society of old New Orleans. Ironically, however, he fell in love with a debutante from an old family, Frances Tobin.

Mrs. Tobin, the girl's mother, wanted a fancy wedding but Morgan would have no part of it. Mrs. Alma Richards, the proprietor of the Broadway Pharmacy, where Morgan and our crowd gathered, had introduced Morgan to Frances Tobin. Alma once said that Frances would make an appearance at debutante parties which was expected of a New Orleans society girl; then, shortly after the party started, she would disappear—to go out with Morgan who would be dressed in an old sweat shirt and pants. Morgan didn't dress up for anybody unless he was going some place special.

To resolve the impasse of the wedding situation, the couple came to me with the problem. I planned the wedding, as I have planned most things in my life, including a few would-be surprise parties which just happened to be in my honor.

Eddie Morgan and Frances Tobin told me their problem, and I had them married before the week was out. The wedding party consisted of Abe Bannett; Carl Lind, an old schoolmate and friend who played second base for the same Cleveland team as Morgan; Dr. Garland Walls; and myself. I got my favorite photographer from the *States*, Leon Trice, to shoot the wedding pictures at St. Stephen's Church.

All of this occurred at a time when Morgan was a holdout from the Indians over a dispute in salary with Billy Evans, the general manager of the team. Naturally the situation was a topic of major discussion on the nation's sports pages.

On the day of the nuptials the *New Orleans States* had the exclusive story of Morgan's wedding to the prominent debutante, complete with pictures. The sporting world, however, could not find Morgan and his bride; but the national press splashed my exclusive across its sports pages. Get the story! That was the name of the game. It was ruthless journalism, a very competitive era. And then a by-line meant something; it wasn't stuck on for just anybody.

My sports writing and my friendship with Heinemann placed me in the company of numerous ballplayers on their way up to the major leagues or on their way back down. I was well acquainted with Mel Ott, the New York Giants' star from Gretna, a small community across the Mississippi River from New Orleans; Larry Gilbert, the manager of the Pelicans, who sent his two sons, Charlie and Tookie, to the major leagues; Buddy Myer, whom I put on a train to the nation's capital where he became an outstanding infielder for the Washington Senators and led the American League in batting in 1935; and Dazzy Vance, whom I persuaded to return to New Orleans to pitch an exhibition game after that fireballer made it big in the big leagues.

I also made the acquaintance of Kenesaw Mountain Landis, the gruff, no-nonsense commissioner of baseball who liked to run a bluff on the press, not to mention the men who played the game under his jurisdiction. Once, when Landis was running roughshod over the press in New Orleans, I met him under the grandstand in Heinemann Park. "You know," I told the baseball czar, standing there with his dishevelled hair, crushed hat and frozen mein, "you're not so tough at all." Later I blistered Landis in a column for refusing to allow a young man named Alabama Pitts to play professional baseball after he served a sentence in Sing Sing prison. I wrote:

> I wonder if the pharisaical hand that snatched from Alabama Pitts the chance to earn an honest living has ever turned the pages of the book called the *Bible* . . . and paused at the story of Mary Magdalene and the Man whose feet she bathed and wiped with her tresses . . . I wonder if this "holier than thou" magistrate of baseball, this mighty dictator of the diamond, ever heard the words, "Let he who is without sin cast the first stone!"
>
> What kind of law is it which says that after a man has paid his debt to society he must forever be a shunned leper of sports? What kind of law is it which says that a prison sentence in expiation of a crime is merely the foundation for life-long persecution? What kind of law is it which says that Alabama Pitts must be society's Jean Val Jean and baseball its ignoble Javert?
>
> Why teach convicts right from wrong if we fail to practice it ourselves? Why attempt to restore lost ideals and give inmates of prisons football and baseball instructions and lessons of character if we are to snatch them all from their hands as they leave the prison gates? It all seems so wrong. It's all so unfair to this boy who erred and now that he has paid his debt cries for a chance to make good.

My faith in rehabilitation unfortunately failed to move Mountain Landis. Alabama Pitts did not play. I guess I was years ahead of my time on this matter. Now some former convicts are even major league stars.

I've always appreciated humane leadership, and I saw the benefits of it as my hometown baseball team, the Pelicans, finished in the first division of the Southern Association sixteen consecutive years. That success made manager Gilbert one of the greatest idols in local baseball history. But, being a local idol was no insurance against being booed by rabid New Orleans baseball fans. According to Bob Dowie, a catcher who had been traded to Memphis and then returned to New Orleans, Gilbert was booed at least once. Dowie's hitting ability was very suspect, but following his return to New Orleans, Gilbert sent him in to pinch-hit during a very tight ball game. Cries of derision filled the air.

"You hear that?" Gilbert asked Dowie. "Show 'em. Go in there and get a hit. Don't let 'em boo you."

"Boo me? What in the hell do you mean?" Dowie asked. "They're booing you for sending me in."

Gilbert was a favorite of Heinemann. He had hocked a personal insurance policy as a neophyte owner to purchase Gilbert's contract from the Kansas City Blues. The two men became very close, and Gilbert repeatedly turned down offers to manage major league teams. Heinemann handled investments for Gilbert and had him on the road to becoming a wealthy man when 1929 crashed down upon them and the rest of the country.

Heinemann had also made investments for some of his other close friends. Before the crash Heine told me he had bought some stock for me. It was Vivadou, and he said for me to watch it rise. It rose half a point the next day and then plunged. Heine also bought into the market for his old friend, Jake Atz, who was another famous baseball man. He had won his spurs and fame as manager of the Fort Worth Cats of the Texas League. Atz, whose entire career was in baseball, once told me that he changed his name from Zimmerman because "when I started out in this game they paid off according to the alphabet and when they came to the Z's the money had run out. So I decided to cover the whole alphabet from A to Z and change my name. I've been at the top of the payroll ever since."

When the market began to drop, Heinemann reassured his friends that it was only temporary. But Heine had a peculiar idea about profit and loss. If he bought at fifty and it went to a hundred, then fell back to seventy-five, he figured he had lost twenty-five when in reality he had made that much profit.

One day after the stock market began to drop, Heine asked me how to write a will which did not need a witness. He was talking about a holographic will, which I explained how to write.

About a week later he told me not to come for him the next afternoon as I usually did. He said he had something he wanted to do.

He did that something: he put a pistol in his mouth and pulled the trigger.

I wrote the story of Heinemann at three o'clock in the morning, and described his peculiar life and the melancholia which I had recently detected in him. In fact, I wrote twenty pages of copy on the Heinemann suicide. I began:

"My best friend is dead.

"Because my best friend is dead means nothing to the world, but my best friend is the best friend of thousands, perhaps personally unknown to them, but still their best friend; he is the best friend of the orphans and the needy and the worthy and that does mean something."

I went on to cite the huge amounts of money Heinemann had given to and raised for charity, saying, "There will never be another more true, loyal, charitable, sterling character than A. J. Heinemann."

As my eulogy continued, I discussed the why of Heinemann's suicide, and it was this which landed me in court. "It was not a sudden, rash act," I wrote. "It was fully premeditated and determined on the part of Mr. Heinemann. He had been becoming more depressed with the passing of each day and then he seemed to be obsessed with the thought that his friends were turning against him. It was the loneliness of a worried mind harassing him.

"True, he lost heavily in the stock market but the thought and the worry that perhaps he had wrongly advised some of his friends worried Heine. He became a changed man—he was not the jovial, gay, humorous Heine of other days. He became a sullen, dejected, brooding man, aging quickly."

I noted that Heinemann soon "started thinking that his closest friends frowned on him. He who laughed at the jeers of the bleachers and enjoyed it—began to cringe at the thought that his friends were turning against him. The thought worried Heinemann. If he had been married, if he had had a wife or a child to steady and comfort him now in his declining years he would never have killed himself.

"This idea that his friends were leaving was the result of a natural disposition to worry. He allowed the thought to get the best of him.

To Larry Gilbert, one of his closest and most bosom friends, he repeatedly declared, 'Larry, you won't leave me will you?' "

I noted that Heinemann had told Eddie Morgan, "All my friends have gone to the country," and how he telephoned Jake Atz in Texas at 1:00 a.m. several months before his death to tell him he was going to kill himself. Heinemann had also inquired among his friends about the best method of killing oneself. My story continued, relating Heinemann's activities shortly before his death, discussing the hints he dropped of the impending suicide, and how Gilbert sought to guard him.

Then, before I concluded, I pulled out all the stops in my heartfelt sorrow over this friend's demise.

Wednesday afternoon in that office, stalwart, strong men openly cried as they viewed his body. Men whose muscles are of iron found tears streaming down their cheeks. Their best friend was dead.

Many are those who are going to miss Heine now that he is gone; many hearts which he gladdened will return to sadness.

Heinemann Park will never be the same again.

Heine parading up and down the aisles, laughing sometimes, sometimes unmindful of the joking crowds; jumping up in his chair and yelling "Pocahontas" when the Pelicans were in the rear—all the little characteristics of Heinemann are now gone but their memory will last forever.

My best friend is dead.

Following Heinemann's death, one of the most publicized law suits in Louisiana judicial history exploded. It was based on the holographic will which I had shown him how to write. In the will Heinemann had left his estate to his brother and sisters and had set aside enough to cover "whatever Larry Gilbert has lost in the stock market."

It was a bitterly fought case, contested by a disgruntled nephew who wanted to break the will by proving his uncle incompetent. As a result of my instructions regarding the will and my story on Heinemann's death, I was the star witness at the trial. On direct examination by the defense attorneys, my close relationship with

Heinemann was established, and then I was asked to characterize
Heinemann's opinion of Jay Weil, the nephew who was trying to
overturn the will.

"He spoke harshly of Mr. Weil," I testified. "He told me he didn't
like him, that he was mercenary and cold-blooded, and one or two
other things I would prefer not to say in the presence of ladies."

The judge then instructed me to write the expression Heinemann
used to describe his nephew. "Mr. Heinemann said that Mr. Jay Weil
'pissed ice water,' " I wrote.

The attorney representing Weil, Eldon Lazarus, then tried to establish that Gilbert, who had testified prior to me, and I both lied.

> LAZARUS: Is it a fact or not that Mr. Gilbert used to wait at the ball
> park until you got there, so as not to leave Mr. Heinemann alone in the
> afternoon?
> HÉBERT: I don't know that to be a fact.
> LAZARUS: Is it a fact that Mr. Gilbert did meet you out there for the
> last several weeks, in the afternoons, when you went to get Mr.
> Heinemann?
> HÉBERT: Sometimes.
> LAZARUS: How often?
> HÉBERT: Maybe three or four times a week; maybe less or more.
> LAZARUS: We are not concerned with "maybes" or "perhapses."
> We want to get the actual facts, and you are a witness produced by the
> defendants to give facts, and I am entitled to get facts, and not opinions.
> HÉBERT: Perhaps if you will tell me the exact language you want
> me to express it in, I might tell you.
> LAZARUS: Are you accustomed to doing that?
> HÉBERT: For you, yes sir.
> LAZARUS: Now, Mr. Hebert, can you tell me how many times a
> week you met Mr. Gilbert at the ball park when you went to get Mr.
> Heinemann to bring him to town.
> HÉBERT: I don't know.

With me trying to protect my friend's last wishes, and Lazarus
pressing me, the testimony took a convoluted and often humorous
tack. Lazarus began questioning me from the article I had written on
Heinemann's suicide.

> LAZARUS: Now I read you this excerpt from your signed article:

"He became a changed man—he was not the jovial, gay, humorous Heine of other days. He became a sullen, dejected, brooding man, aging quickly." Was that statement true or not when you made it?

HÉBERT: Again you change your question to me.

LAZARUS: That is my privilege.

HÉBERT: I will answer the same thing. At the time it was written, yes, it was true. Before the suicide, no.

LAZARUS: You don't mean to say that his disposition changed after three o'clock in the morning when you wrote the article?

HÉBERT: I don't get you.

LAZARUS: He was dead then.

HÉBERT: Yes, but you are asking me different questions to contradict me. I will not let you contradict me if I can help it. We both know what you are up to. I am telling you the truth as I know it.

LAZARUS: I ask you again whether or not it was true, from your own observation, as stated in this article, that Mr. Heinemann changed from a jovial, gay, humorous man to a sullen, dejected, and brooding man, aging quickly.

HÉBERT: I can have my last answer read . . . or I will answer again. At the time the article was written, it was true, before the article was written, it wasn't true; and I changed my opinion from what I heard or learned after his death.

LAZARUS: You say that . . .

HÉBERT: Let me have a piece of paper, please. I want to write down what I have said already.

I obtained a piece of paper and wrote my answer, which I read repeatedly in response to the attorney's future questions. Lazarus was forced to go on to other points in my news story, still trying, of course, to pin me down.

LAZARUS: I now read from the article as follows: "Two months ago, at the New Orleans Athletic Club, night after night, he paced up and down the main corridor, apparently in deep thought and obviously worried." Was that statement written by you?

HÉBERT: Yes, sir.

LAZARUS: It was written on hearsay?

HÉBERT: Yes, sir.

LAZARUS: Will you give the source of the hearsay?

HÉBERT: General conversation of the N.O.A.C.

LAZARUS: Will you particularize them?

HÉBERT: I have no one in mind particularly.

LAZARUS: That is not the question.

HÉBERT: Well, the answer is no, sir.

LAZARUS: Can you now tell us the name of one or more persons who gave you the information on which this statement in the article is based?

HÉBERT: No, sir.

LAZARUS: Did somebody—some living person give you that information?

HÉBERT: Yes, sir.

LAZARUS: You didn't get it from any spooks?

HÉBERT: I don't remember whether I did or not. I don't think I did. I am rather hazy on that subject now, but I don't think I did.

LAZARUS: Are you accustomed to getting information from spooks?

HÉBERT: I don't think so.

LAZARUS: Are you sure about this?

HÉBERT: No, sir, I can't be too sure, when your method of cross-examination is the same. It is rather a foolish question to ask of a normal man if he got information from spooks, and my answer was just the same.

I had written that shortly before Heinemann ended his life, the baseball owner had avoided me by cancelling the daily ride which I provided for him to the athletic club. Lazarus then turned to that section of the story.

LAZARUS: In the article you say, "I became suspicious," and as a result of that, you went to the ball park thereafter. Is not that correct?

HÉBERT: Do I say "thereafter,' in the article?

LAZARUS: I don't want to misquote you. "I became suspicious, and finally one afternoon I went to the ball park and asked what was the matter?" Now, was that thereafter?

HÉBERT: No, sir. You are incorrect. I said, "one afternoon" I went. "Thereafter" would presume I went every afternoon thereafter, but I didn't.

Unable to break me, the attorneys for the nephew were unsuccessful, and the holographic will stood as written.

After two years in the *New Orleans States* sports department, I left to handle public relations for Loyola University of the South. I had a $3,500-a-year contract which permitted me to handle publicity for other groups also. I took advantage of it and publicized the Tulane Theater, the Orpheum Theater, boxing matches, the Pontchartrain Beach amusement park, and wrote brochures for the Pelicans. I was really in clover in those days, and I never saved a dime. I'd throw it away as fast as I'd make it. Hoarding money meant nothing to me.

The Loyola job included sports publicity for the university, and one of my jobs was broadcasting football games. Bill Coker, a well-known New Orleanian, and I announced the first football game broadcast over WWL, the Jesuit-owned station in New Orleans. The star of the Loyola club at that time was Elton "Bucky" Moore, who had been dubbed "The Dixie Flyer." Bucky was a fine halfback with a fantastic change of pace and elusive hip movement when carrying the ball. In that first game broadcast, he was given the ball on about the ten-yard line and broke around his own right end and headed for daylight.

Coker was at the mike and he was getting excited: "Moore's got the ball. He's off the wide right end and cuts in. There he goes, he passes the twenty, the thirty, the forty—LOOK AT THAT SON OF A BITCH GO!" Coker screamed into the microphone of the Jesuit-owned radio station. Coker and I managed to suppress our laughter and somehow continued the broadcast. Not only was Coker's *faux pas* the talk of the town, it went down in the history of radio bloopers.

While at Loyola, I was hired to handle the publicity for the first professional football game played in New Orleans. Professional football was in its fledgling stages, and its main attraction was Harold "Red" Grange, the "Galloping Ghost." A big-time promoter, C.C. "Cash and Carry" Pyle, had signed Grange to a contract and hit the road with the Chicago Bears, playing select teams across the country.

In New Orleans the Bears were to play the Southern All-Stars, a group of former college players. Grange was the main atraction, but George Halas, who eventually owned the team and is called the father of professional football, was in the line.

I pulled out all the stops with every publicity trick I knew to get a crowd out to the newfangled game of pro football. One of my inducements was to claim that the fans would see "the greatest collection of football celebrities ever assembled on a local gridiron." The lineup of the team from Dixie included five former Tulane stars, Alfred "Brother" Brown at halfback, Bill Besselman at center, Gene Bergeret at guard, Johnny Wight at left end, and Lester Lautenschlaeger, who has been enshrined in the Football Hall of Fame, at quarterback. Despite losing 14-0, the Southerners played themselves proud, holding Grange to one touchdown. His longest run was twenty yards.

Although they became restless, local fans assumed that the new game of professional football demanded a half time of forty-five minutes. Actually Lautenschlaeger, still in his uniform, spent the rest period haggling with Pyle over the payment he had been promised. He had assembled and coached the Southern All-Stars on the promise of a $6,000 fee by "Cash and Carry."

"I agreed on the condition that $3,000 would be paid in advance," Lautenschlaeger said, "and $3,000 on the day of the game. Pyle's reputation was so bad I told him if I did not have the second $3,000 during the half there would be no second half." Lautenschlaeger got the money.

Pro football was so frowned upon in collegiate circles in those days that Brother Brown, who was an assistant coach at Tulane, was fired, and an agreement Lautenschlaeger had to become an assistant coach the next year was cancelled. However, time healed the rift and Lautenschlaeger later became a Tulane coach and a member of the university's board of administrators.

I guess I should have learned from Lautenschlaeger's experience with "Cash and Carry," but I had to deal with him firsthand to find out how he got his nickname. Not long after the professional football debut in New Orleans, Pyle returned to the city promoting professional tennis. His star was the great woman player, Suzanne Lenglen, who had been Wimbledon champion from 1919 to 1923 and again in 1925. When Pyle arrived with his caravan, he sought me out, for he felt that I had done a good job for him in publicizing the football game. Everything went fine until it came time for me to get paid. Pyle had carried his cash to Texas.

My career as a press agent also required me to promote some of the top operettas of the day, *The Student Prince, The Desert Song, Blossom Time, Maryland, My Maryland,* and *The Merry Widow,* among others. Road shows making the rounds included *Rio Rita* and *George White's Scandals.* All played to packed houses. Nudity, contrary to youthful opinion, is not new to the stage. It was done when I was a press agent, and was not innovative then. However, it was slightly more daring at that time. I asked one of the dancers in the *Scandals* how she had the nerve to bare one breast in the show's big scene. "I'm doing it for art's sake," she replied seriously. Usually never at a loss for words, I was struck dumb by her response.

I handled the publicity and was the "front of the house" for such stars as Mrs. Minnie Maddern Fiske, a native New Orleanian, Fritz Leiber, Walker Whiteside, Otis Skinner, Guy Bates Post, Ezio Pinza, De Wolf Hopper, Ethel Barrymore, Billie Burke, Lou Tellegen and others. As the press agent for the Tulane Theater (which had no connection with the university) I was again working for Colonel Thomas C. Campbell, the man in whose "army" I had been a soldier as an usher in my early teens. The colonel was getting up in age by this time and asked me to ghostwrite his memoirs. Campbell had been an outstanding figure theatrically, socially, and politically, and the memoir I wrote was a saga of show business in New Orleans from the turn of the century through the twenties, filled with lists of the plays Campbell had produced and the stars who performed in them. It cited the colonel's part in the establishment of the Police Relief Fund, the reopening of the city's famous race track, the Fair Grounds, and countless other activities.

The colonel had discussed his memoirs with me, but the first time he read them was when they appeared in the Sunday newspaper where I had planted them. They were published in installments, as fast as I could write them. I suddenly realized when I was about to close the book that I had forgotten to mention the fact the colonel was married. I hadn't given a clue to his wife's identity. I had to get something about his wife. I therefore made up something entirely in keeping with the colonel's opinion of himself.

And through the entire story I have failed to make reference to one party in particular. I have told of the players and the great stars of stage and life whom I have met, but I have not mentioned the one greatest person of all whom I met thirty-one years ago at New Bedford, on Buzzard's Bay, and who has been my pal and friend, most of all in times of gloom as well as sunshine. That one person is greater to me than all the illustrious people I have had the pleasure of meeting.

The name?

The name is Ann Olstine—or rather that was the name thirty-one years ago, but since then it has been Mrs. Thomas C. Campbell.

And what play would be complete without sweet romance and a love scene as the curtain falls? The person whom I met thirty-one years ago is the romance of this play of my life, and as the curtain falls, we will be going up the lane together, hand in hand, arm in arm, each a mate to the other. For thirty-one years, she has been a friend and a wife to me and she is going to be my greatest star, my greatest play, my greatest personage until the curtain of life falls, never more to rise.

The Sunday night that the last chapter of the memoirs appeared, the colonel, who was not adverse to a few drops of the grape, was feeling its effect when Althea Wuerpel, a local drama critic, came into the front office. The colonel was sitting there with the paper in one hand and a well-filled glass in the other when he saw Althea. He rushed up to her, threw his arms around her, and asked her in a sobbing voice and with tears in his eyes: "Oh, Althea, have you read the beautiful thing which I wrote about my wife today?"

I was also press agent for the famous Leona Powers and her actor husband, Howard Miller. She had long been the toast of Washington at the national theater when they came to New Orleans to play at the Tulane Theater. They later moved into the St. Charles Theater, and I moved with them. I was unable to save their investment, however. Howard and Leona blew their life savings, and lost everything in the venture.

The second man and manager of the company was named George Clark, and his wife, Georgia Neese, was the second lead woman. She became the first woman treasurer of the United States—Georgia Neese Clark. Harry Truman appointed her. Well, I was her press agent.

Mrs. Clark was not the only performer I knew who went into government service. In the late 1960s, I invited Congressman Dan

Flood of Pennsylvania to be the principal speaker at the annual banquet of the Louisiana Historical Society on the anniversary of the Battle of New Orleans. Flood, who has a wide reputation in Congress for hamming it up, was a big hit with the Louisiana folks. Following the banquet, Flood, who was wearing a top hat, a cape draped about his shoulders, and was brandishing a walking cane to complete his ensemble, and I were talking on the sidewalk outside Antoine's Restaurant in the French Quarter.

"The first time I was in New Orleans," Flood mused, "was in 1925 and I was playing in a show called *White Cargo.*"

"I am Tondelayo," I purred in my sexiest voice.

"My God," Flood said, "that's the first time I've heard that curtain line in years."

I had just realized and explained to Flood's amazement, that I had been the theater's press agent when Flood played in *White Cargo* at the Tulane. Until that time neither of us had realized, even though we had spent years together in Congress, that our paths had crossed forty-odd years before in a different milieu.

Shortly after the Powers-Miller acting company folded I went back to the *New Orleans States* because the money ran out at Loyola too. But instead of going to the news desk, I wound up heading the promotion department. I was bickering with Jim Crown, the city editor, to go back on the general news staff and with Jim Ewing, the publisher, to go into the promotion department. I wound up with seventy-five dollars a week downstairs in the promotion department without Crown knowing I was trying to get that job.

It was not long, however, before the Depression forced me back into the newsroom, which is one good thing that can be said for the Depression. When the bubble burst, the newspaper knocked off all the big-salary people. That included me. So where do I go? I go upstairs to the newsroom. Forty bucks a week, as a general assignment reporter. But it was not long before I was made a page-one columnist in the Walter Winchell tradition.

Indeed, I eventually became the paper's jack-of-all-trades. I did all of the reviews—the motion pictures, and I was the theatrical reviewer as well. I was doing the shows, the political reports, writing a column, and I was on the rewrite desk. I even dressed up as a clown to do a feature on the last circus parade held in New Orleans. That's how we would operate. It was a plain case of the survival of the fittest. This was no kid's game. I was doing everything imaginable. I'd be writing the column on one typewriter and have to leave it to do rewrites on another one.

During that period bathing-beauty contests became fashionable, and they were promoted locally by Gladys Moore, the original bathing beauty around New Orleans. Somehow, I became a perennial judge at the contests along with Mel Washburn, a rival columnist for the *Morning Tribune* (which is no longer in circulation).

One of the contestants we selected was a pretty young girl named Dorothy Dell Goff. Runner-up in the contest was a girl named Dorothy Lambour. Through Gladys Moore's influence the girls went to Galveston, Texas, to participate in one of the first Miss Universe contests. Dorothy Dell Goff went over there with only a $3.98 white bathing suit. And while I would not indicate or suggest anything untoward, John Held, Jr., the famous wood-cut artist who was Gladys Moore's husband, was one of the judges. Dorothy won Miss Universe. This was a great thing for New Orleans. She was a lovely thing, too. Rather buxom, and she had a personality, a smile just as big as anything in the world. They had a private coach for her to come in from Galveston.

The night she came back, Union Station was jammed with people. Everybody was down there to welcome this New Orleans gal. I got on the train ahead of them. I'll never forget that fresh young thing coming down the aisle of the train with Dorothy Lambour following closely behind.

At the time, Big Boy Peterson, the first guy Primo Carnera knocked out when he came to America, was after Dorothy. I was right in the aisle and Big Boy rushed by me and threw his arms around Dorothy and said, "Baby, I'm sure proud of you." That was a great original line.

After she returned to New Orleans, Vic Meyer, the manager of the Orpheum Theater, tried to get me to tie Miss Goff to a personal appearance contract, but some other guy was talking bigger money, and she wouldn't listen. Vic said, "The hell with it; she'll never amount to anything anyway. This is just a flash in the pan."

I didn't agree because I had already paid her sixteen dollars to appear in a style show I was staging. Did she amount to anything? Well, as we say in Congress, "let the record speak for itself." She went on to the Ziegfeld Follies. She took Ruth Etting's place and introduced the song, "Was I Drunk, Was He Handsome, and Did My Ma Give Me Hell." That was Dorothy's great song. Then she went to Hollywood and played in *Wharf Angel* with Victor McLaglen.

When the movie opened in New Orleans there was a runner preceding it in which Miss Dell, who had dropped the Goff and had become actress, Dorothy Dell, thanked the people who had helped her on the way up, Bill Coker, Mel Washburn, and Eddie Hébert.

Her next picture was *Little Miss Marker* with Shirley Temple and Charles Bickford. She was just on the threshold of what promised to be a spectacular career when she was killed in an early morning automobile accident.

We had no pictures of her at the *States*, but two days before she was killed she had sent me two autographed pictures, and they were very warm autographs, too. We used one of those pictures in the paper.

The girl who placed second to Dorothy Dell in the beauty contests had a longer run in show business after she dropped the "b" from her name and became Dorothy Lamour. She started with Edgar Bergen and Charlie McCarthy on radio and finally made the sarong famous with Bing Crosby and Bob Hope.

The bathing beauty contest which I relish most came during the summer of Dorothy Dell's death. I had never offered any advice to my fellow connoisseurs of beauty during my tenure as a judge, although the competition was then so keen that charges and counter-charges led to an investigation of the contests. Charlie Campbell, the city editor of the *Morning Tribune*, and I were called before a grand jury. We were accused of trying to fix the contests. Whenever I judged a contest, I would sit down and just vote and pay no attention to the other six or seven judges. However it came out didn't make any difference.

But this particular night there was a girl there, a bit chubby, but sweet, and she reminded me so much of Dorothy Dell that I argued with the judges. She was not their selected first choice, but I argued with them before they put their ballots in the box, and I won. They then selected her. She was representing the Four X Brewery in New Orleans. Promoting her were Dandy Flynn and Martin Burke. Burke was a former heavyweight fighter and had been Jack Dempsey's sparring partner. His son, Paul Burke, became a film and television actor.

They had found this girl in a stenographic pool. She was Mary Healy. She was only sixteen then, but she had a lot of charm and she never lost it.

I knew the man who would eventually marry Mary Healy long before I met her. While a columnist, I had several jobs on the side, a usual practice, one which was not only condoned but encouraged by the editors as a means of keeping the wolf away from the door. I was press agent for the Suburban Gardens Club, a nightspot and gambling casino in Jefferson Parish.

When I began visiting the clubs in Jefferson, next door to New Orleans, the "Noble Experiment" of Prohibition was being conducted, but liquor flowed, dice rolled and the music rarely stopped. The Suburban and Club Forest were having band wars. Top entertainment was engaged. Ella Logan, who went on to Broadway fame, made her American debut at Club Forest. Singer Tony Martin was then a saxophone player in the band there.

I got to know all these people: Louis Armstrong, who used twelve dozen handkerchiefs during his nightly performances, Vincent Lopez, George Olsen, Fred Waring and His Pennsylvanians, Ted Weems, Jan Garber, Henry Busse, Tom Gerun. These were the days when Joe Brown had the Suburban, before he became famous for his race horses.

I'd even shill for them sometimes. They'd give me a lot of money for shilling those dice games. I had more fun shilling because it wasn't my money. I would just lose all of it but it didn't make any difference to me. I was having fun shooting dice and then doubling up. I bet more people looked at me and said, "Where is this guy getting that money to bet like that?"

At this time there was a great star at the Club Forest named Grace Hayes. She was the most gorgeous thing around; raven hair, diamonds all over her. She got a thousand bucks a week just singing at the Club Forest. Can anyone imagine that kind of money back in 1931–32? She was a great star. She would never come on stage from her dressing room. She had her table reserved right in the middle of the ring of tables. She would be introduced from her table.

I got to know her when Vincent Lopez and Hayes and I went out one night. We made the town. I mean we *made* the town upside down, inside out. Here is this beautiful woman, wearing all those diamonds, burning the honky-tonks up. We made all the back honky-tonks. We were showing her the town.

From then on I became—I won't use the word enamoured or anything like that—but I thought Hayes was one of the greatest-looking women I had ever seen. So here is old Hébert, nothing but a broke columnist who didn't know where the next nickel was coming from, sitting at her table every night. Grace sang a song to me that I loved, "Stardust." To this day, whenever I hear "Stardust" and Gladys (the gal who became Mrs. F. Edward Hébert) is around, she'll say, "Down boy, down boy."

Grace Hayes eventually left the New Orleans area to perform elsewhere, but she returned to do a stint at the Orpheum Theater, where I was handling publicity. This time she had her little kid with her. I always called him Lind. He was the first kid I ever knew who studied while the radio was playing. The kid was Peter Lind Hayes, who would eventually marry Mary Healy.

Several years later I was traveling for the national office of my fraternity, Delta Sigma Phi, and Hollywood was on my itinerary. Grace Hayes had opened a club on Ventura Boulevard, called Hayes Lodge, and Bill Coker, who was a close friend of Hayes, wrote, telling her of my impending visit to the city. "Who's Coker trying to kid?" Gladys, who was by then Mrs. Hébert, asked, "You need an introduction?"

When we got to Hollywood, of course, I wanted to see Hayes. Cecil B. DeMille's top press agent was a fellow named Bill Hebert, only he pronounced it Hee-burt. I met him through Quentin Reynolds when DeMille came to New Orleans to shoot the movie *The Buc-caneer*. I told Bill I wanted to go to Hayes' club. Bill and his girlfriend and Gladys and I went out there. There was a big bar with a huge mirror behind it, and I looked up and saw Grace come in. I told Gladys I was going to see somebody. I went up there and stood at the bar next to Grace. She looked in the mirror and didn't even bat an eye. "How in the hell did you get here?" she asked.

I said, "Well, honey, didn't Coker write you?"

She replied, "You never needed Coker to talk for you before. Why should he talk for you now?"

Sometime after I went to Congress, Mary Healy was performing with Milton Berle at the National Theater in Washington. Senator Warren Magnuson called me. He was hot for Mary. I had known Maggie when he served with me in the House. He said, "Mary won't go to lunch with me unless you go with us." I ended up having to go with them so he could have lunch with her in the Senate restaurant.

Two other good friends of mine were singers Wini Shaw and Gloria Grafton. Wini Shaw became famous singing "Lullaby of Broadway." She became famous in World War II as the "Sweetheart of the G.I." Her song for me, however, was "Love For Sale."

Gloria Grafton, who later starred in several movies, and the great Broadway hit *Jumbo*, had two looks. Offstage she looked like a movie-cast schoolteacher with big eyeglasses and a rather prim attitude. On the nightclub floor, she was something else. She was glamorous, vivacious, and captivating. She used to dedicate to me the song, "You're So Wonderful, So Divine and You are Mine, All Mine." It sounded good in those days.

Another group of show business friends of mine were The South-land Rhythm Girls, a quartet made up of a clarinet, cornet, piano and bass. They played with Ben Bernie, "The Old Maestro," at the College Inn in Chicago, and in New York with Vincent Lopez, and for years at Leon and Eddie's in New York. One member of the group, Dixie Fasnacht, later owned Dixie's Bar of Music in the French Quarter, and Betty Giblin, the attractive pianist who looked like a prettier version of Joan Crawford, came to work for me in my congressional office.

She had married William T. Harter, a good friend of mine, and when he entered the Navy during World War II, she joined my staff when I had a job opening. Betty and Gladys, my wife, were good friends, so we had Betty move in with us and she became for all practical purposes a member of the family.

Besides playing the piano by ear as well as reading music, which made Betty the hit of our parties, she proved to be an excellent office assistant. When the title of administrative assistant was established for the top office personnel in congressional offices, Betty Harter became the first person to hold that title in the House of Representatives. She remained on my staff some twenty years, until her death.

I was closely associated with many other entertainers: Chaney and Fox, known as the Roosevelt Dance Team because of the favor they held with the President, and especially his wife, Eleanor; Peppino and Rhoda, the latter whom I "warmed up" by waltzing her around the dance floor prior to her show; June and Cherry Blossom Priesser, who went on to Broadway and the *Ziegfeld Follies* after getting their start in New Orleans where their mother brought them up to the *States* office seeking publicity and told them to "kiss Uncle Eddie." Cherry eventually married the son of Harry Hopkins, President Roosevelt's famous "brain truster." I was also a friend of the Boswell Sisters, natives of New Orleans, especially Connie.

I befriended movie magnates like Cecil B. DeMille and Woody Van Dyke. When DeMille was in New Orleans to research the life of Jean Lafitte for his film, *The Buccaneer*, the director and I visited the grave of Dominique You, Lafitte's cannoneer and lieutenant. Much of Lafitte's life—and even his death—is shrouded in mystery, but DeMille wanted the film to be as authentic as possible. As he stood next to the tomb, the movie producer sang a line from a popular song: "If I could spend one hour with You."

As for Woody Van Dyke, he would never be accused of looking like a movie director. He dressed like a bum. He drank Van Dyke cocktails—gin with a gin chaser. We became pretty good friends when he was visiting in New Orleans. He got married in New Orleans. He told me he was getting married and I had the only picture of the ceremony. I had a clean beat.

Over the years I maintained friendships with entertainers such as Al Hirt, Pete Fountain, Papa Celestin, the Dukes of Dixieland and many others who played in New Orleans. I can usually recognize talent. Once though, I reviewed the opening of a young arranger who had become a band leader at the Blue Room of the Roosevelt Hotel. The review I wrote was a doozy. I panned the band from the first to the last note. Too much brass. Too little string. I said the leader would never be heard from again. I thought I really knew my stuff. Nobody ever heard of him again—his name was Glenn Miller.

The next time I heard Miller play was in Washington. I was then a congressman and Miller was the hottest musician in the country. I sent him a note following the performance: "Well, Glenn, I was right. You never were heard from again."

I have always enjoyed being around talent. I have always enjoyed the company of achievers in show business and, in fact, in almost any other endeavor. But I am no sycophant. Once, when Ethel Barrymore arrived in New Orleans for a personal appearance, arrangements were made for me to interview her. I arrived promptly with a photographer at the appointed time. She was still asleep. When she awakened, she sent word that she could not be disturbed. She would summon me at a later hour to be named by her. Well, I've never considered that to be a way to endear oneself. "Tell her," I instructed the messanger, "she needs the publicity for her show far more than I need her interview. You tell her there will be no later hour." With that I left.

Throughout my career I have believed in the tenants of journalism. I have tried to be as fair, as objective as possible, and have never tried to use my columns to line my pockets. Everyone in New Orleans did not share my outlook, however. Mel Washburn, the *Morning Tribune* columnist, was hustling all these people around. He was a ten percent man with the hula dancers and the strippers. Mel used to burn me up because I thought he was a disgrace to the profession. And here I was writing a column opposite him, and I thought I was being honest. I wasn't hustling these people, or doing those things. It just burned me up.

Whenever either of us was in the audience at one of the plush

Jefferson Parish casinos, the master of ceremonies would introduce us. I don't deny that I enjoyed it, and I would beam each time I would be asked to stand. But I never took all that seriously. I'd get introduced every night that I was out there because they liked me; that column didn't mean much. (I'm being facetious.) Washburn found that out when he got fired.

He was fired as the result of a loan episode which occurred when he was visiting Hollywood studios. I never kidded myself. Take that column away from me and I would have been a stranger when I walked into the front door of those clubs. Those characters might have liked me, but they loved my column. The publicity was their bread and butter and a great stimulus to their ego.

Many years have passed since those days, but I still keep in touch with entertainers and athletes because they are an interesting and fascinating breed to me as they are to almost everyone. The movie industry has changed and sports have been streamlined and have become a big business. Nevertheless, the glamour remains. That glamour or awe, if you will, also surrounds those of us in politics, providing, I guess, a common bond with entertainers and athletes.

One of moviedom's lasting stars is Eva Gabor, the beautiful and charming actress who is married to my good friend, Frank Jameson. I have spent many enjoyable hours with Frank and Eva. At a celebration in my honor in New Orleans, Eva brought the house down when she quipped, "Eddie is not 'a-bear,' he's just a pussycat."

Ed Nelson, who graduated from Tulane where he was a cheerleader, often stops by my Washington office. Ed gained stardom in the popular television series "Peyton Place," and he has also done a superb job in the road show of *Give 'em Hell, Harry*.

Old memories were rekindled when Connie Boswell's niece was an intern in my Washington office in the summer of 1974. She reminded me so much of Connie.

Bourbon Street, which was my beat when I was a reporter and part of my congressional district for so many years, is still a special place for me. I enjoy taking big-shot visitors down on Bourbon Street to see a dear friend, the vivacious and fantastic dancer, Chris Owens. She really puts on a show when I am in the audience and has a special rendition of "Hello, Eddie," sung to the tune of "Hello, Dolly" which she belts out when I walk in. I love it.

And I still make the rounds at the clubs owned by my long-time friends, Pete Fountain and Al Hirt, where they perform regularly when they are not on tour. They always have a special table for me: and make my presence known to the audience. As in those days when I was introduced to the crowds at the Jefferson Parish casinos, I still enjoy taking that bow. I guess I'll always be a ham at heart.

Some may wonder how I got reelected if I was always seen out nightclubbing on Bourbon Street. If you know New Orleans and its people, you know that those people who see me when I'm out are votes in the box.

Al and Pete both presented me with portraits which hang in my Washington office. Pete also gave me a fine work of art which is displayed in my office foyer, and he gave me a unique lamp which is made from one of his clarinets.

Neither has my love for sports diminished. How could it when I was so involved with them as a youngster and was writing about sports from the time I was a teenager when I was working on the New Orleans papers.

I already mentioned my friendship with the great Gene Tunney, and now I am serving in the Congress with his son, John, who is a United States senator from California.

Because of my background, I became fast friends with some outstanding athletes who serve or served in the Congress, not the least of which is Gerald Ford, who was a standout center on Michigan's football team. There is Wilmer "Vinegar Bend" Mizell, the former St. Louis Cardinal and Pittsburgh Pirate southpaw hurler, who was elected to the House from North Carolina. He is now an assistant secretary in the Department of Commerce. Bob Mathias, who won the Olympic decathlon event in 1948 and 1952 and was known as the world's greatest athlete, was a member of Congress from California, and we spent countless hours talking sports. Still serving in the House is Jack Kemp of New York, a good friend, who quarterbacked the Buffalo Bills when the team was in the American Football League.

He spent 13 years in professional football, was AFL Player of the Year in 1965, and was twice an all AFL quarterback. Ralph Metcalfe, still a representative from Illinois, was a famous sprinter and participated in the 1932 and 1936 Olympic games. With Ralph on the relay team which won a gold medal was Emmett Toppino of New Orleans. Ralph and I often chat about Emmett, who is deceased. Also of interest is that Ralph was track coach and a political science instructor at Xavier University in New Orleans from 1936–42. When Edwin Dooley served in the House, he and I were great friends. He was a famous quarterback at Dartmouth. Another good friend was Jack Westland of Washington who was the United States Amateur Golf Champion in 1952. In 1953 Gene Littler won it, and in 1954 Arnold Palmer. However, Jack never turned pro. Hamilton Fish, Jr. of New York was an All-American at Harvard, and we served together in the 1940s. Now his son and I serve together.

My ties with Tulane, where I was manager of the football team, remain strong. I attend every football game I can and follow the team's fortunes religiously. I often speak at the T Club breakfast preceding the homecoming game.

While in the Tulane arena, I recall two former Green Wave gridders who have a new claim to fame. Maurice and Sidney Legendre are the uncles of Anne Armstrong, the ambassador to England. Anne's father, Armand "Cajun" Legendre, was an All-American football player at Princeton. Prior to becoming ambassador, Anne served a tour as special assistant to then President Nixon.

I am also an avid New Orleans Saints fan. Who isn't in New Orleans and Louisiana? Hanging on my office wall is the picture of Tom Dempsey kicking his record-breaking 63-yard field goal against Detroit. Tom, now with the Los Angeles Rams, is a friend I admire greatly for his courage.

My friendships remain with other former greats of the sports world, such as Connie Ryan, the major leaguer who managed the Atlanta Braves, and Mel Parnell of Boston Red Sox fame. My friend and fraternity brother Fritz Crisler was a great coach. Marchmont "Marchie" Schwartz of New Orleans was an All-American on the last Notre Dame team Knute Rockne coached. It's rather amusing, perhaps, that I introduced Marchie to Crisler at the Blue Room in New Orleans just before Fritz left Princeton, where he put that university on the football map, to take the head coaching job at Michigan. The two former All-Americans had never met. Henry "Zeke" Bonura is another friend who comes to mind. He spent several years in the big leagues.

That all-time coaching genius who guided Army's gridiron successes when West Point was a powerhouse, Red Blaik, is one of my dearest friends, and we get together whenever we can. We often remember the time his assistant coach, Harry "Fats" Ellinger, died unexpectedly in his sleep at my home in Alexandria, Virginia. I know all the academy coaches because of my interest in sports and my position on the House Armed Services Committee where I was chairman of the Academies Subcommittee. There is Ben Martin of the Air Force Academy, the dean of academy coaches, and Rick Forenzo, who was at the Naval Academy, and now guides the fortunes of the Detroit Lions.

And how can I help but mention three close friends who wound up in the College Football Hall of Fame. I'm talking about Claude "Little Monk" Simons, whom I wrote about when he was a kid playing sports and with whose father I was a friend, and Lester Lautenschlaeger and Clark Shaughnessy.

I could go on and on, but I merely wanted to show that these things are an intricate part of my life. Like a reporter with printer's ink in his blood—and I certainly know about that—the entertainment industry and sports flow just as heavily through my veins today in memory and in real life.

CHAPTER IV

THE REPORTER

THE ENVIRONMENT OF the New Orleans newsrooms in the late 1920s and 30s differed from their modern counterparts in a number of aspects. Whether they were better or worse depends on one's point of view. Which is preferable: Walter Winchell or Jack Anderson? Ben Hecht and Charles MacArthur or Bob Woodward and Carl Bernstein? In each case, the latter no doubt considers himself on a higher plane, takes himself more seriously. The former, in contrast, offered lively writing, wit, and a more understanding attitude of the foibles of human nature.

In New Orleans in those years, reporters with faults and flaws roamed the city rooms, making no pretense at perfection. While they reported wrongdoing, it was with the attitude that it was their job, not a holy crusade conducted by morally superior beings.

There were few college graduates on the staffs, and it was not unusual to find reporters who had not finished high school—not that they were not bright; rather time, place, and circumstance often dictated on-the-job training instead of formal education. This route often produced a newsroom full of "characters," individualists who lived by their wits, shunned convention, pampered their hedonistic impulses, and did not give a whit for "job security."

Colorful may be a trite description of the habitués of the New Orleans newsrooms, but it is an accurate one. And perhaps the most colorful one of all, Major James E. Crown, became simultaneously the editor and managing editor of the *New Orleans States* when the legendary Captain J. Walker Ross died in 1937.

Crown, a rotund, bespeckled son of a Methodist circuit rider, was a real character. When Captain Ross was honored on his fiftieth anniversary at the *States*, Crown said, "Hell, I've been on fifty papers in one year."

It was not far from the the truth. Stanley Walker, perhaps the greatest city editor ever to run a New York newsroom, once said, "You haven't been around unless you've worked for Crown." In Denver, where he was city editor of the *Republican*, Crown hired a young man because he liked the looks of a raccoon coat he was wearing. The young man, Harvey Deuell, in the late 1930s became the highest paid newspaper staffer in the country when the *New York Daily News* gave him a salary of $142,000 to be its managing editor. Crown himself was a fine editor when he saw fit. He also was a gambler, a drinker, a hypocrite, and a chiseler. His staff loved him.

One day Walker Ross couldn't find Crown and he sent Allen Dowling out to look for him. That was a mistake. They both got drunk and stood out in the street in front of the paper yelling and cursing Ross, and singing, "Hey, Johnny Ross. Oh, Johnny Ross."

Dowling later told me this story:

> When Ross approached me about finding Crown, I knew exactly where he was. He was right across the street in a Greek hat-cleaning establishment. They had a poker game in the back room. But I said, "Well, I'll see if I can find him."
>
> I told Crown, "Captain Ross is raising hell. He wants you back." I don't remember Crown's exact language, but it was obscene. I said, "Well, I've got to give him some kind of story."
>
> Crown said, "You'll play poker."
>
> I said, "I gotta get back to the office, we're short-handed."
>
> "If you don't play poker, you're fired."
>
> I said, "If I don't get back I'm fired."
>
> I played. I figured getting fired for playing poker is better than getting fired for going back to work. But Ross had no idea of firing Crown. He was a cracker-jack man, the old-time fire and brimstone editor.

The people running the *States* today would never recognize the old *States*. They couldn't have gotten a newspaper out under those conditions. We were hardened pros, guys who had grown up the hard way. I mean we hadn't been to any journalism school. Flying by the seat of your pants. The old *States* had one police reporter, a federal run reporter, a civil district court reporter, a city hall reporter, and about two general assignment reporters. They had two men on the copy desk, a rewrite man, a women's society editor, three men in the sports department. When Ross died, Crown became editor and managing editor, and I became city editor and news editor. I mean the combinations you would get on that paper. Most papers would have four men in those slots. We had two.

When I was city editor, my desk abutted Crown's. He'd be snoring or stealing copy and filing it until the paper came out. He was always second-guessing me. He was always saying I was wrong on the headlines. The other paper played this or that. When Knute Rockne was killed, he played that down and instead headlined an earthquake in Nicaragua. I told him he was wrong. Nobody'll remember that earthquake but years from now people will still remember Rockne.

Crown was trying to second-guess me, but he was either making bets or stealing AP flimsies (carbon copies) and selling the stories to other papers. We used to file flimsies with the Associated Press. Well, Crown wouldn't do it when there was a good story until he could clear it with other newspapers. He'd query the papers: "So and so shot. How many words?" The papers would wire back, "three hundred."

And the people who had the by-lines, like Meigs O. Frost and myself, well, if he'd get a great big story, he'd scratch Frost's name off or my name off, and write James E. Crown at the bottom and file the damn thing. We never got a dime. When Huey Long was killed, I must have written a million words. Crown was filing them under his name to the *New York Daily News* before he was putting them in the *States*.

One day, Lon Yancey, a famous pilot of the day who had made his reputation flying from Old Orchard, Maine, to Rome, Italy, shortly after Charles Lindberg made his celebrated nonstop flight across the Atlantic, was visiting New Orleans. He invited me to take a ride in his revolutionary autogiro. It was somewhat like a helicopter—Amelia

Earhart had been flying around in them. At that time they were considered the safest thing in the air, but they turned out to be the most hazardous thing next to Icarus' wings.

Anyway, I knew Lon and he invited me to take a ride with him. I thought it would be a good idea, and I planned to take Leon Trice with me to get some fine aerial photos. When I proposed the idea to Crown, he turned me down cold. It was a Saturday and there was a big race at the Fair Grounds. And Crown had ordered a picture of the winner. He said he needed me at the desk and Trice at the Fair Grounds. Well, I knew I couldn't win.

But a short time later John D. Ewing, the son of Colonel Robert Ewing, the owner of the paper, came into the newsroom and engaged in conversation with Ross and Crown. I saw my chance and moved in. "Too bad, Jim, I couldn't make that flight today," I told Crown.

"What flight?" Ewing asked. I explained the invitation to him. Before anybody could say anything, Crown jumped in. "That's great, Eddie, that's great. You take that flight." Crown was not about to be exposed to Ewing, but he followed me out of the room with a warning: "You better be back here in time for Trice to get that picture for me!"

When Trice and I got to Menefee Field, we found that something in the autogiro needed to be repaired before we took off, and that took about an hour.

Finally we took off and within a few minutes after we were airborne, I noticed billows of smoke coming from a raging fire on the west bank of the Mississippi River. I signaled to Lon to head for the fire. He was in the rear of the open tandem cockpit and Trice and I were in the front. I laid down on the floor of the cockpit while Trice stood over me and shot pictures of the fire.

It was late when we got back and both Trice and myself knew we were going to catch hell. Crown was waiting for us at the head of the stairs. He started screaming at me, calling me every kind of son of a bitch and bastard in the book. He backed me across the newsroom, shouting that he had warned me to be back in time for the Fair Grounds picture. All the time I was trying to explain that I had pictures of a big fire.

"To hell with a fire," he kept shouting. "I told you to get back." This went on until he had backed me in front of the photographers' dark room. He suddenly stopped and asked, "What fire? What pictures do you have?" When I told him he became a changed man, very calm and collected.

"Now, Eddie, you go home and get some rest and come back and give me a hell of a story for Sunday. I'll tell Trice to get me a couple of pictures."

When I came back that night, more than one hundred pictures were stacked up on the floor, all addressed and ready to be mailed out to papers around the country. Crown had made another sale.

Ralph Wheatly, the chief of the Associated Press bureau, had watched the whole performance with glee. "I never saw a no good stinking reporter become a saint in such a short time," he told me.

I wrote a big story on the fire and Crown sold that too. Trice and I never saw any of that money. Not a cent.

The motivation for Crown's thefts of his staffers' work came from the necessity of obtaining money for his gambling activities. As Allen Dowling recalled, "Crown bet every race. Fifty cents a race. And Crown would put on these anti-gambling campaigns, in the midst of which he kept making bets on every race."

James W. Guillot, still in his teens when I first hired him as a photographer, recently recalled that the anti-gambling tirades usually resulted from a bad day with the horses. Then Crown would write a scathing editorial about the horrors of gambling. "You remember how Crown used to sit up in his office with a Bible in front of him like he was getting a quote for an editorial or just reading it, and he would have a racing form inside it. Remember that copy boy he had for years and the only thing he did was run bets for him."

For a number of years, Crown did not need a runner. Hell, he had a bookie running on the city desk, Andy Ojeda, the rewrite man. I used to call in the results of baseball games from the Alhambra Baths on Poydras and South Rampart streets, which was a cover for bookmakers. Imagine a metropolitan newspaper getting its news from a bookie joint. Imagine the paper not having its own sports wire. Just get the results for nothing and call them in. It was not infrequent that I would have to tell Andy, "Wait a minute, they're raiding the place." The police would come in, and there I was on the telephone, calling in the results of a ball game.

Ojeda's handbook ran for years in the newsroom without interference. It eventually had to go underground when the publisher had a bad run of luck. Ewing lost his shirt one day so he closed it down. I don't remember the horse but he shut the bookie down. No matter, there was another one running in the composing room, and Ojeda still made book on the side.

It was really a fabulous newspaper. Old Lee Edwards, who was a character, was the civil district court run reporter. He used one of those old revolving typewriters. He'd mark every piece of copy "exclusive up to this point."

He was the yachting expert—for all the papers. He worked for the yacht club. Practically every Sunday they would have a sailboat race, the Lipton Series. Edwards' leads would be, "Old Boreas whipped up a spanking breeze on Lake Pontchartrain today, and the Southern Yacht Club, largest in membership, second oldest yachting organization in the United States. . . ." All that was in the lead. Old Boreas spanked up more leads than one can imagine.

Lee and Crown would always get into some kind of fight on Saturday nights. Lee was always coming in loaded. One night they got into the damndest fight. So Lee goes down to the classified desk and grabs the telephone. He dares Crown to come downstairs and fight him. Crown starts spouting all over the place and he goes downstairs to fight it out. As soon as he stepped out of the elevator Lee cold-cocked him. Crown didn't have a chance, not a chance.

There was no danger of Edwards getting fired because Crown wouldn't fire anybody. But those were rough and ready characters in those days. John "Greaseball" Sullivan was on the rewrite desk sometimes, but he also covered the fights for out-of-town papers. He'd be at ringside for every fight, smoking those stinking five-cent cigars. He'd sell two paragraphs for a buck, saying who won the fight, and made the whole thing sound like he was Westbrook Pegler at a big event.

Old Sullivan would tell everybody his wife thought he was king of

Mardi Gras or something, in her estimation. He'd call his wife, and he'd be saying, "Yes, my love. Yes, sweetheart. Yes, my pet." The telephone operator at the paper would listen in, and old Greaseball's wife would be giving him hell, saying "You dirty son of a bitch. You dirty bastard." And he'd be saying, "Yes, my love."

Sullivan, like many of his contemporaries, had a penchant for drinking. Phil Guarisco, who became the paper's chief photographer, said that when he was a copy boy he made most of his money running to a nearby speakeasy to buy Sullivan's whiskey. "It used to cost sixty-five cents for a coke with whiskey in it. They'd mix whiskey in with the coke and I'd carry it back wrapped in newsprint. The deal was I'd get to keep the thirty-five cents change. I was running down there all day for him, and Crown would get mad at him and say, 'Get out of here you goddamned drunk.' You could smell him all the way across the newsroom. And once, Chris Eichon, the head engraver at the paper, painted a sparrow yellow and sold it to Sullivan as a canary. Boy, his wife gave him hell when he got home with it."

Sullivan never bothered to pay his bills. One day a collector came up to see him. Sullivan was sitting next to Ojeda on the rewrite desk, and this guy was bothering Ojeda and Sullivan. Crown was sitting there with his teeth out, drinking coffee from a tin can. Never in a cup. He got up and said, "Cut it out," and interjected himself into the argument.

The collector said, "Mr. Crown, I don't have any argument with you."

"Well," Crown said, "Goddamnit, you can't come in here like this." He really gets bully, and the fellow keeps backing up. Crown realizes he has the advantage by this time. That fellow's backing away. He backs him all the way out on Camp Street saying, "Don't you know you can't do this to my reporters," and so on. When they got out in front of the building, this fellow gets tired of Crown yelling at him. He hit Crown right in the nose. Put his nose all over his face. I can still picture Crown sitting there at the desk with that plaster all over his face. Everything was covered but his eyes.

It may be difficult to believe that the brawling city which spawned the rambunctious reportorial types also supported the first operas performed in America. Of course, that was long before Crown and company made their impact on New Orleans. The city had one of the oldest opera houses in the country, an ornate old building in the Vieux Carre. It was known as the Old French Opera House, and was pointed to with pride by local citizens until it was reduced to ashes in a fire which authorities said was of "undetermined origin." It may have been undetermined to authorities, but most of the *States'* staff knew who was responsible for the demise of that symbol of upper-class decadence.

Jim Crown burned the opera house down. A bunch of drunks were down there and started the fire. Allen Dowling was with them. Dowling told me that he; Crown; Roy Aymond, the *States'* cartoonist who expressed his individuality by not showing up for work for months at a time; Frank Holloway, the paper's wire editor; and Andy Ojeda were drinking in the patio of a cabaret adjoining the opera house. Some brandy barrels still containing their packing straw were lined up next to the opera house wall.

Dowling said, "Crown smoked three or four packs of cigarettes a day—an odd brand called Home Runs, the strongest straight Virginia tobacco. And Aymond smoked cigars. One of them started that fire flipping their ashes into those barrels. It must have smouldered awhile because we were gone before it started. I had to go back and cover the fire."

Crown had innumerable facets to his personality. One of his favorite stunts was when things were not going right—a couple of us might have got beat on some stories—he'd do what we called "selling the paper." He would walk up and down, tell us what a tremendous investment the paper was and what an obligation we had to the public and what the Ewings were doing for the community and other things of that kind. We paid no attention to him. The *States* was operated strictly for the financial benefit of the Ewings. We were always underpaid compared with other papers, and Crown had a favorite line. The *Item*, the *States'* afternoon rival, always had twice as many men as we had, and most of them were higher priced than we were. Crown would say, "Those people are journalists—you're newspapermen." He'd give us pep talks and of course we'd break our necks for him.

As a storyteller Crown would sometimes relate accounts of his amorous adventures and at other times would go off on religious tangents. On Saturdays he would dictate vigorous "Go to Church" editorials. It was the major's practice to dictate all of his editorials to a reporter. He punctuated his intonations by slapping desks as he paraded up and down the newsroom, booming out the gospel according to Crown.

The late Dave McGuire, one of my reporters who became New Orleans Mayor deLesseps "Chep" Morrison's chief administrative officer, wrote of Crown that he would occasionally begin his editorials by announcing to his news staff: "Gentlemen, this is the damndest thing ever I did hear tell of."

That happened whenever he was in an indignant mood and about to let fly with no punches pulled. His black horn-rimmed glasses would slip down on his nose, he would twirl his watch chain furiously, and his hair would fall in disarray on either side of a river-like part down the middle of his head.

As he concluded his dictation, McGuire wrote, Crown would light up into a grin, take off his glasses, slap his thigh, and boom out, "Now that's telling 'em, ain't it."

Walter Cowan, the associate editor of the *States-Item*, relates how one day Crown was pacing up and down dictating when suddenly he whirled around and ordered a recently hired cub reporter to "answer that telephone."

"But it's not ringing, Major," the reporter replied.

At that instant the telephone rang. "You've gotta anticipate those things if you're gonna make it in this business, son," Crown said as he picked up dictating where he left off.

Aside from his "Go to Church" editorials, Crown also enjoyed conversations with local clergymen, probably as a result of his upbringing by a Methodist circuit-rider in Virginia. Once he bet the pastor of the Carrollton Avenue Methodist Church he could preach a better sermon than the minister.

Called on his bet, Crown showed up Sunday morning in his best suit topped off by a new derby. His topic was "Don't Sell God Short." His style was the antithesis of Dale Carnegie—he believed in telling people what was wrong with them. In fact, he embarrassed several reporters who, on a lark, had gone to hear him preach. He made them stand up and pointed them out to the congregation as examples of sinners, men who drank, gambled, and consorted with women of loose morals. Before the sermon was over, Crown had most of the congregation in tears.

He also took considerable pride in his acquaintanceship with noteworthy personages of the day. And at that time the *States* habitually interviewed numerous celebrities. No matter who the celebrity was, Crown would pretend to know the person. He would pretend that they were big buddies. The truth was that they had never heard of him.

One day Channing Pollock, dramatist of *In The Bishop's Carriage,* was at the St. Charles Hotel. I got a call he was there, and told Crown I was going to interview him. Before he could say anything, I said, "Oh, it's all right, I'll tell Channing hello for you. It's okay." I was giving him the business.

Before I could get out the door Crown said, "Ed, wait a minute." I went back; Crown reached into his pocket and pulled out a five dollar bill. He said, "Here, give this to Channing and tell him that's the five I got from him in Chicago. I just want to be sure I pay him back."

Channing Pollock never heard of Jim Crown. Pollock and I took the five down to the St. Charles bar and drank it up. I got a picture of Pollock begging for his money and me holding the five dollar bill. When I got back to the paper I told Crown that Pollock said, "Thanks," he "knew you'd come through."

It was in an atmosphere such as this that I thrived. I became, I believe, a good reporter of the city. My city background, aptitude for language, enjoyment of the work, and philosophy of life all collaborated to make me the newspaperman I was and am.

From time to time my friends at the paper, and in other walks of life, would congratulate me on a story or some other piece of reporting. While I appreciated their remarks, I was discomforted by too much flattery. Once I told a friend, "Look here, I'm not the Archangel Gabriel. I would be embarrassed to be painted as an archangel. There's a little Lucifer in me. I mean I'm a human being, just like everybody else. I'm no saint. I don't even pose as a saint. I just want to be somebody who will express an honest opinion. Moreover, I don't love everybody. I don't love everybody at all. On the other hand, I don't hate people. I dislike some, and I keep away from them. That's all.''

Still, taking my ability to speak into consideration, I guess it was inevitable that I would gravitate toward politics, despite my love of newspapering. I never intended to enter politics and after being elected to Congress I often repeated the contention that I was just a reporter on sabbatical. Even after having been in Congress several terms I would awaken at night, having dreamt I was back on the *States*, running the city desk.

My first major political undertaking after my successes in school elections was my bid to become president of the Young Men's Business Club, then a civic organization with exceptional political clout. In those days politics were hot over there in the Young Men's Business Club. Louis Riecke was running one crowd and I was running the other. They called Louis "Little Dick" and me "Big Dick." (Riecke, who later unsuccessfully challenged me for Congress, went on to become a highly respected president of the Orleans Parish School Board.) During this period Abe Shushan, who was president of the Orleans Levee Board, was a power in politics. I told him, "Abe, I want to run for president and I want you on my ticket."

Shushan said, "No, I don't want to be on any ticket. I'll give you all the money you need, but I don't want to be on the ticket!"

I said, "No, sir, I want you to be on my ticket. I don't want any money. I want you on the ticket." And why did I want him on the ticket? Why didn't I want any money? Because when the fight got hot and the going got tough, he could leave me. But if he was on the ticket, he couldn't leave me. He had to stay with me. And that is exactly what happened. He was on the ticket as a board member.

Well, it developed that Frank Stich was my opponent. Louis Riecke was on his ticket as vice-president. Stich was a floor leader for the Old Regulars in the state house of representatives. Well, Shushan and all these people were Long people. There was a truce between the Old Regulars and the Longs. They put it to Frank: "Do you want to be a floor leader? Pull out of the race. You can't run for president of the YMBC and be floor leader."

So Frank pulled out. The Long people were all supporting me and I was fighting the hell out of them on the paper. Anyway, when Frank pulled out, that left a headless ticket. But then I made a mistake. There was a rule at the time that a candidate couldn't discuss his candidacy for a certain number of days. I went to see Forrest Pendleton, and I talked the situation over with him. As a result, they tried to disqualify me.

The case was taken before the board of directors. I was represented by Dick Leche, who was later to become governor of Louisiana. They met for three hours, and finally I made my pitch. I made a grand speech. I said, "Now, I know how an innocent man feels when he goes to the gallows." I cried all over that place and I won. I made a hell of a speech that day. I went to the presidency of the YMBC without ever being in an election.

This was in 1932, and I was still struggling up the reportorial ladder. I worked hard and had my own methods. I never took notes. I went on assignment and talked to people, just carried on a conversation. I got more information that way because I've always thought that a pencil and paper scared people and made them clam up. I always carried a piece of copy paper with me, and following an interview, I would jot down a word or two.

While taking notes may have disconcerted some people, not taking them disconcerted others. My brother, Gordon, who was handling the *Times-Picayune*'s automobile advertising at the time, recalls that when I was sent to interview Charles F. "Boss" Kettering, the inventor of the automobile self-starter, I never used a pencil or paper on the story; that I just sat around talking to Kettering. After awhile, Kettering's press aide came over to Gordon and whispered, "When is your brother going to start taking notes?" Gordon told him, "He never takes notes."

I have always preferred that technique to the popular conception of the reporter spit-wetting the end of his pencil and writing madly. Fortunately I was blessed with a phonographic memory. Rival reporters covering the same story often remarked that they were amazed at my accuracy.

One of my strongest points as a reporter, I believe, is the fact that I like people. My acquaintances and friends have come from all strata

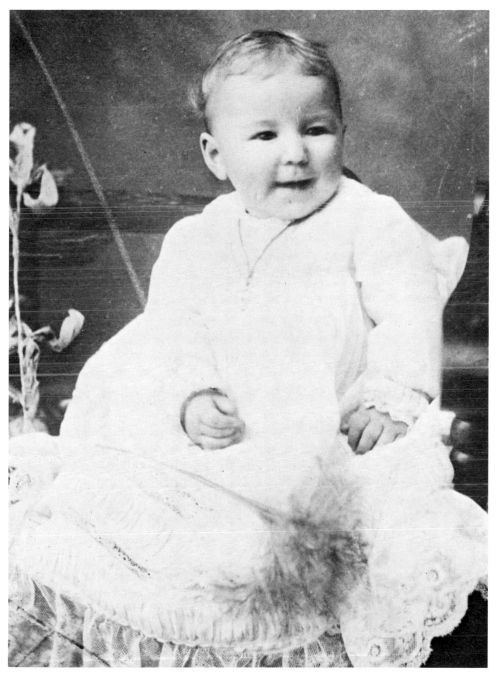

Always a clothes horse, I'm dressed in style for my first birthday, October 12, 1902.

Me, at age five.

My brother Gordon, age three.

My mother, haughty but with humor.

My father, an honest, dignified man.

On my twenty-first birthday.

With my mother.

My father.

My father and brother.

*En route to New Rochelle,
N.Y., in 1914, I check out the
White House. Woodrow Wil-
son was President.*

*I returned to the White House many times at the invitation of seven presidents, including this visit
with my wife, Gladys, for a reception given by President John F. Kennedy in 1963.*

At ease, Gladys, myself, and our daughter Dawn at our Alexandria, Va., home.

With my Duhe grandchildren, Edward Malcolm, Martin Bofill, Jeanne Louise and Kim Marie in Speaker McCormack's office.

After the hanging of my portrait in the House Armed Services hearing room in 1971, President Nixon posed with my family. From left: Mrs. Gordon Hebert, Gordon, Dawn, myself, President Nixon, Gladys, my niece, Mrs. Renée Hebert Bryant, my son-in-law, John M. Duhe, Jr. In front are my grandchildren: Kim, Martin, Edward, and Jeanne.

Dawn, as Queen of Hermes in 1955 with the King, Harry Batt.

As Queen of the Washington Mardi Gras Ball, 1952, she was escorted by Vice President Nixon. They posed with Gladys and me. Walter Cronkite narrated the ball.

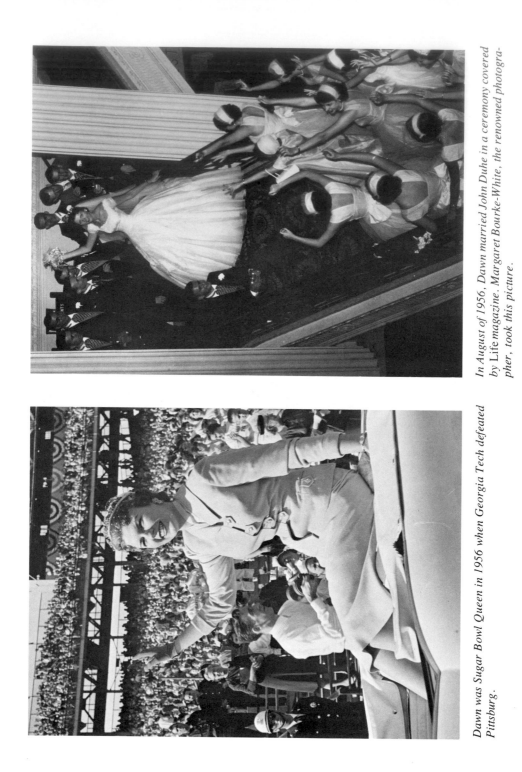

Dawn was Sugar Bowl Queen in 1956 when Georgia Tech defeated Pittsburg.

In August of 1956, Dawn married John Duhe in a ceremony covered by Life magazine. Margaret Bourke-White, the renowned photographer, took this picture.

At the Louisiana State Museum on the occasion of my 25th year in Congress. Hugh Wilkinson (left) gave the principal address. Seymour Weiss (next to the flag) sponsored my portrait hanging behind me.

It took me 25 years in Congress to get two of my biggest supporters together. John F. Tims, Jr., the publisher of the Times-Picayune (standing), and Leander Perez, the Plaquemines Parish powerhouse, came to my silver anniversary luncheon at Antoine's.

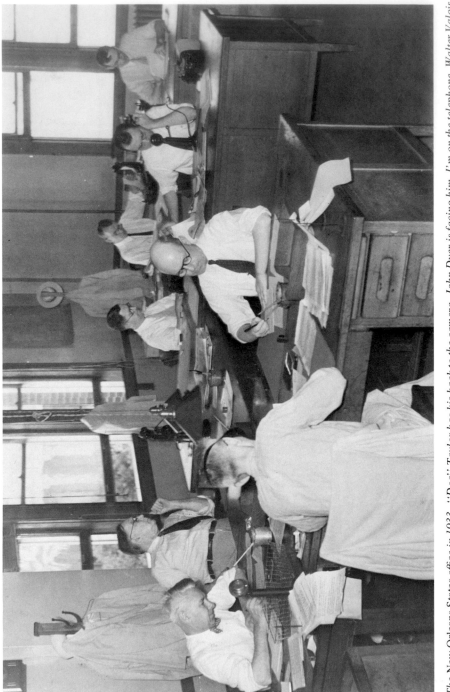

The New Orleans States office in 1933. "Doc" Taylor has his back to the camera. John Dyer is facing him. I'm on the telephone. Walter Valois is behind me. Thomas Ewing Dabney is in the corner. Andy Ojeda is next to him. Major James Evans Crown surveys the scene while Frank Holloway edits copy. It was a typical city room of the day.

Me, banging out the story of the Huey Long assassination.

I'm interviewing Sheffield Clarke, Jr., of Memphis who had just flown into New Orleans as the result of his father's murder. The man in the straw hat is Police Captain Jock Malone. Hal Boyle, who also was a States reporter, is at far right.

Murder scene. Walton Tomplain (left) had just shot to death "Big Jim" Clark in a bootleg war when I arrived on the scene in my Panama outfit. Captain Malone is at far right.

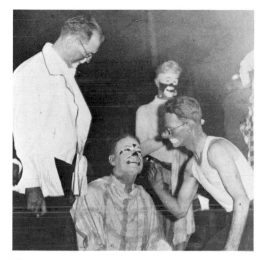

Clowning around. Roy Aymond (seated) and I get the finishing touches put on for the last circus parade Barnum and Bailey held in New Orleans. The story I wrote, "A Clown for a Day."

I dress for the story covering a New Orleans Riding Club horse show.

Col. Jack Jouett (right), the head of Standard Oil Air Division in New Orleans and who later was a flight instructor in China, took me for my first plane ride.

At the Fairgrounds racetrack with Bruce I. Hayer, Tulane baseball coach and major league scout.

The cream of the Louisiana press corps at the trial of U.S. Sen. John H. Overton of Louisiana. In the foreground, Times-Picayune reporter George Vandervoot, wearing the light suit, talks to fellow T-P reporter Frank Allen. Alexander Gifford, Sr., also of the T-P, is taking notes. Others are: John Femrite, United Press, listening to the proceedings; William Gaudet, International News Service, facing the camera; Margaret Dixon, of the Baton Rouge Morning Advocate, partially obscured by Gaudet's head; Herman Deutsch, of the New Orleans Item, mugging for the camera; unidentified; Charles "Chick" Frampton, also of the Item; me, with pencil in hand; Edward Desobry, of the Associated Press; and Capt. Henry Assett of the New Orleans Police Department. (Insert) Covering the Louisiana Legislature with Billy Fitzpatrick, a future Pulitzer Prize winner and my successor at the New Orleans Daily States.

Mrs. Eleanor Roosevelt holds a press conference in New Orleans. I'm the reporter (standing at left) who is not taking notes. Other reporters (from left): Mac Darling, of the Times-Picayune; *Elizabeth Kell, society editor of the* States; *and seated next to Mrs. Roosevelt, Podine Schoenberger of the* Times-Picayune.

As a judge of the city marble championship, I (at right) was photographed with fellow judges Nicholas Bauer, superintendent of schools; Mayor Martin Behrman; and Leon diBenedetto, director of playgrounds.

of society. And I think that my contacts and friendships opened many doors for me as a reporter. In 1936, for example, there was a special train going to Washington, D.C., with Richard Leche, the governor, and other Louisiana dignitaries aboard to attend the inauguration ceremonies for President Franklin D. Roosevelt. I was assigned to cover the activities for the *States*. Before I left, Crown is reported to have said, "I'll bet that son of a bitch Hébert gets in the White House."

When I checked into the Mayflower Hotel, there was a message from my friend, Mayris "Tiny" Chaney, one half of Chaney and Fox, the Roosevelt Dance Team. A charming couple, they became friends with the President and his wife, and Mrs. Roosevelt was the godmother of Tiny's first child.

I had known Chaney and Fox since the couple's first appearance at the Club Forest, and when Tiny learned I would be in Washington for the inauguration, she left a message at the hotel for me to call the White House.

I called and Malvina Thompson, who was Mrs. Roosevelt's secretary, took the call. She said Mayris Chaney had been talking so much about me that Mrs. Roosevelt insisted that I come to lunch the next day. The luncheon was set for the day before the inauguration, but I had already planned to share the noon meal with an old friend, Arthur "Dutch" Defenderfer, the mayor of Chevy Chase, Maryland. I told Dutch I couldn't keep the luncheon date, that I had to go to the White House for a luncheon. He didn't believe me. He didn't believe I was having lunch at the White House, so he drove me right up to the front door. I left him watching me as I went in.

There were about ten people gathered for lunch. Very interesting people. We talked for awhile and then went into the private family dining room downstairs. I was seated between Elliott Roosevelt's wife, who was on my left, and Malvina Thompson, who was on my right.

The meal progressed with amiable talk. Prior to dessert, a small bowl with a fancy doily beneath it was placed on a plate before each person. I noticed others removing the finger bowl and I followed suit. Except I left the doily on the plate.

I didn't know what that damned doily was and nobody told me anything, and the dessert was chocolate ice cream. I just poured that chocolate ice cream right on top of that doily, which, at the time, I thought was a silly thing to do.

Undaunted, however, I ate the ice cream and continued conversing with Mrs. Thompson, learning that Mrs. Roosevelt was planning a trip to New Orleans. After the meal I made a point to escort the First Lady across the hall to the private elevator which provided access to the family's living quarters. I told Mrs. Roosevelt I understood she would be visiting New Orleans shortly.

She looked surprised and asked, "How do you know that?"

"Mrs. Thompson told me."

"Yes, I am," Mrs. Roosevelt admitted.

Hardly pausing to make polite good-byes, I tore out of the White House, making a mad dash to the first telephone I could find. The next day the *States* had an eight-column headline across the front page trumpeting the fact that Mrs. Roosevelt had confided her plans to one of the paper's reporters.

When the paper came out, Major Crown beamed at the headline with satisfaction and bellowed across the news room, "I told you that son of a bitch would get into the White House."

Getting back to the ice cream, pouring it on top of the doily naturally was embarrassing, but I tried to be nonchalant about it. No one said anything. They were too polite. Years later, I was attending another White House dinner. Among the guests were actress Joan Crawford, the famous acting team of the Lunts, Henry Cabot Lodge, Supreme Court Justice William O. Douglas, and the very young girl who had just become his bride.

It was *déjà vu* for me when the youthful Mrs. Douglas neglected to remove her doily. Joan Crawford, however, reached across in front of her, picked up the doily and set it under the finger bowl. It was all very embarrassing for that young girl.

When I was a reporter, crimes of violence got more attention than they do today, perhaps because there were fewer of them. They were, nevertheless, my bread and butter. I had scooped the city on the marriage of a well-known local amateur star, Aline Richter. When I learned of the marriage, I also learned that my friend Aline was not overjoyed by the union. She had even implied that only her suitor's persistence had pressured her into marrying him. The man was exceptionally jealous. Early one morning this guy shot and wounded Aline and then killed himself. I was working on the story so I went out to this boy's house; his name was Sullivan. He was from a very prominent family and I wanted to get a picture of him for the paper. I lied like hell to his mother. I wanted that picture. I told her she should let everybody see what a fine-looking boy he was. I got the picture, the frame, everything. Before I left that place I had his picture, the story, everything there was. In those days, it was "get the story."

As I progressed up the reportorial ladder, I would take young reporters under my wing. One young man, John Klorer, who later became a night city editor of the *Times-Picayune*, was hired by Crown at my suggestion. Shortly afterwards, I was in the office when the police reported a murder-suicide in the uptown section of New Orleans.

I'd usually cover the murders so I said, "Come on, John, go with me." When we got there it was the bloodiest mess I'd ever seen. The guy had killed his wife while she was at the table preparing liver for breakfast, then shot himself. Klorer looked at the mess, the woman and the man, blood everywhere. Then he said, "Who's gonna cook the liver?"

As a political reporter, my first assignment was to cover Huey Long when he opened his campaign for the United States Senate standing under the Evangeline Oak at St. Martinville. This was the first time a sound truck was used in a political campaign. Huey introduced it and later used the same truck to stump Arkansas to elect Hattie Caraway to the United States Senate.

Anyway, things were all right until Huey started getting on the "lying newspapers." Then it got a little crowded around there.

I was with Long the night he got the manuscript of *Every Man a King*, the ghost-written book which spelled out how the Kingfish allegedly was going to Share-the-Wealth. He asked me, "What do you think I ought to call this book?" Then he read the last paragraph which had the line "every man a king" in it. He said, "That's what

I'm gonna call it.'' Of course he already had his mind made up what he was going to call it. He was just trying to con me.

The day the book was published, I ran into Huey in the lobby of the Roosevelt Hotel. Long gave me a copy of the book but made me pay for the damned thing. He autographed it in green ink. He borrowed a pen from Seymour Weiss, who always wrote in green ink. He wrote, "To my good friend, F. Edward Hebert, from his friend, Huey Long, United States Senator, National Democratic Committeeman, and best wishes . . .'' and on and on with that stuff. He handed it to me, then said, "Give it back," and he wrote, "Among these wishes are that more respectable employers will sign your pay check. HPL.''

Long was always at war with the newspapers, and it was not long before I fell from grace. Jack Dempsey the former heavyweight champion, was in town. I went over to the Roosevelt Hotel to interview him. I had Phil Guarisco with me. As I was walking in the lobby, the elevator door opened and here was this man covered with blood—a terrible split over his eye. I looked at him and said, "Senator Overton, what happened to you?''

Burt Henry, a very prominent lawyer, a socialite leader in the fight against the Long machine, had hit him. Senator John H. Overton of Louisiana had made a speech saying he had "torn the mask of hypocrisy'' from Burt Henry. Henry demanded an apology; to him Overton's statement was an insult. Overton wouldn't apologize and Henry hit him. I took Overton to his room, called Seymour Weiss, and got a doctor to come up.

Then, for some unexplained reason, one of Long's hatchet men, Maurice Gatlin, who later took on Hale Boggs, went on radio and said that I had struck Senator Overton. He could talk like Huey. He went on radio and described me as a big six-foot-two prize fighter who beat up the senator. And I never knew Gatlin except by name.

The next indication I was not a fair-haired boy of the Long machine also occurred at the Roosevelt Hotel, where I was living and paying my rent by doing public-relations work for the hotel. Suddenly, I was presented a bill for my rent. Apparently some of my news stories had riled Huey who ordered Seymour Weiss to charge me for my room. I got the message, paid the bill, and moved into the St. Charles Hotel where I worked out a similar arrangement to pay my room rent.

During my stay at the Roosevelt, I met a very attractive young woman, Gladys Bofill, an assistant to the comptroller of the hotel and the daughter of a well-to-do Cajun family. When I first saw Gladys I thought she was the most gorgeous woman I had ever seen in my life, and she still is. How she could have given me the time of day I can never figure out. She was such a striking woman and here I was, a tall, skinny guy. I had no attraction that I could imagine, for such a glamorous woman. I can't explain something like that. As far as a woman is concerned, I am very much an introvert because I can never accept the fact that a woman would be attracted to me. I can see myself in the mirror. I am not a physically attractive man to a woman, as far as I can see.

When it became generally known that Gladys and I were dating, she was fired from her job at the Roosevelt, another casualty of Huey Long's democracy. In August, 1934, Gladys and I were married, and I took her on a news story for a honeymoon. It probably was not too dangerous. The rebellion was almost over in Cuba and photographer Leon Trice and his wife were there for company.

In one day I obtained exclusive interviews with Colonel Fulgencio Batista, the late Cuban dictator; Carlos Mendieta, who was the figurehead president of Cuba; and United States Ambassador Jefferson Caffery. That was probably my best day's work as a reporter. Caffery, a fellow Louisianian, told me that it would be impossible for him to secure an interview with Batista because the rebel leader was conducting operations in the mountains. When I left Caffery, I told the chauffeur that I really wanted to meet Batista. The driver replied that he knew where Batista's headquarters were, and that the colonel was there.

"Let's go," I said, and we sped off to secluded Camp Columbia in a Havana suburb. I talked my way into the camp and, escorted by what appeared to be half of the Cuban army, I was received by Batista in his stronghold and granted one of the first interviews given to an American by the island chieftain. As usual, I took no notes, and waited until I returned to New Orleans to write the articles on my three interviews.

When the *States* published my story on Batista it had hard news value and human interest. Today it remains valuable from a historic point of view, describing early Batista as seen by another man his same age, 33, who had yet to make his own political move. In addition to providing much information, I think, the story is still interesting and entertaining.

The article began:

I would rather be Sergeant Fulgencio Batista than Dictator Fulgencio Batista.

It is a bold challenge to a world of dictators that this once humble and meek Cuban sergeant flaunts in the faces of the Hitlers, the Mussolinis, and the Stalins. It is defiant refutation of the charge that patriotism has been supplanted by selfishness and ambition for power in a strife-torn world. It is the answer of a man who could be dictator or king if he wishes. It is an answer from the heart and soul of Cuba's iron man, Colonel Fulgencio Batista.

The frank, sincere, and straight-forward declaration came almost shot-like from the former army sergeant as he sat comfortably in a rocker one afternoon recently in a cellar in the officers' club at Camp Columbia, outside the city of Havana. I had been chatting amicably with Colonel Batista for the better part of an hour when he issued the statement which startled me with its naive positiveness and finality. During that hour I had been trying to get behind the mask of this young thirty-three-year-old revolutionary leader to find out, first-hand, just what sort of stuff Batista was made of. I sought him out to ascertain for myself the difference between Batista, the man, and Batista, the mutinous sergeant and revolutionist of Cuba.

"You can be a Hitler," I told him. "You can be Mussolini. You can be a Stalin. You can be president. You can be king. You can be dictator."

He drank in every word as it was uttered. He half-slumped in his rocker as I spoke. He placed a clenched fist to his chin and closed his eyes. At the mention of each dictator's name he grunted in assent and nodded his head affirmatively. Each grunt and each nod told of his own full realization that he possessed the power which I attributed to him. He made me understand I was not paying him overdue compliment.

When I had finished, he opened his eyes. There was fire in them. He tensed his hands and the bones bulged through the dark skin. He gripped the rocker's arm with both hands. He didn't wait for the interpreter to answer. In that characteristic, imperfect though positive English, he answered for himself.

"I would rather be Sergeant Fulgencio Batista than Dictator Fulgencio Batista.

"I don't want my people to think of me as a colonel. I want them to always think of me as a sergeant. I want them to know and believe that today I am the same as I have always been. I am one of them and I am no better than the humblest Cuban. I was born a Cuban and I am going to die a Cuban. Anything that I may do or accomplish is not for my personal benefit but for the benefit of my people.

"I want my people to live under a rule of kindness, and justice, and democracy."

I wrote on and on. Not surprisingly, Batista liked the story. I sent him copies along with photographs, and in return received a courteous reply signed by the colonel. However, it was addressed to me in "New Orleans, N.Y.," but then few Cuban leaders have ever been experts on North American geography.

The next time I met Batista was in the office of Speaker of the House of Representatives Sam Rayburn. I was then a congressman, and had been asked to escort Batista to the House floor to address a joint session of the United States Congress. Sergeant Batista had become President Batista.

An entirely different aspect of my journalism is found in a column I wrote on June 2, 1936. I admit it is sentimental, a little gushy, but what should a reader expect from a newspaperman when his first and only child has just been born.

She's unquestionably the queen of the House of Hebert and surely you and you and you will pardon me while I prate at length on her arrival because after all, one doesn't become a father every day—even columnists. I know there have been millions of babies born before this one and there will be millions of others born in years to come, but I am positive none could be such an adorable, charming, precious, coy, beautiful bundle of loveliness as this package . . . Now, wouldn't I be a helluva pappy if I didn't think so!!! And why shouldn't a guy who writes about other folks for 365 days a year be allowed to write one day about his first offspring?

If it had been a boy it would have been F. Edw. Hebert II. If a girl I pledged to give her the name "Dawn" in commemoration of the many dawns that her pop had wandered aimlessly homeward and finally, hesitatingly crawled under the soothing white sheets and rested a rather enlarged and airy head on downy pillows. Sure 'nuf, it was a girl and Dawn it will be.

The mother? Oh, she had the baby.

During her infancy, Dawn lived with us at the St. Charles Hotel, and was therefore reared in the atmosphere of adults. Her playground was the lobby of the St. Charles. As far as she was concerned Santa Claus would arrive from the lobby. As a small child, she had no playmates, only her maid, Myrtle Wright. Myrtle would put her in a then-fashionable harness and walk with her down to Lafayette Square. That's the reason we built the house on the Mississippi coast, to take her there in the summer.

Dawn attended Catholic elementary schools, and when she approached high-school age, we wanted to send her to the prestigious Sacred Heart Academy on St. Charles Avenue in New Orleans. A person practically had to register their child before birth to get her in there in those days. When I decided to send Dawn there, a friend of mine said, "Hébert, you're crazy, you can't get that kid in there."

I therefore went to the Academy to speak with the mother superior. She was very gracious, but said, "I'm sorry, Mr. Hébert, we can't accept your daughter. As you know, we are overcrowded."

I said, "Mother, give me the application, please."

She said, "I'm sorry, I can't."

"Will you give me the application and let me fill it out at least?" I asked. So she agreed and I took the application and filled it out. In about a week I got a very nice note from the mother saying that there was no place open, that they were oversubscribed, and had a long waiting list.

Then, about two weeks later, I got this beautiful note from her: "Dear Mr. Hébert, the Blessed Mother has smiled on us. There is a vacancy. We would be delighted to have Dawn."

Well, that was the first time I knew that Our Lady wore the red robes of an archbishop. I went to see Archbishop Francis Rummel, and I told the archbishop, "Let's get going here. They're not going to accept my daughter."

Glenn Conrad, who compiled and edited *Creed of a Congressman*, an evaluation of my congressional career, concludes that my "ideals are based squarely on the concept of fair play.'' I've tried to let few transgressions stemming from the human condition unsettle me, but, on rare occasions some act has been so grossly unfair as to outrage me. Huey Long accomplished that. In a charade and mockery of the political process, the Kingfish had called a mass meeting on the campus of Louisiana State University where he was to name the school's star halfback, Abe Mickal, to the state senate. The action moved a clear-sighted and courageous student to write a letter to the university's newspaper, *The Reveille*, criticizing Long's shenanigans. The decision by the student staff to print the letter set off an uproar which led to the dismissal of seven journalism students whose youthful ideals would not permit them to submit to the dictates of Huey Long. The man who actually expelled them was Dr. James Monroe Smith, the Long-appointed and controlled university president. On June 9, 1935, I had had enough and gave vent to my feelings about the shenanigans in my front-page column.

> The greatest tragedy that can befall youth is to lose faith in its ideals . . . When ideals perish, life becomes a drab, meaningless existence . . . When ideals are shattered there is nothing that we can hope for . . . When our tabernacles of ideals crash we find ourselves broken in spirit . . . weakened in courage . . . clasping only to a straw of life . . . The loss of idealism is sad at any time in life, but its loss in youth is irreparable . . . The hope of a nation is embedded in the idealism of its youth . . . Humanity must of necessity turn to the idealism of youth for its betterment . . .
>
> Only too short a time ago, seven youths at Louisiana State University . . . were expelled from their university because they fought for their ideals . . . because they believed in the principles of the freedom of the press and free speech, the foundation on which the structure of democracy has been built . . . And when one of those seven youths told a professor that he was fighting for a principle, he was told: ''When you get as old as I am you will learn that principles don't mean much!'' How brutal! How inhuman!
>
> But principles do mean something after all. There are ideals and there are principles and there are men and women who preach idealism and live up to the standards of their ideals. The story that hasn't been told is that $1200 has been raised by an unnamed group of men and women in order to finance those boys through [the University of] Missouri . . . to

prove to them that their fight was not in vain . . . That fund stands as a monument to idealism and principles.

Those boys today know that "He who dies for an ideal is not a lost soul." They know that, despite what one professor said, principles do count for something. They know that there are still clean and decent things in life. They know that idealism is still alive in the world and that there is still hope for the future.

Sports, of course, were included in my columns. I had been a boxing fan most of my life. As boys, Gordon and I climbed over the fence in our backyard on Canal Street and slipped into the Tulane Athletic Club where we saw some of the top fighters in the country perform—Sam Langford (the Boston Tarbaby), Harry Wills, the Moran brothers, Joe Azevedo, Mexican Joe Rivers and many others. I grew up watching the local greats of the era—Joe Mandot (the French Market Baker Boy), Pal Moran, Martin Burke, Tony Canzoneri, and numerous topnotch club fighters. I covered as a sports writer such stalwarts as Jack Dempsey, Gene Tunney, Harry Greb, the Gibbons brothers.

Perhaps the most courageous of them all was a little man whom Mother taught when she was a school teacher in Houma. He was born Pete Gulotta, and when his family moved to New Orleans he paid his way as a bootblack. Under the name Pete Herman, he twice became the bantamweight champion of the world. He was going blind when he lost his title for the second time, but he hid the fact from his manager and continued to fight another year, going out a winner when he beat Roy Moore in Boston in 1921.

By 1935 Herman was completely blind. He sought help in Memphis, and he sent me a card from the hospital: "Hello, Ed, feeling fine. Leaving in a few days." Almost as an afterthought, he added, "Operation, I don't believe successful. Regards, Pete Herman."

I was particularly moved by the courage shown by this little man, possibly because I myself had some insight into the world of the sightless since I had lost an eye. It moved me to write: "In that simple message on the back of a postcard from Memphis is the story of faith, courage, hope and undying spirit. The spirit of a mighty little man who wouldn't quit and who in the face of eternal darkness has the courage and the fortitude to write, 'feeling fine.' "

Perhaps our view of human nature was more naive and sentimental in those less sophisticated and cynical times, and in some regard, I know it was. But that's the way it was, and I loved being a part of it.

CHAPTER V

THE LAST MILE

MY FORTE AS A reporter was drama, and there are few stories that conjure up more histrionics than an execution, so I made hangings my beat. Few contemporaries, outside of an executioner, and certainly no other member of Congress, have witnessed as many men drop from the gallows as I have. I have been present at hangings when society extracted its vengeance upon one, two, three, and four men. Some of them, whose death was sought in keeping with the Old Testament fiat of ''an eye for an eye,'' were interesting individuals. It was the change and development in their personalities during their incarceration on death row which I chronicled for my readers. As I wrote of their careers right up to the final moment, I discovered that my piece was not a news story, but a passion play.

One of the most interesting men I accompanied to the gallows was Kenneth Neu, a swashbuckling, defiant double murderer. The twenty-six-year-old Georgian also possessed an excellent baritone singing voice. By the time he was scheduled to die, Neu had become the main topic of conversation in New Orleans, largely because of my columns. Neu had entered prison singing and vowed to leave it the same way. As the time of execution drew near, Neu became sullen and refused to see members of the press, which tended to indicate the face he had shown to the public was merely a façade. The date of the execution was February 1, 1935. In my January 16 column, I discussed the apparent changes in Neu:

> The thing that is important is how this man is going to die. Will he go to the gallows with the audacious bravado that has characterized him?

Will he wilt under the strain of approaching death and die a cringing coward? Will he walk to the gallows with a song on his lips in the manner that he has bellowed popular ballads while fellow prisoners have been led to their doom, or will he be carried to the trap by the strong arms of prison guards?

If he is sincere in his statement that he has repented and has embraced religion, he will die bravely. If he is sincere, he will die buoyed by the comfort of religion. If he is not sincere, he will be carried to the gallows—he will collapse. Kenneth Neu's only chance for a brave death is his heart—his only hope is religion.

I have never seen religion fail men on the gallows. I have seen murderers die—I have walked up the gallows' steps with men who have killed and I have heard their last words—I have spent the last night on earth with men who were to be killed because they have killed.

I had stoked interest in Neu's execution by being dramatic, by making the reading public anxious for my account of the events which were to occur on the first day of February. When the time came I was prepared. Looking back, it seems I wrote almost as if the executions were held for my benefit. I felt it was my duty to chronicle the minute details of the condemned man's last hours, to record those final moments as if anything less would be an insult to the condemned man and a violation of my obligation to my paper and its readers.

Louis Kenneth Neu kept his word Friday at noon on the gallows of the Parish Prison and died without a whimper.

Until he was prepared for the death march Neu remained in lively spirits and within five minutes of his death was reading a popular magazine and jesting over the cartoons in his cell.

With him at the end were two priests, two Sisters of Mercy, two prison workers and two newspaper reporters. He denied himself to all members of the press except the two who bade him good-bye just before he asked that he be allowed to place his own handcuffs on his wrists.

Before he went to the gallows Neu received a telegram from his father in Savannah, Georgia, which bade the murderer God-speed.

"God bless you until we meet again," it said.

Louis Kenneth Neu, braggart killer, became Louis Kenneth Neu, penitent sinner the last night he spent on the earth he had roamed as adventurer, soldier, killer, but withal he kept his word and sang songs as he had never sung them before.

For months Neu had promised to go out of prison as he came in—singing. During recent weeks there were reports and rumors that he was breaking and had lost the braggadocio which had characterized him since his apprehension. His determination not to see newspaper reporters added to the rumors that he was breaking. Louis Kenneth Neu contradicted those rumors with a rich baritone voice shortly after midnight when strains of "June in January," the popular ballad of the moment, filled the barred walls of the death chamber only a few feet removed from where the murderer sang his last song at night.

There was nothing about Neu to indicate that he was going to die within 12 hours when at midnight he turned the radio on in his cell and listened intently to the broadcast of Barney Rapp and his orchestra from the Hotel Gibson in Cincinnati.

And a big smile spread over Neu's face as he listened to two numbers, "Blue Moon" and "Love in Bloom," which were especially dedicated to him by Rapp on the eve of his death. The orchestra leader and Neu had been friends. They became acquainted when Rapp's band played at the Club Forest here last year and visited Neu in the condemned tier at Parish Prison. At that time Rapp promised to play for Neu the night before he was hanged. Thursday night at midnight Rapp kept his promise and dedicated the two favorite melodies of the killer to Neu.

The voice of Rapp over the powerful Crosley radio station carried the word that the orchestra leader had kept his promise to Neu. He announced that the two numbers were being dedicated to a "friend in New Orleans."

Shortly after the two numbers had been played over the air, Rapp's orchestra played "June in January." Neu stood up in his cell, his face wreathed in smiles, and accompanied the orchestra in the lilting melody of the catchy ballad. He never sang better or with more feeling than he sang that number.

He asked for a telegraph blank and sent the following message to Rapp in Cincinnati:

"Thanks, t'was swell. God bless all. Bon voyage. Kenneth."

That was Kenneth Neu's last written message on the last night he spent on earth alive.

Although Neu was not aware of it, Henry Meyer, the hangman who pulled the lever which sent Neu to his death through the trap, slept near the cell of the victim in the prison. The hangman arrived at the jail early

Thursday night and was taken to a cot on the third floor of the prison. Palsied from age and weakened from a recent illness which endangered his life, Meyer was obviously nervous on the eve of what was to be his 39th hanging.

Even though Neu kept his word and faced death with a song, he walked on the gallows a penitent sinner, reciting the Litany of the Dead and begging for mercy on his soul. He had not lost his nerve but had gained religion as a bulwark of strength in his fast ebbing hours.

Even today I can remember the sight of Neu clutching those iron bars with both hands and singing in the most beautiful baritone I think I have ever heard, "I'll Take You Home Again Kathleen."

In adjacent Jefferson Parish, famous for its gambling casinos and nightclubs, I had sources of information denied other reporters, who, as a group, were generally slightly less popular than Carrie Nation. Parish officials and proprietors of the clubs knew me and were confident I would not take advantage of our acquaintanceship.

I used these sources in Jefferson Parish (or "The Parish," as it was known colloquially) to obtain stories unavailable to other newsmen. On the night before two men were scheduled to hang, a new executioner arrived to perform the job. I particularly wanted to interview him. I found the men who performed this unenviable task interesting subjects to write about, but in this case I had another reason for wanting to see what kind of man had been retained for the hanging. The last execution I had witnessed was bungled by an inept hangman, Henry Meyer, the old man who needed whiskey to steel himself for the effort. He had prepared the noose in such a manner that it cut into the necks of the two condemned men, John Capaci and George Dallao, leaving a bloody mess.

As the first of those two men headed for the gallows, I witnessed one of the most startling incidents in my career of covering hangings. "In the last meeting between the two confederates in crime," I wrote, "just as the death march for Dallao began, Capaci, reaching his hand through the cells as Dallao passed, pulled Dallao close to the bars."

"Kiss me, George," Capaci said.

The two kissed and then waved farewells to each other.

But it was the botched hanging itself which concerned me. I wrote:

Witnesses, including me, were waiting atop the gallows when Dallao came up and stepped upon the trap door. Father Wynhoven began praying, followed by the other three priests. Dallao repeated the prayers just before the hangman adjusted the black cap, then the rope.

Then, as the hangman stopped to adjust the sash cord about his feet, Dallao said:

"Wait a minute; let me remove my slippers." A deputy removed the bedroom slippers he wore in the march, leaving Dallao barefooted. After waving goodbye to Sheriff Clancy, deputies and others gathered about, Dallao requested that he be told just when the trap would be sprung. Deputy Cassagne shouted back, "All right, George, I'll let you know."

Cassagne had hardly gotten the words out of his mouth when the hangman crouching in the corner of the gallows, pulled the lever and Dallao shot downward to his death.

From my position alongside the trap door, I could see quite clearly the hanged body. It was a shocking sight. The neck was cut to the vertebrae and the blood was gushing out. It was something never to be forgotten.

Blood that spurted from the jagged wounds in Dallao's neck, made by the rope which seemed to cut deeply into the flesh, was washed away quickly by prison attachés. So much had flowed from the wound that a hose was employed to wash it away.

Capaci was hanged a short time later, and the results were the same. The entire incident had thoroughly disgusted me, and I was anxious to see the new hangman who had been hired to preside over the execution of two murderers, Gladstone James and Ralph Eisenhardt. But I was not the only reporter who wanted to talk to the new hangman. The other three papers also had representatives at the Jefferson Parish Prison seeking interviews. Paul Cassagne, the sheriff's chief deputy, called me aside. "The hangman just arrived but he won't see reporters. But you stay back here and I'll chase those other guys out of here."

"Don't do that, Paul. You're in enough trouble with the press already. Throw me out with them. I'll be right back."

I joined the other reporters and a few minutes later Cassagne walked into the room. "Okay, you guys, school's out. The hangman says he won't talk to reporters. You gotta go, and that includes you, Hébert.''

A cub reporter with the rival *Morning Tribune* called his city editor, Charlie Campbell, who was a personal friend of mine. He told Campbell that every reporter, including me, had been forced to leave. Knowing me, Campbell was skeptical but the reporter reassured him that I, the man with all the contacts, had been told to leave also.

Of course, I returned immediately after the other reporters had gone, and the next day the *States* published an exclusive interview with Bush Jarrett, the new hangman.

Of Jarrett, I wrote, ''His presence means a distasteful (but essential) job done calmly and deftly with the steady nerves of a man who knows his job and all its ramifications and takes a peculiar pride in doing well with whatever he does.

''The hangman has a job to do and it is best that a good hangman does it.''

After Jarret had performed the task for which he had been retained, I wrote: ''In striking contrast to Henry Meyer, who officiated at hangings in New Orleans and nearby parishes for many years, today's hangman is a giant of a man in stature. Meyer was a cringing, frightened little man, extremely nervous and always keyed himself for his task by drinking heavily before each hanging. Today's hangman is methodical and businesslike in his manner and preparation.''

And that is the way in which he dispatched Gladstone James and Ralph Eisenhardt, both of whom were dead within twenty minutes of each other. ''Not the slightest sign of strangulation for either; not a drop of blood was visible. Besides, each of the wretched men died within the usual period in which death comes to those whose necks are properly broken through expert manipulation of the noose.''

The new executioner also performed well the next time his services were needed several months later. Three men, Joseph Ugarte, Owen Cauche and Anthony Dallao, a brother of George Dallao who had been hanged with John Capaci, were all executed without the attendant gore which had marked Meyer's jobs, and I provided graphic descriptions for the avid readers who devoured the details of this ritual. ''There was not the slightest tremor as Cauche hung at the end of the rope which stood rigid through the opening. The crack as Cauche's neck snapped could be heard even above the voices of the crowd in the execution chamber.''

In addition to the effectiveness of the hangman, I was always impressed with the role religion played in the personalities of the condemned men. The transformation of killers intrigued and practically mesmerized me. In fact, in reporting the hanging of four men, religion became the main subject upon which I concluded my account of these executions.

Whatever the beliefs of the group of men who gathered behind that stout rail in the death chamber of the Parish Prison Wednesday at noon to see four men drop through the steel trap to death at the end of the hangman's noose, not one of them could deny that after all there is something to this thing called religion.

Atheist, non-believer, infidel, pagan, if there were such within those close confines of the smoke-filled and over-heated barred room, they must have had a tingling of doubt as to the fallacy of their beliefs as they saw Ito Jacques, Herman Taylor, George O'Day, and Donald Rylich march unflinchingly to death with prayer on their lips, unassisted by human hands and buoyed for the death march without the aid of stimulants.

The four men died on the gallows for the crime of murder. Even if men be bandits, robbers, thugs, or hoodlums, one cannot but admire courage and fearlessness, and the courage and fearlessness exhibited by the four men who died Wednesday on the gallows was the chief topic of conversation not only by those who witnessed the executions, but over the dinner tables in thousands of homes in New Orleans Wednesday night. And the one answer to that fearlessness is religion.

It was a priest whom the men asked for at the end although only two were Catholics, a third a Jew, and a fourth a Baptist. The priest, Father George McNamara, was loved by the men because he had buoyed their spirits up so highly. Even two hours before they hung Wednesday the priest was leading the men in song, singing the popular tunes of the day, and death apparently the farthest thing from their minds.

Spending the last night in a death cell with four men condemned to die on the gallows, you find out something about what men think about just before they are going to die. The reaction is strange.

Ito Jacques was selected as the first man to die because he was thought to be the weakest, and yet he turned out to be the second strongest of the four. He walked onto the gallows with a smile, which was covered only by the black hood as it was slipped over his head by the hangman. For eight minutes he was forced to stand on the trap because somebody had forgotten to get the key to the trap lever, and yet not once did he falter. He recited the entire Litany of the Dead while he waited with the black hood over his head.

In the little prison chapel where Jacques was brought to hear Chief Deputy Michael McKay read the death warrant, he said:

"I hope this will be the last death warrant you'll ever read. Society has demanded my life and I suppose they'll get it. But I have this consolation—they can't have my soul."

Religion, again, his last thought.

Herman Taylor, who one would suspect of being the most fearless, alone showed signs of faltering on the gallows when he was selected to die. Until 3:30 the morning of his death, he had played checkers with this writer and never once gave an indication of fear. He was cynical, bitter and stoutly boasted that nobody could deprive him of the kingdom of heaven.

It was Taylor who furnished the most dramatic moment of the entire hangings when just before the black hood was dropped over his head he closed his eyes, lifted his head upward and in clear tones which ran clarion-like through the gallows declared:

"Oh, God, be with me in Paradise," and then as the hood was dropped over his head, "Goodbye, everybody."

Again, religion was his last thought.

George O'Day, the Jew who wanted to be known as George O'Day although his real name was Harold Stone, sent for this reporter to give him his last message to the world. It was a message of love, the keynote of his Jewish religion.

Throughout the morning he had sat quietly on his white prison cot with Rabbi Emil Leipzinger and chatted pleasantly. Together O'Day and Rabbi Leipzinger had smoked and talked until just a few minutes before twelve o'clock when O'Day decided to send his last message out and sent for me.

"This is the last request I am going to make," he said. "Everything is over now and I know it, but I want you to promise that you will deliver this message for me. Tell everybody who believed in us and believed in our innocence, that we appreciate everything that they did for us and I want all of them to know that we love them."

Love—the keynote of Jewry.

Again, religion to the very end.

Donald Rylich, the last of the four, went to his death the least fearful. During the morning hours at Mass in the prison chapel he seemed to be weakening. His eyes had a wild stare in them and he gazed about the walls of the building. Prison attaches at that time thought that next to Jacques he would weaken the quickest, yet he listened to the clang of the trap three times while Jacques, Taylor, and O'Day went to their deaths and walked out of his cell with a smile on his face and a joke on his lips.

"Give me the keys, Jimmy," he asked Deputy Sheriff James Taranto with whom he had joked often.

"What's the matter, Charlie, don't get nervous," he chided Deputy Sheriff McNamara.

Rylich's last words were the responses to the Litany of the Dead which Father Horwath recited at his side.

It is of note that when Rylich was first arrested he refused to see priest, preacher, or nun.

"I didn't pray when I was out there and I'm not going to do it now," he had said. But at the end, he and Jacques were the most religious of the quartet and the most respectful of the priest.

Reflecting, more than forty years later, on the experience of covering so many hangings, I cannot now recall exactly how many men I have seen hanged. It was all messy and gruesome stuff. But it was the news of the day and it had to be written as accurately as possible. It was my job.

CHAPTER VI

THE NIGHT HUEY LONG WAS SHOT

IT WAS A TYPICAL September night in New Orleans.

The year was 1935.

The time was a few minutes after nine o'clock on a Sunday night.

The radio in my St. Charles Hotel suite was playing typical Sunday night sweet music.

Suddenly the music stopped.

"This is a special news bulletin" came the voice through the tube.

My ears perked. Subconsciously I turned to Gladys, my wife, and said, "Now what is this?"

The voice through the tube almost blended into the dying sound of my question.

"Senator Huey Long has been shot at the Capitol in Baton Rouge by a man tentatively identified by the name of Weiss."

It was unbelievable. It was impossible. It was incredible.

Huey shot by a man identified by the name of Weiss. Seymour, the first name to cross my mind. Ludicrous. Never Seymour Weiss but the announcer distinctly said Weiss.

Waiting for clarification of the original news flash I rapidly reviewed the few hours which had just passed.

On Saturday morning Gladys and I had returned from vacation. We had been to Mackinaw Island in Michigan to a Delta Sigma Phi Fraternity convention.

As political editor for the *New Orleans States* I had been covering Huey Long and the Louisiana legislature for years.

The first time I personally met Huey Long was in a Shreveport

Hotel coffee shop where I was breakfasting before going to the ball park to cover a baseball game between the Shreveport and New Orleans teams. There was no doubt in anybody's mind when he entered the door with his blustering fanfare as to who he was. My old friend Sam Roccaforte introduced me to him.

The first time I covered Huey politically was when he opened his campaign for the United States Senate against Senator Joseph E. Ransdell. He opened the campaign under the Evangeline Oak at St. Martinville. It was the first time a sound truck had ever been used in a political campaign. He then went to Abbeville and closed at Erath.

O. K. Allen was governor of Louisiana but in name only. The Kingfish, as Huey had dubbed himself, was the overlord and boss. He had been elected to the United States Senate and was absolute dictator of the state of Louisiana.

When special sessions of the legislature were called, and they were frequent, they were of course called in the name of the governor but it was Huey who gave the orders to call and he ran the whole show.

Under the law special sessions were to last a minimum of five days but any reporter covering them knew they would last only three days in fact and the action taken would be a mere formality.

Allen J. Ellender, who later became United States senator, was the speaker of the Louisiana house of representatives.

Huey always kept himself surrounded with a group of bodyguards but nobody ever thought seriously that an attempt would be made on his life. The bodyguards were used for the part to push reporters around, slug photographers and simply act tough like bodyguards were supposed to act. They rode with him on the train to and from Washington. They escorted him to the floors of the House and Senate.

One time there was a lot of publicity given to an alleged plot to kill Huey—where? At Dead Man's Turn on the highway into Baton Rouge. Where else?

This was the atmosphere in which I had lived covering Huey. Understanding this situation it is easy to understand my reaction on the Saturday morning before Huey was shot when a friend of mine boarded the Panama Limited on which Gladys and I were returning to

New Orleans. He got on the train at Hammond and informed me during the general conversation on what had been happening in Louisiana during my absence. Huey had called a special session of the Legislature for Sunday night. So what's new?

I was scheduled to report back to the office on Monday morning but I could have reported in a day earlier in order to cover the opening session of the special session. Under the circumstances I saw no reason to do the normal thing because there would be no advantage to it. It would only be a routine coverage which would be covered in a perfunctory manner by the wire services.

That decision robbed me the opportunity of covering the biggest political story of my career up till that time—the assassination of Huey P. Long, the greatest political dictator in the history of the United States.

The news was now coming over the radio more clearly.

Of course it was not Seymour Weiss, Huey's very close friend, who had done the shooting. It developed the alleged assassin was a highly respected young doctor named Carl Weiss.

Huey had been talking to Speaker Ellender in the house and had been called to the telephone in connection with a huge train wreck of veterans in Florida. He had left the house chamber and started walking down the corridor to the governor's office accompanied by the usual entourage of bodyguards and Justice John B. Fournet of the Louisiana Supreme Court.

What actually took place must be described with more accuracy by those reporters who were on the scene. I had missed my chance of being there when the great tragedy took place but I had not removed myself from covering the story which followed in the echo of that lone bullet fired from the gun of Dr. Carl Weiss.

Of course it was to no avail to go to the *States* office at that time of the night and it was foolish to think of going to Baton Rouge and become embroiled in the mad confusion.

At about 11 o'clock my telephone rang. It was my friend Pascal Radosta, owner of famed Manale's restaurant in New Orleans. Pascal was perhaps the most knowledgeable man on the inside of the political arena. He called to inform me that Dr. Russell Stone, one of the

finest surgeons ever to practice in New Orleans, had stopped by
Manale's to pick up some cigars. He was en route to Baton Rouge to
attend the wounded senator who had been taken to Our Lady of the
Lake hospital.

I later learned that it was Jimmy O'Connor, a public service
commissioner, who had driven Long to the hospital.

Jimmy later explained the situation to me. He said he had been in
the cafeteria in the basement and was returning to the house floor
when he heard the shots ringing out. Suddenly he looked up and Huey
was running down the steps saying "I'm shot." Jimmy grabbed him
noting that he was bleeding from the mouth. He put him in his
automobile and took him to the hospital. On the way Huey kept
asking Jimmy "Why did he shoot me? Why did he shoot me?"

I did not sleep during the rest of the night and at about four o'clock I
went to the office. Major Jim Crown, the city editor was already
there. We started to gather follow-up copy for our first edition. All
avenues of information in Baton Rouge were closed. Nobody would
talk. The bodyguards were really in charge. The only information
was that Long had been operated on by Dr. Arthur Vidrine, superintendent of the great Charity Hospital in New Orleans. It later developed that Dr. Vidrine, a Long follower, had insisted on doing the
operation. I was told later by my good friend Lucille May Grace, then
register of the Land Office, that Huey kept asking Vidrine if he really
had to do the operation and Vidrine insisted.

I knew my best contact as to what happened would be Dr. Stone,
who was an old friend of mine. I learned that he was at Touro
Infirmary operating. Time was about eight o'clock Monday morning,
September 9.

I got Dr. Stone on the phone.

"What happened, Doc?" I asked him.

"I didn't touch him," replied Stone.

I placed my hand over the mouthpiece of the telephone and looked
at Crown.

"He won't make it, Major. Stone didn't touch him."

Dr. Stone then explained to me what had happened. He said that
when he arrived at the hospital Long had already been operated on by

Dr. Vidrine. He and Vidrine then became engaged in a technical medical discussion. Stone asked him why he had gone into Huey when he was in shock, a very dangerous approach. Stone was told that the lone bullet had passed through the colon and clipped the kidney. Stone inquired as to whether or not Vidrine had looked at the kidney, and he told Stone he had not. He then challenged Stone to open up Huey and look at the kidney himself.

"I don't kill living patients," Stone replied.

After Huey had died and the burial date and time had been set he told me that on the day of the funeral he had run across Dr. Vidrine on the Charity Hospital campus and Dr. Vidrine had asked him, "Are you going to the patient's funeral?"

"I don't go to patients' funerals and anyway he was not my patient," Dr. Stone replied.

"I would not mention that kidney," replied Dr. Vidrine.

Dr. Stone told me Long died from a hemorrhaged kidney.

I never left my typewriter on the rewrite desk all that day. I was constantly on the telephone talking with contacts and with our Baton Rouge reporters. I wrote new lead after lead for all editions. Before the story was to be put to bed I was to write thousands upon thousands of words about the shooting and the burial. In addition to the pieces for the *States*, Major Crown was selling copy all over the country and, as was his custom, he was merely filing the copy which I was writing except he put his name to it.

It was on Tuesday morning, September 10, 1935, that Huey P. Long died of an assassin's bullet.

Whose bullet?

No autopsy was ever allowed on the body of the dead Senator.

My own summation which I have said and repeated for the past forty years is that a good district attorney could convict Dr. Weiss of firing the fatal shot and a good defense attorney could acquit him of the murder.

Then came the flamboyant funeral. I continued to cover it from a distance. I wrote and I wrote and I wrote and I wrote, never thinking or realizing that what had happened was to have such an effect on my own life in the years to come and that I would be writing this from my

Congressional office in Washington where I have sat for more than 35 years, longer than anybody in Louisiana's history. That shot which was fired out of my hearing because I chose not to shorten my vacation began the ill-fated succession to the dictatorship which resulted in what has become known as ''The Louisiana Scandals.''

The reaction of the *New Orleans States* is worth noting.

No editorial on the death of Huey Long was ever written.

The paper remained editorially silent.

On the front page there was no silence.

Major Crown, ever the headliner, didn't hesitate to publish the news. Oscar Valeton, one of the better photographers of his time, had stolen a spot in the huge gallery in the State Capitol where the body of Huey Long lay in state and from which photographers were barred while thousands of mourners and worshippers of the dead Kingfish passed. He sneaked a picture of the slain dictator in his coffin. Crown, without hesitance, published the picture on the front page of the *New Orleans States*.

But it was not the end of the Long story.

I moved from the rewrite desk as job of political editor to city editor.

Jimmy Noe, who was lieutenant governor at the time and had given his blood in transfusion to his friend and was a pallbearer, subsequently broke with the heirs to the Long machine and fed me the information which was the basis for breaking the Louisiana Scandals.

The echo of that bullet which I did not hear is still heard in the political halls of Louisiana.

CHAPTER VII

THE LOUISIANA SCANDALS

The most unfortunate act Huey Long's political heirs committed—technically, not morally—was to thwart Jimmy Noe's ambition. The most fortunate mistake I ever made—journalistically and ultimately politically—was to print an inaccuracy about Noe in a front-page column.

James A. Noe had been lured from his old Kentucky home at Bear Wallow by the excitement of battle during World War I. "I signed up as soon as the fightin' started," he once said. Although largely uneducated, he rose in rank from private to lieutenant, serving under the illustrious Hamilton Fish. After making the world safe for democracy, Noe returned to Kentucky and began putting his native intelligence to work buying oil leases with a certain amount of success. Eventually, sensing the greener pastures of other geographical strata, he migrated to Ouachita Parish in North Louisiana where he fit right in with the country boys.

His activities soon caught the attention of that astute judge of men, Hucy P. Long, a country boy himself. They eventually formed a mutually advantageous oil corporation with Seymour Weiss (Huey's money man, influence peddler, entertainment chairman, and the proprietor of the Roosevelt Hotel) and Earle Christenberry, Huey's secretary, confidant and aide. It was called "Win or Lose," and while the whole matter may be still controversial today, it has never lost. Almost immediately after an investment of two hundred dollars, indeed, the next day, the company had assets of almost $30,000. In less than a year stockholders were being presented dividends of $2,000 per share, and there were many shares.

Eventually, Huey persuaded his newfound friend to represent his adopted area as a state senator, the only office to which Noe was ever to be elected, though he was to serve as governor. He became the state's chief executive through a chain of events which culminated when Oscar "O.K." Allen, the man Huey had picked to be governor after he had moved on to the United States Senate, died four months before his term of office ended. Noe, as president pro tem of the state senate, had assumed the lieutenant governor's office when John B. Fournet left that post after winning a seat on the Louisiana Supreme Court.

Noe obviously grew to like being governor for he used his four months in office preparing to run for a full term. His tactics were primarily to entertain rural voters with whom he has always had a great deal in common. Years later, he was squiring a visitor around his North Louisiana land, and his conversation indicated he still had the common touch:

> You take a fine bull and breed it to a scrub cow and you'll have a pretty good calf. You can take a scrub bull and breed it to one of my finest cows and you'll have a scrub calf. It's all in the man—it's in the bull. It's the bull that puts the deal over. It's ninety percent. She's just reproducing the damn thing.
>
> You reckon it's that way in human beings, too?
>
> Sure it is. No question about it. What the hell is the difference between human beings and other people?

Despite Noe's common touch, or possibly because of it, the powerful political axis of Long heirs had plans for the governor's office which did not include him. It did not matter that Noe had given Huey a blood transfusion when the senator lay mortally wounded by a bullet from the gun of a brilliant but driven young surgeon, Dr. Carl Weiss, or that Huey had promised Noe that he would be his choice as the next governor. Those were the childish and sentimental posings of a romantic. Pragmatism called for the next governor of the Great State of Louisiana to be Richard W. Leche, a judge of an appeals court. According to the kingmakers, Huey had selected him to be the next governor.

That selection proved to be a mistake. Not because of Leche's character, particularly—any one of the dozen or so claimants to the

reins of the Long-established dictatorship, given their past performances, would have come to the same end which lay in store for
Leche. But if Noe had been selected, none of the others would have
gone after him in the bulldog fashion with which he pursued them.
He collected every scrap of information he could lay his hands on
concerning the remnants of the Long machine's venality and corruption, and there was plenty of it. His main attack was to obtain
affidavits from informants alleging wrongdoing on the part of politicians. At one time he had more than a thousand of them. He was
dubbed "James A. Affidavit Noe-Noe Nannette" by an opponent in
the 1940 gubernatorial campaign.

I had met Noe casually in the lobby of the Roosevelt Hotel,
Seymour Weiss' bailiwick and the home and headquarters of the
Long men in New Orleans. Of course, at that time, I got the usual
brushoff from Jimmy which he would give any young reporter he
didn't know.

One day after Noe had become lieutenant governor, the pardon
board, of which he was a member in his new official capacity, was
meeting in New Orleans. I got a report that Noe had had lunch at
Antoine's with Freddy Rickerfor, a big rackets man, a lottery man in
town. Well, it's not difficult to imagine what crossed my mind: the
lieutenant governor of the state of Louisiana is having lunch with this
well-known racketeer who is interested in some of the boys trying to
get paroles. My God, *this is* big news, so I led with it in the next day's
column.

The paper had hardly hit the streets when Noe called me at the
office. Was he ever burned up.

"Eddie," Noe said, "you know I want to be governor of Louisiana
more than anything in the world, and this sure is ruining me. Can you
come over and see me about this?"

I went over to Noe's room at the Roosevelt, and Noe was raving
when I walked in. "I want to know where you got this from. Where
did you get this pack of lies?"

"You know damned well that I am not going to tell you where I got
it," I replied, protecting my source as any good reporter will do.

"You tell me and I'll punch the lying son of a bitch in the nose,"
Noe yelled.

"Don't worry about doing that," I said, "I'm not going to tell you where I got it. But I'll do one thing. I'll check my source, and if I am wrong, and if I've said something that's not true, I'll take it back."

"I'll tell you, Eddie, it's not true. I didn't have lunch with that man," Noe insisted.

I went back to the office and called my source, George Vandervoort, a political reporter for the *Times-Picayune*, who had thought the tip would make good column material for me. Vandervoort said he would double-check the report. He did and came back with the story that Noe had shaken hands with Rickerfor as the gambler was leaving the restaurant and Noe was entering it.

"Well," I said, "that's nothing. I mean a man shakes hands with everybody, especially when he is in politics."

The next day at the top of my column was an apology and a retraction. From that day on, there was an affinity between Noe and me. He appreciated the fact that I had taken it back, and our friendship really grew.

One of Noe's first acts as governor was to make Charles E. "Chick" Frampton and me colonels on his staff. Frampton was the political correspondent for the *States'* biggest rival, the *New Orleans Item*, but a close personal friend of mine. With our designation as "colonel," we felt we were really big shots.

In fact Frampton and I were the only reporters with access to the governor. On occasion Noe would barricade himself in his capitol office—sending out for fried chicken, his favorite food—and refuse to talk with reporters other than the two of us. We would have to *make* him talk to other reporters.

"You've got to talk to them," we'd tell him.

"Why can't I just give it to you boys?" Noe would whine, not comprehending the situation, but eventually giving in to the friendly persuasion of Frampton and myself.

What he did understand, however, was the fact that Seymour Weiss and Robert Maestri, the powerful mayor of New Orleans, had brought the various and sundry factions of the Long machine together and had decided that Noe was too much of a rebel, a man with too many unpredictable traits of character, to be the successor to the dynasty. As governor, he had been uncontrollable, refusing to appoint Allen J. Ellender to the Senate post vacated by the departed Huey Long. Instead he had crossed the new power brokers and named Huey's widow, Mrs. Rose McConnell Long, to represent Louisiana in Congress. In the minds of the Longites, there was no telling what that crazy hillbilly would do.

But Richard Leche was a horse of a different color, a dark horse in the scramble for the chief executive's office and a jovial hedonist whose actions could be predicted. He was a big, pleasant-looking man: gregarious, fun-loving, with a liking for the good life, just what the power brokers were looking for, someone they could trust. Earl Long would be his lieutenant governor, and Noe would be the state senator from Ouachita, if he could get reelected.

Immediately Noe broke with his "allies" and stood as one man opposing the successor to the Long regime. After that, vote counts in the senate would always be thirty-eight to one, Noe being the dissenting one.

Noe methodically set about to break up the Long people. He meant to get them, and he was willing to spend God knows how much money to do it. His first open attack against the machine came on the floor of the senate. He accused Leche of firing the inheritance tax collector in the central Louisiana city of Alexandria because he wouldn't kick back half of his revenue, and of replacing him with someone who would, a species which has never been endangered in Louisiana.

After Noe made his charges, the capitol reporters clammered for a press conference with Leche, and they got one. But the head-bashing days of Huey were still a vivid memory, and some reporters present were reluctant to brace the governor with such charges. However, I had known Leche since childhood and therefore did not hesitate to speak up.

"Governor," I said, "Senator Noe has just made some serious allegations against you on the floor of the senate," and I repeated the charges.

"Well," said Leche, "I deny the allegations and I defy the alligator."

As I left the press conference, Leche called me aside. There had been rumors that the huge mansion Leche had recently built across Lake Pontchartrain from New Orleans, in the exclusive ozone belt of St. Tammany Parish, had been constructed with bricks taken from the demolished old Charity Hospital in the city. The bricks were said to be identifiable by the iodoform, a light yellow crystalline compound used as an antiseptic at Charity, which had infiltrated them. Leche knew that I, too, was building a weekend retreat, on the nearby Mississippi Gulf Coast. "Hey, Eddie," Leche grinned, "you got any iodoform in your bricks?" I appreciated the crack, as I appreciated most of Leche's wit. Dick Leche was a fantastic character.

Leche was a great companion who loved good food and drink, blooded horses and registered cattle, baseball and a successful hunt. Unfortunately, his governor's salary of $7,500 annually was not adequate to sate his appetites. A federal investigation eventually revealed his income for the three years he served as governor approached one-half million dollars. But he was a likeable rogue, and it was not in his nature to brook the rough stuff which Huey had employed, the head-knocking and camera-smashing which had become reflex with the Kingfish's boys.

In fact, he had called off the dogs on occasion when Huey was still running the show. During a special session of the legislature, an almost routine occurrence during Huey's reign, I was working with photographer Leon Trice. Orders from on high, however, had been given—no pictures! But Trice, a gutsy little guy, tried to steal one during a committee meeting. His argument for doing so is typical of the profession—it is a free country after all. When the camera flashed, Huey yelled to Joe Messina, one of his bodyguards: "Get that man!"

It was like telling a hungry dog to get raw meat, and Trice took off like a rabbit with Messina right behind him. While Trice took Messina on a tour of the capitol, I headed for the pressroom, which I knew would be Trice's eventual destination. Trice dashed in breathlessly with barely enough time to hide the photo plates before Messina roared in.

"You're under arrest," Messina yelled.

"Oh, for Christ's sake, Joe," I said, "what do you want to do that for?"

"Come, now!" Messina ordered Trice.

"Aw, Joe," I pleaded.

"You too," he said to me.

Herman Deutsch, a star reporter for the rival *Item*, was in the pressroom, and he almost died, because he would have liked nothing better than to get himself arrested. Almost any reporter likes nothing better than being arrested.

Messina took Trice and me back to the committee room and presented us to Huey. Trice and I began denying Trice had taken a picture when Leche stepped in.

"That's right, Huey," Leche said, "nobody took any pictures. Somebody lit a cigarette lighter. Those boys didn't take a picture." Huey was skeptical, but let us go.

Despite the role I was to play in Leche's political and social demise, we liked one another personally. It was Leche who first introduced me to Franklin D. Roosevelt. I had covered the president previously when Roosevelt had toured the Gulf South, and had written a glowing account of his visit. The president's reception was, I wrote, "a most remarkable tribute to certainly a most remarkable man and a remarkable president whose ideas and ideals will cover many pages when the histories of the future are written."

I changed my opinion later, but in those days I held the president in high esteem. I was, therefore, pleased to meet Roosevelt in person when Leche provided the opportunity. It was in Dallas. Leche had called a meeting of the Louisiana legislature to journey to Texas to pay its respects to the president.

Louisiana had practically withdrawn from the Union during Huey's heyday and Leche was negotiating what was to become known as the Second Louisiana Purchase. The Roosevelt administration had been one of the main targets during Huey's tumultuous rule as the Share-the-Wealth evangelist, a gimmick which he counted on to propel him into the White House. But Leche sought peace where his mentor had sought battle. Money appealed to Leche more than unlimited dictatorial power. And Roosevelt was only too happy to buy back Louisiana's influence and the ten votes the state cast in the Electoral College. Money poured into the state from the federal cornucopia in staggering sums, and Leche began to pay court to Roosevelt. Huey's archenemy became Dick's fast friend.

Naturally, Leche developed vice-presidential aspirations. He had the labor vote going for him, was in and out of the White House with Roosevelt. Harry Hopkins was pushing him as the labor candidate for vice-president.

It was as part of his campaign to charm Roosevelt that Leche had convened a session of the Louisiana legislature in Dallas where the president was visiting the Texas Centennial Exposition, in addition to doing some fishing. Every member of the legislature showed up except Noe. Leche was also conducting a good public-relations campaign with the press when he invited Frampton and me to meet Roosevelt. When we walked into that room the president was sitting in a chair with that big hearty Roosevelt smile, his head tilted back. Leche said, "Mr. President, I want you to meet two polecats, Chick Frampton and Eddie Hébert."

"But sweet ones," I countered.

Roosevelt laughed, knowing that Huey had referred to reporters as polecats, then said, "Hello, Chick. Hello, Eddie."

It was like he had known us all of our lives.

Things were going so well for Roosevelt in Louisiana under the guidance of Leche that he decided to visit New Orleans in the spring of 1937. It was a mutually advantageous arrangement. Huey's heirs loved federal money, any kind of money in fact; and Roosevelt loved being loved by Louisiana for a change. He did not mind that he had to pay for the affection with WPA and PWA funds. And his gratuities were more than welcome.

One of the highlights of the presidential trip was lunch at Antoine's. It was served in the Mystery Room, a long, narrow chamber approximately fifteen by forty feet. The diners were seated at a single table which bisected the room. Leche was to Roosevelt's right. To his left was Maestri, the taciturn and almost monosyllabic mayor. I was seated directly across the table from the president. Among the others in attendance were James Thompson, the editor and publisher of the

Item and the son-in-law of Champ Clark, a former Speaker of the House of Representatives; the president's son, Elliott; and a number of other dignitaries and reporters.

A luncheon at Antoine's always takes about two hours. The first course is the traditional Oysters Rockefeller for which Antoine's is world famous. The meal got underway, and, despite the fact that he was seated beside the president, the laconic Maestri did not address Roosevelt until the guest of honor had eaten his oysters. Then he glanced at the president, and asked, "How'd you like the oysters?" For the mayor, who only had a third-grade education, but was sensitive enough to know it, the question was a speech. He would talk well enough in the traditional smoke-filled rooms, and was savvy enough to have become one of the largest property owners in the city, but around strangers like Roosevelt the thickset son of a neighborhood grocer took on the characteristics of a cigar-store Indian.

Roosevelt was apparently glad for the opportunity to reply to the mayor of New Orleans for the president, in his effusive, expansive grand manner, began to extol the virtues of the oysters and his great enjoyment of them. To this Hyde Park outpouring, Maestri withdrew into his stoic, swarthy countenance, making no further effort at conversation. Leche, always bubbling himself, sized up the situation and intervened with small talk.

The luncheon lasted for the normal two hours. There was much banter and conversation across the table on every conceivable subject, but the mayor did not participate. It was not until the conclusion of the meal that Maestri turned to the president for the second time. "How did you like the meal?" he inquired. Again the President replied in superlatives, and again, Dick Leche took the conversation away.

As Roosevelt was wheeled out of the room, I leaned across the table and asked the mayor, "Say, Bob, how did you like the President?"

Without hesitation, Maestri replied, "That guy's full of bullshit, ain't he?"

When I got back to the paper, I couldn't wait to relate what the mayor of New Orleans had said about the president of the United

States. Major Crown was talking with Harry Costello, a former football great at Georgetown University and the director of publicity at Louisiana State University when Huey was using the school as an extension of his personality. I related the story and they got a hearty laugh out of it. The next time I heard the story was when I read it in Drew Pearson's column, with the language cleaned up a bit. I didn't know Costello was working for Pearson at the time.

Later, in 1937, when Major Crown, that paradoxical combination of sinner and reformer, became managing editor of the *States*, I was named city editor through the insistence of the publisher of the *Times-Picayune*. The *Picayune* had purchased the *States* in 1933. But my dealings with that autocratic publisher, John F. Tims, had not always been good. Jack Tims, a man accustomed to having his own way, was the son of a New Orleans assessor, a politically powerful breed in the ward politics of the Crescent City. That background served Tims well in his rise through the ranks to a position as the major domo of the state's largest newspaper where he wielded more influence and power than most politicians.

My dealings with Tims got off to a dismal start. I had left the *States* sports department to handle publicity for Loyola University of the South under a $3,500 a year contract, which presented few restrictions on my other activities.

This left me free to handle publicity for other endeavors, including style shows, which were considered big events in those days. To publicize the event, I planned to put out a special section in a local paper, which would mean a good advertising dollar for the paper selected. Tims wanted the action, but he wouldn't give me the prices.

"Well, Mr. Tims," I finally said, "I'm going to go to the *States*," which was then an independent newspaper.

"Hébert," Tims said, "I don't like your attitude."

I guess I had inherited a certain degree of "haughtiness" from my mother, with whom insults did not sit well either. "Tims," I shot back as I stood up to leave, "I don't like your attitude."

We didn't speak for years. It was a bad falling out. Tims, who had my brother Gordon working for him in the advertising department, continued his ill will toward me for a number of years. And when I gave up my stint in the publicity business to return to the *States*, Tims told Jimmy Ewing, the *States* publisher, "Well, you got the bastard of the Hébert family."

Several years later the *Times-Picayune* purchased the *States* and only five reporters made the transition. I was one of them, but only because the bureau chief of the Associated Press in New Orleans, Ralph Wheatley, interceded for me. However, it was not long before Tims and I began to see eye to eye. In my capacity as former president of the Young Men's Business Club, the civic organization which then wielded an unusual amount of political clout, I was asked to address the club after returning from covering one of Huey's special sessions of the legislature. This session had provided some unusually wild scenes.

During the speech, a stocky, well-groomed man in the front of the audience expressed particular pleasure whenever I would let go with a well-chosen barb. His applause was excessive. I was wondering all the time I was speaking who that fool was. After the meeting, the man walked over and threw his arm around me. "Eddie," he said with easy familiarity, "I'm Gerald L. K. Smith. You know, you and I can make a lot of money. You're a real crowd pleaser. We could get up a good circuit. You could go into a town and rap Huey. Then I could come in and praise him. We could clean up." I laughed off his suggestion and left Smith, a preacher-turned-politician, to his own devices. They eventually grew to include being Huey's Share-the-Wealth front man and organizer, and later he evolved—if that's the word—into being a vicious anti-Semitic who published an offensive hate sheet which saw communistic Jews under every rock.

Smith was not the only one apparently impressed with my YMBC speech. Jack Tims had been in the audience. He, too, thought I showed possibilities, different possibilities to be sure. To show his appreciation of those possibilities Tims gave me a five-dollar-a-week raise, which was really being impressed for Tims, particularly in those tightfisted days of the Depression.

Huey, ensconced in his suite upstairs in the Roosevelt, heard about my talk. His reaction was: "What does Eddie want to do that for? He knows I would take care of him."

Huey always operated on the theory that everybody had his price. Unfortunately, too many people did. It never occurred to him that this was the way I felt—and that *was* the way I felt.

Russell Long later told me—before he went to the Senate— "Eddie, you know how you used to vex my father."

I looked at him and said, "Russell, if I only vexed your father, I was a failure."

Over the years I have tried to remain consistent about most things and that includes Huey Long. Huey was a dangerous, unscrupulous but effective operator. Just because he's dead doesn't change anything. The way some people think, if Judas Iscariot had been assassinated, that would have been cause for canonization.

Tim's assessment of Long and my own were not dissimilar, and he saw a like-minded man in me. I think it was that speech, more than anything else, which attracted Jack's attention to my possibilities. He took a very vital interest in me after that, and when Captain Ross died, it was Jack Tims who made me city editor.

After getting back into the good graces of the publisher and owners of the *Times-Picayune*, I was encouraged to represent the newspapers whenever a speaker was requested. The Queen City Club of Cincinnati requested one of the owners of the papers, Leonard Nicholson, to provide them with a speaker who would talk on the political situation in Louisiana. One morning, Nicholson walked up to my desk and asked, "Say, Eddie, how would you like to go up to Cincinnati to make a speech?"

I jumped at the chance. Hell, I'd go any place to make a speech and get a trip. Before I left, I received a letter from the club acknowledging my commitment and inquiring about my honorarium. I told Nicholson about it, but he said the paper would cover all my expenses.

When I got to Cincinnati my hosts took me to the Queen City Club. That was something. I was to have lunch there, and I suppose that in order to put me at ease, they had called in a reporter from the *Cincinnati Enquirer*. Throughout lunch, I felt my way along, trying to get their reactions. The more I called Long a son of a bitch, the better they liked it.

Then they asked me about Marvel Logan, the senator from Kentucky. "That guy," I said, "I gave him unshirted hell." I had met Logan in New Orleans. The senator had a great reputation as an investigator, and all the reporters in New Orleans were trying to see the great Senator Logan as part of a senatorial investigation of state politics. He was the most unwashed, filthiest-looking person I ever saw in my life. The reporters were all around him and he was asking these stupid questions about how could Long do these things as a senator, and I thought, "So this is the great investigator! If I were he, I'd have at least known that much." And so I related my opinion of Logan to my hosts during lunch.

Following the meal the club members asked me to play golf with them, but I said I would rather see the *Ziegfeld Follies*, which was playing in Cincinnati. Two friends of mine, June and Cherry Blossum Priesser, a dance team, were performing. They arranged it for me, and again, they sent the reporter with me. We were sitting in the third row, right in the middle. This reporter turned to me and said, "Mr. Hébert, I hope you're not too hard on my old man in your speech tonight."

"Who's your old man?" I asked.

"Senator Logan."

I was talking to Spud Logan. We went out that night and got drunk after my speech. I didn't say anything about the senator, I let it go, but that had been an embarrassing moment. Anyway, the next day, Hulbert Taft had a reception for me. Imagine, Hulbert Taft, the owner of the *Cincinnati Enquirer*, had something like that for a reporter, a big reception in his home. I felt like a big shot indeed. Ethan Allen, the head of the American Laundry Machine Company, picked me up, and at once apologized for having to use his town car. His big car was out, and there he was apologizing for me having to sit in the back seat with a lap robe and everything, being driven around by a chauffeur.

He showed me through a number of parks, and then took me to a museum and discussed all the art, the heroic figures and everything. Then, as we're riding along, he said, "Mr. Hébert, the matter of an honorarium."

I said, "Oh, forget it."

But he said, "How much do you usually get when you speak? Two hundred and fifty?"

"Oh, quite all right. Quite all right," I said. I could have told him that for a ham sandwich I'd make a speech if somebody would listen to me.

Two weeks later columnist Clayton Rand spoke to the Queen City Club and received two hundred dollars. It turned out he was fifty dollars cheaper than I was. Now, there was a great speaker. Rand, a Pulitzer Prize winner, could talk on any subject, for or against.

When I took over the city desk of the *New Orleans States* the nation was still digging out of the Depression, but the citizens of Louisiana were burdened with the highest tax rate in the history of the state. The state payroll had burgeoned to $20 million a year. Every employee of the state had to contribute five percent of his monthly salary to his immediate political boss. Where it went from there was a mystery, but it was allegedly a contribution to the Louisiana Democratic Association. Educated estimates put the amount deducted at one million dollars a year. In addition, each state employee had to subscribe to the *Louisiana Progress*, a political propaganda sheet begun by Huey. Under Leche, it played the same tune, but it was accompanied by the jingle of money. Huey had given the *Progress* away, but Leche saw to it that every state employee enjoyed a yearly subscription; and those in supervisory capacity were saddled with several copies to sell to acquaintances. Another source of income for the *Progress* was the exceptionally large number of firms doing business with the state which elected to advertise in the paper. They understood the adage that it pays to advertise.

State employees were assessed for countless items: flowers for funerals of politicians, "gifts" of automobiles to state officials, and countless other indignities. Graft and corruption were the guiding lights of the state's elected and appointed officials. State jobs multiplied, and the jobholders in the higher brackets raised their own salaries beyond the bounds of credulity.

The routine and regular deductions from the salaries of state employees became known as "de-ducts," and the phrase, "the de-ducts are flying again, boys," became a byword of the day. Cynically, the practice was called job insurance.

The *States*, and other Louisiana newspapers, had been reporting allegations of corruption and challenging the dictatorial adulteration of democracy editorially for years. But they were dismissed as just the whinings of the big-money corporations that were incensed because Huey, and then his political heirs, were going to soak the rich and share the wealth. Those editorials were just the palaver of those "lying newspapers."

I knew that if the *States* was going to have any real effect on conditions in Louisiana, I was going to have to obtain cold, hard, incontrovertible facts. I set out to get them even though some of these politicians were my friends. This fact didn't bother me at all, for I have always been able to like someone without countenancing his activities or morality. Recognizing my own imperfections made me less of a zealot in judging the actions of others. I always regarded ferreting out wrongdoing as a part of my job as a newspaperman or as a congressman, not a holy crusade. Emotion has seldom found its way into my investigative articles and exposés.

I therefore sent reporters out to interview indignant state jobholders, but the facts I sought were difficult to come by. State employees would talk in confidence, but were afraid to permit use of their names, for instant discharge followed any public complaint. But the *States* was able to reveal, while still protecting its sources, that even nurses and minor employees of Charity Hospital, a state institution, were subjected to the gouges.

These stories, without names to back them up, brought official denials, of course, and left many of Huey's true believers convinced it was just some more bull from those "lying newspapers." The only course was for the *States* to keep plugging away. The paper did, and as is often the case in journalism, I finally got a break. Not the big, knockout haymaker for which I was longing, but one which carried a good solid punch and would weaken the midsection of the state's political machine, for—to continue the boxing metaphor—when you kill the body, the head dies.

Chester Martin, an employee of the Louisiana State Highway Department, had decided he had had enough. Willing to forfeit his job to expose the truth about the "de-ducts," Martin consented to be quoted, and I had some hard news. My story told how Martin had to pay five percent of his $155 monthly salary as a "voluntary contribution" to the Louisiana Democratic Association, and how he was coerced into purchasing from five to ten subscriptions of Governor Leche's popular newspaper, the *Progress*.

When the *States* hit the streets with this exclusive, Leche lost some of his insouciance, and had Martin fired, and once again "denied the allegations and defied the alligator."

Martin filed charges, paralleling his statements which I had run in the *States*, with the United States Attorney for the Eastern District of Louisiana, Rene A. Viosca. Martin accused state officials of violating Act 324 of the 73rd Congress which made it a crime to shakedown any employee involved with federally financed projects. Backing up his charges was evidence that he had been employed on thirteen projects in which federal funds or federal labor had been involved.

The United States attorney turned Martin's charges, and the cancelled checks which backed them up, over to Paul Hansen, the agent in charge of the WPA investigation unit in Louisiana. Evidence of the rapprochement between Washington and Louisiana became even more obvious, blatant, in fact. Despite Martin's proof that WPA funds were involved in the shakedowns, Hansen ruled his office had no jurisdiction. Viosca then passed on the charges to the Federal Bureau of Investigation, which "studied" them for a while and announced no action would be taken in the case. The WPA seemed to stand for "Won't Prosecute Administration." Martin lost his state job, and it was business as usual in Louisiana.

I shrugged, had a couple of drinks after work, and the next day had a crew of reporters out digging. The *States* kept hammering away at "de-ducts," citing case after case and detailing the resultant hardships to the donors. Stories recounting how the circulation of the *Progress* was increased also appeared. Owners of bars said they were forced to buy from one to ten subscriptions, or their radios (which were the customers' entertainment) would be turned off at 8:00 p.m., or fictitious health regulations would be enforced.

Owners of other small establishments backed up the stories. One man claimed that his friends were avoiding him "for fear I'll try to sell them some of the five *Progress*es I have to take."

Following a series on "de-ducts" in the *States*, Leche sent me several mallards he had shot. He attached a note: "Dese ducks are not flying." However, the pressure continued, and Leche was forced to admit that deductions were routine. He made the admission during a radio address in which he launched a blustery verbal attack against the *States*, and said he was merely continuing a practice started by the now deified Huey P. Long in his campaign to help the poor. Leche said he, too, was a friend of the poor man, and that the big corporations were out to get him, out to prevent him from attaining a federal judgeship for which he was rumored to be in the running.

The verbal attack only caused the *States* to redouble its efforts to expose what can undramatically be called the sordid truth. I sent my staffers out time and again on tips of graft and corruption, only to have them report back that, "Yes, it is true, but we don't have the proof." Finally, persistence paid off, and I got what I wanted, a story which would rattle the foundations of the Long machine and eventually collapse the remnants of the malignancy.

It was a typically warm, humid summer's day in New Orleans on June 7, 1939. The first edition of the *States* had gone to press, and the usual morning lull prevailed in the newsroom. I was at the city desk island, working in shirt sleeves, tie loosened, leaning back in a swivel chair chatting with Major Crown who was seated across the cluster of desks from me. The telephone rang, and I reached for it. "*States* city desk."

"Eddie, this is Jimmy Noe."

"How you doing, Jimmy?"

"Eddie, I got something you oughta check out right now. A truck just left LSU loaded with WPA material. It's headed for Jim McLachlan's place in Metairie."

I knew McLachlan was a colonel on Leche's staff, the governor's personal friend and advisor on purchases of blooded saddle horses and registered livestock. But I did not know where McLachlan lived.

"How do I get there?" I asked, being unfamiliar with the exclusive suburban residential area growing up in adjoining Jefferson Parish.

"Call Ray Hufft at the station. He'll take you. Eddie,'' Noe added, "this is what we've been waiting for.''

Ray Hufft had met Noe as a young lieutenant in the Louisiana National Guard when he had been part of Huey's "partial martial law'' mobilization in September 1934. The Guard had been called out in New Orleans to "oversee'' the congressional elections. They did, and Huey's boys won. Noe, who had been as staunch an ally of Long's as he was an enemy of his successors, visited the troops nightly, seeing to it that they were well fed and cared for, while Huey romped. One day following the mobilization, Hufft walked into Noe's radio station and told him, "I'm working for you.''

"You are?'' Noe asked. "You don't have a job.''

"Yes, I do. You just hired me,'' Hufft replied. And Noe did. It was a fortunate friendship, and it grew to include me. Hufft became one of my closest friends and staunchest supporters during the years that we both rose to prominence. Hufft, a medium-sized, well-knit man of superior muscular coordination and mental toughness, was to become Louisiana's most decorated soldier during World War II, and the first infantryman to cross the Rhine River when the allies made their final push into Nazi Germany. As a colonel, he not only led his command across the river, but first paddled across the night before on a reconnaissance mission in a rubber raft, becoming the first American to cross into Germany in the final Allied push which led to the capitulation of the Nazis in World War II. He returned home to become the youngest adjutant general of a state National Guard in the history of the United States. Despite his courage and swashbuckling heroics, or perhaps as an offshoot of them, Hufft was intensely loyal to his friends and his country. He could shed tears by looking at the American flag or upon hearing the "Star-Spangled Banner'' recited, which he actually did once when I, then a congressman, concluded a patriotic meeting with a recitation of the national anthem.

Hufft rose fast in Noe's organization and at the time I called for help in finding the McLachlan residence, Hufft had already become president and general manager of WNOE. Hufft was out of the office when I called, but a secretary traced him down. Hufft agreed to meet a reporter and photographer in front of Charity Hospital on Tulane

Avenue and accompany them to the construction site of McLachlan's home.

I looked around the city room for a reporter. The only one available was Meigs O. Frost, a hard digger whose prose could sing, but whose principles were a little too flexible to suit me. However, he could be an excellent reporter when so moved. I called Frost and photographer Wilfred D'Aquin to my desk and said, ''Listen, you guys, we've got something which might be what we've been looking for. Ray Hufft is going to meet you in front of Charity. He'll take you to where McLachlan is building a new home. Get me a good picture of the LSU truck on his property, and make sure you get a clear shot of the license plate. No slip ups. I want pictures and I want them damned clear.''

The journalists picked up Hufft and headed for Metairie. D'Aquin, who became photo editor of the successor of the *States*, the New Orleans *States-Item*, later said, ''We passed the truck on its way to New Orleans, so we turned around and followed it. We watched the truck pull into its destination at 170 West Avenue, and then drove around a corner and parked behind the construction site.

''Meigs stayed in the car with the motor running, just in case we were spotted. Ray and I crawled across a vacant lot and hid behind a clump of bushes. We knew if we were seen we were in real trouble because the house was situated on one leg of a U-shaped street and there was only one way out.''

The truck, which was loaded with window frames, sashes and other construction material, had come from the LSU campus in Baton Rouge, ninety miles upriver from New Orleans. It bore no identifying marks, a violation of state law, and the rear license plate was smeared with mud. The front plate wasn't covered, however, and D'Aquin zeroed in on it. He also shot pictures of the truck being unloaded by two of the dozen workmen on the site. After getting those photos, Hufft and D'Aquin made their way back to the waiting Frost and drove to a more advantageous spot where they photographed the workmen's vehicles parked in front of the construction site.

Back at the *States* office, the pictures developed perfectly. They plainly showed the license number of the truck. I then had my capitol correspondent check the number with the secretary of state's office.

The records showed it was issued to a truck which was the property of Louisiana State University. The license plate of the workmen's automobiles showed some of them to be employees of George Caldwell, the superintendent of construction at LSU.

Next I checked the homes of the workmen. Relatives said the men had been "sent down to New Orleans on a job." Another reporter was sent to research the assessment records of the McLachlan property. The records, which were photographed by *States* photographer Jimmy Guillot, revealed that the property belonged to Mrs. James McLachlan. And finally, residents of the Metairie suburb confirmed that the McLachlans were building a new home there.

I held the story until every conceivable angle could be checked out, and then called Frost to my desk, two days after the tip had been received. "Now, listen, Meigs," I said, "there will be no by-line on this story. Too many people have worked on it, and above all, there will be no adjectives. I want just the barest facts. I want it simple and short."

By not letting Frost put his by-line on that story, I made an enemy, for the first thing Meigs would ever put in the paper was "By Meigs O. Frost." Once Meigs put his by-line on a one-paragraph story and Major Crown saw it and said, "If the son of a bitch has the guts to put his name on it, I've got the guts to run it."

But this story ran unencumbered by a by-line; it told in simple language that state material was being used by state employees to build a home on the private property of a close personal friend of the governor of the state. Two of D'Aquin's photographs were spread across the front page, one showing a general view of the truck being unloaded, and the other a close-up of the truck with the license-plate number legible. The pictures made it difficult for the governor to holler "lying newspapers."

Well, all hell broke loose. That story and those pictures were like the lantern Mrs. O'Leary's cow kicked over to start the Chicago fire. When the flames started licking around him, Leche went into a tantrum in Baton Rouge. "The *New Orleans States* is blackguarding the McLachlans because they are my friends. This sort of thing has got to stop," he screamed.

Unfortunately for Leche and his cohorts, things were just getting started. As for himself, Leche turned to burlesque. In an attempt to imitate his mentor, Huey, the governor instructed the state attorney general to hold an open hearing with a statewide radio hookup in the Louisiana Supreme Court quarters in Baton Rouge on June 15. In preparing for this Circus Maximus, Leche had subpoenas issued for me; Crown; L. K. Nicholson, president and publisher of the *Times-Picayune* and corporate owner of the *States*; Esmond Phelps, the paper's attorney, who was also a member of its board of directors and was president of Tulane University's board of administrators; and Dr. Rufus C. Harris, president of Tulane. Harris and Phelps were called apparently in an effort to show that the city of New Orleans had done special favors by paving roads around the private university, which was hardly analogous to state workmen and materials being used to build a home for private citizens. But Leche thought it was real finesse. When asked why Dr. Harris had been called, the governor replied darkly, "That will be disclosed."

"I'm a lawyer myself," Leche added, "and I'm going to be the assistant prosecutor of Attorney General Ellison at this public hearing. I'm going to be counsel for the defense, too."

"You're going to be prosecutor and defense counsel both?" a reporter asked.

"Sure," he said. "Somebody's going to need defending before I get through with them." As things turned out, Leche was right, but those who needed defending were not those he had in mind. In the meantime, he was becoming paranoid about the tip to the *States* which led to the McLachlan incident. Word came to me that Leche thought someone on his staff had supplied the information. I sent word back to him that he was wrong.

While waiting for Leche's open-hearing extravaganza, I had reporters get in touch with Dr. James Monroe Smith, the bald, dignified, slow-speaking president of LSU, who, when he was appointed to the post by Huey, became known among the anti-Long forces as "Jimmy Moron." Later he earned the sobriquet, "Jingle Money." When questioned about the use of LSU materials and equipment, Smith told a *States* reporter, "I know nothing about it, but if the university materials or vehicles have been used, I'm sure adequate compensation has been made.'' In addition to the McLachlan incident, Dr. Smith had other concerns. He was perplexed as to how he was going to explain the diversion of almost $500,000 of university funds which he used for speculation in wheat futures. Not only did Smith use poor judgment in forging LSU bonds for his adventures, the price of wheat fell, marking another area of his shortcomings.

Then two days before the June 15 open hearing was scheduled, Leche had second thoughts. Apparently realizing that mimicking Huey did not make him Huey, Leche announced that the hearing was postponed ''indefinitely.'' Attorney General Ellison, he said, was investigating more serious matters.

He then declared that the sale of LSU products to private individuals ''was not unusual.'' The university's dairy sold its milk, after all. The entire McLachlan matter was trivial; less than $300 was involved, including nine dollars a trip for the truck and payment of wages to the workmen in the LSU carpentry shop. The materials, Leche continued, had been purchased by the McLachlans from a commercial lumber yard.

On June 14, I sent *States* reporters to corner George Caldwell, the superintendent at LSU, the man directly responsible for assigning workmen to the McLachlans. My interest in Caldwell was stimulated by Leche. The governor had issued a statement saying Caldwell had explained the facts—those being that the McLachlans had paid for all materials and work—to a *States* reporter prior to the publication of the story. Leche, in a pretty fair country ploy, was trying once again to show the *States* was just attacking him because he was a friend of Huey's and the poor people. ''For some reason entirely beyond my comprehension,'' the governor said, ''those who make such decisions for this newspaper decided to ignore completely the true facts of which they were aware, and publish instead a story containing cheap and untrue insinuations, apparently designed to damage the reputation of two citizens [Mr. and Mrs. McLachlan] of this state.''

When the *States* reporters confronted the obese Caldwell, they asked, ''Will you state the name of the reporter to whom you say you talked, giving the day, the time, and the number of the telephone over which you spoke?''

'' I made my report to the attorney general; I have nothing to say,'' Caldwell replied.

"How about checking your records," one of the reporters suggested.

"My books were open once, but they're closed now," he replied.

The reporters then sought out Dr. Smith to inquire as to why Caldwell's books were closed, since they were public records. But the good doctor was nowhere to be found. His secretary said he was out, and did not know when he would be back.

On June 19, Dr. Smith was finally "in." He met with *States* reporters in his office and told them he had merely been taking a hard-earned rest. The work done at the LSU carpentry shop, he admitted "was against LSU policy." He said he did not know what Caldwell was talking about when he said the books had been open but were now closed. Mr. Caldwell, Dr. Smith said, did not keep any books at all. He told reporters that Caldwell must have been "befud dled."

This, of course, not only explained why Caldwell had been mistaken about having records; it explained why Caldwell had built a beautiful mansion near the governor's home on the St. Tammany Gold Coast (so dubbed by me) which had gold fixtures in its black-marble bathroom, among the other splendors. Caldwell must have been "befuddled," or otherwise he would have known he could not afford such luxury on his salary of $6,000 a year.

On the same day Dr. Smith made his explanation to the *States* reporters, the "Washington Merry-Go-Round" column by Drew Pearson and Robert S. Allen printed affidavits charging WPA fraud and corruption in Louisiana. The affidavits, of course, were supplied by Jimmy Noe. He had been to see the United States attorney general, United States Senator Allen J. Ellender, "and all those fellows up there, and nobody wanted any trouble, and they wouldn't even talk to me about it. And I had these damn things [the affidavits] and I was staying at the Mayflower Hotel, and I knew Drew Pearson, and this was one of the first big things that Drew had done. I called Drew to come over to my hotel. I showed him this [the affidavits] and told him about all the graft and all that kind of stuff. And Drew said, 'Well, can you swear to this?' I says, 'Swear to it, every damn one of them will swear to it.' ''

Noe then took out more affidavits and began to display them before Pearson. ''I had two notary publics up there swearing to this damn stuff that we had taken these affidavits from these people. And Pearson come out with this big column that the attorney general wouldn't listen to this, and that's when it broke in Washington. But nobody would have paid any attention to it if you hadn't been running those stories in New Orleans, Eddie.'' Noe boosted my role in breaking the Scandals at every opportunity.

Following Pearson's column, Colonel F. C. Harrington, national administrator of the WPA, ordered a complete investigation of the charges in the affidavits. Included in those charges were allegations that WPA labor and funds had been used on privately owned homes of Governor Leche, Attorney General Ellison, Caldwell, E. N. Jackson, the LSU business manager, and others high in the administration of Leche. These stories paralleled the McLachlan incident whose publication in the *States* gave credibility to the other stories and pried the Roosevelt administration loose from its apathy.

The day after Pearson's column appeared, Paul Hansen, the WPA investigator who had previously decided there was nothing to investigate, was busily inspecting the records of LSU. A day later, Leche announced that he was going to resign his office ''for the sake of my health.'' This would be the first time in the history of the state that a governor had resigned under fire, if he made good his promise. The announcement was two-pronged. Not only was the state stirred by the announcement of Leche's impending resignation, the citizens were aware of what that resignation would mean. Earl K. Long, Huey's brother, would be the new chief executive with all the power of the state machine in his hands.

When Leche became governor and Earl Long lieutenant governor, I realized Earl would in all likelihood become governor himself one day. And, as a political reporter, I knew I had to get along with Long if I was going to be able to operate effectively as a journalist covering the capitol. Really, I had no choice. I was a reporter and if I was going to get anything at all I would have to get along with Earl. That was all there was to it.

One day I was sitting with him when he was presiding as lieutenant governor in his capacity as president of the senate. I was talking to him and a beautiful woman passed right in front of us. Earl saw me look at her as she walked across the aisle. He knew that Chick Frampton and I were good friends, and he leaned over and said, "You and that Frampton get yourselves a couple of broads and I'll put 'em on the payroll and all they'll have to do is what you tell 'em." I said, "Thank you, Earl, but I'll get my own broad." He was being entirely too crude; moreover he would own us.

It was in the cards for Earl to become governor, but not as quickly as he thought. True to Louisiana politics, four days after Leche's announcement of resignation, he changed his mind. He said he would not be able to resign as promised, for Dr. Smith had just submitted his resignation as president of LSU, and he had learned of financial irregularities at the university totaling "several hundred thousand dollars." Under the circumstances, Leche would have to defer his own resignation.

When I sent reporters in search of Dr. Smith and an explanation of the financial irregularities, the academician, whose illusions of becoming a shrewd operator in wheat futures never materialized, could not be found. His wife, who had entertained her way into high society in Baton Rouge, such as it was, apparently had accompanied her husband in flight.

On the next day, June 26, 1939, the district attorney of East Baton Rouge Parish, Dewey Sanchez, accepted a formal charge against Dr. Smith, accusing him of embezzling $100,000 of LSU funds. In an apparent act of beneficence, the DA didn't mention the other $400,000 invested in wheat futures.

The same day, United States Attorney Rene Viosca, apparently having undergone a metamorphosis similar to that of WPA investigator Hansen, announced that a federal grand jury had begun its own probe into the misuse of WPA funds, labor, and materials in Louisiana.

June 26 was fast becoming memorable in the state. To top it off,

Leche announced his resignation at 7:00 p.m. Earl Long took the oath of office that same night. When he entered the governor's office the next morning, Earl's only statement was a Biblical quotation from Proverbs. ''Better a little with righteousness than great revenue with right.'' He had read it in the *Times-Picayune* ''Thought-for-the-Day'' column that morning.

As Long was quoting the Bible, the East Baton Rouge Parish Sheriff's Department and the Louisiana State Police initiated a search for Dr. Smith, and the Baton Rouge grand jury began an investigation of LSU funds. While the probes continued in Louisiana, Dr. and Mrs. Smith were traced to Detroit and eventually to Canada.

On June 30, the grand jury in the state capital returned indictments against Dr. Smith, charging him with embezzling $100,000 in LSU funds. His wife was charged with ''harboring, concealing, and assisting'' Dr. Smith in his flight. Also indicted on identical charges were Owen W. Ware, Dr. Smith's attorney, and J. Emory Adams, Mrs. Smith's nephew, who drove the pair to Memphis.

Smith's New Orleans broker, J. M. Brown, who had full authority over the LSU president's account, which had been flimsily disguised as the ''J. Monroe Account,'' was charged with aiding and abetting Smith in the embezzlement.

The number of investigations underway by various grand juries and state and federal agencies became epidemic. On July 1, Governor Long announced that George Caldwell, ''by fake agreement of which the LSU Board of Supervisors knew nothing,'' had been receiving in addition to his $6,000 a year salary a two percent kickback on all construction work at LSU. Thus the mystery of his Gold Coast mansion was solved. Caldwell had not been ''befuddled'' at all.

I called Leche to get his reaction to the allegations against Caldwell, but the former governor allowed from the confines of his own luxurious St. Tammany show place that Caldwell had done very satisfactory work for him on that estate. He said he would hire him again if he needed any more work done.

As Caldwell was resigning, Dr. Smith turned up in Brockville, a village in Ontario, Canada. He was arrested by a constable who recognized the Michigan license plate on his automobile. It had been learned that Mrs. Smith had purchased the car in Detroit while Smith accompanied her. She had introduced him to the automobile dealer as "J. M. Southern, a friend."

Once Smith was found, an intramural squabble broke out between East Baton Rouge authorities and the state police over which agency would bring the prisoners home. They finally compromised by each sending officers. Major Murphy J. Roden, a former bodyguard of Huey Long's, was sent by the state police, and Special Investigator Bryan Clemmons, who was later to serve as sheriff of East Baton Rouge Parish, went to represent parish authorities. They flew to Canada in the LSU plane in which Dr. Smith had been wont to travel as president of the university, and in which LSU football scouts would "bring back the beef" for the Purple and Gold.

Appropriate with the way things were run in Louisiana, the plane would not accommodate the pilot, the police, and the Smiths. Thus, on the fourth of July, the pair was brought back to New Orleans in a commercial plane, and on to Baton Rouge by automobile. I sent reporter David McGuire to the airport to meet the Smiths. Five years earlier, McGuire had been one of those students expelled from LSU by Smith because of his rebellion against Long-ordered censorship. I thought it was poetic justice.

Dr. Smith told reporters, "I'm not going to be the goat in this case! I'm glad to be back. I'm going to fight this. I'm sorry I went away. I was ill-advised." "Who advised Dr. Smith?" the *States* asked in heavy, black type on the front page.

Hugh Wilkinson, a New Orleans attorney who had worked as a reporter on the old *Times-Democrat*, came to me with a story. Wilkinson had been attacking a "tax racket" in New Orleans publicly, charging that the State Tax Commission employees and officials were granting enormous assessment reductions to individuals and companies. In return they received a kickback of fifty percent of the reduction.

Wilkinson, who had been an ally of Huey's, as Noe had, apparently had a similar change of heart. He provided me with alleged facts, figures, and names of those involved in the tax racket. This was the kind of stuff I wasn't about to publish. Esmond Phelps, the paper's attorney and the father of Ashton Phelps, Sr., the man who would succeed Jack Tims as publisher of the *Times-Picayune*, was so damn cautious that I couldn't have published it if I'd wanted to.

Then I got an idea. I knew that congressmen are privileged to utter on the floor of Congress, and the repetition of that utterance had never been challenged. I went to Phelps and asked, "What if I put the facts in the *Congressional Record*, and made it privileged?" Phelps agreed to the ploy. If it could be inserted into the *Congressional Record*, then the *States* could print the story, quoting the *Record*.

I therefore sent the information in story form to Bascom Timmons, the *States'* Washington correspondent and a top-flight newsman. Timmons gave the story to a friendly senator and called me to report that everything was taken care of. In an abundance of caution, I deleted many names of those allegedly involved in the racket before I published the story. When the story broke, the editors, the publisher, and the attorney were pleased. Everybody was happy. The only problem was that the senator forgot to put it in the *Congressional Record*. But nobody knew any better down here. Everybody thought it was in the *Record*.

The information in the story eventually found its way before several grand juries and resulted in runaway jurors defying the district attorney and a judge. The story also spurred federal investigators and prosecutors to pursue their probes with added vigor. In the end the district attorney was replaced, and the tax racket halted.

On July 17, Governor Long announced from Baton Rouge that he had learned that heads of various state departments and their employees had financial interests in business concerns involved in transactions with the state. He said he ordered the practice halted. On the same day, John M. Fush, assistant to the general manager of the New Orleans Dock Board, admitted to a *States* reporter that he was the collector of the infamous five percent "de-ducts." When pressed as to whether Mayor Maestri was the custodian of the fund, Fush denied it, but refused to comment further.

Long's announcement and Fush's remarks sparked me to run a list of "Pertinent Questions" in black type on the front page.

Who are the officials who have been interested in supply companies selling materials to the state departments of institutions with which they are connected?

Mr. J. M. Fush says that Mayor Robert S. Maestri is not custodian of the "de-ducts" fund. Who is custodian?

All state employees must pay five percent of their salaries to the "de-ducts" fund. To whom is an accounting for the fund made?

How long will Governor Earl Long permit the "de-ducts" practice to continue?

Dr. James Monroe Smith said Tuesday: "I'm glad to get back. I was ill-advised to leave." Who advised him?

Also on the front page that day was a story that the Congress of the United States had prepared to launch its own investigation into the handling of WPA employees, money, and materials in Louisiana. The House of Representatives' WPA investigation committee was sending two of its ace investigators to Louisiana.

But the biggest news of the day was the arrest of the pudgy, former superintendent of construction at LSU who had resigned under fire. As George Caldwell stepped out of a grand jury room in New Orleans, where he had testified regarding WPA graft, fraud, and misapplication of funds, federal agents arrested him. The arrest warrant charged him with the diversion of federal material, labor, and therefore, funds, to the use of private individuals—including himself.

Caldwell posted a $10,000 bond and walked out free, but his arrest signaled the beginning of the end for the politicians who had enjoyed the eleven-year debauch. They no longer laughed at the efforts of newspapers to check their appetites. Former untouchables became tangible to the law.

I kept up the pressure with front-page coverage of the machinations within the state. New revelations of corruption and theft brought indictments, and there were four suicides as a result of the exposé. Dr. J. L. Shaw, the head of the mineral division of the Louisiana Conservation Department, shot and killed himself after testifying in a Dallas court in connection with the running of "hot oil." He was accused of being involved in a scheme to pipe oil from Louisiana fields to a Texas broker in excess of the allowable production. The

Long men had not been missing a trick. Yet, it was a shock when Shaw killed himself. He had a reputation for having a thick hide. Once Earl Long had fired him, but Shaw refused to vacate his office, and the governor reinstated him.

George Heldelberg, who was in charge of youth administration activities at LSU, killed himself when irregularities were discovered in even that department. He was joined shortly thereafter by Lawrence Merrigan, a one-time collector of internal revenue in New Orleans and the auditor for many prominent persons indicted during the peak of the federal investigation.

Monte Hart, a wealthy electrical construction man with political connections, placed a pistol in his mouth and pulled the trigger. It blew off the top of his head. When he was found, a printed quotation by Elbert Hubbard lay before him. It read: "Never explain. Your friends don't require it, and your enemies don't believe you anyway."

Hart was alleged to be the "brains" behind an audacious act of fraud which became known as the "Bienville Double Dip." The case became the first criminal trial of the Scandals, and to report it, I instituted a new style of courtroom coverage. The case involved the old Bienville Hotel, once owned by Hart and Seymour Weiss, but twice sold by them—both times to the state. They had paid $541,000 for the building, but it turned out to be unprofitable. Hart and Weiss did not think to increase profits by having a law enacted requiring state employees to reside there; but they hit upon something just as good: the state, they decided, needed the property. They sold it to good old LSU for $575,000, which included the building and all its furnishings. Hart and Weiss had found a soul mate in Dr. Smith. His wife's nephew, J. Emory Adams, and Louis LeSage, a lobbyist who represented himself as a public relations advisor to Standard Oil, also played a part in the next transaction. This included reselling the furnishings of the Bienville, which the taxpayers of the state had purchased already, to LSU again, at the bargain price of $75,000.

Smith, Weiss, and Hart were sentenced to two and one-half years in the Atlanta federal penitentiary. LeSage and Adams got one year each. The readers of the *States* got all the details.

Although I was city editor, I could not resist covering the trial myself, and I selected Russ Kintzley, a tall, slim, soft-spoken Iowan who migrated South one winter, to assist me. Kintzley, who was to become an associate editor of the *Times-Picayune*, and I dictated the running story over a private telephone I had installed in the court-house to a rewrite man who sat with a headset glued to his ears.

The national newspaper trade magazine, *Editor and Publisher*, wrote a feature about my rather unusual method of covering the trial. The effectiveness of publishing an almost verbatim transcript of the significant aspects of the courtroom procedures was obvious, and interested readers devoured the details. The *States* has continued this practice at all major trials.

As the revelations of the Scandals continued, some intimations of slapstick comedy appeared. In one instance a $500,000 building, which nobody claimed, was discovered on the LSU campus. The state had paid for its construction, but why it was built and under whose jurisdiction it belonged, was a mystery. Actually everybody knew why it was built; it was the alleged purpose which was unknown. However, a counterbalance to this situation soon appeared. The state had paid an equally large sum for another building which nobody could find.

Indictments continued to pile up in federal and state courts. In less than two years since the *New Orleans States* had begun its campaign against graft and corruption, more than 300 charges had been filed against the looters of the state's finances. Almost without exception, every legislator linked with the Huey Long machine was charged with dual jobholding. The magnitude of unmitigated defilement of public trust reached practically all levels of society and is still unique in the history of the United States, Watergate notwithstanding. William Rankin, the conservation commissioner, resigned after it was revealed $11,000 had been paid out of commission funds for a yacht presented to Governor Leche by "friends." A.P. Abernathy, chairman of the State Highway Commission, resigned after he was indicted for participating in the purchase and sale of materials from his own supply company to state agencies of which he was a member. Attorney General Davis Ellison was evicted from his office by state

troopers. The Orleans Parish district attorney, Charles Byrne, resigned during the height of the tax-racket hearings sparked by the
"Congressional Record" story.

The speaker of the Louisiana house of representatives, Lorris
Wimberly; his father, a judge; his brother, an inspector for the State
Highway Commission; a state senator; and a mayor of a small town
were all indicted for a scheme in which they allegedly defrauded a
parish out of a goodly portion of its finances. The case ended in a
mistrial, but Judge Wimberly was found guilty of contempt of court
in connection with jury tampering in the case.

Dr. Clarence Lorio, one of Long's political leaders in Baton
Rouge, resigned from office when it was discovered he was on three
payrolls. Lorio, who was also president of the Louisiana State
Medical Society, had been appointed medical director of LSU, state
penitentiary physician, and medical director of the state tuberculosis
sanitarium. Apparently a real workhorse, Lorio was also a state
senator, at least until he was convicted of mail fraud stemming from a
scheme which involved phony bidding practices for work performed
at—where else—LSU.

A. L. Shushan, a former president of the Orleans Levee Board,
however, had beaten a charge of income-tax evasion. Shushan, who
was, and remained, a personal friend of mine, had been accused of
receiving kickbacks from the Chicago Dredging Company on shell
supplied to build the New Orleans Lakefront Airport, formerly the
Shushan Airport. The firm had been paying a two cents kickback for
every cubic yard of shell purchased by the levee board. Huey sent
Abe up to Chicago to get three cents. Abe figured he'd add a cent to
it—make it four cents—and not tell Huey about it.

When he was acquitted of the charges, I told him, "Look stupid,
why didn't you put that airport out in the middle of Lake Pontchartrain? You could have had a lot more yardage." Shushan could afford
to laugh, having just got away with grand larceny, but later things
were not so funny. He was indicted on charges of mail fraud in
connection with a $500,000 bond deal cooked up by local stockbro-
kers, a plan in which Shushan, being a practical man, could see merit.
It involved Orleans Levee Board funds, and Shushan, as president of

that board, provided the bonds which were refinanced. Shushan shared in the profits of the transaction, and the levee board itself didn't suffer any immediate damages. Forty years later, when the bonds matured, it would, however.

During the height of the *States'* exposure of this graft, I kept a headline on the story referring to it as the "Shushan Scandal." Shushan telephoned me. He said, "You and that Jimmy Crown keep calling it the Shushan case. Why don't you call it some other case?"

I said, "Abe, I got news for you, that man with the whiskers [Uncle Sam] wants you. And when the man with the whiskers wants you, he's going to get you. And it is the Shushan case." But he could never understand that.

I was ultimately correct in my assessment. Shushan was convicted and sentenced to serve two years in the Atlanta federal penitentiary, which by that time was becoming crowded with Louisiana notables. Joining Shushan on his sabbatical were Herbert Waguespack, an attorney and a former member of the levee board as well as the scion of one of the state's oldest families; Henry J. Miller, a certified public accountant; and Robert Newman and Norvin Trent Harris, the stockbroker who invested the levee board's funds so freely.

Leon Weiss, the chief architect for Huey's boys, who actually was an architect, also went to Atlanta. He was sentenced to five years for his participation in a fraudulent scheme involving a building on the Louisiana Tech campus in the North Louisiana city of Ruston.

There were many, many others—politicians, contractors, slot-machine operators, fixers of many varieties, public employees, all of whom found their operations constricted by the massive crackdowns on their intrigues, including George Caldwell. Dr. Smith joined Caldwell and his other cronies in Atlanta. He had attempted to kill himself while incarcerated in a Baton Rouge jail by slitting a leg artery and placing it in a tub of hot water. A jailer had discovered him and saved his life.

Leche, who once said, "When I took the oath as governor, I didn't take any vows of poverty," was alleged to have been involved in numerous illegal activities. He was finally convicted of using the U.S. mails to defraud the State Highway Department of $115,000 on the sale of trucks. After receiving the stiffest sentence of all those convicted in the Scandals—ten years—Leche shrugged it off. "What the hell," he said, "it's an occupational hazard."

As the *States* itself commented in recounting its activities in exposing the Scandals:

> An untrammelled and fearless press had once again saved the cherished freedom of a downtrodden people. Through the irrefutable evidence of word, picture, and editorial on the printed page, the people of Louisiana were given a true picture of what before had existed in their state.
>
> As long as there is freedom of the press and freedom of speech, neither a lasting dictatorship nor a lasting rotten government seething with graft and corruption of public and quasi-public officials can last indefinitely.

The role of the *States* in exposing that corruption and graft was immense, and its work did not go unnoticed. The newspaper won the Sigma Delta Chi award for "Courage in Journalism." It undoubtedly should have been awarded the Pulitzer Prize, but in one of its less admirable decisions, the Pulitzer selection committee was swayed from honoring the *States* through pressure applied by the rival *New Orleans Item*. The prize went instead to a small-town paper which had conducted a street cleanup campaign. But, it should be acknowledged, the campaign resulted in very clean streets.

The voters of Louisiana completed the cleanup of their state themselves. Sam Jones, a young attorney from Lake Charles with a spotless political record, was elected governor. That same year the state sent five new members to Washington to represent them in the United States Congress. I was one of them.

CHAPTER VIII

GOODBYE ROGUES, HELLO REFORMERS

ANYONE WHO HAD NOT been in a catatonic trance for the preceding two years was aware that the 1940 Louisiana elections were destined to be wild even by Louisiana's standards. Libel and slander were the order of the day. Issues of substance were practically unheard. "You're another one," was the most popular campaign slogan.

Still, the gubernatorial candidates lined up early. Huey's brother, Earl Long, was the incumbent—thanks to the resignation of Richard Leche, which allowed Louisiana to save face by having a former governor, rather than a reigning chief executive, incarcerated in a federal prison. And Earl, the incumbent, was running. James A. Noe, of course, had been running since he broke with Huey's heirs when they had the audacity to select Leche, instead of him, to carry on.

Jimmy had moved from the Roosevelt (the bailiwick of the Long forces) to the St. Charles Hotel, where his radio station, WNOE, was located. Since I also lived at the St. Charles, I was always in close touch with him. More often than not, I would see Jimmy in the morning before I went to the paper. We would discuss, among other things, the reason why the *Times-Picayune*, the owners of the *New Orleans States*, would not support him in his drive for the governor's office.

Jimmy, being of his own nature, and believing that Huey was the greatest thing since water and having been part of the Long machine, was unacceptable to the *Times-Picayune*, and that was understandable.

But what is perfectly obvious to one individual often completely

139

eludes another. Thus, Noe kept asking, "Eddie, why can't they
support me? I'm clean as a hound's tooth."

I was completely frank in my response. "Listen, Jimmy," I said,
"I want to tell you a little story. About two thousand years ago, on
Calvary Hill, there was a man crucified on a cross. Two other men
were crucified at the same time. The fellow on the left said, 'If you are
the Son of God, why don't you get me off this cross and get yourself
off?' The fellow on the right said, 'Talk to your Father in Heaven for
me, and ask for His forgiveness for me also.' Jimmy, all you can do is
play the role of that fellow on the right." Noe laughed and understood, but he still wanted to be governor. It was his main desire.

In fact, Noe thought it might improve his chances if I ran for
lieutenant governor on his ticket. Since the breaking of the Scandals,
my name had become fairly well-known across the state. Jimmy kept
urging me to run for lieutenant governor with him. He even offered to
put $5,000 in escrow to cover my salary during the campaign and
cover expenses. If we lost, he offered to make me manager of WNOE
at a salary of $5,000 a year, which was big money in those days, plus
give me twenty-five percent of the station's gross. At that time
WNOE was making about $65,000. On the other hand I was making
$85 a week as city editor, so the proposition was real attractive.
However, I was told by the paper, and properly so, that if I got mixed
up with politics as a candidate, I would have to resign. They didn't
want anybody running for office while working on the paper, which is
understandable. I toyed with this thing, kicked it around, and kicked
it around again. I couldn't make up my mind what to do because the
money proposition was so attractive, even if I lost.

Finally, I went to Major Crown with my dilemma, and after
discussing the possibilities, Crown said, "Why don't you take a shot
at it. You can always come back here if you don't like it."

With that security, I set up an appointment with Noe at the St.
Charles. I walked in there and the first man I bumped into was Mike
O'Leary (Captain John J. Michael O'Leary), the manager of the St.
Charles and a friend of mine.

"Your friend just cashed a bad check," O'Leary told me.

"Was it a $5,000 check?" I asked.

"No, it was a $3,000 check. But he'll make it good."

I realized Noe's predicament. On the way to the suite, I contemplated the situation. I thought to myself, "you are a fine and grateful so and so. Here is your friend, you know he is strapped for money. You know this exposé, which you have benefitted by and made this great reputation on, cost him all his ready cash. Now, you are going to let him carry the load, and you can't lose. He can lose, you can't lose."

By the time I reached Noe's room, I had decided not to be a candidate. When I told him my decision, Jimmy looked at me dumbfounded, like I had lost my cotton-pickin' mind. "I just changed my mind," I told him. "I just don't feel like running."

Then Jimmy started that typical and wonderful Noe persuasive action. He had the $3,000 in a roll stuffed in his inside coat pocket. "Eddie, you sure you don't want to run?" Noe asked, letting his coat fall open to expose the wad of bills.

Well, I was just a poor city editor and I had never seen money like that in my life. Nevertheless, I said, "No, Jimmy," but he persisted.

Finally, I said, "Jimmy, I have a suggestion for you. I have an old friend named Dr. Joseph Menendez. He would be a good man to run for lieutenant governor. He is an honored past president of the Veterans of Foreign Wars. He is very active in civic affairs, and very well-liked. He also is a very fine surgeon." (I also mentioned Joe had the money to run.) Jimmy bought my suggestion, and Joe finally became his running mate.

Thus, two candidates were ready to run, Long and Noe. Soon, James Morrison, a young attorney who had organized the strawberry farmers into cooperatives, joined Long and Noe as a candidate. While he had a clean record, his campaign tactics were too facetious, albeit amusing, to suit the reformers. He would introduce a monkey to an audience as Earl Long, and then apologize to the monkey. Eventually, the monkey suffered a nervous collapse. Morrison said it had been called Earl too often.

Two men in the forefront of the reformers seeking a suitable candidate to back for governor were E. A. Stephens, an automobile dealer, and Preston Foster, a sugar planter from the town of

Franklin in the coastal parish of St. Mary. One day I was sitting in the
bar of the St. Charles Hotel talking to Stephens, who asked me where
the reformers could get a candidate.

"Well," I replied, "there is a man who I don't know personally,
but I have heard a great deal about him. His name is Sam Jones. He's
a lawyer, and a big wheel in the American Legion movement. I
understand he makes one helluva wonderful speech, and he is clean."

The suggestion struck a responsive chord in the reform leaders.
Sam Houston Jones, who had risen from humble origins in the
Southwest Louisiana community of De Ridder to become a successful lawyer in the oil-oriented city of Lake Charles, became the
candidate of the reform movement. He had dignity, a grasp of what
needed to be done to the political apparatus of Louisiana, and he was
untainted by corruption of any sort—all the things which made him
unacceptable to the Long machine.

When Jones registered as a candidate, his campaign leaders approached me with the proposition that I manage their candidate's race
for governor. However, the newspaper would not allow me to work in
the campaign unless I left the paper. I understood and approved the
decision and therefore declined to leave the paper for Jones. I had
refused to leave for Noe's proposition and I wasn't going to leave for
Jones' proposition, particularly because Jimmy was my friend, and I
had to support him.

The campaign, once it got into full swing, lived up to its billing: it
was wild and woolly. Noe considered Huey his sacred province, a
saint whose memory had been desecrated by his followers. And Earl
was campaigning primarily on the strength of having "Huey's
blood" running through his veins. Noe was incensed. "I remember
when Earl ran all over Huey," he said, and read an old statement
made by Earl about his brother: "Huey's a yellow coward. I'll meet
him in front of the Roosevelt [Hotel], and I'll not only beat him one
block, I'll beat him for twenty blocks." "Now," Noe said, "Earl is
going around saying, 'Vote for me. I'm Huey Long's brother.' "
Noe attacked Jones as "a big corporation lawyer" who only had the
interest of big business at heart.

Long, himself, tried to take credit for sending Leche, the man he had served as lieutenant governor, to jail: "I'm sorry I had to do it, . . . but it was my duty." Since becoming governor in his own right, Long said he had spent his time recovering the people's money which had been squandered by Leche and his cronies.

> The legislature voted $300,000 for seven parks and the Leche administration spent it all on a 28-hole [*sic*] golf course on the Tchefuncte River, one of six of its kind in the world. They even built a clubhouse where people could change into those knicker-britches that they play in. I suppose you know what a golf course is. It's a place where rich men go to get exercise. I never wore knicker-britches in my life. I get all the exercise I need hoeing on my farm and pulling potatoes and riding horseback.

Long then got down to the issues, name calling: "High Hat Jones" and "Sweet Smelling Sam."

But Long was not doing all of the throwing, he was catching, too. A particularly sore spot with Long was a small ear of corn that *States'* cartoonist, Roy Aymond, put in all the cartoons about Earl. I had been told that it would rile Long if the symbol was used, and it did. At one rally, Earl called the editor of the *States* "a fat, lazy, do-nothing scoundrel by the name of Jim Crown," and allowed that the ears of corn did not bother him. "Some people just can't stand being blackguarded in the newspapers, but they can't harass me. I can go on for five or six more weeks and battle them in the cold and rain. I would be willing for the campaign to go on for a while longer so the newspapers can keep having fun, . . . They haven't had so much fun since they tried to impeach poor Huey. That only lasted seventy days, but this has been going on for five months."

He said it was understandable that the *Times-Picayune* did not want him to be governor. "It's because I can't eat a sixteen course dinner with a fork about as big as your little finger without spilling some of it on my vest. Sam Jones can do that."

Meanwhile, Noe was fighting hard to attain his goal of recapturing the governorship which he had possessed for so short a time. Noe called Earl an exponent of dictatorship, and he labeled Jones the corporation candidate. On the other hand, Noe was working for honesty and efficiency in government. "I'll let Earl Long take his graft and corruption and thievery, and I'll let Sam Jones take his corporation money—I'll take our Legion of Honor and beat them so bad they won't know what to do." Noe had organized a "Legion of Honor" which was composed of his supporters, who would prove loyal, if too few. They backed his main platform planks of tax relief and clean government, both of which, in all likelihood, he would have provided.

As the primary grew nearer, the oratory got hotter. Jones wore a battered felt hat to prove he was not "High Hat Sam," but he had to spend much of his time refuting allegations by Long that he was supported by the Ku Klux Klan and had voted against Al Smith, charges Long lodged in the predominantly Roman Catholic areas of the state. Both charges were untrue. Jones had even campaigned for Smith. He admitted he represented corporations, which, he said, had the same right to representation as did the farmers and laborers who were also his clients. He attacked the record of the Long machine, which supported Earl, and he charged that as much as $100,000,000 had been stolen from the state by that machine. He offered to lower taxes, liberalize welfare, and grant greater aid to public schools.

Noe, the great detective, had some other things to say about the Longs. He accused them of pre-marking ballots in order to stuff the boxes on election day. "Now, I have just received information," Noe announced shortly before the January 16 primary, "that they have given up trying to put Earl Long over and are trying to get the boys to steal the election. One of the Long men called me and gave me the name and address of the Long organization leader already marking ballots."

"I hope that man is listening to me now," pleaded Noe, who was speaking over the air waves of his own radio station. "I hope his wife and father and mother are listening, too, and I hope he will burn those ballots up before Mr. Rogge (O. John Rogge, the federal prosecutor credited with putting most of the Long men in the penitentiary) gets hold of them a month or so after the election."

"And another thing," Noe said, speaking directly to the God-fearing people of the state on the subject of Earl Long, "he can't say

four words without cussin'.'' Noe was making reference to Long
being cut off the air while making a radio address in Shreveport.

The thing which caused the most ''cussin' '' in the Long camp was
a Gallup Poll conducted prior to the election which showed, among
other things, that the majority of the people in Louisiana did not
believe the elections were honest. But what bothered the Long back-
ers was the fact the poll indicated that if the elections were honest,
Jones and Long would be in a dead heat, with Noe running a strong
third.

The Progress—the newspaper started by Huey to satirize and sully
his opponents, continued by Leche with the extra added attraction of
coerced profits, and maintained by Earl in its vitriolic tradition—was
particularly outraged. It expressed the outward indignation of the
Long machine over the results of the poll. The poll takers, it charged,
were a bunch of nefarious characters from New York, including ''a
Harlem nigger in a double-breasted suit,'' who came to Louisiana to
rig the results.

Jones, for his part, was naturally pleased with the results of the
poll, and said there were plenty of reasons to disbelieve anything the
Progress reported. He said the paper ran a picture of him one week
with a diamond stickpin painted on his tie. The next week it was gone.
''That gang steals even from photographs,'' he said.

Noe was beginning to realize things did not look promising. If the
election were honest, he was in trouble. If it were rigged, he was in
trouble. His best bet, he figured, was to keep on campaigning and
hope he could sway enough voters to put him into a runoff. To do this,
he knew he must have an honest count at the polls.

The other candidate, Morrison, was the biggest crowd pleaser in
the campaign with his ''Convict Parade.'' It was estimated that
100,000 persons turned out in New Orleans a few nights before the
election to watch the Mardi Gras-style performance. The parade
depicted members of the Long machine in striped convict uniforms.
Morrison dubbed them with sobriquets such as ''Sizemore Weiss,''
''Richard (Give Me a Yacht) Leche,'' and ''Robert S. (Sneaker)
Maestri.'' Included in his political caravan were floats designated as
''the Leche-Weiss-Maestri-Long Taxi Cab,'' which was a mobile jail

inhabited by four convicts. On another float two ersatz convicts were being boiled in "hot oil," a reference to the hot oil deals of the Scandals.

While the populace of New Orleans loved a parade, Morrison should have realized that parading had never elected anybody to any public office. In fact it has usually had the opposite effect in the Crescent City: witness the would-be politicos who were kings of Carnival. Election day 1940 bore out this tradition.

It was a day to remember. I had never seen such a high wave of emotionalism as was in the air on election day and I have not seen it since. Everybody was excited. It was really a highly charged atmosphere.

In his effort to get an honest count at the polling places in New Orleans, Jimmy Noe had a group of his supporters with him on January 16, including Ray Hufft and Jim Edgecombe. Edgecombe always struck me as the toughest guy in the world. That group, all armed, would speed to precincts whenever they got word of irregularities, or word that Noe supporters were being prevented from voting.

Jones, too, was watching the polling booths. He had hired photographers to shoot pictures of voter intimidation. One of those cameramen was beaten by Long supporters while a policeman looked on. But Noe was giving out more than he got. He had some of his "Hot Boys" from North Louisiana—as he called them—with him. Somebody—"one of their inside fellas"—told Noe and his lieutenants that a ballot box had been switched and fixed. Noe found out about it, and went over to the polling place and poured ink into the box. He filled it full of ink. Ray and Edge and his other helpers were there and joined in the fun.

The afternoon papers carried front-page stories on the fights which erupted throughout the day. I reported in the *States* on an altercation involving Noe. It occurred at the first precinct in the Second Ward, 1108 Tchoupitoulas, a brawling section of the city: "Side-stepping a blow directed at him by a husky Long supporter . . . Noe dropped his attacker with a right-cross to the jaw." Noe was quoted in the articles as saying his attacker pulled a knife after he knocked him down, "but

Ray Hufft took it away from him and gave him what he was looking for.''

Years later Noe recalled the incident: ''Old Ray hit that fella and knocked him plumb up on a car there. Cold-cocked him. We tore up there. And did you see that spread in *Life* magazine about that fight? Well, that fella that was representing the *New York Times* got hit with a brick. I saw that. Daniels, I believe was his name, Ray Daniels. He told me when I saw him after the Second World War in New York that he didn't see as much action in the war as he did on election day in New Orleans.''

I think it's only fair to add that one fight was started by Noe's supporters for the benefit of *Life* magazine. The *Life* photographers didn't have a picture of an election-day fracas so some of Noe's boys went over and punched a couple of guys. The result was one hell of a fight with pictures galore.

After that brawl, Noe and his ''hot boys'' went to Nina Patorno's precinct, the first in the Fifth Ward. ''They were tough down there,'' Noe said. ''And that was the first time the Old Regulars had really been fought. We went down there because I wanted Patorno. I had my forty-five right here,'' he said, indicating a shoulder holster, ''and old Ray was with me, and old Edge and that fella that used to be a hell of a football player at [Louisiana] Tech, and we all had guns on. There were about two hundred of them on the other side of the street, and they were looking for it. We had sent word we were coming down there.

''And I went up to Patorno and I says, 'now you might kill me but' . . . I mean Ray Hufft and old Edge was right behind me, both of them already had their guns out. Had them in their hands. And I said to Patorno, 'We're goin' in there to check that box and if you make a move, or any one of those fellas across that street, I'm gonna blow a hole in you, and so will my boys.'

''You know what Patorno said? He said, 'Governor, we don't want any trouble. We're not goin' to keep anybody out of here.'

''And Patorno had plenty of guts, too. I had Bob Maestri and a lot of 'em tell me they don't see how in the hell we all didn't get killed.''

Before the day was over, Noe, Hufft, Edgecombe and Scott Wil-

son, Noe's campaign manager, had been arrested. "I got a photographer to take a picture of us in the wagon," Noe said. "I wanted it to
come out in the papers and show what they was trying to do."

When I heard about the goings-on at Patorno's precinct, I sent Russ
Kintzley, my co-reporter on the Bienville Double Dip Trial, to check
out the reports. He was accompanied by Oscar Valeton, a fiery
photographer who seemingly had no inhibitions when it came to
getting a picture. It was Valeton who sneaked up into the balcony of
the rotunda in the state capitol to photograph Huey Long lying in state
and ran for miles to elude pursuing bodyguards intent upon revenging
the sacrilege.

I told Russ, who lived in that precinct, to vote, check the story, and
send Valeton back with the pictures and information if there was
anything to it. Then he was to go home since it was late in the
afternoon. But later Russ called me at the paper, and I said, "I
thought I told you to vote and go home."

"Vote!" Kintzley replied. "They're putting me in jail."

"They can't do that," I shot back.

"I'm calling you from jail!" Kintzley said.

Kintzley and Valeton were incarcerated because the poll commissioners did not want Russ to vote since they knew he was not
supporting Long. The ostensible reason was that they were violating a
law which prevented photographs being taken at polling places, a law
which did not exist. The Long-controlled machine was trying to
prevent the reporting and photographing of irregularities. When I got
my two staffers out of jail, I called Noe, who sent two of his
bodyguards to escort Kintzley back to the polling booth to vote.

As the returns trickled in, Long was in the lead, with Jones running
second. Noe, who received a substantial vote, was in third place.
Morrison was running a poor fourth. During the early morning hours
of January 17, it became obvious that Long would be in a runoff with
Jones. It also became obvious that Noe would be the key man in that
race. The reformers and editors were at the paper watching the returns
roll in. About three o'clock in the morning they wanted me to go
down to the St. Charles and talk to Noe. I didn't want to do it. Noe's
whole empire had just collapsed around him. He had lost the race; he

gambled and lost. But I said I would feel him out, see what his attitude was.

When I got down there Jimmy was raving. He was calling Jones "Sweet Smelling Sam" and everything he could think of. I talked to him. "Jimmy, I'm not asking you to do anything now. I'm not asking you to make any decision. All I'm asking you to do is to keep quiet. Don't do or say anything until tomorrow when I have a chance to talk to you."

To this Noe agreed, and I returned to the paper and reported the situation to the editors and the good-government crowd. The next day a select group of reformers headed by Press Foster met with Noe at the Monteleone Hotel. They agreed to pay Jimmy's campaign debts if he would support Jones, and also agreed to split the patronage with him. I told him to take it, to make the deal, and he did.

In the meantime, Long charged that Noe had agreed to support him for $150,000, but Jones had apparently bid higher. Noe replied that the statement was not exactly correct; he had been offered $300,000 to support Long but had turned it down.

Noe's headquarters was in the Elks Building on Elks Place, just off Canal Street. While it seeemed spontaneous, it had been planned for Noe to lead his "Legion of Honor" down Canal Street on the night of January 19 to Jones' headquarters at the Monteleone Hotel. It was unusually cold for New Orleans. Noe addressed his followers who were gathered in the unheated Elks Building, and told them of his decision to support Sam Jones. "Are you proud of my decision?" he asked the packed auditorium. "Are you with me?" The crowd roared its approval.

"Come on," Noe said, waving his arm toward the door, "let's go get him." He led his people outside into the sleet and on to Jones' headquarters. They marched down Canal with linked arms, blocking traffic and throwing the fear of defeat into the crowd which had gathered at the Long headquarters on Canal Street.

If ever a group resembled the vagabonds of Paris, it was that crowd that night. I know because I was part of the march. I accompanied the Noe partisans on their trek to the Monteleone on Royal Street in the French Quarter. By prearrangement Jones was waiting in the hotel lobby. Noe walked up the steps and Jones came out to meet him. Jones said, "Jimmy, I'm glad to have you with me," and Noe said, "Sam, I'm glad to be with you." Then they joined arms and marched back to Elks Place.

Back inside the frigid building, Noe took the stand to tell of his decision to back Jones: "I said to myself, I said, 'Jimmy Noe, you only have one road to go. That road is the road of decency and honesty and that road leads to Sam Jones.'" Then in the tumult of approval, he called on Jones to speak. "If I had known what I know now, Jimmy, you would be the candidate and not me," Jones said. "Jimmy Noe is the biggest man in this state."

This union caused Earl Long some discomfort. Within a few days, Long had called a special session of the legislature to enact laws increasing benefits to citizens in an attempt to win converts. He was running scared, and he kept up his attacks on "High Hat Sam." As the campaign wore on, Earl approached calling Jones, whose record was unblemished, a thief. "I don't say Sam Jones is crooked, but my old father told me that while there are a lot of men who won't go to hell for a quarter, they will fool around the edge trying to get in until they fall in."

Jones continued to conduct his campaign simply by citing abuses and promising relief. And with the support of Noe, who took ninety percent of the votes cast for him in the first primary to Jones, it was enough. When the results came in on February 10, Jones had defeated Long by almost 20,000 votes, despite what many people believed to have been a crooked election.

"Louisiana has gone back into the hands of the people," Jones said, as citizens celebrated in the streets with the wildest outpouring of exuberance of any election in the history of the state. "A new day had dawned on this state after a long night with foul things happening in the dark."

Noe became the fair-haired boy, and was flushed with victory. He thought he was the kingmaker, and he was dead set that I should run for mayor against Maestri. I wasn't about to compete against Bob Maestri, whom I liked very much and who was a good friend. Also, being realistic, I didn't think I could beat Maestri to begin with.

Anyway, I was not interested in being mayor. I didn't want to be in politics or anything like that. But Noe kept pressing me, and somewhere in the back of my mind, I thought, well, maybe going to Congress would be a good deal.

Indeed, I had begun to consider the benefits which would accrue to a reporter if he served two years in Congress. I concluded that the congressional experience would make me a better reporter. I'd have entree to the national political scene. I realized that once someone serves in Congress he has a lifetime floor privilege. Imagine being a reporter and going back and having the privileges of going into those cloak rooms and listening to all that conversation behind those rails. The conversations which go on there!

The idea grew, and I called Bascom Timmons in the paper's Washington office to get the details of salary and benefits available to congressmen. The salary was $10,000 a year, which was all the money in the world to me. I was making $85 a week. There was a $200 stationery account, and a congressman could employ three people in his office. The total salary was $6,500 for three people with the top one making $3,500. And congressmen were provided also with one free round trip. Timmons thought I wanted this information for a story, but I wanted to find out whether it was worthwhile thinking about going to Congress.

A few days after I received the information, I was sitting with Jimmy Noe in the Recess Club, an organization dedicated to hedonistic pursuits, when we got a call from Major Crown, who told us that T. A. Conway, the secretary of state, had died. He said Earl Long was maneuvering to become secretary of state, which, of course, nobody wanted. Old Uncle Earl could always come up when you figured he was dead. Crown wanted me to rush to Baton Rouge with Noe and check the story.

We drove up with Jim Edgecombe and Ray Hufft. On the way, the subject came up again about me running for mayor. I wanted to get Noe out of my hair about running for mayor, so I said, "Jimmy, I tell you what. I will go to Congress for two years, and I'll be seasoned in politics and then maybe I'll run for mayor."

Noe thought it was a good idea, so I said, "What you do is this: you go to Sam Jones and tell him you want to divide up the jobs. You tell him you want to designate the nominee for Congress from the First Congressional District, and he can name the nominee from the Second District. Tell him you'll join forces and support each other's candidate.''

Jones bought it, but at the moment the Jones people really wanted Paul Maloney, who represented the Second District, to remain in Congress. Hale Boggs wasn't even in the picture. He was being considered for public service commissioner.

But Boggs, who would later become majority leader in the House of Representatives, desperately wanted to run for Congress. He was a young, handsome, intelligent attorney and a former Tulane campus reporter who had worked on the *States*. He possessed an ambition to be a part of something larger than local politics or a law practice.

In the meantime Noe was trying to solidify support for me. He went up to see the two Nicholsons (Leonard and York) and old Major Crown. And why not? They were always talking about good government, wanted good government and all that.

Noe laid the cards on the table. He stated bluntly that he had made a deal with Sam Jones. He would name one congressman and so many judges, and Sam Jones would name so many. They then agreed to support one another's candidates. I was Noe's choice but he could have picked almost anyone. There were at least forty would-be congressmen trying to get him to name them, but he had committed himself to me. Even though Noe had the deal wrapped up, he wanted the approval of the *Picayune*, and so he went to see the Nicholsons and Crown. As soon as the meeting ended, Noe told me what had happened.

I said, ''I want to talk to you about good government. Now, do you agree to support a man that I name as congressman?''

''We'll agree to it if he's a good respectable man,'' they said.

I said, ''Do you want a man that'll really go up there and do something, that's really got a lot of guts and backbone and courage? A young fella who hasn't had the opportunity he should've? He's working for an outfit that don't recognize his ability.''

They said, ''We don't give a damn about that; if his firm doesn't recognize his ability, why that's their fault. They'll just have to lose him.''

I hadn't said anything about you yet. I wanted to tie the bastards up. Tight as a goat. Then I said, ''What kind of people are you here at the *Picayune*? You've never supported me. You've always screwed me. But after Sam Jones got elected I'm the biggest fella in the world. You have me on the front page and all that. But you got some good men here.''

''All of them are good,'' they said. ''We don't keep bastards around here.''

I said, ''Well, I'll tell you who I want to run for Congress. Eddie Hébert.''

Old man Crown said, ''Governor, are you serious?''

I said, ''Major, nobody likes you better than Eddie Hébert.''

He said, ''Well, I like Eddie and I don't want to lose him. He's city editor. He's the best and he's going to be better.''

I said, ''Hell, he's been working here for years and he hasn't gone too far.''

''The hell he hasn't,'' old man Nicholson said. Then he said to me, ''Are you serious about Hébert?''

''Yes, sir. I think he'll make an excellent congressman.''

''Well,'' Nicholson said, ''he can't work for us and run for office. The day Eddie announces for office, he'll have to resign.''

I resigned, and because I had to have a visible means of support between May when I resigned and September when the primary was held, I went to Washington as Sam Jones' personal representative. Obviously the new administration didn't want to have anthing to do with the old Louisiana delegation, which was anti-Jones. There was no representative of the Jones administration, thus it was perfectly valid and logical that somebody should be there to represent it.

At the time the representative of the governor's office was Earle Christenberry, the man who had been Huey's secretary. I had lunch with Earle who had a fine suite of offices in Washington, and I told him I was going to take his job. He said he understood. Whether or not he did, I became the possessor of a $10,000 a year job.

Boggs himself was trying to get the new governor's support, and that was proving difficult. Jones, himself, was very friendly with

Hale, but the Jones people wanted to keep Maloney in Congress because that would insure support for their candidate from the New Orleans machine, the Old Regulars, which was responsible for Maloney being a United States Representative. The governor's advisers were trying to get Boggs to run for public service commissioner. Personally, I thought it was the thing Hale should do. He was a young man, twenty-six years old, and it would have been a good deal for him to become public service commissioner for a term of six years, and to practice law. What more could any aspiring young lawyer want?

Hale would not give up, though. He was fighting for his life. Then, one night, George Montgomery, head of the Old Regular faction, was talking to some people and remarked that he didn't care who ran for Congress from the Second District. He even allowed that Hale Boggs was acceptable to him. When Hale found out, he immediately called Jack Tims (the publisher of the *Times-Picayune*). Tims met Boggs at Major Crown's house and they smoked out Montgomery. Jack Tims put Hale in the race, and after that Jones picked Hale up. I feel certain that if the chance remark by Montgomery had not been made, Hale would not have been the candidate from the Second District.

Eventually Maestri, who was the central power of the Old Regulars, threw his support to Boggs and me, which gave us neophyte candidates a coalition of Jones, Noe, and the Old Regulars. Maestri's action was partly an attempt to decoy federal investigators who were sniffing at his door because of his connections with the Long machine. Still, his political support was welcome and necessary, and when it came, it cinched the election for all practical purposes. How could we miss? With a coalition such as that which had been put together, Joe Blow could have been elected.

Despite this support, I realized that I had problems, and I wanted to establish all the backing I could. My main opponent was a ten-year congressional veteran, Joachim Octave Fernandez, and without the right combination of support, a victory over an entrenched political veteran would be difficult. But my concern was for naught; things began to fall into place. In addition to the already established coalition, C. F. "Dutch" Rowley, the roguish sheriff of St. Bernard, a coastal parish whose rugged inhabitants made their living primarily from the Gulf waters and possessed a Mediterranean tolerance for things non-Puritan, threw his support to me. Rowley was feuding with Judge Leander Perez, the autocrat of adjoining Plaquemines Parish. Aligned with Rowley was a small but vocal group from Plaquemines who disagreed with the Judge's dreams for that strip of land which guides the Mississippi River its last eighty miles to the Gulf of Mexico.

Still there was no doubt who controlled Plaquemines, and when Judge Perez called me, I responded. I had fought Perez all the time as a reporter, but we somehow remained friends. When he called and asked if I could meet him at the American Bank Building, I went to see him. I walked in and he was surrounded by his lieutenants.

"Eddie," the Judge said, "I just wanted you to know we have decided to support you. There is only one thing that I ask of you, let our organization handle your commissioners at the polls."

"You got 'em," I replied.

Of course, Perez' opponents got mad. Well, I figured it this way: Perez is going to win, no matter what I do; and if I gave him the commissioners, he'd have to deliver.

Judge Perez was with me thereafter, for which I am grateful. But I never asked for a campaign contribution and he never offered one. Over the years, I disagreed with a lot of things he said, and I disagreed with the way he did certain things, but I think he was a man of great depth. A man with a sincere purpose.

With Perez support in hand, I went to Washington to represent Governor Jones. A month prior to the September primary, I took a leave of absence, and returned to face my opponents: Fernandez, the ten-year congressional veteran; and Herve Racivich, an independent candidate who was subsequently elected district attorney of New Orleans.

The campaign was a lulu. I have said on many occasions I was probably the worst candidate anybody could think of. But, looking at the cold facts of life, I knew I was a shoo-in because of this coalition which was backing me. Nevertheless, I really wondered if I would click with the people as a congressional candidate. To begin with, there is my own manner. In the opinion of some people, I have a very haughty manner, although I do not believe it to be so. I will admit that I possess a very positive manner which results from thinking things out to my satisfaction. That is to say, I have always been one to draw my own conclusions, to arrive at my own answers, be they right or wrong. Many people, unfortunately, interpret this inherent drive "to be my own man" as crass egoism. I knew this, and I was well aware it could go against me at any time. Secondly, I was working for a corporate newspaper. I was working for a big-money institution. That wouldn't sit well in the Seventh, Eighth, and Ninth Wards (composed essentially of middle and lower middle class laboring people, many of whom were members of organized unions). Thirdly, I lived in the St. Charles Hotel. In those days nobody ever heard of anybody living in a hotel. This was real high-class stuff. Also, I was the product of private schools, Jesuit High School and Tulane University.

Finally, I was saddled with the worst thing I could think of for a political candidate in my district: I loved clothes. I have always had a fetish for good clothes because I can remember the days when I had two suits—one on and one off. But even on the paper, I wore good clothes.

I had all these things going against me. Recognizing this, I made up my mind that I was going to win; but if I lost, it couldn't be blamed on not trying. The first thing I did was buy myself a seersucker suit. I kept that suit on from the beginning of the campaign until the end. I never worked so hard. I'd go to meetings, throw off my coat, roll up my sleeves, pull down my tie, and indulge in all the tricks of the trade to let the people know I was one of them, and not a high-hat city editor from the corporate newspaper who looked down his nose at them.

I opened the campaign with an address on WNOE where I was introduced by Noe amid the cheers of his supporters who had packed the radio station. I followed this up with three open-air rallies at night in the city, a Sunday afternoon parade in St. Bernard Parish, a shrimp boil on a Sunday afternoon in Plaquemines Parish, and an ice-cream party for children in the Eighth Ward, whose parents thought it a nice gesture. My daughter Dawn, then four years old, was the hostess.

Between rallies and speeches, I made the political rounds, and never drank so much dime gin in my life. Fortunately, my background to talk to everybody was good. I had, of course, written sports for years. One night I was down in the Ninth Ward. As I was about to get into my car I heard somebody in a nearby bar say something about Eddie Hébert. I walked over to the saloon, threw open the door and said, "All right, somebody's talking about me. What did you say?" Before the night was over I was sitting with these characters eating boiled crabs and talking about fights and fighters they never even heard of. I could be a gentleman in the living room or a bum in the barroom. I could go either way, as the situation dictated, and this knack helped me a lot.

There was never any question about my ability to speak in public, and I put this to good use during the campaign. Jimmy Noe had given me carte blanche on his radio station, which was located in the St. Charles, where I lived. I would listen to Joe Fernandez speak on the radio, and immediately after he finished, I would run downstairs to the studio and go on the air to rebut his charges.

Primarily, I attacked Fernandez for his failure to obtain benefits for the state. For my part, I was advocating a two-ocean Navy and a standing Army large enough to defend all borders. I encouraged voters to finish the job of cleaning out the remnants of the Long machine by electing candidates sponsored by Governor Jones—in order to make Louisiana the kind of state we think it ought to be.

As the campaign wore on, I continued to concentrate on my stronger opponent, Fernandez, ignoring Racivich, for the most part. During the campaign I nicknamed Fernandez "Bathtub Joe" because when anyone wanted to speak to him on the telephone, he could not talk because he was "in the bathtub." Soon I labeled Fernandez "Joe-Joe Zero Fernandez," the name representing what my opponent had accomplished during ten years in Congress.

Fernandez countered by getting the Speaker of the United States House of Representatives, William B. Bankhead, and the majority leader, Sam Rayburn, to write letters commending him for his fine and dedicated service to his state and his nation. I responded to this by saying, "If I were Speaker Bankhead, I, too, would congratulate Congressman Fernandez. He has coincided with Bankhead's views and assisted him greatly in obtaining appropriations for Alabama, which meant that much was not being appropriated for Louisiana. As for Representative Rayburn, I can well believe that he heartily approved Mr. Fernandez because while the congressman from Louisiana saw to it that Mr. Rayburn was getting fifty to sixty millions of dollars for Corpus Christi, Louisiana was getting not one red dime."

Fernandez, who was backed by organized labor, attacked me as being anti-union and pro-big business, making much of my ties with the Times-Picayune Publishing Corporation. Indeed, many unions were hot on my tail even before I ran for office. I had opposed the formation of a guild at the newspaper on the grounds that the newspaper business was a profession. If a person could make it in the newspaper business, he could make it without anyone, including unions, pulling him up.

Strangest thing, however, was that when the union boys attempted to organize the guild, they sent copies to me. Why? Because of the way I talked up for reporters. I was the biggest supporter a reporter had. I believed they were underpaid. I believed the pay was terrible, and I would pop off about this in the office. I was their spokesman, and they wanted me to be their organizer. I was fighting for the same thing they were fighting for, but I did not believe in that method of organization. Thus, my anti-guild stand was well-known and was translated as being anti-union. In reality, however, I am not against unions in general, only as an adjunct of journalism.

For the purpose of the campaign, I had to show that I was not a labor baiter. I therefore recounted my father's years as a member of the local streetcar union. I even dragged out one of my old high school debates defending unionism and quoted from it: "Long may labor unionism live in this country, as a God-sent benefit to this ever glorious United States of America and to her people, forever waving aloft the banner of democracy linked with the standard of the organized movement in this country, and both marching up the rugged road to success, and both being led by the motto of the greatest nation under God's bright sunshine, E Pluribus Unum."

I was taking no chances, even though I felt certain that labor could not control the votes in my district. I don't know about anywhere else, but in my district, if a man was labor and Old Regular, he was going to vote Old Regular. In those days, it was a combination of support; issues meant nothing.

Toward the end of the campaign, as the rhetoric warmed, I categorized Fernandez as one of "this mob of diehards who can't understand the writing on the wall. They can't believe that after twelve years of ruthless plunderbund they have been counted out by the free and independent people of the state." In reply, Fernandez mounted a personal attack on my work as a journalist. This really got to me because I have always been proud of my newspaper record. I hit back. "Under the pressure of hysteria and facing certain defeat, Congressman J. O. Fernandez tonight became a political maniac. By innuendo and insinuation, because he isn't man enough to come right out and say what he means, he has the effrontery and audacity to attack my record, my character and my reputation as a newspaperman."

I gave Fernandez forty-eight hours in which to prove his charges. I vowed to borrow $5,000 and, if the charges could be proved, I promised to donate it to any charity selected by a Catholic priest, Jewish rabbi, and Protestant minister. I then challenged Fernandez to put up a matching $5,000, which he would be required to contribute to charity if he could not prove the charges. "In answer to Mr. Fernandez . . . I hurl the short and ugly word 'lie' to his teeth. J. O. 'Zero' Fernandez is a political leper unfit to walk among, much less represent, decent people. I challenge him to prove his cowardly and dastardly assertions."

On election day, the newspapers were full of pictures of my family and me voting, all with big smiles, confident of victory. That night a group of supporters from St. Bernard arrived at headquarters in the St. Charles Hotel to bring me news of the vote. I had told the bosses of the political machine that I wanted an honest vote count. In previous elections, when the nabobs were supporting Fernandez, the vote had, an occasion, exceeded the census—in Fernandez's favor. I did not want a recurrence of that, even if I was to be the beneficiary. So I told the St. Bernard people, there is only one thing I want: an honest count.

On the night of the election some fellows from St. Bernard came down to the St. Charles. It was the first time most of them had been inside a hotel, and they were jubilant over the count of a particular box. It showed: Hébert 342, Fernandez 3, and Racivich 0.

I rebuked these supporters with: "Didn't I tell you to give them an honest count?" They looked at me incredulously; and one offered: "Could we help it if the guy who was going to vote for Racivich ruined his ballot?"

The fact was that I had easily carried the parish; indeed, the election, by two to one over Fernandez. I received 35,363 votes, Fernandez 17,587, and Racivich 4,752. But I wasn't the only Jones-supported candidate to win. Boggs won in the Second District, James Domengeaux in the Third District, J. Y. Sanders, Jr., was returned in the Sixth, and Vance Plauché was elected from the Seventh District. Five of the eight congressmen representing Louisiana had been elected as a result of the Louisiana Scandals.

Within two weeks of the election, I was back in Washington representing the Jones administration in my old capacity, waiting for January to get sworn in, a performance which I would repeat eighteen more times before I decided that I had come to the end of the road and was ready to announce my retirement.

CHAPTER IX

THE FRESHMAN

It WAS WHILE representing Governor Sam Jones in Washington prior to assuming office, that I became friendly with one of the most powerful men in the nation's capital, Sam Rayburn, the Speaker of the House of Representatives. It was to prove to be a fortunate acquaintanceship for the state. Of Louisiana's eight-man delegation to the House, five of us were freshmen, and two of those five had defeated a couple of Rayburn's boys. Clearly, the state needed someone who could communicate with the head honcho of the House.

I had trounced Fernandez, a member of the powerful Appropriations Committee, and Hale Boggs had unseated Paul Maloney, who had been a member of the Ways and Means Committee. Defeating a member of the Ways and Means Committee was like ousting a member of the College of Cardinals. Hale's was an unpardonable sin, an unforgivable sin. He really should have known better than to beat Maloney. Obviously, then, Hale was not popular at all, particularly with Rayburn. Indeed, Rayburn had bawled the hell out of Sam Jones for opposing Maloney.

Rayburn had liked Fernandez, too, but during my tenure as Sam Jones' representative, I had fallen into the good graces of the crusty old Texan. "Eddie," Rayburn told me after I was sworn in, "you are the only member of the delegation I am going to talk to."

Not only did the Speaker talk to me, he also took me under his wing. I was not in Congress thirty days before I was presiding over the House. It was really pleasing to have that famous gavel in my hand, but I realized it was all a game they were playing. That was obvious. Here is a freshman congressman from Louisiana presiding over the House, and then what is he supposed to do? He is, according to the rules of the game, supposed to yes Mr. Rayburn to death. Similarly, he is supposed to be awed whenever the President of the United States talks to him. If I had played the game according to the Washington Hoyles, I would have been in the league, and probably would have become majority leader. It was all so easy, so effortless. But I had to be my own man. I may have dreamed of being their leader, but I could not yes them to death. I had the chance, and I quickly gave it up.

Hale Boggs did become the majority leader, despite Rayburn's early dislike of him, because Hale was an ingratiating person. He was always there when Rayburn wanted him. If I had played the game like Hale played it—well, I would have been available at all times. As much as Rayburn originally opposed Boggs, Hale ingratiated himself with Rayburn and became one of Rayburn's most trusted lieutenants.

Despite the reality or cynicism of my views on the honor of presiding over the House, my old paper, the *States*, was ecstatic. The paper commented:

> Dispatches from Washington informed the nation that Representative F. Edward Hebert, of the First Louisiana Congressional District Friday presided over the House of Representatives for forty-five minutes.
>
> This is heretofore an unheard of honor for a representative who has been in the House less than one month. He was called to the chair by Speaker Sam Rayburn. Many men serve in Congress all their lives and never obtain the honor of presiding over its deliberations. It was a splendid introduction for Mr. Hebert to the other members of the House. Useless to say that he presided over the deliberations of the House with dignity, poise, and intelligence.

In less than two years those sentiments would be regretted. Why? Politics, what else. In the meantime, however, I kept busy. I had no trouble getting my name into the Washington papers, after all, I had a natural affinity for the capital reporters and a nose for news. I also had one of the best press agents in Washington working for me—myself. Moreover, I believe that the Washington press corps took some sort of chauvinistic pride in my successes. This was manifested by coverage in society columns, light features on my comings and goings, political articles, and editorials. Almost every reference to me was prefaced with: "former hard-boiled city editor," or "ex-news sleuth," or "journalist-turned-congressman."

I got myself assigned to the District of Columbia Committee because I was told it was the one committee where a freshman could "get himself some action." The committee actually administered the district, but it wasn't long before I realized how clumsy the system was. I proposed changes which were welcomed by the city's newspapers and in doing so got more good press, both reportorial and editorial.

My work on the District of Columbia Committee began with a plan to reorganize the city's police department, which was apprehending few criminals and suffering from a morale problem. In addition, I advocated that more powers be granted to the district's board of commissioners in order that its municipal operations could function more effectively.

Outside Washington, I came to the aid of the beekeepers of my district who had suffered losses as the result of a federal program to eradicate the white-fringed beetle. Simultaneously, I championed the cause of the hard-pressed hardwood forests of Louisiana, and battled to keep afloat the important Higgins Shipyard of New Orleans. On a national level, I worked hard to solve the defense housing problems created by World War II.

Despite frequent trips connected with my work regarding the housing shortage, I managed to be present in Washington on April 25, 1941, the day the statue of Huey Long was unveiled in the Capitol's Statuary Hall. The statue had cost the taxpayers of Louisiana $15,000 by the time it was completed in December 1940. Since then, it had stood draped and undedicated, but not undisputed. Still-strong forces in Louisiana had pushed through the idea of a statue of Long. The idea, however, did not have universal appeal. When a reporter asked me what I thought about the idea of a statue of Long, I shot back: "You couldn't print what I think about it." And, when U. S. Senator Allen J. Ellender, a former protégé of Long, began his oration on the day of the unveiling, Representatives Boggs, J. Y. Sanders, Vance Plauché, and I walked out of the House Chamber.

The New Orleans newspapers approved of the exit, but it was one of my last acts which would be greeted with enthusiasm for some time to come, for the end of my honeymoon with the hometown press was on the horizon. During my next trip to the district, the breach occurred. Naturally, politics was at the core of the matter. The good-government guys (anti-Old Regulars) previously had sent an emissary, E.A. Stephens, the big reformer, to Washinton to ask me to run for mayor against incumbent Robert S. Maestri in the 1942 election. But I had no interest in running against Maestri and no intention of doing so. I was perfectly happy where I was, and why not? When I went to Washington, I was the plumed knight in shining armor on a white horse. I was the great crusading editor who was going to carry on the great search for the holy grail. In addition to not wanting to run for mayor, I fully intended to divorce myself from local politics because the insincerity, the cheating, the lying never appealed to me. I wanted no part of that. Also I had an understanding with the paper that, as a Congressman, I would take no part in local elections. I have never thought a Congressman should meddle in local politics, and I still hold that conviction to this day.

The papers in New Orleans and the reform group continued to look around for a candidate for mayor. And of all people, they picked Paul Maloney (whom Boggs had defeated in the 1940 congressional election with the support of the newspapers). The next thing I knew Maloney had made his formal announcement, and word was that the paper had told him that Hale and I would campaign on his behalf. Now such a suggestion was directly contrary to my understanding with the paper that I would not take part in local elections.

Maloney did not stay in the race long, however. The Old Regulars got to Maloney and promised to send him back to Congress if he would withdraw from the mayoral race. It was Tom Hill, the Rasputin of the Old Regulars, who was doing the conniving. The deal was made with Maloney, and Boggs was dealt out by the Old Regulars. The *Times-Picayune* was left without a candidate in the mayor's race.

They looked around and finally came up with Herve Racivich, whom I had beaten for Congress. He had run third behind Fernandez.

Returning to New Orleans from Washington, I dropped in at the newspaper office, as was my habit, to visit with old friends to whom I was attached and for whom I had affection. On that particular day I was standing between the city rooms of the *States* and the *Picayune*, talking to Charlie Nutter, chief of the AP Bureau, Jim Crown, and York Nicholson, vice-president of The Times-Picayune Publishing Company. Mr. Leonard Nicholson, the president and publisher of the *States* and the *Picayune*, walked up. He was always a very mild-mannered and soft-spoken man, a gentle, refined man, considerate and courteous. He said, "Hello, Eddie, are you down to campaign for Racivich?"

I said, "Mr. Nicholson, it was my understanding that when I went to Congress I would not take part in local campaigns." Now, this mild-mannered man stared coldly at me and said, "Well, if you don't it's your ass." It was like someone throwing cold water into my face, but I did not bat an eye. I said very calmly, "If that is the way you feel about it, I am going to come down here and campaign for Mr. Maestri and I'm going to win reelection to Congress."

From that moment on, the newspaper saw me as a horned frog or the devil or some ogre. I had not told Maestri what I intended to do. Publicly, I was still uncommitted. But I made up my mind that if the game was going to be played that way, I was going to play it that way, too, and stay in Congress.

Shortly after the incident at the newspaper, and after the Old Regulars had made their commitment to Maloney, Maestri arrived in Washington, apparently to test the political waters. He telephoned me, and I visited him at the Mayflower Hotel.

Boggs, who was already frantic over the Old Regulars throwing their support to Maloney in Maloney's attempt to unseat him, had not been called by the mayor. This added to his anxiety. Hale's office was right next to mine, and he kept asking Joe Huddleston, my secretary at the time, where was the mayor.

After I left Maestri, he went over to see Senator Ellender. As I was returning to my office, Hale encountered me. He was carrying a bundle of laundry and looked like a sad sack. I felt sorry for the situation he was in, and when Hale asked about the mayor, I told him, ''You go back to your office and he'll see you.''

Maestri dropped into my office a few minutes later and I told him Boggs wanted to see him. ''I can't do anything for that boy,'' Maestri said. ''I can't help him.''

''Well, you can go talk to him can't you?'' I asked.

''What good is that going to do?''

''Go talk to the man. The man wants to see you,'' I urged.

When Maestri returned about fifteen minutes later he said, ''If that boy doesn't go back to Congress, he jumps out of the window.''

''What happened?''

''I told him I can't help him,'' Maestri shrugged.

The Old Regulars had made a deal without even talking to Hale. They were not concerned about him. They were only concerned about getting Maloney out of the mayor's race.

As for myself, the visit with the mayor resulted in no commitment by either of us, and that was the way I wanted it. I wanted Maestri to need me, to seek my support.

In January 1942, a few days before the mayoral primary, Jimmy Noe called me. Noe said the Old Regulars needed me in New Orleans for the campaign. He said they had to have me to make speeches and if I would come down and talk to them, he would assure me that Maestri and the Old Regulars would support me for reelection. I told him to have Maestri call and tell me that, because at that time I had to wheel and deal.

I was ready when Maestri called. There would be no doubt concerning any agreements reached. Joe Huddleston was listening on one telephone; Alice Fisher, my stenographer, was on another, ready to take the conversation in shorthand. I answered the call as if I wasn't expecting it, and Maestri identified himself.

''Eddie, this is Bob, Bob Maestri.''

''Oh, hello! Robert Sidney. How's the situation down there?''

''I believe it's well in hand, Eddie, but you know we always need help and aid, as I was telling Jimmy Noe . . .''

''Jimmy has been making some damn good speeches.''

"Yes, Jimmy is all right."

"He's a damn good man to have around, isn't he?"

"Listen, Eddie, what I wanted to talk to you about—at a meeting the other night they [the Old Regular caucus] practically insisted that you make one speech Saturday night—you know, at the Municipal Auditorium at the closing rally."

"You know, Bob, I would rather make a speech here in Washington."

"Eddie, we would like for you to just show your face, that's all, and I believe everything will be all right."

"Bob, if I make this speech, do I have your assurance that I'll get the Old Regular support in September [for the Congressional primary]?"

"Oh, that'll be all right."

"Do I have your word for it?"

"Yes."

"Bob, I'll take your word for it—that's good enough for me."

"Listen, Eddie, I tell you what we'll do: when you get in town we'll have those fellows [the Old Regular Caucus] or a majority of them, anyway, and hold a meeting with you and Jimmy Noe. Then we can get them to go on the record for you in your campaign in September."

"Well, in other words, if I appear with you and your candidates at the closing rally, and make this speech, I have the Old Regular support for September?"

"Okay, that's right."

"That's good enough, Bob."

The conversation took another tack for awhile, then Maestri brought the subject back on course. "Eddie, I wouldn't tell the other fellow, you know, B [Boggs], as I can't make any promises to him."

"I know. Of course, they all know up here that I'm coming out for you. I've told them I was coming out."

"That's fine! That's okay."

"I'll get busy, then, and make the speech. Listen, Bob, don't spread it around. Now, Bob, if I do this I will have the Old Regular support in September?"

"Yes, you have. But you're not going to put that in your speech, are you?"

I laughed. "Listen, Bob, how long do you know me? You know me better than that."

Although I was reasonably satisfied with the mayor's assurances of support, I knew New Orleans politics well enough to seek further insurance. I had Huddleston and Fisher make an affidavit before a notary public that the conversation which Fisher had recorded in shorthand was an accurate transcription of the dialogue between the mayor and me.

For my part I made the speech, and Maestri and the Old Regulars won the mayoral contest easily, defeating Racivich and two other opponents by almost 15,000 votes. Soon thereafter, I announced publicly my candidacy.

"I seek reelection," my formal announcement in the newspapers began. "I do so with the pride and knowledge that I have kept every promise and pledge which I have made. I have kept faith with the people who believed in me and elected me to Congress. I intend to continue to support the foreign policy of President Roosevelt until we have won, not only the war, but the peace which is to follow."

For some reason congressional hopefuls reacted to that statement like a bigmouth bass to a grasshopper. At one point I had six opponents: Charles V. Gonzales, Frank De Latour, J. Aubrey Gaiennie, A. Sidney Nunez, J. Norris Henning, and who else but my old friend, J. O. Fernandez.

In short order, however, the would-be candidates found other pastimes to occupy themselves. Only Nunez couldn't bring himself to deprive the voters of the opportunity of casting their ballots for a man of his qualifications. Fernandez was the first candidate to withdraw, but Gaiennie was not far behind, and he left with a bang. As a state senator who was a leader of the Old Regulars in the state legislature, Gaiennie was under the impression he had their support sewn up. When the Old Regulars suddenly announced their support of me, Gaiennie screamed that he had been "double-crossed."

The Old Regulars had signed a "Round Robin" against me, to take me out. The Round Robin was a written pledge by a group and was a technique made popular in Louisiana by Huey Long. Long had used it to defeat an impeachment attempt against him by the state senate. In my case, the Old Regulars had used it as a pledge not to support me. But Mayor Maestri intervened.

He called the Old Regulars into his office one at a time, and they all left happy. They couldn't find their names on that Round Robin after Maestri whispered a few words to them.

Gaiennie was incensed. "Well," he said in a statement to the press, "Jimmy Noe's boy, Mr. Eddie Hébert, was not double-crossed, and [he] set aside a staunch Old Regular like myself, and there is no one who can question my loyalty; and when one thinks of the number of times I stuck my neck out for the Old Regulars, it is pretty tough to sit by and be double-crossed for a first-class in and outer and double-crosser.

". . . I want to correct any erroneous impression or rumor that may exist . . . that I will not stick to the very end [of the congressional race]. The law prohibits dummy candidates and I want it to be known now and forever that I am a bona fide, genuine, Simon-pure candidate for the office of congressman from the First Congressional District." Gaiennie withdrew from the race several days later.

Following his lead was the rest of my opposition, except Nunez, a former state senator. And, as is said down South, he had two chances: slim and none. In the campaign, Nunez sought the labor vote. He charged that I had voted to repeal the wage and hour law. That would have been difficult, for the bill had never come before the House for a vote. My response was: "If Nunez said I voted for repeal of the wage and hour law with the knowledge that I did not, then he knowingly uttered a falsehood, and certainly any purveyor of untruths cannot expect the confidence of the voters. On the other hand, if Mr. Nunez made the statement I voted for repeal, in good faith, then he stamps himself as a man totally unfit for public office since he doesn't know what is going on in Congress, which anybody who knows Mr. Nunez has long suspicioned."

Just to be on the safe side, I got Congressmen Sam Rayburn, Jennings Randolf, Fritz G. Lanham, and John McCormack to write letters attesting to my work in Congress. It was overkill, for with the Old Regular support, plus the strong backing I received in Plaquemines and St. Bernard parishes, I could expect to win by a five to one margin.

In the other New Orleans congressional race, Paul Maloney narrowly defeated Hale Boggs who, despite Maestri's prediction, shunned the suicide window in favor of a commission in the United States Navy.

As for me, I became an Old Regulars hero, and eventually their chief spokesman. Instead of being a plumed knight in the eyes of the press, I was now the most vicious symbol of the machine.

CHAPTER X

TRUTH AND CONSEQUENCES

At the beginning of my second term, I received the most important appointment of my career. Paul Maloney, who had defeated Hale Boggs, regained his old position on the Ways and Means Committee which had jurisdiction over committee assignments. He greased the way for my appointment to the old Naval Affairs Committee which later merged with Military Affairs to form the House Armed Services Committee. On this powerful committee, which controls the authorization for the United States armed services, my steadfast belief in the necessity for a strong military as a deterrent to war would gain meaning; simultaneously, my ability as an investigator and interrogator would emerge as they were needed.

But first I had to contend with the realities of life as a legislator. Shortly after my appointment to the Naval Affairs Committee, I was approached by Sam Rayburn bearing gifts. The Ruml tax plan was before Congress. It was a plan whereby all back taxes owed by an individual would be forgiven and a "pay-as-you-go" policy instituted. The idea was originated by the Republicans, but about a dozen Democrats were in the forefront of its support. Naturally, being a maverick, I was one of the more outspoken proponents of the proposal, despite the Democratic administration's well-known objections to it.

Rayburn called my house on a Saturday morning and asked if I would be at the White House that night. Roosevelt was giving a little party for sophomore congressmen. It was one of those munching-cheese-and-drinking-beer-and-throwing-his-charm-all-over-the-place

171

parties. I told Sam I would be there. "Well, I want to talk to you," he said.

When I got down to the White House, Sam called me over to a corner and said, "Eddie, how would you like to be on the Board of Visitors of the United States Naval Academy?"

I said, "Sure."

He said, "Well, Lyndon has too much to do." Lyndon, of course, being Lyndon Johnson. "He is going to resign. I'll put you on the board."

There was really *big* pressure on Lyndon. All he had to do as a member of the Board of Visitors was attend those big receptions. What really happened is that Sam told Lyndon to get off to make a vacancy for me. Two days later in the House, Sam sent a page down to get me. I went up to talk to him; I knew the payoff was coming. He said, "Eddie, don't you think you can go along with us on this Ruml plan?"

I said, "No, Mr. Speaker, I am committed to the other side." What did he expect me to do? Say "Oh, yes, Mr. Speaker, I am very grateful for having been named to the Board of Visitors."

Sam was a great presiding officer, the finest presiding officer I have ever seen. He was the boss of the House. He dominated the scene, and he was a cold, calculating politician.

But I can also be a calculating politician, particularly when it comes to representing my constituents. In 1943 one would have been hard pressed to find a more patriotic congressional district than Louisiana's First. The people supported the war effort *in toto*, and I had no qualms about representing their views in Congress. Southerners by temperament and tradition are among the most patriotic citizens of the United States, and considering the circumstances of World War II, it was incomprehensible to them that there were those who would not, and did not, subordinate personal ambition to the good of the country in time of war.

Never naive to begin with, I already had encountered those who didn't feel as Stephen Decatur—"my country right or wrong." But for the most part that type had been either well-meaning if unrealistic pacifists, or out-and-out communists who accused the United States of imperialistic fascism—that is, until Russia became an ally.

There were, however, still other types who consciously hindered the war effort. One of them was an egocentric, opportunistic union boss who sought to magnify his power by defying the United States government, a man whose tactics cost the lives of better men than he. Without so much as a tinge of guilt he had announced: "If I had brothers at the front who needed the 10 or 12 planes that were sacrificed [due to quibbling over labor contract technicalities], I'd let them die, ..."

The author of that statement was Thomas Vincent DeLorenzo, the surly CIO boss of Local 365 of the United Auto Workers at the Brewster Aeronautical Corporation's plant in Johnsville, Pennsylvania. It was primarily through the connivance of DeLorenzo, but also due to the ineptness of corporation management and the ineffectiveness of the United States Navy in dealing with the situation, that Brewster was not producing the planes sorely needed by the troops.

The situation at the Brewster plant was called to the attention of the Naval Affairs Committee through the work of a reporter, Mrs. Agnes Meyer. She was the wife of Eugene Meyer, the publisher of the *Washington Post*. Her full-page story on the Brewster mess sparked the congressional investigation. Conservative syndicated columnist Westbrook Pegler, who didn't toss many bouquets to his more liberal peers, acknowledged in this case that Mrs. Meyer had done a fine piece of investigative work. Yet, he wrote, if "the story could be criticized at all, the criticism would be that she failed to run her man down. . . .This coup was left to Eddie Hebert, a congressman from Louisiana, who broke the real story some days later."

It was a complex story. In addition to DeLorenzo's tactics, the Navy had poured $5.5 million into the Brewster plant. It also had extended credit of $55 million more without receiving any return on its investment. In addition, the Navy had forced on the company a president who proved to be incompetent. "The Navy takes the attitude that it is not to blame," I remarked at the time, "but in my opinion the fault rests with the whole triumvirate, management, labor, and the Navy."

Neverthless, DeLorenzo was the main heavy in the sordid in-
fighting which left America's fighting men short of air power during
the hard days of 1943. Besides slowdowns, strikes and inferior
products, DeLorenzo had forced the company to rehire pro-Nazi
sympathizers who had been fired following sabotage at the plant.
Additionally, in an unusual exercise of power, the union boss forced
the company to rehire not only members of his local, but management
representatives as well who had been terminated for pro-Nazi activities. When the Naval Affairs Subcommittee began investigating
the contretemps at Brewster and subpoenaed DeLorenzo, he boasted
to the press, "I ain't scared of those guys. I can handle them all
right."

He was as good as his word under the questioning of the chairman
of the subcommittee, Representative Patrick Drewry of Virginia.
Alternatingly curt and expansive with his arrogant replies, De-
Lorenzo dominated the proceedings until I got hold of him, and, as
we say in Louisiana, "turned him every way but loose." I had come
loaded for bear, and had obtained my ammunition by accident, the
way most news reporters traditionally come by their best stories. But,
like any alert reporter, I knew what to do with the information once I
got it.

The tip came in casual conversation. One day during a luncheon
recess of the hearings (prior to DeLorenzo's appearance) I ran into a
friend, Commander James Reynolds, the brother of famed reporter
Quentin Reynolds.

Reynolds told me he was a security officer at the Brewster plant
and had been called to testify. Over a luncheon cocktail in my office, I
asked Reynolds about the union boss: "What gives with this guy,
DeLorenzo, Jim?"

"You know that's not his real name," Reynolds replied matter-
of-factly.

The conversation continued, but that was all said about De-
Lorenzo; yet, it was enough. If that wasn't his real name, there had to
be a reason why he wasn't using his real name. What was his real
name?

I next called a friend at the FBI. I told him I wanted to know

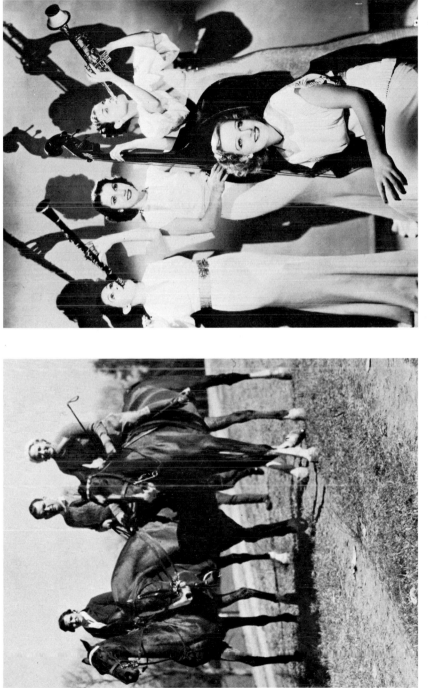

The Southland Rhythm Girls: Dixie Fasnacht, on clarinet; Maxine Phinney, bass; Judy Ertle, trumpet; and Betty Giblin Harter, piano. Betty became my administrative assistant in Washington.

Gladys (left), I and Mayris "Tiny" Chaney —one half of the "Roosevelt Dance Team" of Chaney and Fox—ride on the Mississippi River Levee in New Orleans.

Gladys and I visit Mary Healy (left) on the lot at Paramount Pictures in Hollywood.

The Preisser sisters, June and Cherry Blossom of New Orleans, as Ziegfield Follies stars.

To Eddie —
With my sincere
admiration —
Fondly
Dottie

To Eddie —
from someone
who was to
grateful to
be at this
party @ all
Dorothy
(Right now)

I picked Dorothy Dell (left) and Dorothy Lamour as beauty contest winners long before Hollywood called.

Grace Hayes, a real star(dust)—Mother of Peter Lind Hayes

Wini Shaw, the "Lady in Red." Connie Boswell made it big as a single after the Boswell Sisters of New Orleans disbanded.

Eva Gabor said I was not "A–Bear," but a pussycat. I said she was close, but no cigar. It's tomcat.

Playwright Channing Pollock "begs" for Major Crown's five spot.

My bodyguards, Jack Dempsey and Gene Tunney, two of the greatest champions.

I present the New Orleans Press Club's Roll of Honor award to Bantamweight Pete Herman, the city's first world boxing champion and the game's greatest bantam weight. He was blinded in the ring.

With Coach Bernie Bierman at the 1955 All Star game in Chicago.

Football innovator Clark Shaugnessy, a great coach, and I are reunited at an Armed Forces Day parade in California in 1967. Actor Ed Nelson of New Orleans, a former Tulane cheerleader, joined us.

Eddie Morgan, nonconformist and a great athlete.

A. J. Heinemann, president of the New Orleans Pelicans (left), with Jack Quinn, president of the Boston Red Sox, and Lee Fohl, the Red Sox' manager in the 1920s.

I'm presenting Army coach, Col. Earl "Red" Blaik (center) a check for the Delafield Fund. At right is Capt. "Biff" Jones, who coached at West Point, Nebraska, and LSU.

With the golfing Hebert Brothers, Jay and Lionel, of Lafayette, La., during the National Open in Washington in 1964.

Giving L. Mendel Rivers the word.

Introducing two real tough guys, General Ray Hufft (center) and Secretary of Defense James Forrestal.

Interviewing Fulgencio Batista in Cuba in 1934. And I was on my honeymoon.

I am at left after escorting Batista to the podium when he addressed Congress. Speaker Sam Rayburn is seated next to Batista who is standing at the microphone. Seated in front of Batista are Reps. Sol Bloom, Hamilton Fish, Joe Martin, and John McCormack.

Riding with Gen. Claire Chennault upon his triumphant return to New Orleans after World War II.

Another famous Louisiana high flyer, Astronaut Mike Collins presented me with a picture he took of the earth as his space ship circled the moon. I appointed Mike to the U. S. Military Academy.

Nanking, 1947. Pictured with Generalissimo and Madame Chiang Kai-Shek are: Rep. Errett Power Scrivner, Ambassador J. Leithton Stuart, Reps. Charles Clason, William Hess, Sterling Cole, me, and Albin Walter Norblad, Jr.

In Iran with Mohammed Reza Shah Pohlavi, His Imperial Majesty, the Shah of Iran, are: Representatives Porter Hardy, Samuel Stratton and me.

With the Pope at the Castel Gondelfo outside Rome in 1956 are: Rep. L. Mendel Rivers, Col. Rennie Kelly, Rep. William Hess, and me.

At the dedication of the L. Mendel Rivers Library at Charleston in 1970, Mendel brought the pride of the Carolinas, the Rev. Billy Graham. I brought the pride of New Orleans, Jazzman Al Hirt. Mendel was a Baptist and I am a music lover. Dr. Asa Hamrick, president of Baptist College, Charleston, is in the center.

The Tulane football team of 1923. Standing, from left: Joe Killeen, Coach Bernie Bierman, Brother Brown, Coach Clark Shaughnessy, Fred Hoffman, Peggy Flournoy, Bill Besselman, Benny Wight, George DeGarmo, Walter Carre, Fred Lamprecht, Frank Phillips, Howard Roehl, Dr. Wilbur C. Smith, athletic director, President A. B. Dinwiddie, me, the team manager. Kneeling, from left: Selzer Robinson, Gene Bergeret, Team Captain "Little Eva" Talbot, Barney Hopkins, Leal MacLean, Virgil Robinson, Benny Goldsmith, Joe Henican, Squint Odom, Doug O'Kelley, Tommy Killeen, Irish Levy, George Tunstall, Lester Lautenschlaeger and Claude "Monk" Simons, trainer.

everything about this DeLorenzo. Of course, FBI people are not going to let just anyone look at the files, but I got a good briefing. I could have virtually told DeLorenzo about the first time he wet his diaper.

I quickly followed up the leads provided by the FBI by writing to the people DeLorenzo said he had worked for. I wrote for records.

Once I got the information I wanted, I talked to Chairman Drewry. "Pat, just give me one chance. Just let me check this guy's veracity. Give him to me. He's my pigeon."

When Drewry turned DeLorenzo over to me for questioning, I began by playing to the union boss' vanity, but all the while I was "lying in the gap," waiting to ambush this cocksure, pretentious labor leader.

Mr. DeLorenzo, I might tell you by way of introduction, so that we may understand each other, that I am very inquisitive by nature and profession. I happen to be a newspaper reporter. I was very much interested in your rise to power, which I think is commendable for anybody in our American way of life, which you so vigorously upheld in your testimony this morning about your rights as an American citizen and about your ability to do certain things. I think only in America can we have such men created as you, men who, according to the information I have received about you, are able to rise up from lowly beginnings to positions of power.

I make that preface to tell you exactly what is in my mind. I didn't know anything about you until I read an article in the *Washington Post* some weeks ago by Mrs. Agnes E. Meyer. I think you read that article. It had a two-column picture of you and was a full-page spread. It was entitled "Chaos and Tyranny Compete Bitterly at Brewster Plant— Incompetent Management Is Hopelessly Ensnarled by Shrewd, Ruthless Union Autocrats."

I thought Mrs. Meyer had no regard for you until I read a special insert in that article, and, just to refresh your memory and the memory of the committee, I will read the first two or three paragraphs. Speaking to you, Mr. DeLorenzo, Mrs. Meyer says this:

"After gathering the amazing picture of a beautifully organized tyranny . . . I was naturally curious to see the man whom everybody gave the somewhat dubious credit of being the unquestioned dictator, not only of the union at the Brewster plant, but of the whole situation, Tom De Lorenzo, president of Local 365.

"I expected a forceful personality, but what I could see in this firmly built 35-year-old American of Italian descent was a good deal more than I expected.

"If I am any judge of people, the country is going to hear a lot more from Tom De Lorenzo.

"He was born and grew up in New York, in a section of the city where every boy has to fight his way from the moment he is out of diapers. De Lorenzo is still fighting his way upward. It is my impression that nobody can stop him."

Whether we agree with your philosophy or not, the article shows, Mr. DeLorenzo, that you are definitely a force in your selected field and you have risen to the top. This is most commendable, because whether I agree with a man's principles or not, whether I agree with what he is doing or not, I do have to admire what he has accomplished. You have many friends, and you know very well you have a lot of enemies and a lot of people who disagree with you.

DELORENZO: Yes, sir.

HÉBERT: Before this committee, a lot of people expressed their disagreement with you and said you were not a man of your word, but it seems you have a calf-like devotion from your union. How you acquired it is what I want to know. Would you mind tracing your history as a young man, 34 or 35 years old—how old are you?

DELORENZO: Thirty-five. I was born in 1909, March 20.

HÉBERT: Who grew up on the streets of New York, the sidewalks of New York, if you please, to a position as a labor leader, who can attract such an audience as you have this morning, including more admirals than I have seen before this committee in years. Can you tell me just how you did it? I want to know your surroundings. I want to know about your family and all. I think it would be a very interesting story.

DELORENZO: I think it would be, sir; but I don't know whether it has anything to do with this investigation.

HÉBERT: It is very pertinent because we want to know the type of people we are dealing with.

DELORENZO: I am just as astonished as anyone here at your reference to me. I don't know what is responsible for it any more than you do. All I know is this . . . I never belonged to a union prior to the time that I went to work at Brewster.

HÉBERT: You said you went to work for Brewster. At what time?

DELORENZO: I was in the wholesale wine business for an extended period of time, and my wife insisted that I give it up because I was drinking a little bit too much, and I gave it up and went to work for $22 a week in the Brewster factory on the night shift as a riveter. I had never worked in aircraft before. I didn't know the first thing about it, but my wife insisted I get a job somewhat different. . . .

Here DeLorenzo expanded his pomposities, saying how he didn't mind giving up the substantial money he was making for a lesser salary if it made his wife happy. He then went on to tell about his spectacular rise in the union hierarchy. When he went to work for Brewster he was asked to join the AFL and also the CIO, each of which was vying for control. He said he feared that if he joined either, and the other union won the election, he would be out of a job. At his wife's suggestion he joined both unions. The CIO won the collective bargaining election and, DeLorenzo said, he eventually rose through the ranks.

HÉBERT: I think it is a typical story of the American boy rising up, and nothing succeeds like success. I will agree with you. Certainly you have succeeded.

Mrs. Meyer describes you as of Italian descent. How long were your parents in this country? When did they come from Italy?

DELORENZO: My parents didn't come from Italy.

HÉBERT: Where did they come from?

DELORENZO: My father came from Poland and my mother came from Hungary.

HÉBERT: They were born outside the United States then?

DELORENZO: That is right.

Having set the stage, I was now ready to drop a bombshell, so I asked the question in a tone of voice just as cold and hard as I could manage. According to reporters there, DeLorenzo's face dropped and his demeanor began to crumble when I asked:

What is your real name, Mr. DeLorenzo?

DELORENZO: My real name, legal name, morally, physically, and everything else, is Thomas V. DeLorenzo. I have used other names as the occasion has arisen. I have used various names. I don't believe there is anything wrong with it. If you would like to know, I would tell you the names. I have used James Harris, Harry Posner . . .

HÉBERT: How do you spell that?

DELORENZO: P-o-s-n-e-r—and half a dozen others as they came in handy.

HÉBERT: What do you mean, came in handy? Isn't that unusual, for a man to be changing his name?

DELORENZO: I don't think so.

HÉBERT: I don't know what league you play in, but in the league I play in, the people keep their own names. Why did you change your name legally?

DELORENZO: I felt that it was the proper thing to do.

HÉBERT: How did you happen to select the name DeLorenzo? What appealed to you in that name?

DELORENZO: Nothing in particular. I just selected it out of a telephone book or a hat, call it what you will.

HÉBERT: Now, Mr. DeLorenzo, you were taken with the euphony of the name of Thomas Vincent DeLorenzo. You say you just picked that name out because it was a pretty sounding name, because you liked it?

DELORENZO: Yes.

* * *

HÉBERT: When did you decide to legally change your name to Thomas Vincent DeLorenzo?

DELORENZO: I don't remember exactly; possibly two years ago, maybe three.

HÉBERT: After you got into union activities?

DELORENZO: That is correct.

HÉBERT: Did you think that DeLorenzo was a better name in union activities than Posner or Harris or some other name? What other names did you use? When did you use the name of Harris?

DELORENZO: I said I have used a half-a-dozen names.

HÉBERT: What other names, I would like to know? James Harris is one. Harry Posner is one.

DELORENZO: I used the name of Sid Traurig.

HÉBERT: Isn't there a Sid Traurig at Brewster?

DELORENZO: That is correct, sir.

HÉBERT: Why did you impersonate another individual?

DELORENZO: Well, there are certain reasons for it.

HÉBERT: We would like to know those reasons. It is not usual for a man to walk around and impersonate other individuals, although I can understand taking another name sometimes.

DELORENZO: I deny that I impersonated an individual. I used his name.

HÉBERT: You know a Sidney Traurig, don't you?

DELORENZO: Sure I do.

HÉBERT: And you used his name, didn't you?

DELORENZO: That is right.

HÉBERT: Would they think you were Paul Jones if you gave the name of Sidney Traurig? They thought you were Sidney Traurig when you represented yourself as Sidney Traurig.

DELORENZO: That is probably right, but they didn't know Sidney Traurig.

HÉBERT: Therefore they thought you were he.

DELORENZO: If I gave any name and nobody had reason to question it, they would believe that.

HÉBERT: That you weren't impersonating that man?

DELORENZO: I don't believe I was.

HÉBERT: What was the occasion for using his name?

DELORENZO: I would like to refuse to answer the question.

After much beating around the bush, DeLorenzo eventually whispered his big secret in private to the committee members—he used Traurig's name when he registered at hotels for assignations.

HÉBERT: Did you use any other names on any other occasions?

DELORENZO: I did, sir, but I can't remember. . . . .

HÉBERT: What was your father's name?

DELORENZO: Posner, Ike Posner.

HÉBERT: Therefore your real name is Harry Posner then? That is the name you were born under?

DELORENZO: That is correct.

HÉBERT: And then you became very esthetic and took the name of Thomas Vincent DeLorenzo. Did the fact that that name had an Italian background have any effect in your union activities?

DELORENZO: No. As a matter of fact there is a contributing factor. My sister was studying Italian in college, and she liked the name of DeLorenzo, and she used it, so I used it. Period!

HÉBERT: As a matter of fact, then you didn't just pick it out of a hat or telephone book?

DELORENZO: It may have been that that is where she got it.

* * *

HÉBERT: I am just trying to get the facts. When you went to Brewster, that was your introduction to airplane manufacture and to union activities?

DELORENZO: That is right.

HÉBERT: I have here, Mr. DeLorenzo, what purports to be your application to go to work at Brewster. It contains what is purported to be a picture of you and what is purported to be your signature and your complete health record at Brewster. I will ask you to identify that and tell me if that is correct.

DELORENZO: That is right, sir.

HÉBERT: This will be put in the record. Hébert reading: Name: Thomas Vincent DeLorenzo. Are you a citizen of the U.S.A.? Yes. Religion? Catholic. Present address? 4526 Avenue H, Brooklyn, New York. Social Security account number? 115-05-8960. Date of birth? August 17, 1902.

You just told me you were born on March 20, 1909. When were you born?

DELORENZO: March 20, 1909.

HÉBERT: Why did you put August 17, 1902, on this application?

DELORENZO: For the same reason I put the name and everything else on there, in order to get a job.

HÉBERT: Was it necessary for you to lie about your age to get a job?

DELORENZO: It was necessary to lie about everything to get a job.

HÉBERT: Is that the country you boast that you live in, where it is necessary to lie to get a job?

DELORENZO: That is correct.

HÉBERT: Is that the kind of country you live in, Mr. DeLorenzo, that you proudly claim you are a citizen of?

DELORENZO: That is the kind of country I live in still, sir, and I am trying to change it in my own way.

HÉBERT: I think that gives a very deep insight into your philosophy of what kind of government you really like.

"Birthplace of father? U.S.A." Did you have to lie about your father's birthplace?

DELORENZO: So that it may be perfectly clear, I don't believe that I put anything on that application that is true outside of my Social Security number, in order to obtain this job.

HÉBERT: You have answered everything, sir. We are just trying to establish how much we can believe you . . .

You put on here your name, "Thomas Vincent DeLorenzo," which wasn't really your name, so nothing on it is true except your picture?

DELORENZO: And the Social Security number.

HÉBERT: Why didn't you change that, too?

DELORENZO: Well . . .

HÉBERT: Because you were going to get some benefits out of it?

DELORENZO: No, because I couldn't get another card in time to change it. Otherwise I would have requested a change.

HÉBERT: If you had thought you would have gotten more money out of it you would have put another Social Security number on it, if it suited your purposes?

DELORENZO: I disagree with you.

HÉBERT: I want to talk to you about another matter now. Since you said everything on that was a lie, I may as well put something in the record which will keep things straight. I want it to be my testimony and not yours, because I want it to be believed.

On this application you are asked to tell where you had previously worked. You said you worked at Fairchild Farmingdale, wing and fuselage assembler, from 1929 to 1931. Of course, this is just substantiating the fact that you lied, but I am going to read this letter. This is from the Fairchild Aviation Corporation, addressed to this committee:

". . . a preliminary investigation of our records discloses that no such person was employed by us during this aforementioned period."

I read several other letters from firms which DeLorenzo had claimed he had worked for. All said he had never been in their employ.

HÉBERT: Let's get this record straight so we know how much of his testimony to believe. I have in my hand a certified copy of an application of Harry Posner asking to change his name to Thomas Vincent DeLorenzo, from the City Court of New York. It is sworn to, under oath, just as you are under oath right now to tell the truth. Section 7 of that petition of Harry Posner to change his name to Thomas V. De-Lorenzo says this, and it is sworn to by you under oath:

"Petitioner was never arrested or convicted of any crime or ever filed any petition in bankruptcy or insolvency?''

Is that a true statement?

DELORENZO: I think I was arrested, but I don't remember whether it was before or after that. I was arrested twice as far as I can remember, perhaps three times.

HÉBERT: I will refresh your memory. You were arrested for homicide, for vehicular homicide, that is what you were arrested for, under the name of Harry Posner, living at 79 Ashford Street, in 1933. You were arrested with another man. Why didn't you put that in there?

DELORENZO: Put what in where?

HÉBERT: In your petition to change your name. You swore to this statement before a court of New York. Why didn't you put that in there? Were you trying to get a job in the City Court of New York?

DELORENZO: No.

HÉBERT: Why did you lie?

DELORENZO: I didn't draw the statement up. Some lawyer did. He drew it up and asked me to sign it, and I signed it and paid him the fee, whatever it was, fifty dollars, or so.

HÉBERT: You didn't read what you signed? A man who changes his name as a convenience must be pretty cagey; he doesn't sign a thing when he doesn't know what he is signing.

DELORENZO: I didn't read that.

HÉBERT: You just signed it?

DELORENZO: That is correct, sir.

HÉBERT: He filled this from some source. He must have asked you a lot of things about yourself. I will read you section III: ''Petitioner is unmarried and his occupation is that of a machinist.'' You were married on the 22nd of December 1929, at the home of your wife's parents, weren't you?

DELORENZO: I think I was.

HÉBERT: Yes, that is where you were married by a man named Reverend Chioff, I think the name was.

DELORENZO: I don't remember.

HÉBERT: Why didn't you tell your lawyer you were married? He didn't assume you were unmarried, did he?

DELORENZO: I don't know. He made the petition up, and I am saying I didn't read it.

HÉBERT: I will give you one you did read. Did you ever have a federal job?

DELORENZO: No, sir; I don't think I ever had a federal job.

HÉBERT: Did you ever apply for one?

DELORENZO: Yes, sir.

HÉBERT: I want to place in the record, for the purpose of identification, the immigration papers of his father who came from Grodna, Poland, on the steamship *St. Louis* in 1898 and was naturalized and gave the date of birth of his son as March 4, 1909, which again varies from the date given. It was the same year, just a difference of a few days. On the date of the birth given on the Brewster records, his father and mother weren't married. They weren't married until 1908, being seven years later.

HÉBERT: Will you identify this?

KLINE (Committee Counsel): Is this your signature, Mr. DeLorenzo?

DELORENZO: That is right, sir.

[The document identified was an application for federal employment.]

HÉBERT: No lawyer filled this out for you?

DELORENZO: I filled this out myself.

HÉBERT: Are you positive of that?

DELORENZO: Positive.

HÉBERT: So you won't give that alibi this time that you gave before when you were shown how many times you had lied. Will you identify yourself as the Thomas V. DeLorenzo of 2946 Northern Boulevard, Long Island City, referred to in this document?

DELORENZO: I am.

HÉBERT: You gave the date of birth here as March 20, 1909, one of the three dates. I will read you question number five [from the federal job application]:

"Have you ever been arrested or summoned into court as a defendant or indicted, or convicted, or fined, or imprisoned or placed on probation, or has any case against you been filed, or have you ever been ordered to deposit collateral for alleged breach or violation of any law or police regulation or ordinance whatsoever . . . If appointed, your fingerprints will be taken."

Your fingerprints were taken, and that is how you were identified as the Harry Posner arrested in 1933 on the vehicular homicide charge.

Your answer to a previous question was that you filled this form out yourself, so you can't say a lawyer filled out these answers. Your answer to that is, 'received summons and tickets for traffic violations in

New York City in last four or five years and either paid fine or received suspended sentence.' You don't say anything about the vehicular homicide arrest, do you?

DELORENZO: I was discharged.

HÉBERT: You were arrested.

DELORENZO: I was discharged.

HÉBERT: This question five, which you already testified you read, tells you of arrest and disposition.

DELORENZO: That is right.

HÉBERT: Why didn't you put that down?

DELORENZO: I just didn't feel like putting it down, I guess.

HÉBERT: Oh, you didn't feel like putting it down? Why didn't you feel like putting it down?

DELORENZO: I can't think of any reason. I just didn't feel like it.

HÉBERT: You didn't want to tell them about that vehicular homicide charge did you, because you didn't feel like it? Why didn't you tell them that you were arrested for inciting a riot and indicted? You didn't feel like it?

DELORENZO: It was strictly a matter of a labor dispute, a strike.

HÉBERT: Sure, throwing bricks at policemen was strictly a labor dispute. Turning over an omnibus and breaking it up was strictly a labor dispute.

DELORENZO: I did that myself, turned over an omnibus?

HÉBERT: That is what you were charged with. You didn't want to put that down either, did you? You put down just a casual few traffic violations that you had. As a matter of fact, you had fifteen of them, Mr. DeLorenzo, and I will give you the dates and exactly what happened. If you didn't put it on the application, I will put it in the record for you. . . . [I read the citations and concluded:] On March 15, 1933, you were arrested on a charge of disorderly conduct and interfering with a policeman in the performance of his duty. That was in 1933. You were not interested in labor matters then. . . .

HÉBERT: Now, you lied to get a job at Brewster, didn't you? Why did you lie in your civil service examination?

DELORENZO: What civil service examination?

HÉBERT: The civil service application. Mind you when you filed this application, you knew what you were filing for, to get on the War Labor Board panel, didn't you?

DELORENZO: That is right.

HÉBERT: Of course. In that application in which you took this oath and just admitted you filled out yourself, you tell you worked from February 1940 to the present time at Brewster's, and you tell you worked at Seversky. Why did you put that down? Did you have to lie to get a job with your government?

DELORENZO: Just to make it correspond to the previous one. . . .

HÉBERT: I said in the beginning when I started to talk to you I knew you were an amazing man, and I am still of that opinion. Question forty-one: "Were any of the following members of your family born outside the continental United States: Wife, husband, father, mother?" Your answer is "No," another lie. Your father and mother were born outside the United States, your father at Grodna, Poland, and your mother in Austria.

DELORENZO: Is that part of my family, my father and mother?

HÉBERT: I should say it is. I accept my father and mother as part of my family, and I will get along a little later and show that you think so, too, when you claim your income-tax exemption. I am just starting.

So that is another lie, isn't it, that application to the United States government under oath?

DELORENZO: So far as that last question is concerned, if you consider my father part of my immediate family, it is.

HÉBERT: They ask specifically, "Were your father and mother born outside the United States?" You said, "No."

* * *

Now, we get back to Brewster—I hope we are not boring you—you worked at Brewster. You went to work, I think the date was July 2, 1939. That is when you first started at Brewster.

Anyway, the records show you went to work in 1939 under the name of Thomas DeLorenzo.

DELORENZO: That is correct, sir.

HÉBERT: Mr. Posner—I mean Mr. DeLorenzo, you filed an income-tax return in 1940 under the name of Harry Posner, and gave your occupation as a salesman. That is an income-tax return, Mr. DeLorenzo. You are supposed to tell the truth. The money you said you received was in the amount of $1,647.60, and you received it from yourself. What about the money you received from Brewster?

DELORENZO: That was the money I received from Brewster.

HÉBERT: Why did you say you received it from yourself?

DELORENZO: If you start something, you just can't get out of it; you have got to continue with it.

HÉBERT: How far are you going with this? Are you going that far dealing with Brewster and the Navy, lying about contracts or running out on them?

DELORENZO: I didn't lie about the finances on the income-tax return.

WELLS (Committee Counsel): Is that your signature?

DELORENZO: Yes.

HÉBERT: I understood you to say this morning, Mr. DeLorenzo, that your wife persuaded you to get the job at Brewster though you were making less money, that you wanted to agree with her so you got the job making less money. You filed an income-tax return for 1940.

Why didn't you file an income-tax return for 1938 and 1939? That is the law of the land, the law of the government.

DELORENZO: I don't believe I earned enough in those years to file an income-tax return under the statutes.

HÉBERT: How much did you earn?

DELORENZO: I don't remember, sir.

HÉBERT: You testified here this morning, Mr. DeLorenzo, that the reason you went to Brewster was to satisfy your wife, and you made enough in 1940 to file a return.

DELORENZO: That is right. I think I did.

HÉBERT: So you must have made more money in 1938 and 1939.

DELORENZO: I believe my wife was working at that time.

HÉBERT: But 1940 doesn't show her filing any return—1940 is a single return in the name of Harry Posner, so you can't alibi on that.

I continued the pursuit, catching DeLorenzo in more lies, deceptions, and evasions concerning his income tax forms and employment records. I then turned to statements DeLorenzo had made to his draft board.

HÉBERT: You told the draft board that you worked from 1937 to 1939 as a riveter, aircraft assembly. You told your draft board that you work as a riveter from 1935 to 1937. Did you have to lie to the draft board to get a job with the Army?

Having shown DeLorenzo to be a compulsive liar in case after case, I then returned to the union boss' methods of bargaining with the management of Brewster. DeLorenzo defended his bargaining methods by charging that congressmen bargain with the President. It was an irrelevant statement, but it irritated me, and I shot back:

I, for one, am a member of Congress and that Congress belongs to the people and the people own this country, not the President or anybody else. Let's get on an even meeting ground and know what we think and don't put words in the mouths of members of Congress. You said Congress bargained with the President.

DELORENZO: I said it was my opinion that there are groups in this country bargaining with the President, whether Congress or various government agencies; it is done every day of the week, and I can't see there is anything wrong with it. It would put our international president in a better bargaining position.

HÉBERT: Did you ever hear of a battalion of soldiers or regiment of soldiers going to General Marshall and trying to bargain with him and saying, "General Marshall, if you don't give us what we want, by God, we won't go in the trenches today?"

DELORENZO: That is an unfair comparison.

HÉBERT: It is not an unfair comparison. We are fighting this war on the front as well as at home.

DELORENZO: We are fighting it at home in the way we always fight it, that is bargaining collectively, whether it is through the President, or across a table.

HÉBERT: You prated this morning about your rights as an American citizen. The soldier is an American citizen. Why doesn't he have the same rights to bargain with his commander in chief?

DELORENZO: You cannot compare the military with the civilian.

HÉBERT: You cannot compare the military with the civilian when the civilian is not engaged in war production. You are engaged in war production over there, and your 600,000 strike-hours destroyed thirty-three planes of ours. When Captain Westervelt [a mediator assigned by the U.S. Navy to Brewster] was on the stand I tried to paint the picture to him, to show where raids on production centers in Germany are for the purpose of deterring production, curbing production, and that in effect those thirty-three planes which were not produced would have been the same as if the Luftwaffe had come over Philadelphia with you in the lead airplane. He agreed with me that was substantially correct.

Not a German soldier's life was risked in destroying those thirty-three planes which you and your organization did.

Did you ever make a statement like this? "Our policy is not to win the war at any cost. The policy of our local union is to win the war without sacrificing too much of the rights which we have at the present time."

DELORENZO: I did, sir.

HÉBERT: Do you still want to make that statement?

DELORENZO: I am of the opinion that that is the policy of our local union—to maintain those things that we have here at home.

HÉBERT: And when you say the policy of your local union you are talking about the policy of Thomas Vincent DeLorenzo?

DELORENZO: I am not.

HÉBERT: You control the union, Mr. DeLorenzo, and you know you do.

DELORENZO: I disagree with you on that and I would still like to have you come down to a membership meeting to satisfy your mind that there is no control such as you speak of in the matter of dictatorship.

HÉBERT: I have never heard a dictator yet admit he controlled them. I have lived in Louisiana, and I think I know a few things about control.

HÉBERT: Did you ever make this statement: "If I had brothers at the front who needed the ten or twelve planes that were sacrificed I would let them die."

DELORENZO: That has been the statement that I have heard so much about in the last month or so. I would like to explain the circumstances, and I must again ask the committee to realize the circumstances under which that statement was given.

HÉBERT: You did make the statement, though?

DELORENZO: I made that statement. The English isn't perhaps as well couched as it should be . . . I made that statement in substance along those lines. Perhaps I didn't put it as well as I should have put it.

HÉBERT: You would rather retract that statement today?

DELORENZO: Well, I would rephrase it, if you will permit me to do so.

HÉBERT: You rephrase it.

DELORENZO: I believe in trying to recall the exact conversation, but I don't believe I can because it is kind of muddled over. The general term used in fighting this war is for democracy. Democracy is a broad term to me. I have a letter from some of the boys in the Army and they each have different thoughts on what they are fighting for. One of the boys came home to a small town in Pennsylvania where he lived and couldn't get any chocolate ice cream and he wanted to know what the deuce he was fighting for the war for, if he couldn't get any chocolate ice cream . . .

HÉBERT: They may have a different idea of what they went over there to fight for, but they haven't got a different idea when they write home thousands and thousands of letters talking about strikes when they are out there giving their lives. They are unanimous in that thought, that the people back home should sacrifice something, and don't you think that the people of this country are sacrificing? Should labor unions and organizations such as yours be exempt?

DELORENZO: We have sacrificed our people, too.

HÉBERT: I am talking about rights and privileges.

DELORENZO: We have sacrificed some of our rights and privileges.

HÉBERT: In the new contract you signed you gained a couple more.

DELORENZO: I disagree with that. . . .

CHAIRMAN DREWRY: Regardless of what may happen in the future—that you don't know and I don't know—wouldn't you rather give up every advantage you have in this contract that you have than to lose this war?

DELORENZO: If that was all that was involved, just the advantage of the contract, I would say yes.

HÉBERT: This morning, Mr. DeLorenzo, you said the reason that you lied, and that was the petition for changing your name, was the fact that you didn't read the petition. In the next document, when you were caught in a lie again, it was shown you had read it and signed it. Then your excuse was that you lied because you wanted a job. The third document that caught you in a lie showed you didn't need the job; that was a government job on a labor panel. Then you answered to that, well, you just kept lying because you started to lie and had to keep it up. Then when you were shown your income-tax variances and discrepancies, I think your answer was, "Well, when you get in that deep you have to keep going on." My final question to you is, how far are you going to continue this lie.

DELORENZO: I think I answered that.

Westbrook Pegler, referring to me in his column, wrote that "a former reporter played to the vanity of a lying, arrogant imposter in the Brewster sabotage case in Washington, blew him up with compliments and then suddenly began to bounce him off all four walls like a handball."

Drew Pearson also had some kind words: "Most members of Congress are lawyers. However, it took a journalist-congressman to conduct one of the most searching cross-examinations in recent Capitol Hill probes and to expose labor racketeering in the Brewster airplane plant." Pearson went on to say, "Hebert's cross-examination was one of the most devastating ever heard since the days of Tom Walsh and Teapot Dome, but to him it was just a news reporter doing another story."

The *Washington Post* editorialized: "Congressmen who had spread the disgusting story of Thomas V. DeLorenzo on the record are entitled to a vote of thanks from the workers of America. Apparently the great majority of the 18,000 unionized employees of the Brewster Aeronautical Corporation did not know that their leader used a string of aliases copied from 'a telephone book or maybe a hat' and that he made false claims to get a job as an aircraft worker. Like various unprincipled opportunists who have come to the top of the mushroom unions in war industries, DeLorenzo has left behind him a slimy trail of deception that will make thousands of honest and sincere union members sick at heart."

"The report shields nobody," the *New Orleans Item* reported. "The Naval Affairs Committee is close to the Navy, but the Navy was blamed without hesitation for its part in the failure. The management is condemned for lack of ability to manage. And labor is chastised for submission to the dictator's whip of a self-confessed, shameful and shameless liar and perjurer."

The upshot of the investigation was that DeLorenzo was ousted from the union after being fined and jailed upon conviction of perjury in the United States courts. He tried to say that he had purged himself before Congress and therefore couldn't be tried for perjury, but the courts held that he couldn't purge himself because I told him when he was lying; he didn't tell me. By the process of questioning, I had nailed him.

The whole episode had an ironic twist. His draft board inducted DeLorenzo into the army. There one assumes he became more concerned with the needs of the military and less willing to let servicemen die to increase the power of corrupt union bosses.

CHAPTER XI

FUSILLADES AND FINESSE

At the same time I was reaping the spoils of my brush with DeLorenzo and basking in the bouquets tossed by the bards of editorial rooms across the country, I was fielding flack from my old flagship, the *New Orleans States*. Not that the *States* didn't consider my exposé of DeLorenzo an honorable piece of work; it did, and said so. But my actions vis-à-vis Judge Leander Perez left a different impression with the *States'* major domo, Major Crown.

Although I was insulated somewhat by distance from the severity and bitterness of the political battle between Plaquemines Parish and the State of Louisiana, I eventually found myself in the middle of the squabble. The parish-state war began with death, and intensified. The sheriff of Plaquemines Parish had died a natural death. The parish thus required a new sheriff, a fact about which practically everyone agreed; it was the question of who would pin on the badge which caused the dispute. Governor Sam Jones and Leander Perez were never political allies. The battle lines were drawn long before the sheriff succumbed to the laws of nature. When the governor claimed the right to appoint a new sheriff, Perez naturally disagreed. He held that it was necessary to either hold an election or have a new sheriff appointed by parish authorities, meaning himself. The result of the brouhaha was that the Louisiana Supreme Court ruled the appointment to be the governor's prerogative, and Jones dispatched National Guardsmen to Plaquemines to keep his man in office.

Shortly thereafter I received a telephone call from Perez. He was raising hell about the people in Plaquemines buying war bonds and everything and then having equipment supplied by the federal government being used by the National Guard to enter the parish and install a sheriff.

Perez then went on statewide radio and made one hell of a speech attacking the governor's action. But that wasn't enough; next, he wanted the speech put into the *Congressional Record*, so he sent it to me.

I called Maestri and asked him what it was all about. Maestri said to give Perez what he wanted but not to get him involved, which was typical Maestri. So the speech arrived in Washington, and I went onto the floor of the House to get what is termed "permission to revise and extend one's remarks, and include therein extraneous matter," which in this instance would be the speech by Judge Perez of Plaquemines Parish.

A congressman, however, can only "revise and extend" his remarks for two pages in the *Record*. Beyond that he is supposed to pay for it. After it is submitted, the printer notifies him it is beyond the limit and will cost him X number of dollars to print. The next step in the procedure is for the congressman to go back to the House and state that his extended remarks will cost X number of dollars, and that fact notwithstanding, he wants to have the work done. The final step in these formalities is that the extended remarks are printed, and nobody pays anything.

Anyway, I got the damn speech from Perez, and I knew it was going to be a tough deal because of the newspapers. I knew what they thought of Perez, but I went through with it and got permission to put put the speech in the *Record*. The next day I was notified that it exceeded the two-page limitation and that publication would cost me one hundred and twelve dollars. I wrote Perez right away: "Dear Judge: I am returning your manuscript, . . ." and I explained the situation, concluding with, "I would not dare edit your copy."

Well, to the ordinary man that would have been the end of it, but not Perez. As fast as it could get back to Washington, I got a special delivery envelope. There was a check to pay for the cost of inserting his speech into the *Record*. I went before the House with the check and got unanimous consent to print the speech and pay for it. The only problem was that nobody in the House knew how to accept the check.

Nobody ever paid for anything like this before. As far as the members were concerned this whole matter was like a dream; anyone wanting to pay for printing work was something out of this world.

So, I had Perez' check and couldn't give it to anybody. John McCormack, majority leader at the time, called me outside and said, "Eddie, listen, let me tell you something, and I'm talking to you as a friend and not as your leader. Do you know what you have done? You have embarrassed everybody in this House because nobody ever pays for that."

I said, "Yes, John, but you don't understand the situation."

He said "Eddie, I don't care about the situation. You just make up your mind that you live up here and your life is with these people in the House. You have to live with them everyday. Now, you make your decision."

I went back and got unanimous consent to withdraw my request, and I got permission to print the speech regardless of price. I sent the Judge his money back.

From then on the *States* attacked me. The paper claimed that all anybody had to do was hate Sam Jones and I would put anything they wanted into the *Record*. That, of course, was not the truth, but anyway, that was what they wanted people to believe.

Following the appearance of the Perez speech in the *Record*, I sent copies of it to many of my constitutents, at the judge's request, needless to say.

Major Crown didn't wait for the letters to be mailed before launching a salvo at me. Crown was incensed by the printing of the speech in the *Congressional Record*, and he wasn't hesitant to say so— particularly since he felt no restraints against attacking me after I had refused to campaign for the newspaper's mayoral candidate. In an editorial entitled "Misinformation," the major set his reading public straight on the true nature of the *Record*.

> The *Congressional Record* is an account of what Congress is and does and says and thinks. It is also the occasional receptacle—the ash can or waste basket, so to speak—of a nauseating quantity of drivel, froth, trash, litter, demagogic flapdoodle, political quackery, and, at times, mendacious and deceitful twaddle.

A case in point: On Tuesday, November 2, the *Record* contained a speech by the General Pipsqueak Perez, swashbuckling insurrectionary of Plaquemines Parish.

It was a speech vilely and senselessly assailing the governor of the State of Louisiana. And it was a monstrous perversion of truth and fact.

And now that speech becomes part of the "history" of the proceedings of Congress. You ask how come?

The Pipsqueak is not a member of Congress, of course. Nor does his speech refer to any national legislation nor action or matter pending before Congress. But he had a friend in the House. The friend is his congressman, the Honorable F. Edward Hebert of the First District. The speech ran over two pages in the *Record*. By Mr. Hebert's admission, it cost the taxpayers $112.50 to print the Pip's piffle.

Crown went on and on, and, as one can surmise, cackled joyfully and slapped his leg in conclusion.

Then, before too many days had passed, the major learned that I had mailed copies of the speech under my congressional franking privilege. That bit of intelligence, which wasn't exactly a secret, called for another editorial. Accompanying it was a mixed-media editorial cartoon. It featured photo copies of the speech as it appeared in the *Record*, plus copies of the speech mailed under my frank. The artist's contribution to the cartoon was amateurish, as were most drawn by Roy Aymond, who was appreciated more for his camaradarie than for his cartoons. It depicted an Uncle Sam who looked more like a constipated Father Time. The message: "No Wonder Uncle Sam Scowls His Displeasure."

"We know that this is common political practice," Major Crown wrote. "We know that members of Congress with probably very few exceptions use their franking privilege and the *Congressional Record* to fight their political campaigns and strengthen their political fences. But in the Plaquemines case, District Attorney Leander H. Perez was conducting a personal political campaign against the Sam Jones administration."

Well, I decided that the time had come to strike back. I fired off a letter to Major Crown, who refused to print it. After waiting a few days, I sent a copy to the *Plaquemines Gazette*, a small, Perez-controlled weekly, which was happy to publish it . I wrote:

I do not challenge your right to criticize me for any act in my public life. I welcome criticism at all times, as you well know. Whether or not I did the proper thing in inserting Judge Perez' speech is, of course, a matter of personal opinion. In my opinion it was most proper. . . .

I not only had the legal right to insert the matter in the *Congressional Record* and to send it out under my frank, but I also had the moral right, which I exercised.

I have known you for many years and some of the most pleasant years of my life were spent on the *New Orleans States*. I know that you inherently want to be honest, fair, and impartial, and above all, I know your greatest desire is to be consistent. . . .

I next cited five previous occasions when I had inserted the newspaper's editorials or Governor Jones' letters and observations into the *Congressional Record* at taxpayers' expense.

A search of the editorial files of the *New Orleans States* does not disclose any criticism of my having done this. . . . I am sure that if it is wrong now to have inserted in the *Congressional Record* certain matters relating to activities in my district, it would, in your opinion, have been wrong [before]. I am sure you do not want to leave with the reading public that it is wrong to insert something which Mr. Perez has to say, while it is perfectly proper to have inserted something which the *Times-Picayune* and the *New Orleans States* and Governor Jones had to say on another occasion.

In conclusion may I say this to you, that if it is your desire to have this exchange of correspondence printed in the *Congressional Record*, I shall be happy to do so upon your request. Further, if you care to bear the expense of reprinting and addressing of envelopes, such as Mr. Perez did, which was certainly not at government expense and did not cost the taxpayers one penny, I shall be very happy to do so upon receipt of your check to cover the same.

While the First Amendment guaranteed me the right to write the letter, it did not require the *States* to publish it. Only a sense of fair play could do that, and the letter did not appear. But several weeks later in an editorial concerning an unrelated subject, a reference to the Perez matter cropped up parenthetically. It prompted me to act against such arbitrary remarks. I launched a verbal assault against

Major James Evans Crown on the floor of the United States House of Representatives that required a full thirty minutes. I think everyone gathered from my remarks that I considered Major Crown to be somewhat less than perfect.

Thereafter there were no more editorials concerning the placement of certain speeches in the *Congressional Record*. Crown's lone reply to my attack came in an Associated Press story of the event. The editor said only that he was saddened by the remarks, a comment calculated to win sympathy and at the same time indicate a good reporter had gone bad.

Meanwhile, I had gone off on a trip with two congressional buddies, Sterling (Stub) Cole of New York and William Hess of Ohio, incidentally, both Republicans. Stub and Bill were two of my closest friends on the old Naval Affairs Committee. They were the ones who arranged for the big portrait of Carl Vinson, the committee chairman, which hangs in the committee room. And in the typical Vinson manner, right away Carl gave them a trip. I was pretty new to the committee, but Cole, Hess and I had struck up a solid friendship. Thus, one day when I was in New Orleans, I got a call from Cole who was in Washington. He said, "How'd you like to go down to Trinidad?"

I said, "Sure, I'd like to go to Trinidad." I hadn't been properly initiated then, because on this junket we ended up in Rio instead. I didn't know at the time that Cole would start out with one destination in mind, but end up at the other end of the world before he returned. Later I accompanied him on a trip, ostensibly to China, but we ended up going around the world.

Well, what Stub and Bill really wanted—and had to have because it was a Democratic administration—was a Democratic chairman for the trip. They hadn't figured out a way to have a Republican chairman. So, in essence, they were taking me along for the ride. When I realized what was going on, I said, "You bastards. All you got me for is to be the protocol chairman for you characters. You've got a two to one vote on anything I don't want to do."

We got down to Recife, the American base on the South Atlantic, and Jonas Ingram was the admiral commanding the whole area. This was the time when he made all the newspapers because he took the cruiser *Memphis* into the harbor of Rio de Janeiro without authority and announced to those characters down there that if they weren't for us he was going to shoot the hell out of them. He was a real sea dog. He later became president of the All-American Football Conference. He was a real hot-shot guy, a go-getter, a real blusterer.

When we got down to Recife, the planes were taking off on a mission to get the last of the German submarines in the area. Old Jonas said, "Look at those boys go. Look at 'em go. They're gonna get 'em." All that kind of stuff, but he was right. They sank the last German submarine in the South Atlantic. Jonas promised us—we were going on to Rio—that he would wait until we came back so that we could award the medals to those flyers. When we got back to Recife, he had the men line up and delivered a speech to the troops which ran something like this, "Now, I know you guys got the red-ass because you think the action is over, but you get that goddamn red-ass out of your system because you've got a hell of a lot more action coming. We've got to clean up the Pacific next." And we pinned the medals on those boys.

One night, about nine o'clock, I was in my quarters when a knock came to the door. It was the admiral. He said, "I gotta talk to you." I invited him in and he sat down. "I've got a message for you to take to the President—about what to do with these goddamn Bras [the Brazilians], and it can't go through diplomatic channels because Roosevelt will never get it. But he's got to know what's going on. He's got to be told, and you're gonna tell him!"

I looked at him, and going through my mind was the fact that I'm only a sophomore congressman, a protocol chairman on a junket, and I'm supposed to go to the White House and tell the President of the United States how to run the world.

I said, "Well, admiral, I'll be very glad to tell him, but may I say that you told me to tell him?"

"Goddamn right," Jonas said. "Tell him I told you to tell him."

He then told me how he wanted to deal with the Brazilians in postwar relations, which is all quite vague to me now. Nevertheless, when I got back to Washington, I called General "Pa" Watson, the appointments secretary at the White House, and I told him I had a message from Admiral Ingram for the President. He arranged for me to have five minutes. I rushed over to the White House.

Whenever a person talked to Roosevelt, he had to talk fast because if he didn't the President would do the talking and the visitor would leave there in five minutes wondering what the hell he had come to the White House for.

When I went in Roosevelt was sitting behind his big desk and he began to tell me about "my cotton," and "my oil." The country was his: "my army," "my navy," "my country." But that was Roosevelt.

I listened for a little while and then said, "Mr. President, I want you to understand one thing. I'm not here giving you advice. I'm only here for one reason. Admiral Ingram has asked me to give you a message personally, and I'm only carrying the message to Garcia."

"Ho-ho-ho," he laughed. "Old Jonas. He's a helluva guy. You know President Vargas of Brazil wants me to make Jonas vice president of the United States."

Well, I gave Roosevelt the message. Slowly he pushed that big cigarette holder back into his mouth and said, "I'll tell you what I'll do, Hébert. My missus is going down there in a month, and I'll tell her to take the message down. She'll deliver the message and bring back the reply."

It was as though he was saying, "My old lady is going down to the corner to get a can of beer and she'll stop off and give you a sip on the way back."

Jonas Ingram, however, disliked Mrs. Roosevelt; in fact he couldn't stand her. I knew this because of the things he said about her when I visited with him. I therefore wrote him that I had delivered the message and that he might expect a pretty important guest. After Mrs. Roosevelt delivered the President's reply, I got a note from Ingram. He said, "The lady delivered the message. It was a costly delivery but it was worth it."

Besides playing messenger boy for presidents and admirals, I had to run for reelection in 1944. This time I won hands down, being offered even less of a contest than in 1942. It was my third time to win public office, and I was beginning to understand the game, so much so that I wrote a little piece on how to win at politics. It got wider play in the press than I expected.

So far as I have been able to ascertain, after years of exhaustive research, no man ever gets to Congress because the people wanted him. And certainly never on his own merits. I have estimated that it makes your ego drop anywhere from fifty to sixty per cent.

You arrive here [in Washington] full of your own importance, confident you are the people's choice. But you are speedily disabused. Before you have been on the job long enough to distinguish Sam Rayburn's scalp from a searchlight reflector you begin to hear how you really got to Congress.

It develops you owe it all to a motley array of characters, of whose very existence you were hitherto unaware. I have catalogued them as follows.

1. The fellow who discovered you. It matters nothing that you never saw him before; he discovered you. It seems he recognized your true worth when everyone else was blind, and started the ball rolling.

2. The fellow who not only discovered you, but forced the big bosses—much against their will—to accept you. He convinced them it meant political disaster if they didn't.

3. The fellow who cleared the way. It seems the opposition was considering a strong candidate who would have beaten you hands down, but this guy worked it so they put up a weak candidate.

4. The fellow who held back a huge block of votes until the last minute and then threw them to you, starting a stampede. Later you discover this punk doesn't even live in your district.

5. The Machiavellian character who pretended to be working for the opposition but secretly was all the time for you. He wormed into the foe's inner councils and employed their secrets against them.

6. The real kingmaker. The guy who went quietly to the "right people" and forced them to put up the dough. Without this money, which you never knew about, you couldn't have gotten to first base.

Those are the men who really got you to Congress. And they all come to see you not once, but continually, until you learn to bar the door. They are practically selfless, demanding little for themselves. All they want in return for their efforts is your integrity and maybe your heart's blood.

Perhaps the biggest mystery of all was how an opponent bagged even one vote. You never encounter anyone who voted for your opponent. For all you can discover, nobody did.

During these years I naturally was supporting the war effort, and when I returned from Brazil I advocated President Roosevelt's reelection to a fourth term to insure continuity in the fight against the Axis powers and the maintenance of unbroken relations with the Allies.

I also returned to my committee work. As a member of the District of Columbia Committee, I was sorely concerned about the lack of parking facilities in the nation's capital, and sought to correct the situation. Representative Clarence Cannon of Missouri, however, objected to my inclusion of $5,000 for off-street parking facilities in a $1,400,000,000 appropriations bill. Editorially, Washington's newspapers backed me. They had previously noted my other efforts to improve the administration of the District, a generally thankless task for congressmen whose constituents aren't as a rule overly ecstatic about their representatives spending time improving the government of a city foreign to their immediate concerns.

The newspapers took a dim view of Cannon's reluctance to alleviate the parking problem. His statements in the House concerning the parking situation indicated he did not grasp the seriousness of the problem. I therefore informed him that I intended to challenge him on the floor of the House. I later addressed the House, saying, "If what the gentleman [Cannon] has said indicates his knowledge of the items in this appropriations bill, then it's no wonder he is having so much trouble getting it passed, because he evidently knows nothing about anything in it."

At this juncture my old nemesis, the *Congressional Record*, came into play again. When it appeared the day after I spoke, it carried my remarks—but they had been altered by Cannon. So had those of Congressman George Bender of Cleveland, who had challenged Cannon on another section of the appropriations bill.

But Cannon apparently was not satisfied with altering our remarks, for he charged me with a lack of "sportsmanship." He said I had spoken against him while he was absent from the floor. I had, however, plainly forewarned him that I intended to speak against his position. "I smile," I said, "When I consider that he, of all people, should challenge the sportsmanship of any member of the House." I quoted Omar Khayam's reference to the "inviolability of the written word," in the *Rubaiyat*, and charged that if Cannon had been a contemporary of the Persian poet, he "would have revised and edited that." Nevertheless, Cannon, as chairman of the Appropriations Committee, prevailed, as chairmen often do. The parking problem remained.

I next took on Secretary of the Interior Harold Ickes, a self-described "old Curmudgeon." I preferred to call him "an old sour puss." What had me upset was Ickes' refusal to cooperate with my plan to consolidate the District of Columbia police forces. Every time a crime was committed, there were six varieties of cops stepping on each others' flat feet. I therefore introduced a bill which would combine the District police with the park police. The latter came under Ickes' jurisdiction, and Ickes did not cotton to the idea of losing any of his powers. He refused to cooperate.

So, the issue boiled down to whether Congress was going to make laws or turn the process over to the heads of government agencies. I was prepared to take Ickes on, and said so: "This Ickes is not going to tell me anything. Ickes wants everything he can grab. He probably wants to put the District under his National Parks Service. He is the only man I know who enjoys being an old sour puss."

Despite its merits, the consolidation proposal died in the House. I later gained some satisfaction when I discovered that I was not alone in my opinion of Ickes. It came when President Truman was signing a bill which I had introduced.

In those days, the newspaper room at the White House was where the reception room is now. All the reporters hung out there, and anyone going in to see the President had to pass through the group of reporters, through a smaller room, then into the Oval Office.

Naturally when an individual who had an appointment with the President came out, he was swamped by the reporters who wanted to know what the President had to say.

The purpose of my visit to the President was to attend the signing of a bill I had written for the District of Columbia. While I was there I asked that a picture of the two of us be made, which I could use in my approaching campaign, plus I requested an autographed picture of him for my daughter, Dawn. He sent Matt Connolly, his appointments secretary, to get a picture for Dawn, leaving us alone in the room.

At this time, he and Ickes were having a real down to earth battle. Without anything better to talk about while waiting for Matt to get a photograph, I said, "Mr. President, I understand you're having some trouble with your Secretary of the Interior." The President looked me straight in the eye and replied, "Hébert, there's a no good, counterfeit son of a bitch. My father always told me that when someone calls himself honest, lock the cupboard doors because he is going to steal something."

I wonder what the headlines would have been that day if I had come out of the Oval Office and told the waiting reporters what the President had said?

CHAPTER XII

I WENT, I SAW, I HEARD

Ten days after the surrender of Germany, I left Washington for a tour of war-ravaged Europe as a member of a five-man select committee appointed by Naval Affairs Chairman Carl Vinson. Lyndon Johnson, a representative from Texas, was chairman of the special subcommittee. Its other members were Congressmen Sterling Cole of New York and William Hess of Ohio, old traveling companions, and Mike Bradley of Pennsylvania.

In his formal authorization of the trip, Chairman Vinson said it was necessary for the our group to focus on the problems of handling the "naval properties used in the great victory just won. . . . Naval properties capable of being integrated into the Navy of tomorrow will be the subject of our urgent study and inquiry."

On the day the subcommittee returned, it filed an official report entitled "Navy Surplus Property in the Mediterranean Area and the British Isles," a title not calculated to hit the best-seller list. But shortly afterwards, another report was published, my diary of the trip. I arrived at the "Caesarish" title, *I Went, I Saw, I Heard,* from the prologue: "I have tried to bring back a true and accurate picture of that which I went to see, and which I saw, and which I heard." And I noted: "It goes beyond the official report and attempts to make the trip a personal one to each and every individual who reads this diary."

I preferred to write the account, for the most part, in a chatty style, much like a letter home to a good friend. Best-selling author Harnett T. Kane, who wrote the foreword to it, said, "the diary has the positive merit, I believe, of honesty, and also clarity. And it is refreshing, and a bit wonderful, too, to find a congressman who can sit down at a typewriter and produce something that doesn't sound like a loud speech in a heavy wind.''

While undoubtedly there were political benefits which could accrue from the diary, I really wrote it as a reporter, not as a politician. Perhaps that is why the diary has held up well in the face of history and has proved to be a window into my early thinking about this nation's defense posture. More immediately, the diary reveals how I changed my mind regarding foreign aid and how, at that early date, I perceived the danger of Stalin's imperialistic hunger. What I saw in Europe at the end of World War II also indicated clearly the role which the United States would have to play as the major world power in the decades ahead. As I stated in the prologue, ''The course of the world will be charted in the not distant future. That course will depend more on what America does than anything else.''

After stopovers in Bermuda and the Azores, our party rested in England for part of a day, and then moved on to France where I was greatly troubled by what I saw and heard.

Unlike London, Paris is little scarred by war. Only a few places are visible where bombs have fallen. Paris, at least physically, has been spared the agony of war. The tricolor of France increased in display from window after window as we entered the city of Paris. Everybody seems to be a patriot now. Where are the collaborationists? Where are the minions of Pierre Laval and his ilk?

We are billeted in the Hotel Rafael. The Germans took it when they were here. The ghost of a German officer stands beside me at the writing table where I sit and write this at 1 o'clock in the morning. In this room rattle the skeletons of German debauchery. It is a suite of seduction. The elaborate and ornate decorations of the walls and the furnishings boldly suggest lasciviousness.

There are permanent German telephones installed in the rooms. Undoubtedly the Germans expected to stay here a long, long time. Some of them will stay a long, long time—the dead ones.

I wonder what kind of German occupied this suite? I wonder what his thoughts were as he rested on the bed which I will occupy in a few minutes. If only these walls could speak, even in a whisper. I wonder what they would say? I wonder what they would reveal.

Everything, we are told, is to be had in the black market at black market prices. American cigarettes are for sale at twenty cents each and souls are for sale for a package of cigarettes. My driver, a Frenchman who escaped the slave labor of the Nazis, told me it took 5,000 francs a month for two people to eke out an existence.

But there's no sign of war in the Montmartre. Except for the congressional party no other Americans in the Montmartre were in civilian clothes. All other Americans were in uniform and most of them were beardless striplings. They laughed, they drank champagne, and they petted pretty girls. God forgive me if I judge wrongly, but how many of those same girls gave their lips just as freely to their temporary masters—the Germans, when they were in control?

There is something unreal, something definitely phony about this whole business. I am not laying indictment to the French people of the unyielding underground, to the valiant who refused to choke the throat of France—I mean those who laughed and sang and made merry without interruption in the gay cabarets of Paris during the occupation. The Montmartre never closed during the reign and rule of the Germans. Life was normal, and except for the color and nationality of the uniform, soldiers ruled the roost as they rule the roost now at this moment.

Surely these French mademoiselles must have pleased or else the Germans would not have allowed them to continue operations. Surely their lips must have been just as sweet or else the Nazi overlords would not have taken them, much less paid for momentary ecstasy!

Yes, it all seemed a mockery when a tableau of smiling La Belle France was presented as a closing number in the cabaret in which we sat. They wouldn't have sung that song to a German audience. What then did they sing? Damn such hypocrisy!

I talked with one of the girls of the chorus line. She came to our table. She was beautiful—dreamy eyes, full round lips, blonde tresses carefully coiffured, a slender figure, beautiful teeth encased in a frame of oval crimson.

Where was she born?

"Vichy," she replied in broken understandable English and with apology at the mention of Vichy.

"And how long have you been in Paris?" I asked.

"About a year."

"How did you get in here with the Germans in control?"

"I don't like the Germans. My mother was a Pole and my father came from Odessa. I am a White Russian and I hate the Germans."

What lady of the evening doesn't tell her gentleman what she believes he wants to hear in the hope that he will be generous and she will be satisfactory. I hope I do this girl no wrong, but I have heard the same approach before from the lips of equally attractive girls who sit in the parlors of bagnios and attempt to please the customer in a business where he must always be definitely right.

I hope these American kids, these American boys were not taking too seriously these mouthings which had been poured into German ears and were now being honeyed into youthful American ears with the same insincere earnestness.

I was truly troubled by the actions of all too many Frenchmen during the war, perhaps my feelings were due in part to my French ancestry. I found it disquieting that a significant segment of France would acquiesce in a situation in which it found itself, if not join in outright collaboration with the enemy. Such thoughts nagged me, and I concluded the diary entry for May 18 with,

Get the hell to bed yourself before you prate too much longer on patriots whose patriotism is devotion to the cause which flies a flag of gold.

Thank God the inside of France is made of sterner stuff! Thank God real Frenchmen will lift their country out of the dregs into the sunlight of a world which would rather be silenced in death than sing the song of the conqueror or dance to his tune.

The next morning our party met General Dwight David Eisenhower at Rheims in the "little red schoolhouse" where Germany had surrendered unconditionally to the Allies only a short time before. A great deal of my May 19 entry is taken up with a discourse on Associated Press reporter Edward Kennedy. At the time, I had little respect for this man who apparently broke his word and leaked the story of the Nazi surrender despite an agreement not to do so until arrangements were finalized. Later, however, correspondence between Kennedy and myself allowed Kennedy to explain his side of the story and to document his reinstatement by General Eisenhower.

While we visited with Eisenhower, I also met and chatted with General Lucius Clay. We discussed the devastation of Germany.

Having seen the wreck of France and heard of the situation in Germany, I wrote:

> The greatest problem now posed to General Clay and the American Army of Occupation is to restore as far as possible normal operations and activities in the overrun sections of Europe. Provisions must be made, first of all, to feed these people. America must do its share, there is no alternative!
>
> Industries must be restored in France as quickly and orderly as possible. American brains must be utilized—the best American brains available and not OPA clerks and bureaucratic second-graders. Here is a job for men of ability, a job of construction which has got to be done and now. It's a job for realists and practical men, not a task for theorists and screwball idealists.
>
> The coal mines of France must be reopened. Destroyed bridges and railroad communications must be rebuilt. The people themselves must be given every opportunity to work out their own salvation. It's a new challenge to America, but under men like General Clay I have no fear—if we but do our part.

The necessity of foreign aid, a new concept to me, was becoming obvious. I was really being conditioned to support the yet-to-be-devised Marshall Plan.

My colleagues and I, operating under the theory that all work and no play is un-American, took in the Follics Bergère one night. I was impressed.

> They [the dancers] lived up to all expectations and reputation. Just imagine sitting in a huge overstuffed chair in your living room, casually puffing a good El Trelles triangle cigar and watching beauty parade in nudity before your eyes and you have the Follies Bergère.
>
> The French chorus girls haven't much talent, or maybe it was because I couldn't understand French, but there wasn't anything wrong with their curves—and in the right places.

Later that night I visited a countess who had been a member of the Maquis, "the underground which refused to die." She added to the information which was beginning to increase my concern for the future politics of France.

> She revealed that France today is swinging to the left but will never

remain completely in that direction. Her faith in the future remains although she admits that if communism comes to France they of the valiant Maquis will have fought in vain and the United States will likewise have contributed to a futile cause. Because of the fundamental Catholicism of France she is firm in the conviction that her country will never succumb to Communism or the rule of Moscow.

"What are you doing about the Russians?" is her question of the moment. There's fear in her voice when she talks of the Russians. Why?

Her explanation of the popularity of Russia on the streets and in the theaters of Paris springs from admiration of the great contribution of the Soviet soldiers against the German invader. When the United States and Great Britain are presented in tableaux or moving pictures the applause from the audience is complimentary; when Russia is presented, the applause is deafening.

A few hours before at the Follies Bergère in the closing number of the performance, the Hammer and Sickle was given the position of honor in a grouping of the flags of the United States, Great Britain, France and Russia. What is the reason? Will the Fourth Republic be engulfed by waves from the Third Internationale?

The cliché that travel is broadening buttresses the argument that clichés often become clichés because of the basic truth they expound. "It's Sunday morning," I wrote on May 20. "Last Sunday morning it was Mother's Day and I was at home in Virginia. Today it is Pentecost Sunday and I'm going to the historic Cathedral of Notre Dame in Paris with Bill Hess and Sterling Cole. Between these two Sundays, I have been to Bermuda, the Azores, London, and now Paris. In a world which has shrunk so small how can men of tomorrow ever hope to again isolate themselves from their neighbors?" A sense of the necessity for expanded responsibilities was developing within me and it would grow, contributing to a belief that it is in the best interest of the United States to shed its isolationistic preoccupation problems and assume its responsibility in world relations.

After visiting the United States ambassador to France, Jefferson Caffery of Louisiana, whom I had last seen in Cuba, I wrote:

I am sure we all came away more fully impressed that the challenge facing America in Europe did not end with the unconditional surrender of the Germans.

Let's be realistic about the whole thing.

France is hungry and empty stomachs only too often in the past have been filled with the food of revolution. This has unfortunately been particularly true of France. Advocates of Communism ask no better ground on which to toil. Everywhere I have turned since arriving in France I have been told that France is swinging to the left. The Communist Party is the best organized and the best financed in France today. The Communists are making hay while the sun shines, they are striking while the iron is hot. Control of France by the Communists means control of France by the Soviet Union. Control means domination of the continent by one power and such domination will lead to war sooner than we want it.

Russia prides itself on being realistic and I admire them for it. I like their way of doing business and I think it is about time we start doing business the same way, especially with the Russians.

Oh, the nature of nations isn't so different from the nature of human beings. After all, nations are composed of human beings. How could they act otherwise?

I have no argument with Russia's attempt to communize France. That's Russia's way of belief. . . . I believe America can and must get along with Russia, but to get along with Russia we have to meet the Russians on their own ground and that terrain is paved solely with realism.

This 1945 view has never changed, and has placed me in a position to accept détente with the USSR in more recent days.

The next day our congressional party became the first American civilians to land in Bremen, Germany, following its capitulation. It was a sight not easily forgotten.

Can you picture cities the size of Milwaukee, New Orleans, Cleveland, Los Angeles, St. Louis, Atlanta, laid waste, end to end? If you can, and you cannot, you would have an idea of the path between Paris and Bremen.

There was Aachen (the first city in Germany captured by the Americans), Cologne, Bremerhaven and the rest, all razed to the ground.

What a fight it was! What a siege! What destruction!

Between Paris and Bremen the land is scorched by war. Gaping holes scar the earth. From the sky there is nothing but devastation below. What were once cities are now graveyards of civilization. City after city—town after town--village after village we flew over. Our pilot skimmed the ruins of what once were the homes of families and factories of a misled people.

From the sky we saw the great four-lane highways of Hitler's Germany, now pale strings draping the wreath of a dead nation.

There is hardly a building below us which has not been hit by a projectile of destruction. Here is indeed a nation destroyed. How can Japan resist such force? How long will these stupid fanatics resist the inevitable?

Bremen from the air is destroyed. Bremen on the ground is no more. It is unbelievable that a city can be so destroyed and yet they tell us that in Berlin not a stone stands on a stone. Even after you see Bremen you refuse to believe what is before your eyes.

It just can't be possible, but it is possible because it has happened.

Did you ever attend a prize fight and wonder or marvel at the ability of one of the fighters to stand up under an unmerciful beating? How many times have you heard the expressions: "He's being hit with everything but the bucket." "What's holding him up?"

Defenseless, helpless, he takes punch after punch. His eyes are closed, his lips are split wide open and his nose runs blood and yet he stands up taking, taking, taking, the unending pummeling and beating, finally collapsing under the murderous attack of his opponent, and he is stretched out on the canvas, a bleeding, discolored, broken pulp beaten into unrecognizability beyond recovery.

That's Germany as I have seen it.

That's Germany's cities. Not one, not two, not three but every city I have seen from the air and from the ground. There isn't a city of importance left standing.

In curious, aimless, continuous processions the survivors of this visitation of hell walk about the mess that once was a great city. They are dazed. There is an expression of wonderment on their faces. I did not see one of them smile. They walk in a listless stupor. As our cars drove by they paused momentarily to gaze at us. What was behind those cold blank stares? What were they thinking if they could think at all? What will be their reaction when they recover from the shock?

At the moment they are meek, humble and docile. They take and obey orders without trouble. They have been doing that so long it has become a habit. I did not see a single German who appeared underfed. They all seemed well fed and well nourished.

Has their spirit been broken or merely bent?

There was the little urchin who shot his hand up in the air as our car passed and shouted "Heil, Hitler!"

Did he know what he was saying? Did he know that riding in that caravan were the conquerors of his country or did he associate uniforms and automobiles with the only life he had ever known? Will this youth accept the opportunity for redemption from a life which can only ultimately bring not merely destruction and devastation to his children or his grandchildren, but complete and total annihilation?

What are the German people thinking?

Unable to continue our travels in Germany because of severe weather conditions, we postponed a trip to Munich and headed back to Paris before going to Italy and North Africa. During the Paris stopover, I noted:

> Tonight Charles de Gaulle speaks to the French people for the first time since the day of victory. Lyndon Johnson brings a Polish newspaper woman and a charming Red Cross girl to luncheon. Tonight we had a dinner party at the Royal Monceau and talked with more French people when we could get somebody to tell us what they were saying.
>
> The more I hear people express themselves, the more firmly convinced I am that now is the time to "talk turkey" with Josef Stalin and Russia. There's going to be trouble and plenty of it from Russia unless we deal firmly while our power is at its height. Power is the only language Russia knows and respects. Reports now have it that Russia does not intend to release that section of Germany which is under its control but will make it the 19th State of the Soviet Union. Nice going!

I have never laid claim to gifts of prophesy, but my views on the future of what has become the People's Republic of Germany as well as my recommendations on how to negotiate with the USSR could not have been more accurate. Considering the Cold War and United States-Russian relations since World War II, it certainly would be easy for me to say, "I told you so."

> It was realism which placed Russia on our side as an ally. Russia could just as easily have been on the side of Germany.
>
> I, for one, will not blame Russia for trying to get all it can at the peace table when the time comes, but I will lay the blame at the door of America if our diplomats allow Molotov or whoever else represents

Russia, to get away with it. I never blame the other fellow for winning. I blame myself for losing. So it is with this situation.

If only we had been realistic after the last war, we would not have had to come back here again twenty-five years later to do all over, and at a greater cost of life, what we had done before. It has been only repetition with emphasis—death and destruction being used for the emphasis.

The next day the weather cleared and we flew south to Italy. "Who said, 'See Naples, then die'? I've seen Naples but there's nothing to want to die about," I commented. "The people are half naked and dirty looking. I haven't seen such poverty in all of Europe—not even in Germany where cities don't exist anymore."

In Rome we arranged for an audience with Pope Pius XII.

The private audience with the Pope will always remain an event to be spoken of and described for as many years as I am privileged to live. There were twelve in our party and we were taken through a series of halls and rooms, past Swiss guards, papal Chamberlains, and costumed attendants, into the private office of His Holiness. Mike Bradley led the way and in devout Catholic custom knelt and kissed the Papal ring. I followed him and then came the rest of the party, Catholic and Protestant alike, genuflecting and kissing the ring. We remained for half an hour. It was a charming and interesting conversation. . . . His Holiness demonstrated a keen interest in our visit to Germany. He asked questions and listened attentively to the replies.

The Pope also presented to each member of the party a copy of a statement he had personally prepared and blessed rosaries and medals which were presented.

On May 27 the committee viewed more evidence of the Nazi's solution to everything.

Will the barbarism of Nazi Germany ever cease to be revealed? Today I saw and walked in the cave outside Rome where Italian hostages were machine-gunned in March 1944. Crude pine coffins, lined against the walls of the cave, contain the bodies of those who were murdered a year ago by the Germans for no reason other than they were Italians.

Today grieving families still make pilgrimages to this fantastic mausoleum. Pictures of the murdered men have been placed on top the primitive coffins. Vigil lights burn before them. Fresh flowers are placed atop the pine boxes and I even saw one woman lying prostrate over the box which contained the body of him whom she loved.

And this was supposed to be a civilized nation, a nation of supermen—superbeasts would be a better description.

Italy has six political parties and once again the best organized are the communists, and the finger of organization points in the direction of the Kremlin.

The shadow of Moscow definitely darkens the harbor of Trieste and throws its mantle about the shoulders of Tito. In Rome, many wonder if Tito is being used as the trial balloon of Stalin to find out just how far the Allies will go to back conversation with action. It's all very interesting.

The United States is in this thing up to its neck. Never again can we withdraw into our shell of retirement and isolation. George Washington is dead. His ideals live, but a different kind of fuel must be used to keep the fire burning.

We can't wish for things to happen or not happen any longer. We must prevent them from happening if it is to our interest and national welfare, or we must make them happen if it is necessary for our future happiness and prosperity as a nation.

Leaving Italy, we journeyed to North Africa and experienced a change of pace and environment, but it was no holiday.

I have seen human beings in a form lower than animals exist. Today I have witnessed the unbelievable.

I have known life in the raw. Until today I thought there was little remaining of life to see. I was positive that the form and manner in which I have seen the individual debased and degraded had touched the lowest level. I was wrong.

First, I saw the Medina of Rabat, the native quarter of the capital of Morocco. Through narrow winding streets I rode on an army jeep through filth, disease, stench, human garbage. Water and the bath are unknown to them. Torn, tattered, ragged and stinkingly unclean garments, bearing only the semblance of clothes, cover pitifully dirty, smelling, odorous bodies.

As low as these Medina residents have reached in the pit of human existence, the most revolting and fantastic experience was saved until I stepped within the gates of the Bouse-Bier, a walled city of prostitution, degradation and corruption in Casablanca.

Here prostitutes picked up on the streets of Casablanca are sentenced to confinement and paradoxically to ply the very trade for which they have been confined. Under the strong protection of the Shore Patrol we dared enter this place. Before entering we were warned to guard our pockets and to protect ourselves. The admonition was no indication of what was to happen.

We were set upon by blabbering, screaming women. Actually set upon! Pulled here by one, pulled there by another, propositioned in monosyllabic American words. We actually had to cuff them off or run the risk of being dragged into filthy cubicles. Except for the flashlights of our armed guards and the puny streak of light which struggled through slits in covered doors, the streets were pitch black.

I have never in all my experiences witnessed anything like this. Here was life in its most degraded form, a form lower than the lowest animal which in his own fashion and way must have some respect. Here was none.

I don't recall ever having been as uncomfortable and uncertain as I was in this place called Bouse-Bier, a place just a stone's throw from where Franklin D. Roosevelt and Winston Churchill talked about the Four Freedoms and the preservation of civilization. I wonder what segment of civilization is composed of in what I have witnessed and experienced this day.

On June 4 our caravan finally returned to Germany and to Munich.

Today has been another story of devastation and destruction of that which man has created and built, but devastation and destruction of something far more important, that which has been created by God—man himself.

I saw Dauchau!

Dauchau, the concentration camp near Munich where every dignity of the human existence was violated and degraded. The story of their horror camps is old yet ever new. They cannot be repeated too often lest we forget.

If all other crimes of the Nazis could be forgiven, the crime of the atrocity camps could never be washed from their blackened souls. God, how can men do to other men what these beasts have done, not only to men from other countries, but to their own people. And the crime for which the victims have been convicted is that they dared believe differently from Godless Nazis.

I walked, or more accurately, I edged my way into what was supposed to have been dormitories. Bare rooms with double-sized bunks four high. . .one to a bunk? No, five and six men in each bunk cross-wise. And these were not men I saw today. They were only shells of men. Gaunt frames, sunken eyes, protruding bones—at least they had survived and some have the hope of release and at least partial recovery.

Among them are names which were listed among Europe's men of medicine, law and statesmanship. At one time 32,000 were crowded into this one camp, one of many in other parts of Germany.

Every known physical torture was practiced. Studied starvation always took its toll. One loaf of bread was divided among eight men each day. Breakfast was a choice of not too hot water called coffee or tea. Lunch was soup, and dinner was soup again with a piece of sausage tossed in for good measure. And these men who created such things were supposed to be supermen by their own announced standards.

First there was a crematory of two ovens and then four additional ovens were built—built especially for the purpose of burning the bodies of the dead. The bodies were placed on two stretcher-like pipes and shoved into the flame-licked oven where they burned for three hours. Internees died so fast it became impossible to burn them as quickly as they died and huge surplus stock piles of dead soon accumulated. These were the bodies found by the Americans when the torture camps were first discovered.

Today there were still bodies, but they died only yesterday. They were placed row on row and given the decency of a sheet covering awaiting to be consigned to the earth. The stench of the dead which have been cremated in the oven lingers long in the nostrils after departure.

Dauchau is destruction and devastation of human decency beyond the imagination of the human mind. Munich, the city which gave birth to the brain which created the instrument of this desecration of the dignity of man, is a city of the dead. The Shrine of Nazism is today a hollow sepulchre of destroyed Germanic fanaticism.

We walked the streets of Munich less than an hour ago and we walked the streets alone. The fury of God has been unleashed on this city which dared call itself a shrine.

Leaving the eviscerated remains of Nazi Germany behind, our

party flew to London. Even the antidote of politics could not erase from my mind the lingering image of the depressive nightmare orchestrated by Hitler.

> Today's London papers opposed to Churchill, are filled with blasts against him. It is democracy in its truest style.
>
> In Hyde Park I saw a crowd gathered around a man on a soap box. He had listeners. I wonder how many followers he had? At least he could say what he wanted to say. In Germany too they now can say what they want to say, but the price they paid is the destruction of their country.
>
> They, too, unfortunately, listened too well and too long to a funny-looking guy with a moustache. He destroyed that which gave him the right to talk from a soap box, only to have that right returned to his people by the peoples of other lands who never gave up the right to talk from a soap box or a front porch.

One of my characteristics, for whatever it is worth, is unbridled candor. Therefore, I will freely admit that I did things on this trip for my own pleasure, pure and simple. For example, I have never pretended that every waking moment of this trip to Europe was passed in the pursuit of high governmental studies. It wasn't, and such trips seldom are; but I wonder how many congressmen will admit the fact. Such a "day off" from congressional duties was my trip into Scotland.

> It was a day of long automobile rides but we were more than compensated, and we saw Scotland.
>
> Our plane put down at Prestwick from Exeter, and we immediately started for Resenneath where we lunched. Bill Hess, Lyndon Johnson and myself stopped in Glasgow to call on Frank Quinn's good friend, William Grant Gordon. A most productive visit. A case of Scotch with the compliments of Grant's.
>
> Then to Inverary for some purchases and next along the Loch country and Loch Lomond. "The bonnie, bonnie banks of Loch Lomond" from the song is an understatement. Here is undoubtedly one of the most beautiful spots in all the world.
>
> We paused momentarily in Stirling, a small Scot mining town. We wondered what Scots were thinking of the approaching election between the rival parties of Churchill and Attlee.

Along the street strolled a young Scot. I stopped him, offered him a smoke and engaged in conversation.

"What do you think of the approaching election?" I asked.

"I'm for Attlee," he replied.

"And why?"

"Oh, Mr. Churchill is all right for war but he is no good for peace. Attlee will keep our factories open," he continued. "You see that factory down the street. If Mr. Churchill wins it will be closed."

"And Attlee will keep it open?" I inquired.

"Oh, yes," he replied unhesitatingly.

"What does it manufacture?" I asked.

"Ammunition!"

Isn't human nature the same the world over?

On June 11 our party departed England for home, and I penned the final entry in my journal, a summation of the trip.

This would be a better world and it would be much easier to maintain peace if each and everyone of us could have the chance and the opportunity of seeing how the other fellow lives.

We can get along with any people in the world but we would get along better with them if we could only meet them and sit across the table on even terms and an equitable basis.

We are so complacent. We accept so many things as being just what they should be, when in reality they are only a heritage entrusted to our care which we must protect every day of the week, every hour of the day and every minute of the hour.

Americans insure everything except their independence.

We have waged war and waged it successfully. Far more important is to wage peace.

Talk with those boys who will return from Europe. Listen to what they have seen and observed. Take a page from their book of experience and then thank God you are an American privileged to live in America.

All that I have written could be rewritten today, more than thirty years later. I am still speaking the same philosophy and ideology and giving the same advice and sounding the same warning as when "I Went, I Saw, I Heard."

CHAPTER XIII

BEHIND THE LINES WITH LYNDON

WHEN I FIRST went to Congress, I didn't know Lyndon Johnson. I didn't even know him as a name, although he had been up there quite some time. He was secretary to Congressman Dick Kleberg of Texas before being elected himself. He was always very active on the Hill, in the secretarys' club. At one time he was speaker of that organization. In fact, he was always organized and right in the middle of everything.

During my first two years in Congress, I was on the District Committee and some minor committees and naturally I did not come into contact with Lyndon, although by then I knew who he was. I remember Lyndon when he first returned from the war. He was a tall, gaunt fellow, and he ran for the Senate against Pappy O'Daniel. Sam Rayburn went all out to elect Lyndon. When the votes were coming in, although Pappy had passed out more biscuits, Lyndon was in the lead. Sam Rayburn remarked at the time, "That's one plow we cleaned in Texas today," meaning O'Daniel's plow. But his plow wasn't cleaned very well, for when all the results were in Lyndon had lost.

Of course I got to know Lyndon when I went on the Naval Affairs Committee. We were just thrown together in that we were committee members.

Lyndon and I became much better acquainted when he headed the committee to Europe in 1945. This was a highly select committee. By highly select I mean it was a handpicked committee by the men who were going. In those days I used to travel with Bill Hess of Ohio and Sterling Cole of New York. We were a threesome.

However, there was a halt on congressional trips to Europe several weeks before Germany surrendered, but Rayburn had promised as soon as the war was over he would allow a committee to go, which would be the Naval Affairs Committee. Well, Lyndon was my friend. Stub Cole was my friend. Hess was my friend, and we picked up Mike Bradley of Pennsylvania. He was a very fine person. We knew each other and were friendly, which is very important when traveling together.

We had a Captain Donald Ramsey as the escort officer. Ramsey selected Colonel Joseph Knighton as another aide. He was the legal adviser to General Vandegrift, commandant of the Marine Corps. Lyndon wanted a young man named Donald Cook to go along with us. Stub Cole, for reasons of his own, preferred not to take Cook. Hess and myself agreed with Stub, but Lyndon prevailed. What Lyndon wanted was for Donald Cook to do his work for him, to do really everything, to be an assistant to him. Lyndon was cute in those days. He wanted, in effect, his own secretary, his own man with him.

Well, from the beginning, I won't say there was animosity, but there was a lack of enthusiasm for Cook. But before that trip ended we were all Cook men. He turned out to be one of the finest young men I had ever met, a real fine person. He later turned down an offer to be secretary of the treasury. When he came back from Europe, Lyndon made him a special aide to Tom Clark. And he was alien property custodian at one time. Today, Don Cook is one of the most highly respected public utility executives in the country.

When we were in Paris Lyndon received a letter from Tom Clark. He showed it to me at the time. Clark told Lyndon that Truman had called him in and told him that he was going to name him attorney general and he got so excited he walked through a plate-glass door in the White House.

Anyway, it turned out that everybody had aides but Hess and myself. When we got to England, Mike Bradley picked up his son who was in the service, and when we got to Paris, Stub picked up a young Navy lieutenant for his aide. One night we had dinner at the Royal Monceau, and Admiral Alan Kirk, who later became ambassador to Russia, was with us. Hess and I were complaining we had no aides. The admiral said to pick an aide and he would assign him to us. We said we wanted the boatswain's mate who had been driving us around. The admiral wrote orders and Hess and I ended up with the boatswain's mate as our aide.

The next morning we got to the airplane and Ramsey, who was a very proper officer, looked at the boatswain's mate and said, "What in the hell are you doing here?"

The boatswain's mate said, "I'm the aide to Congressmen Hess and Hébert." And he got on the plane and went to Bremen with us. By the time we came back I had Leander Perez, Jr., summoned by Eisenhower to Paris and he became my aide. We all had aides. There were more aides than members of Congress.

During the whole trip Lyndon was very gracious and extremely friendly. He liked to be friendly. I'll never forget him telling me about little personal things, like the fact that he always wore expensive suits. In those days his suits cost $200. Lady Bird's mother had money. I think she gave them the house they lived in at that time.

Lyndon knew all the big men. There was no doubt about it. He knew everybody who was a big shot. For instance, he knew Lucius Clay, who was with Eisenhower. We went to see Eisenhower in that "little red school house." Here we were in a room in the school house with no more than twelve people in it, and in that room were two future presidents of the United States. Now, who would have thought something like that—two future presidents of the United States in a schoolroom in France?

When we went to Scotland, I had a letter from Frank Quinn, who was the distributor in New Orleans for Grant's Scotch. The distillery was in Glasgow, right in front of the railroad station. Lyndon and I took this letter and went to the distillery. We went up a rickety staircase, and an old man with glasses on and another fellow were in there. I showed them the letter and right away they pulled out a bottle and gave us a slug. Then the younger boy blurted out to the old man, "Boy, get them a case."

Lyndon looked at me and said, ''How old do the boys grow around here?'' Anyway, we got the case of scotch and toted it downstairs and put it in our car. We were traveling to Edinburgh to spend the night. You never saw such a bunch of characters. We had a caravan of three cars. This was when the elections were in progress. We stopped along the way and talked to the people on the highways and byways of Scotland and then we'd take another slug.

When we finally got to a lodge on Loch Lomond we were a rare bunch of soused Americans. I mean we were having a good time. We walked into this little Scottish lounge. It was the most severe place in the world. All these Scots were sitting there reading the papers and in comes this group of boisterous Americans. The Scots would take their papers down and look at us and then put their papers back up and whisper something to each other. We didn't know what they were saying, but it must have been that we were outrageous cowboys from the Wild West of America. We nevertheless had a good time. When we finally got to Edinburgh, we wouldn't give the fellow at the hotel any information on ourselves. We were just being difficult. We had our liquor. I brought one of those bottles to Ray Hufft, who was in the hospital right outside Paris. Of course, in Paris you could get all the liquor you wanted. The Germans had confiscated it from the French, and the Americans took it from the Germans. Lyndon had it all— Benedictine, and all those high-class French liqueurs. I still have a bottle of that Benedictine at home.

In Bremen I had the most interesting conversation I ever had with Lyndon. We were quartered in the only standing mansion, and it was a mansion. Lyndon and I had cots. We were the only two in the library and we had a bottle between our cots. We would sip a little and talk. Lyndon was very pleasant, and very outspoken. He told me about his association with Roosevelt.

Lyndon substantiated to me that when Roosevelt came to New Orleans in 1936, on his way to Texas where he supposedly was going to fish, he was in reality going down to see Lyndon Johnson, who had just been elected to Congress.

Lyndon thought Roosevelt was the greatest guy who ever lived. Lyndon said that one day he was at the White House and Jesse Jones came in. He was head of the Reconstruction Finance Corporation and secretary of commerce at the same time. He wouldn't give up either job. He was a very independent Texan. The President told Lyndon to go in the outer office and wait because "I've gotta see God." Jones is the subject of a book by Bascom Timmons.

Lyndon told me how much he had learned from Roosevelt. It was plain that he basked in his reflection. Looking back it is plain to see that if Lyndon had opportunistic tendencies it was in the way he cultivated powerful friendships. After all, the President of the United States can make or break a person. Who is not going to cultivate the man? No one can fault a person for that. But Lyndon definitely took the President's position into consideration.

In Paris we all went to the Follies Bergère, and Congressman James Wadsworth of New York accompanied us. He had been a United States senator and later served in the House. He would have been President of the United States had it not been for Prohibition. Wadsworth was perhaps one of the most highly respected men I have ever met, a truly fine person. His son-in-law, Senator Stuart W. Symington of Missouri, is an old and dear friend of mine.

We were sitting in the front row in those big leather chairs, which are a big thing at the Follies. All one has to do, which is quite enough, is look around, smoke, drink, and watch the show—look at the nude women, which is about all they've got.

We saw the sights, and Lyndon was always enjoying them. I went back there later with Mendel Rivers and we had a box seat. They had a Negro singing "Sonny Boy" to a little angel that was black, and Rivers, who of course was from South Carolina, said, "Jesus Christ, let me get out of here. They're gonna have Christ black next." The worst thing about the whole affair was that the singer was way off key.

After Paris, we went on down to Rome and saw the Pope. That was the first time I saw Pius. When we were preparing for the audience, Lyndon looked at me and said, "You left-handed Catholic, you can't be chairman of the Pope's committee. We have to make Bradley chairman. He's a real Catholic."

I told Lyndon, "Just be careful you don't bite the Pope's ring, old buddy."

He made Bradley the chairman and we went in to see Pius, and I looked around and thought sure Johnson had taken that ring off. But by that time he had genuflected behind the Catholics.

After our trip, I had a big reunion of the group at my home. And later, when Lyndon went to the Senate, I had contact with him because we were in the same field; I was named chairman of the Armed Forces investigating committee and he was chairman of the Senate investigating committee.

Lyndon, of course, was a big conservative in the House. He was a real Texan, a political philosopher. He opposed all the civil rights bills—as the voting records will show only at that time they weren't labeled civil rights bills. The first indication I had that he was switching his political stance came during his early days in the Senate. I was making radio reports from Washington at the time and I noted in one of them that I was very sorry about Lyndon's changing position. I had always felt very kindly toward Lyndon, I really liked him, but this whole business took me aback. It was a shock to see that he could so completely alter his political philosophy. I heard from somebody who was in a position to know who said, "Well, if that is what he wants to do to be President," and then shook his head.

Lyndon then became leader of the Senate. Dick Russell, of course, should have been the leader, because Dick Russell was the real boss of the Senate. But Dick, being as knowledgeable as he was and being as resourceful as he was, realized the situation he would find himself in as a Southerner. He is the one who maneuvered Lyndon into the leadership. But Lyndon was already out in left field as far as I was concerned. I couldn't go along with him any longer.

Still we remained on a first-name basis, and the nights at the White House remained very pleasant. I have had the best times at the White House when Lyndon was President. Until then I never really enjoyed going to the executive mansion. Lyndon had those bars running like booze-was-going-out-of-style-tomorrow-and-we-were-going-to-dump-it-all-in-because-Prohibition-is-coming-back. His gatherings were usually informal things. He was a master in that area. He conned all these characters around there, and it was interesting to see him in operation. For instance, he would get about forty or fifty members of Congress, sprinkle in about ten freshmen, and then have McNamara and Rusk there. Everybody would have all the drinks they wanted and would usually be in a very relaxed mood. It was a very folksy atmosphere. Then Lyndon would start talking; soon Rusk and McNamara would chime in, and finally Lyndon would say, "Well, Bob, I'll field that one." That meant no one else was going to have a chance to talk the rest of the night. Lyndon had taken over. He would survey the crowd, spot a freshman congressman, and address his remarks to him. Well, the freshman would be ecstatic. Imagine, the President of the United States talking to a freshman congressman. And Johnson was convincing. He was the greatest salesman in the world.

If someone didn't agree with Lyndon, he would break him down. He could be very persuasive; he could also be very mean. Personally, he never called to ask me anything—maybe because he knew I couldn't be had, and he probably knew what I would say.

One of the first parties he had at the White House, I happened to be walking up the corridor with him and we both had a drink. I was griping about McNamara's handling of my home Eighth Naval District. We were practically in a corner together, as sometimes happens when the crowd just falls away, and I said, "Listen, keep that goddamn McNamara off my district, off the Eighth Naval District."

He said, "Oh, I can't do anything with that Republican. He wants to save money."

I said, "That's not saving money. That's not economy, not what he's doing."

Lyndon said, "He will convince you."

I just looked him right in the eye and said, "Bullshit." He just shook his head, and that was all there was to it. Of course he understood that language.

Another time we had sort of a conference before Lyndon sent the troops into Santo Domingo. He was giving us the business. He had the key men there that morning, a very small group, ten or fifteen men from the proper committees, that's all. He gave us his five alternatives, but he didn't say what he was going to do. So I said, "Mr. President, you have given us all these alternatives. What are you going to do? You don't mean to tell me you haven't made up your mind yet? You don't want us to believe you haven't made up your mind?''

He said, ''Yes.''

I said, ''When are you going to make it up?'' This is about 11 o'clock or 11:15 in the morning. He said, ''I will announce it on the air this afternoon.''

''And now you haven't made up your mind?'' I said.

''Nobody is going to beat me to my news,'' he said.

This, I think, is an indication of how sensitive he was. When the crowd broke up, I said, ''I was trying to help you.''

He said, ''I know you were. You did a good job, too.''

One night we were at a party over at the White House and Lady Bird, as was her custom, took all the ladies upstairs. Under other presidents very few people went above the first floor. Eisenhower had us there a couple of times. I was up there with E. A. Stephens and Harry Hopkins when Roosevelt was in—when I first went to Washington, before I went to Congress, as a matter of fact. Those were the only times I had ever been on the second floor of the White House, but Lady Bird took everybody up there. Gladys tells me that Lady Bird is a most gracious person. That was always true, whenever receiving, the Johnsons were just as gracious as could be. They always had a personal word to say to Gladys and me. One time Lady Bird took Gladys aside and said, ''I have just been looking at some pictures of the old days.'' But that was a con game. I have that picture of Lady Bird, Lyndon, Gladys and myself in my office, but it is not exclusive. Every member of Congress has a similar picture.

That night at the White House, Lady Bird had all the women upstairs and when they started back down, Lady Bird said, ''If you want to use the 'john,' it's over there.'' So the ladies got in line and Gladys said, ''Oh, I can't wait that long, I'm going downstairs.'' The woman in front of her said, ''Well, I don't have to go, I just want to see what it looks like.'' Now, what in the hell does a presidential ''john'' look like, but a ''john?''

When Gladys came down, Lyndon was just coming into the room

and he grabbed her and they danced. The next day somebody called from the *New York Times* and asked Gladys how she enjoyed dancing with the President, because this was the new Johnson treatment.

Well, of course, it was Liz Carpenter who gave the *Times* our name, knowing we were both friendly with the Johnsons and naturally we would say only good things about them. When they asked Gladys what was the topic of discussion at the White House, she said, "You'd better ask my husband." I wonder what the *Times'* reaction would have been had she repeated the conversation.

The last time I saw Lyndon at the White House was one morning when I went there for some affair. I would come and go so often, I have forgotten the particular reason. I don't even go over anymore for the signing of bills and things like that. The hell with it. I mean, what for? The President just comes in and signs a bill. But the last time I saw him as president was after the Gridiron Dinner when Russell Long had been putting the needle in Bobby Kennedy, a deep needle. And the whole time Russell was speaking, Lyndon was saying, "You going good, Russell. You going good." And Russell was giving Bobby Kennedy hell. When I saw Lyndon a day or two later, he said, "How'd you like Russell the other night?"

I have an opinion of Lyndon's relation with Sam Rayburn which has no foundation except general conversation. I believe Rayburn very deeply in his heart resented Lyndon's climb. Lyndon was a protégé of Rayburn's, and, of course, they had the San Francisco convention rigged where Hale Boggs was to become chairman and Lyndon was to be nominated. Kennedy beat them to the punch. Rayburn didn't want Lyndon to take the vice-presidency. I always had a feeling that Rayburn saw in Lyndon that which he wanted to be and never became. And that would start with the vice-presidency. I had an interview with Rayburn (when I was doing the radio interview broadcasts from Washington) in which I asked Sam about his availability for the vice-presidency under Roosevelt. We had discussed it before we went on the air and Sam said for me to ask him about it. And during the convention he waited in a hotel room in Chicago for a call to come from Roosevelt, asking him to run as vice-president. When the call did come, it was Roosevelt asking for nominations for Henry Wallace. That was a shock. This opinion of Rayburn's jealousy of Lyndon of course, is without foundation, but I've always had the feeling.

Sam was a fine opponent. I disagreed with a lot of things he did. He was an opportunist. He was expedient, but he was a strong man. No doubt, the greatest speaker that we have ever had in Congress. We had our disagreements, but I admired him. I will never forget one thing he said. One day we were sitting in his little private office. I think Congressman Overton Brooks was there, but I don't remember the occasion. I think the governor of Louisiana, Jimmie Davis, was also there, as well as someone from Alabama. Sam was talking about potential presidential candidates and mentioned Governor Robert Meyner of New Jersey. Someone said, "How about Jack Kennedy?" I'll never forget Sam's reply: "Jack Kennedy will always be a little boy to me." Later, of course, events pitted Lyndon against Kennedy and Kennedy won. Rayburn, being the loyal party man that he was, was loyal to Kennedy. But I could never get over the feeling that Rayburn resented Johnson's climb. Lyndon was a pretty fast operator. He saw early what Sam Rayburn had, and Lyndon had Roosevelt's support. He was able to walk in the shadow of both men, and they cast big shadows. Lyndon took advantage of that. I think Lyndon was a consummate politician.

The last time I saw him was shortly before his death. It was at the Presbytère, adjacent to St. Louis Cathedral in New Orleans, the day of the memorial services for Hale Boggs (who was lost in an airplane crash in Alaska).

Colonel Heywood Smith of the Marines, who had been a very influential aide to Lyndon when he was President, came over and told me the President wanted to see me. I walked over to where Lyndon was standing with Lady Bird.

Joking with him, I said, "Why do you want to see me?"

"Because I love you," he said, "and I want you to tell Carl Vinson something. I understand the old man has criticized my long hair. Tell him I don't go to Warner Robins [Air Force Base] to get my hair cut for nothing [alluding to Vinson]. Tell him I have to drive twenty-five miles and I pay for it."

I never saw or talked to Lyndon Johnson again.

CHAPTER XIV

THEN I WAS A POLITICIAN

Before 1945 ENDED, my concerns shrank from global politics to the equally intriguing stratagems of politics New Orleans style. There were two political races to be decided in 1946 which particularly interested me: the mayoralty election in the Crescent City and the balloting in which the voters of Louisiana's First Congressional District would select me or my successor.

Mayor Robert S. Maestri also had more than a passing interest in the elections, and near the end of 1945 I had him in Washington lobbying for federal programs for New Orleans and paying court to President Harry S Truman. Maestri told Truman the Old Regulars had supported his selection as vice-president in 1944 and would back him for the Democratic presidential nomination in 1948, intelligence which must have mollified an anxious chief executive.

New Orleans was abuzz with politics. Before the first month of the new year was over, on January 22, 1946, the mayor's race would be decided, and I, whose election would not be contested until September, was well aware that Maestri's fate would have a definite effect on my own political well-being. Despite having gone into politics as a reformer, I was by now an easily identifiable Old Regular. After being pushed into the Old Regular's camp by my former employers at the newspaper, I had become an important figure in the organization, even though I did not attempt to make policy or wield power. I represented "class"; that is to say I was literate and could speak in public. (The late newspaper columnist and personality, Dorothy Kilgallen, named me, along with other orators such as

Everett McKinley Dirksen, as one of the ten best speakers in Congress.) Moreover, I had also received excellent press nationally, for the most part, and was respected among my peers in Washington. With credentials such as these, I felt sure I could sway a certain number of votes.

The anti-Old Regulars, or Reformers, as they liked to be known, were hoping to mount a serious challenge to the Old Regulars' hold on the city, a grasp which was personified in Maestri. The mayor was considered the stereotype of big-city "bossism," a largely uneducated but very cunning Grand Sachem. In an article written the day Maestri died in 1974, Jim Gillis, an astute *Times-Picayune* political reporter, stated:

> Lack of book learning notwithstanding, Maestri was a highly intelligent man, with sharp business acumen, a shrewd sense of the value of money, particularly as it related to real estate, and a lively wit.
>
> Among large groups of people, he was basically a rather shy man. However, in the company of a few he became an extrovert capable of sharp repartee often interspersed with salty phraseology.

There is no doubt that Maestri was one of the wittiest men I have ever known. It was actually a satiric wit which spotlighted the truth of a situation rather than the joke which provoked the belly laugh. He once told Gillis that a certain unpleasant city official had "a woman." That could be said about many people, Gillis replied. "I know," Maestri said, "but can you understand what a woman could see in him."

The Reformers didn't find Maestri in office particularly humorous and, as the election approached, they sought a candidate whom they felt could seriously challenge the powerful mayor. They searched high and low, and the latter is where some say they came up with their candidate, J. O. "Bathtub Joe" Fernandez, the Longite I had unseated in 1940 and defeated thereafter. Fernandez being put forward as a reformist candidate almost defies imagination, but clearly demonstrates how silly politics was in New Orleans. It was not only a ridiculous thing to do, but it almost proved disastrous for the Reformers. The Old Regulars, it was charged, made a deal with Fernandez to withdraw from the race. As I understand it, Fernandez was to wait until the deadline for qualifying and then announce he had withdrawn from the race, and that would leave the Reformers without a qualified candidate. Instead, he announced five days ahead of time. I have no evidence of this plan, except for what I have been told, but there was an alleged pay-off. Frank Ellis (a judge who was later named to the federal bench) was supposed to have handled the pay-off. I got a call from Jim Comiskey (a powerful Old Regular ward leader). He told me Fernandez had withdrawn. My reaction was, "You should pay him to stay in. He is the one man Bob [Maestri] could beat."

After withdrawing from the mayor's race, "Reformer" Fernandez pulled a complete flip-flop, publically announcing his "unqualified support" for Maestri. Based on past performance it was the only support he had to offer.

Obviously, when Fernandez withdrew, the Reformers were frantic. They were searching for a candidate. On Sunday afternoon Jack Tims was at the New Orleans Country Club. The papers didn't have a candidate. The Reformers had no candidate when suddenly a fine-looking army colonel walked into the club. He was in uniform, having just arrived in the city from Camp Shelby, Mississippi, where he was stationed. Jack looked at him and said, "There is my candidate—a young hero."

Tims, later publisher of the *Times-Picayune*, liked to think of himself as a kingmaker, and, to a great extent, he was. The day after he saw Morrison he told Mr. Leonard Nicholson (the owner of the paper), "I got a candidate for you."

DeLesseps S. Morrison had been elected to the state legislature before joining the army and serving with distinction in Europe. He was reelected in absentia while on active duty, as were a number of other legislators. Instead of their presence, a small American flag flew on the desk, at the state capitol.

When the Reformers got Chep in the race nobody thought he had a chance. I certainly did not think he could win. As a result, with this attitude of overconfidence, the Old Regulars failed to unite their forces; and while the Reformers didn't have the political savvy of the machine, they had practically lucked into the best of all possible candidates. Handsome, intelligent and charming, deLesseps Morrison also had a successful politician's instincts. In addition, the newspapers unflaggingly supported Morrison as a God-sent saviour while characterizing Maestri as a dictator and a failure as an administrator. There were few ideological or philosophical differences between the candidates. Style and reputation were the main distinctions.

While Maestri had faults aplenty, he also had been faced with legitimate problems, the same problems which had beset other mayors as the result of wartime economics. However, when Maestri mentioned the difficulties resulting from the war, the newspapers reported his speeches satirically, saying he was still blaming everything on the war. But Maestri, the shrewd politician, knew how to fight fire with fire. That was where I came in. In that campaign I was perhaps more deeply involved than anybody except Maestri. I wrote everything Maestri said. I was his ghost writer. The papers were fighting Maestri and me and giving us a bad time. Of course, Maestri was answering them, and they didn't have to read beyond the first line to know who was writing the copy.

Before the Young Men's Business Club, Maestri read a typical Hébert-prepared speech:

> The newspapers, which admit they know all about everything, were curtailed during the war. Their newsprint was cut down, their circulation held down, their advertising held down, and their staffs depleted. If such perfect institutions as newspapers cannot function at top efficiency during wartime, how can we ordinary, imperfect human beings accomplish what these admitted supermen cannot accomplish?

The newspapers reacted to my ghosting of Maestri's material as if no other politician ever employed a speech writer. Admittedly, it was unusual for a mayoral candidate's speech writer to be an incumbent congressman, but the newspaper reports of Maestri's campaign speeches were unusual also. Generally, news stories do not begin with the information that someone other than the speaker wrote the speech, as did one story in the *States*.

Ghost writers haunted Mayor Robert S. Maestri near the end of his political campaign address before a Mid-City rally last night and the mayor had to leave the speaker's spot before he could finish reading his speech.

The mayor had been speaking about 20 minutes when he began to falter while reviewing his platform promises. Suddenly he declared that time was running short, and that he would again come before the public, either on the air or at ward rallies, to discuss his program.

That was also the night Jim Comiskey introduced me right out of the blue. He called on me to close the meeting. Well, once I was on that platform, once I was on stage, I was up there for keeps. It wasn't going to be a second-rate performance. I decided to pull out all the stops, and made one of those hell-raising speeches, a real cheerleader speech, one of those rousing closing speeches.

When we left that night Maestri and I went to District Attorney Jimmy O'Connor's house. Vic Bono was the driver. When we got out to Jimmy's house, I told Maestri to go on in, I would wait in the car. I didn't want to see a thing. I didn't want to know what they were talking about. It was none of my business. I did not want to be involved in all this political maneuvering. Here was the district attorney and the mayor politicking, and that was all right by me. My job was in Washington and I didn't want to be a power down here.

Anyway, Maestri went in for fifteen or twenty minutes and when he came out he was very happy. He had accomplished what he wanted to accomplish. He had come to an agreement on whatever it was he wanted. We were riding down Canal Street and when we passed Sacred Heart Hall, where the rally had taken place, Maestri said, "You see that bullshit you threw in there tonight, that's your racket. What I did out there at O'Connor's, that's my racket. That's where I shine."

From that night onward, I got deeply involved in the campaign. I would always close the meetings. When someone would tell the crowd they were going to hear from their congressman, I was their congressman, regardless of whether they lived in the First or Second District. Mr. Paul Maloney, being the gentleman that he was and everything, didn't participate in all this stuff. But one night we went up to the Mater Dolorosa auditorium. There was a meeting up there, and, of course, the crowd would always anticipate my introduction. I would always color it up, give a rousing speech, and they would go wild when I made my pitch.

Anyway, we were on the platform at Mater Dolorosa, which is in the Second District, at the time Paul Maloney's district. Bob Elliot, Maestri's co-campaign manager, was the master of ceremonies, and he began to give this great build-up, a terrific build-up about the congressman, and we are in Maloney's district. The crowd was beginning to cheer and Maestri leaned over to me and said, "They think they're getting you." When Elliot finally said, "Your Congressman, Paul Maloney," the crowd went, "Aaaah." I felt sorry for Maloney; it wasn't his fault.

While Maestri was the main target of the newspapers during the campaign, they also indulged in the practice of killing two birds with one stone by attacking me. A picture of me seated on a campaign stage with Maestri appeared in the *States*. Under the photo was a story headlined: "Won't Go To Congress Until After Election, Says Hebert." The story cited legislation being considered in Washington by the Naval Affairs Committee, saying that "all [of the bills being considered] are important."

It would, of course, have been more newsworthy if Vinson had said, "None of them are important," but the *States* knew what Vinson's reaction would be when the question was asked. The paper also knew what reflection his answer would cast on me; and while it is a newspaper's prerogative to report on the activities of a congressman, it is doubtful the *States* would have shown as much enterprise if I had been in New Orleans campaigning for Morrison.

This particular exercise in the freedom of the press wasn't the work of Major Crown. That fiery character had quelched some of his flames, made his peace with God and his wife—if not with evildoers—and died with his boots on, still the fire-and-brimstone editor of the *New Orleans States*. The major was replaced by William (Billy) Fitzpatrick, who proved to be a worthy successor, a wild character in Crown's mold, with the exception that he was slim and attractive where Crown had been portly and homely. Once, when the *States* was conducting a campaign against nudity in the Bourbon

Street strip joints, Fitzpatrick took some out-of-town newspaper friends on a drinking tour of the French Quarter. Anxious to please his guests, Fitzpatrick made the rounds and enjoyed the evening to the point where he was arrested for disturbing the peace. He printed the story on page one of the *States* and identified himself. Later, Fitzpatrick would win what the *States* deserved on a previous occasion, the Pulitzer Prize.

Fitzpatrick, aware that I didn't relish being referred to as Felix, began calling me Felix Edward Hébert in print. As my campaign approached, it became Felix Hébert and eventually Felix. Our first big brawl erupted as a verbal spitting contest in the form of a series of letters. Ostensibly, the letters were an exchange between Fitzpatrick and Maestri, but of course I was writing for the mayor. The letters, which will never be set forth as models of decorum or rectitude on the part of either party, received an inordinate amount of newspaper space for their importance. Their main value was entertainment. The first one was sparked by a Fitzpatrick editorial asking Maestri "Where the Money Went?" This brought an exchange of correspondence which remained unpublicized until I mentioned the letters in a campaign speech. Then Fitzpatrick struck back editorially "[Hébert] did not dare read the letters at the meeting for reasons which will become apparent when you look them over," Fitzpatrick wrote, and then he printed the letters.

What is apparent to some isn't apparent to all. In the first letter, writing under Maestri's signature, I said the question of "where the money went?" would be answered if he could be assured the reply would be published "unaltered and unchanged, in the same spot in your newspaper, with the same display in size, type and makeup as you gave your editorial." If there was any doubt who was writing the letter for Maestri, the technical knowledge of newspapering evidenced in that epistle dispelled it.

Fitzpatrick replied that "your inferences of unfair tactics are just a smokescreen on the political horizon, and nothing more." Nevertheless, he concluded, "We shall be glad to publish your answer, on your dictated terms, and we agree to all of them, provided, Mayor Maestri, that your answer is factual and truthful. . . ."

Hébert/Maestri replied:

I am sure that the people of New Orleans, who have been reading
the colored, distorted, slanted, purported news stories, can judge for
themselves whether or not your veracity or mine shall be challenged.

Unlike your newspaper, I do not make a practice of making
misstatements, misrepresentations, and uttering untruths. All I want to
know is simply this: Will you or will you not publish my reply in your
editorial, which appeared on Page 1, in your edition of January 11, in
the same place and position as your editorial?

You can answer that "yes" or "no" without attempting to evade
the issue by confusing verbiage. I will appreciate it very much if you
will reply directly. I only want a simple answer, that is all.

Fitzpatrick's reply was equally sarcastic. It cited unsubstantiated
allegations of wrongdoing by Maestri and said, in effect, that if the
mayor would answer truthfully whether he was still beating his wife,
then the newspaper could comply with his demands for printing the
letter. "I have tried to make this letter simple enough, and trust you
will find it so," Fitzpatrick concluded.

I wrote back: "Obviously, I cannot expect an honest, forthright,
straightforward reply from you in connection with the request contained in my letter directed to you on January 11."

The exchange of letters ceased a day or two before the election
without Maestri being given the space and display he wanted, and
without him answering the questions of the newspaper.

Meanwhile, Maestri's opponent, Morrison, was campaigning
hard. Among his foremost supporters were a large number of women
who formed symbolic "broom brigades" to "sweep the city clean."
Things began to look bad for the incumbent who had appeared
unbeatable only a short time before.

Everything went wrong. The Old Regulars did not fight, except
among themselves. They had a fight over who would be criminal
sheriff; Comiskey had a fist fight about it with Joe Skelly, a member
of the Commission Council, one night at Martin Burke's place.

Nobody figured how strong Johnny Grosch was at the time. Maestri ignored Grosch. I surely have no idea why, but he did, and it really
fouled up the campaign. Grosch had been Maestri's chief of detec-

tives and was an extremely efficient solver of crime, although his methods were sometimes questionable. In the election's post mortems, it was generally concluded that the women's organizations had defeated Maestri, but the mayor confided to reporter Gillis that the reason for his downfall was Grosch, who was elected criminal sheriff on Morrison's ticket after having been rejected by the Old Regulars.

"I don't know if you know it," Maestri told Gillis, "but that fella Grosch was raised in the river precincts of the twelfth and thirteenth wards. Now the lowest people in the world live in those precincts. In other elections those people voted for me. This time they voted for Grosch and they voted for Morrison."

On election day I knew something was wrong. Maestri and I rode together that day. Bob did not want to go to the places where we would have trouble. He wanted to go places where we were winning. But that is foolish. On election night, when the boxes came in, in a half hour I knew we were gone. We were winning in the early returns but not the way we should have been.

When it became evident that Morrison would be the new mayor, Maestri, Bob Elliot and I went out the back door at City Hall to get away from the newspaper guys, but there was a damn photographer right at the door. I told Maestri, "Damn it, smile, laugh!" Well, Maestri put on the biggest grin of his life. We were all laughing like we were overjoyed. We appeared happy. Hell! we felt terrible, but we all laughed. That night Morrison was quoted as saying that the two most surprised men in New Orleans were Maestri and himself. He was probably correct.

When Elliot and I dropped Maestri off that election night the last word we said to him was to give no statement to the press, under any circumstances, until the election results could be assessed. After leaving Maestri, Elliot and I parted company, Elliot went to meet some acquaintances and I dropped by one of my stop-off places. Despite my disappointment at the election results I couldn't resist a joke. I telephoned Elliot:

"Didn't we tell Maestri not to give any statements to the papers?"

"Yeah," Elliot replied.

"Well, he did."

"Oh my God, what'd he say?''

"He said, 'Them broads beat me.' ''

The statement was so in character that it spread across town as gospel.

With the election of Morrison and other reform candidates marking the beginning of the end of the Old Regulars, I recognized the difficulties I would face in the Democratic primary in September. The newspapers were predicting, or, more specifically, urging a total victory by the reform forces that would "complete the job" begun by Morrison in January. *Times-Picayune* humorist Pete Baird suggested I retitle my European diary "I Came, I Went, I'm a Goner." But to paraphrase Mark Twain, reports of my political demise proved to be greatly exaggerated.

Despite the growing pressure in New Orleans, I had work to do in Washington. Representative John McMillan of South Carolina, the chairman of the District of Columbia Committee, selected me to head a subcommittee to investigate the scandal-racked Washington, D.C. jails. The probe was sparked by a well-publicized jail break in which two condemned murderers escaped from death row after incarcerating the guards with whom they had been playing poker. One revelation led to another and the capital's newspapers headlined the exposés: "Safecracker Masterminded Jobs While In Jail," "Gill Calls Jail Life One Orgy After Another—Beautiful Models, Gambling, Drinking Figure in Testimony," "Deputy Warden Named as Grafter," and so on. I got into action, grilling every prison official and many of the system's employees. I almost walked the legs off the committee members, dragging them down every corridor of the capital's jails.

I concluded that the problems in supervising the penal system resulted from "an octopus of divided responsibility." The penal institutions were administered by three agencies—the Metropolitan Police, the Board of Public Welfare, and the Civil Service Commission, which was appointed by the Congress as a quasi-city council to the District.

During the investigations I questioned one of the commissioners about whether Welfare Board members were required to have expe-

rience in penal matters. I found out they were not. "Then as I
understand it," I observed, "a person could go down to the local
sewing circle and pick nine well-meaning ladies and put them on the
Welfare Board. Then they would have complete control of the District Jail?" The commissioner nodded his head.

Before the subcommittee was through—and it wasn't long, less
than one month—it had pinpointed the problems and cited solutions
to them. The committee recommended a sweeping reorganization of
the entire penal system and the replacement of all prison officials. In
addition, it placed much of the blame for the squalid situation
squarely at the feet of Congress itself. As the *Times-Herald* aptly put
it in a banner headline: "Jail Report Raps Everybody." Editorially
the newspaper said, "Thanks are due to the House subcommittee
headed by Representative F. Edward Hebert (D. of Louisiana) for its
prompt and convincing report in what should be done with the D.C.
Jails."

The *Washington Post* wrote: "We owe an apology to the Hebert
Committee. On the eve of its inquiry into the District Jail imbroglio
we said it was safe to predict that the committee would not probe into
'the shocking negligence of Congress itself in this matter.' We
misjudged its temper, for the committee has done precisely that."

As a result of the probe, I introduced a bill into Congress establishing a new department of corrections under the direct control of the
District commissioners, and withdrawing control of penal institutions
from any supervision of the Welfare Board. After the measure passed
Congress, President Truman invited me to witness his signature of the
bill into law.

Shortly after the prison investigation, I was selected to give a
Memorial Day address to Congress. I used such opportunities to
express my true feelings. I've always thought of such events as
moments when a man can come face to face with himself. I called on
my colleagues to steer a course between the rock of "a liberty of
indifference" on the one hand and "totalitarianism" on the other. I
elaborated on this point with reasoning which was certainly foreign to
a so-called rock-ribbed conservative, as I am frequently labeled.

On one side there is the dangerous rock of Scylla. It has often been camouflaged as Liberty, but we must know that it is a liberty of indifference—indifference to truth, indifference to justice, and more than all else, indifference to the social good. It is an alleged vaunted right of the individual to say, to do, or to think anything whatsoever he pleases—no matter who or what might suffer. It is based on the assumption that there is no absolute standard of right and wrong; it sets up the individual as the supreme authority; it regards all regulation of liberty as unwarranted and unjustifiable restraint. We need not look far to find the various manifestations of this dangerous Scylla.

We find it in the ideologies which maintain that there is no such thing as Truth—there is merely a point of view; and their profound reason for such philosophy is because each man is his own measure of what is truth or good.

We look to education and find it indoctrinating even the young with the principle that all discipline is a restriction of the individual's right of self-expression. We come to the political order and we find it assuming that the State has a merely negative function—that is, to protect the individual's rights. Finally, in the economic order, it argues that if individuals are left free to run their businesses as they please without any social interference on the part of government, the maximum good of all, will, in some miraculous way, be the outcome.

There were some who tried to avoid Scylla and they steered a course to Charybdis. They felt that in some way or other men had to be lifted out of their individual desires and brought to a regard for the good of all; some remedy had to be found to divert economic forces to the common good. Some means had to be invented to equalize inequalities and to recall an almost forgotten tie which bound men as brothers. And in looking for these avenues of escape they were dashed against the rocks of Charybdis.

They forgot that men were "yearning to breathe free." To them there opened but one course and that was to force them to live for the general welfare . . . On the rocks appeared the barnacles of dictatorship. Dazzled by siren calls they proclaimed if individuals cannot be responsible to the voice of conscience prompting them to recognize social responsibilities, if unity did not come from inside men, from their minds and their hearts and their souls, then it would be made to come from outside—through compulsion, through force, through dictatorship.

Can you see the ship freighted with the destinies of men, swaying
from one side, where the individual was called supreme to the other
where the State was crowned with the laurels of supremacy? There is
nothing surprising in that twist, for where there was no guardianship
over the mind and heart and soul of liberty, the principle that the strong
individual is permitted to devour the weak one will naturally lead to the
principle that the strong state may devour the weak one. So it was that
liberty began to take on a meaning which we emphatically refused to
accept or recognize—the liberty which Frederick Engels called ''The
liberty of necessity.'' We have heard it shouted from high balconies,
from crowded market places—''man is free when he acts according to
determined laws;'' man is free, so long as he obeys the will of the
dictator, and the dictator is always identified with the common good.
Men will have freedom to think, to will, to desire if they think and will
and desire what the dictator thinks and wills and desires; and thus the
''total man'' is absorbed by the State. Yes, the ''total man,'' body and
soul, and for that reason we have called this not liberty of necessity, but
Totalitarianism.

The point of these sentiments is not that I pretend to be ''a
statesman, or the saviour of the country, or anything like that,'' as
I have repeatedly stated, but I do, in private moments, think these
thoughts. Perhaps more than anything else, the fact that this country
has elected enough men who, despite their flaws, faults and foibles,
think similar thoughts, is the secret of American success. Despite
''cynicism,'' despite ''realism,'' and despite occasional callow acts,
the possession of a pristine spark of idealism can be redemptive. As I
noted in my Memorial Day address, ''American liberty is based on
the recognition that freedom is not merely a constitutional right, not
merely a natural right, nor a social right. It is, above all else, a
spiritual right.''

Not even Lincoln thought constantly in terms of the Gettysburg
Address, and for the next several months my speeches and writings
certainly would take a less lofty direction than the Memorial Day
address. Coming up was what would prove to be the toughest political
battle of my career. The *New Orleans States*, serving as an expedi-
tionary force, fired the first volley. It was in the form of the newspaper's lead editorial. Entitled ''Felix Now Wants a Pension,'' the

editorial was adjacent to a cartoon of a cat wearing eyeglasses. The cat was dubbed Felix Edward Hébert, and it was purring, "Me-I-I-I."

The editorial began: "We see by the Associated Press where Felix Edward Hebert . . . has voted to provide a pension for himself.

"Felix was the only congressman from either Louisiana or Mississippi to vote for the pension plan.

"You also might wonder why Felix Hebert is so anxious to get fixed up with a pension. Sometimes we wonder why, too. Can it be he thinks maybe he will not be returned to Washington next fall? Could be."

The editorial explained the "Me-I-I-I" purring: "We try to keep our cartoons as true to character as we can, and everyone who knows Felix Hebert knows that his favorite noises are 'Me' and 'I'." It continued in the same classy vein and ended by dubbing me "Felix 'Pension Me' Hebert."

If they wanted it rough and tumble, and no holds barred, they selected the right opponent for a protracted battle. I loved it.

Editor, *New Orleans States*:

If you will get your head up out of the gutter of distortion for just a few minutes and stand up in front of me at a safe distance so you won't spoil my clothes, I will give you a little lesson in truth.

You poor, pitiful character. Don't you know that no pension bill in any manner, shape or form has been voted on by the 79th Congress? Your editorial entitled, "Felix Now wants a Pension" is typical of your ignorance, for which you can be excused, but not for your malicious misrepresentation which is so sordid and venal. Let me state here and now that I did not, nor did any other member of Congress vote FOR or AGAINST any pension. The vote which you describe as "a pension plan defeated 217 to 113," was not a vote on the "pension" at all. It was a vote on what is called in Congress "The Rule."

Since you have not taken the trouble to find out, (or have again deliberately lied) when you vote for a rule, which is what I voted for, you vote to bring a bill before the House for consideration. In other words, voting against a rule is a parliamentary maneuver. Therefore, every member of Congress who voted against adopting the rule . . . voted not to consider the so-called Pension Bill. Whereas the 113 who voted in favor of the rule voted to let the bill come up before the House and either be accepted or rejected on its own weight.

Of course, I can easily understand that you would condone voting in favor of refusing to allow the consideration of any subject on its merits. That is obviously your saffron-hued policy of procedure which is constantly being demonstrated.

In a more commanding space on the same page, Fitzpatrick struck back editorially. He admitted that I was technically correct in pointing out that I voted on a resolution to consider the bill and not the bill itself. However, he stacked the deck by citing quotations from other Louisiana and Mississippi congressmen in which they said they considered that by voting against the resolution they were voting against the pension.

"That mass of evidence," the editorial concluded, "gives lie to Representative Hébert's statements quoted herein. Those six men were opposed to the bill and they voted then and there to kill it. HE WAS THE ONLY CONGRESSMAN FROM LOUISIANA OR MISSISSIPPI TO VOTE THAT WAY."

In reality it was an insignificant, trivial matter and probably wouldn't have come up in the first place if Fitzpatrick had had anything better to do the day he wrote the first editorial. But now war had been declared. I lost no time in rallying support from the congressmen who were quoted in the editorial. All backed me and said their statements either had been taken out of context or misconstrued. James Domengeaux, of the Third Congressional District, admitted he did consider that by voting against the resolution he was voting against the bill. But, he added, "this is only part of the statement which I gave. What I told your Washington correspondent was '. . .a vote for the rule would not necessarily mean a vote for the pension.' I know many members of Congress who follow the practice of always voting for a rule because in doing so they consider that legislation should always be given the opportunity of being argued and discussed by the House as a whole. Obviously, neither Mr. Hébert nor any member who voted for the rule in this instance can be said to have voted himself a pension."

Dan McGehee of Mississippi was blunt: "Fitzpatrick, I have read

Hébert's letter to you which you quoted along with the editorial, and he is absolutely correct in his statement, and I am sure that every member of Congress will bear me out in the interpretation that he gave you, and that which I tried to convey to you over the phone."

That was the end of it, right? Wrong. I had an issue and I intended to make the most of it. I placed an ad in the newspaper which asked in bold, black print, "WHO LIED? Listen to Congressman F. Edward Hebert tonight. WNOE 7:30 p.m."

I was at my acerbic best and, after some preliminaries, I got to the point.

> During recent weeks, the *New Orleans States* has seen fit to deliberately lie and misrepresent, as well as distort, my public record.
>
> I use the word "deliberately" advisedly because after the true facts were made known to them and they cringed under the lash of truth, this Ananias not only repeated his venal lie, but brought to the witness stand, through trickery, six of my colleagues in the Congress of the United States, in a vain effort to persuade unsuspecting readers that the lie fell to me rather than to the editor of the *New Orleans States*.
>
> Tonight, I ask, Who Lied?
>
> And I shall unravel as the minutes pass, irrefutable documentary evidence of the malpractice of the editor of the *New Orleans States* insofar as I am concerned, because I refused to take political dictation from this newspaper. I shall attempt to present the case impassionately, without histrionics or oratory. The facts which I am about to present speak more eloquently than any phrase I could possibly put together. Tonight I shall take this editor apart bit by bit and then let you, who are good enough to listen to me present my case, decide who lied.

I attacked the paper for saying the Associated Press reported I voted for a pension, when, in fact, it did not, and I chastised the paper for misrepresenting the statements of the six congressmen. I went on and on, building my case, citing delays by Fitzpatrick in publishing the letters from the congressmen and challenging the use made of the letters.

> And why were they published two weeks after the editorial appeared and NOT when they were received?
>
> That's an easy question to answer.

The editor of the *New Orleans States* never had any intention to publish any of the letters—he never had any intention until he learned that I was going to make this radio broadcast tonight.

Chills went up and down his spine when he learned the question I was going to ask tonight.

Who lied?

He knew who lied and he immediately decided it was time to again try and explain away the truth and take a long shot at preventing my broadcast tonight.

I then read the six letters from the congressmen in their entirety, and cited a statement from Lewis Deschler, the parliamentarian of the House of Representatives, saying that I had not voted for the pension bill. With that I began the build-up for the curtain line.

Now, ladies and gentlemen, you have heard the evidence. You have been good to listen to me, and having listened and having heard the evidence, I ask you, WHO LIED?

As I leave you this evening, I leave you a vivid picture in your mind, I leave you the picture of a journalistic Rasputin seeking to cover a black heart with the armor of a Galahad. I leave you a picture of a knave posing as a knight, hanged by a rope of truth and dangling on a gallows of public scorn and contempt, and I caption that picture in the lines of Tennyson:

"Ay, Knave, because thou strikest as a Knight,
Being but a Knave, I hate thee all the more."
Yes, ladies and gentlemen . . . WHO LIED?

I made the formal announcement of my candidacy for reelection on June 27. My main opponent, Louis Riecke, the proprietor of a lumber yard and the administrator of Charity Hospital, had announced his candidacy for my seat several days earlier.

"The issue in the approaching campaign is a simple one," I said. "It revolves around the answer to the question of whether or not I have made a good representative of my people in the three terms I have served in Congress. If, in the opinion of the people, I have given intelligent, courageous, and honest representation to their problems in Washington, I sincerely hope they will reelect me." And, I added, that if the majority of voters considered that I had not served them well, it was their duty to vote me out of office.

However, the campaign became a little more personal than that. To manage my campaign I called on my old friend, Ray Hufft. Hufft was in the hospital at Kennedy General in Tennessee recuperating from several wounds he had received on separate occasions while leading his battalion in Europe. I knew that the veterans' vote would be a deciding factor so Hufft, who had a leave from the Army, came home from the hospital to run my campaign. When the campaign was over he went back to the hospital. The campaign was a real tough fight, the only tough fight I had. Morrison had just been elected. That is why it was so tough.

Assisting Hufft as co-campaign manager was Hugh "Buddy" Wilkinson, Jr., a decorated Naval flyer and the son of a prominent and colorful New Orleans attorney. Hufft wanted the name of Wilkinson to be associated with the campaign.

Making the first pitch for me was the senior Wilkinson, who besides being Louisiana's most noted and flamboyant criminal trial attorney, had been intimately involved with Huey Long and his regime. In fact, he had been Huey's law partner. But Wilkinson had broken with Huey's heirs and worked with me to expose the New Orleans tax racket during the Scandals. His support for me was aired in what he called "The Court of Public Opinion," a radio program in which he made his case for me. As Hufft explained at the time, "The listening public will represent the jury and Mr. Wilkinson, the trial attorney, will be addressing the jurors." Riecke noted Wilkinson's participation in the campaign by remarking that "When you're in trouble you should get an attorney, but when you are in real trouble you get Hugh Wilkinson."

There were really no substantive issues in the campaign, no philosophical differences between Riecke and me. My opposition was led by Morrison and stemmed from the fact that I had supported Maestri. As the winner of the mayoralty contest, Morrison had tasted blood and wasted no time in becoming the sole boss of his new political machine, which he was determined to strengthen and expand. If he could influence the outcome of a congressional race, it followed that it would increase his power.

While Morrison was praised as a reform candidate, received good press, and was generally considered a good mayor, he was every inch a politician, to which his fifteen years in office attest. He failed twice in his efforts to become governor—partially because of the bucolic prejudices of rural Louisiana—but he only left the mayor's office to become ambassador to the Organization of American States. He had New Orleans locked politically.

Chep had a bigger machine than Maestri, and I think he was more ruthless than Maestri. Chep was cold-blooded as hell. I personally think Maestri was a better mayor than Morrison ever hoped to be. Maestri knew the value of a dollar. Of course Chep was the salesman and brought the Chamber of Commerce style to the city. But Dave McGuire (the reporter who had been expelled from LSU for opposing Huey Long's censorship) made him. McGuire was considered the mayor's right arm while he served as the city's chief administrative officer. Some said he was the mayor's "right mind."

Morrison was respectable but he had a halo he did not deserve. He had a lot of ability, but I have seen Chep come to my office in Washington, put in a couple of telephone calls and in the next day's papers there would be stories of how he had had a conference with this man or that man, and all he had done was to call and say, "I'm in town and I wanted to say hello to you." He accomplished plenty but look at the money he spent. With Maestri the city would never have ended up in the fouled-up situation Morrison left it with.

During the campaign Morrison endorsed a group of candidates who termed themselves the "Combined Independent Ticket." I took to the airwaves and compared Morrison and his candidates to "the proud Pharisee" of the Bible who thought he was better than other men. "Today," I said, "it has come to pass in New Orleans that the City Hall is filled with political Pharisees."

From Biblical lands, I moved on to France for my next analogy.

Mayor Morrison, in a radio address in behalf of Mr. Riecke the other night, referred to his "hundred days" in office. Naturally possessing a Napoleonic complex of dictatorship and vindictiveness, Mayor Morrison would suggest such a phrase as "one hundred days." I suggest that he learn a lesson, however, from Napoleon's hundred days which took "the Little Corporal" from Elba to St. Helena in one hundred days. The "Big Colonel" might be headed in the same direction judging by his "hundred days."

Now we recall that when Mr. Riecke's crowd was campaigning for election last January, the same crowd which is yelling for Mr. Riecke at the moment, you were promised economy in city government, reduced sales tax, protection of civil service, and above all, non-participation of the payroll boys in any election.

Now, one hundred days later, what do we find? A city budget greater by more than a million dollars than any other in the city's history, no attempt to reduce the sales tax, civil service a myth, and municipal employees being threatened and intimidated to get right or lose their jobs, and exclusive participation of the payroll boys in the congressional campaign now in progress as managers, publicists and hatchet men.

They call themselves the "Combined Independent Ticket." Independent of what—truth, independent of kept promises, independent of campaign promises. If that is what they mean by "Combined Independent" then I agree with them.

Then, as was customary with my radio addresses, I concluded with: "Good night and God bless you." When the announcer flipped off the microphone, I turned to Hufft, who was in the studio, and with a big grin said, "Now, how did you like that?"

"Don't you think you're hamming it up too much," Hufft replied

"No, I don't think I'm hamming it up too much," I said, confident of my style.

Riecke opened his campaign against me by charging that the First Congressional District "is tired of eloquence and wants action and results. They are determined to get rid of, once and for all, the old parasitical political machine. The people of this state are not going back to the type of obstructionist who would stunt the growth of New Orleans, if necessary, for their own personal and political advantage."

He called me a "self-styled national figure" who had left the party of good government which had been instrumental in electing me to office. "He left them and joined hands with Maestri, sat on the public platform with him and urged the reelection of the worst city government New Orleans ever had," and in doing so "exercised the prestige, influence and power of his office in an attempt to deprive the people of continued good government in Louisiana. He failed in this attempt. His candidates were not elected."

Considering there were few specifics Riecke could hammer away at other than my allegiance to Maestri, he was forced to complain that

too many times we have elected booming orators who talked their way into office.

It was all right some years back to have a traveling ambassador whose mileage was second only to Mrs. Roosevelt's. Then we had wartime industries here giving employment to our people. Salesmanship, spectacular publicity and pure bluff may have been necessary then.

But the time is coming when we are going to need a man representing our district who is short on speeches and long on performance.

In essence, Riecke said, his candidacy was "in opposition to the last hope of the bosses of the old machine, their congressional Charlie McCarthy."

Besides Riecke, I had three other serious opponents: George Sladovich, Jr., an attorney who ran on a pledge of "full benefits for veterans" and a promise to work toward "maintaining the right of unionism in collective bargaining;" Sidney Massicot, a businessman who ran as a "friend of labor;" and the ubiquitous J. O. Fernandez. I dismissed them as "preliminary boys" in the prize ring and concentrated on Riecke/Morrison.

During the campaign Riecke obtained publicity by examining the voter registration rolls in Plaquemines and St. Bernard parishes. In Plaquemines, Judge Perez, as an exercise in power and because it amused him, refused to allow Riecke to peek at the rolls until he had abided by the letter of the law and observed all technical niceties. The action brought newspaper coverage and editorials denouncing Perez—and a one-day delay in Riecke being allowed to check the registration lists. In St. Bernard, Sheriff C. F. "Dutch" Rowley didn't place any obstacles in Riecke's way when he ventured into the parish to photograph the rolls. Rowley declared to reporters, "You won't find any muskrats or ducks, or even a Donald Duck, Mrs. Drake, or Mickey Mouse" among the voters listed on the rolls. There had been accusations of such names being listed in the past.

One night Hufft and I attended a political meeting at the courthouse in St. Bernard. When we arrived, Sheriff Rowley was presiding. He was instructing the poll commissioners on how and when he wanted the ballot boxes switched in order that I would have no chance of being defeated down there. I looked at Hufft and Hufft looked at me, and Hufft said, "I think we'd better get out of here."

I said, "I agree," and we left that courthouse in a hurry!

As the campaign progressed, I finally latched onto a touch of scandal. I charged that the city's fire chief, Howard Dey, had taken Morrison-supported candidates on rounds of the fire stations "in his official car, driven by a city-paid chauffeur, and lined up the firemen, telling them these were the candidates to vote for."

Morrison, who had pledged to do away with such practices, reacted by saying, "Fire chiefs have been campaigning for political candidates for 35 years. Such complaints coming from the headquarters of Hébert, who spent six weeks of his time as a congressman actively campaigning for Maestri, are rediculous."

Dey publicly acknowledged that he had driven Riecke and Hale Boggs, who was trying to recapture the congressional seat he had lost to Paul Maloney, on tours of the fire stations; but he denied that he had intimidated anyone or told the firemen how they should vote. The *States* was forced to condemn the practice and printed a two-paragraph editorial, saying such activities should be halted. The rival *Item* published a longer editorial which chided the mayor, but both newspapers, even the two-paragraph *States* effort, gave more space to the fact that such practices had been routine during the reign of the Old Regulars. The allegation, and a statement by Morrison to the same effect, brought a stinging rebuke from retired fire chief Frank Rivard: "I want to go on record now, that I have never during all the years I spent on the New Orleans fire department, driven any candidate on visits to any fire station, either in my own personal car or in any car belonging to the New Orleans fire department."

Besides the stem-winding speeches, allegations of wrongdoing, and strong political support in Plaquemines and St. Bernard parishes, I brought a little innovation to the campaign—drama.

It's Dramatic!
It's Entertaining!
It's True!

The
"Hébert Real Story"
Hear Behind the Scene
Events in the Life of Your
Congressman Dramatized

EVERY NIGHT

WDSU—7:30
WNOE—8:15

This was real ham. It was a series of fifteen radio skits. I got my old newspaper competitor, columnist Mel Washburn, to write the skits, and some of his old acting friends to perform in them. One story told about when I was the football manager of Jesuit in 1919, and Dan Levy was the star of the ball club. He was the biggest playboy in the world and he wouldn't come out for practice. He was dating this Irish girl named Claire Casey. In the skit, I asked her, "Claire, get that Dan out for practice. The team needs him. You get him out and I promise you anything in your life that I'm ever able to provide. I'll give it to you." So Dan comes out for practice and the big game is re-enacted. You hear the crowd cheering and all that kind of stuff when Dan leads 'em on to victory.

Then the phone rings in my office. I'm a congressman now. "Eddie? This is Claire."

"How are you, honey?"

"Do you remember what you promised me?"

"I do."

"Well, I want you to keep your promise. Little Dan wants to go to Annapolis."

"I'll appoint him."

There was a promise kept after twenty years. That was the point of the skit which was designed to appeal to the public.

Another good one was about how I got some woman out of Greece after World War II. It was real ham, but she appeared on the show with me. The skit was entitled "The Jewish Refugee," and began with Stella Dallas music, sinister and forbidding. The story of Irma Blumna, a German Jewess living in Greece, was recounted, complete with the rappings of the Gestapo on her door in the middle of the night, and their accusations: "You are a Jewess!" And the meek protestations of a frightened woman alone, "No, no. I am Swiss."

Mrs. Blumna had survived the Nazi occupation but was about to succumb to the desperate food shortages of peacetime Greece. She had been unable to obtain a passport in order to join relatives in New Orleans because her records had been destroyed in Allied bombing raids on her hometown of Manheim, Germany. "Month after month Irma Blumna pleaded, but it was no use," the sonorous narrator intoned. "The war was over, yes, but there was red tape, insurmountable red tape. She was literally starving in Greece but could not get out."

Finally, her nephew went to his congressman—who happened to be F. Edward Hébert—as the family's last hope. Voila! She was miraculously provided with an immigration visa. "And that's how Irma Lloyd Blumna finally got to New Orleans, because her loved ones had a representative in Washington who could get things done when they needed to be done. After living in terror under the merciless Gestapo, enduring every suffering, and finally almost starving, her nephew's congressman in New Orleans found a way to get her to America when the American embassy in Greece said there was none. He's a representative who represents ALL his people. A congressman who can and will heed the appeals of those who need him, ..." and more Stella Dallas music.

At the conclusion of the drama, Mrs. Blumna and I shared a few words, and while they were calculated to serve my cause and were coated in sentimentality, there was nevertheless a sincerity in them. Mrs. Blumna had arrived from Greece only a week before the broadcast.

HÉBERT: I know you must be happy now, Mrs. Blumna, that you have finally been reunited with your sister and other loved ones here in New Orleans.

MRS. BLUMNA: I will never be able to thank you, Congressman

Hébert, for what you have done for me. After so many terrible years you have made it possible for me to live again.

HÉBERT: I am happy that I was able to persuade the State Department in Washington to let you out of Greece.

MRS. BLUMNA: And I am happy, too happy, to be in America where any person can ask and get help from a congressman they do not know. I thank God for that kind of a government and that kind of a man.

HÉBERT: Thank you, Mrs. Blumna. When the people of this country elect a man to represent them, he is their servant. It is his duty to do everything he can for the people he represents even though that duty offers many obstacles, such as those which prevented your getting out of Greece and to America. May you be happy here, always.

In the background the strains of "God Bless America" wafted across the air waves as the announcer intoned,

And that, ladies and gentlemen, is why we must send F. Edward Hébert back to Congress when we vote on September 10. We need a man to represent us in Washington who does get things done, no matter what the obstacle. Listen again tomorrow night for another dramatized episode in the life of Congressman F. Edward Hébert—the man WE MUST KEEP IN WASHINGTON!

And Morrison thought he was going to beat this with a fire chief? Despite the apparent lack of sophistication in their appeal, the dramatizations were, in fact, as compelling as soap operas and as professionally done. They apparently drew a sizeable listening audience, and were well received.

On election eve, I closed my campaign with a radio broadcast in which I repeated the message which I had used to open the campaign: "No matter what herrings are dragged across the trail; no matter how many irrelevant matters are brought into the discussion; no matter how the truth is distorted—it still all boils down to the one issue of whether I have made you a good congressman.

"I like being your congressman and I want to continue being your congressman."

I then recounted my campaign efforts: twenty radio programs personally presented; sixty-five programs in my behalf; fifty precinct, ward and parish meetings; and personal contact with constituents.

"I await your decision with confidence. I want your vote tomorrow if you feel justified in voting for me to continue as your congressman.

"Good night and God bless you."

When the votes were counted almost 13,000 more ballots had been cast for me than for Riecke, who was the runner-up. The other three "major" candidates received a sprinkling of votes. I had survived the most serious challenge of my political life with a clear majority.

As soon as the verdict was in, I said, "Now that the fight is over may I renew my pledge of cooperation in whatever is best for the city, the state and the nation. I hope it will be accepted, especially by those connected with the city administration who heretofore have refused this offer. The city of New Orleans and its progress is bigger than any candidate or organization."

On the morning after the election I had breakfast with Riecke at the St. Charles Hotel dining room where we rehashed the campaign and resumed our friendship. As in so many instances, I regarded the political contest impersonally, as many courtroom lawyers do trials, or boxers fights; there was nothing personal in it, it was simply part of the game.

As for Billy Fitzpatrick, he and I maintained a friendship over the years. In 1974 Fitzpatrick was named a trustee of the F. Edward Hébert Foundation which will build the F. Edward Hébert Library to house memorabilia from my decades in the House of Representatives.

I have some ideas about my successes in so many political campaigns. I believe that my appeal to my district, if there has ever been an appeal, is the appeal of independence, and not conservatism versus liberalism. That is the best answer to my success—my independence.

Using independence I had overcome the defeat of Maestri and the new-found power of Morrison to win reelection against the toughest opponent I would ever face. It gave me a new perspective and a new freedom. I only became politically mature when Morrison fought me and I beat him. Then I was on my own. At that stage I could talk for myself. Then I was a politician.

CHAPTER XV

KENNEDY, EYES, UNCLE EARL

Safely tucked into office for another two years, I indulged in my penchant for becoming embroiled in controversy, which seemingly followed me like a loyal dog. At the end of 1946, I was getting national publicity for proposing that bribery of athletes be made a federal crime. My proposal stemmed from reports of gamblers approaching National Football League players prior to a play-off game, plus the involvement of minor league baseball players in Louisiana's Evangeline League with unsavory characters.

My logic behind this proposal was that "sports have become big business and just as much a part of interstate commerce as cross-country trucking." I introduced a bill, and Republican Congressman Leo Allen of Illinois proceeded to introduce an almost identical measure. Neither bill, however, managed to pass the GOP-dominated Congress and I gave little thought to Allen's plagiarism. The Illinois representative's attempted theft was significant, nevertheless, for it signaled the beginning of a new policy by the Republicans, who had captured control of Congress in the 1946 elections. That policy became glaringly evident early in 1947.

The District of Columbia at the time was staggering under the financial burden which an inordinate number of chronic alcoholics were placing on the judicial system and its "revolving door" method of dealing with the problem: arrest, sentence, confinement, release, *ad infinitum*. To combat the excessive cost of the ineffective system and to aid the victims of intemperate alcohol consumption, I proposed that the District of Columbia subcommittee on Health, Education, and Recreation pass legislation which would provide for the treatment of alcoholism as a disease rather than a crime.

"At a time when the District's fiscal situation is bordering on a huge deficit," I said, "the savings that can be realized under this measure cannot be sneezed at. The present method of healing alcoholics is futile and wasteful." Thus, I proposed that alcoholics be treated scientifully in clinics supported by a tax on the gross sales of liquor. My legislation would have set up the first public agency of its kind in the United States, and heavy drinkers would thus be treated "just as if they were suffering with pneumonia."

I worked out the legislation in collaboration with James V. Bennett, the chief of the Federal Bureau of Prisons, and came up with a plan calling for an alcoholic clinic with a diagnostic center. Every alcoholic arrested would be sent there for observation, examination, and classification. Also a study of each patient would be conducted to analyze his mental and physical condition, pertinent circumstances of school and family life, and any criminal experience or other factors contributing to his addiction to alcohol. Additionally, advisory and psychiatric out-patient care was called for.

The measure was praised in the District press as forward, progressive, and much-needed legislation. "Representative Hebert is to be congratulated on introducing a bill which has revised thinking on the problem of alcoholism in the District," the *Evening Star* said editorially, and the paper ran a series of articles which were prompted by the bill. The Public Health Service, private physicians, and criminologists also voiced support for the bill. Advocacy of it was fast becoming widespread, and practically everybody who didn't own stock in a distillery backed the measure.

When the Republicans gained control of Congress, they naturally took over the committees. Dr. Arthur Miller of Nebraska took over as chairman of my District of Columbia subcommittee. Everything went along well for a month or so. Then I picked up the *Times-Herald* one Sunday and all my bills had been introduced by Miller. Every one of the bills that I had been working on for eight months. Well, that was a hell of a note as far as I was concerned. The chairman usually steals the bills when the committee rewrites them. It is customary for the chairman to introduce the measure, but these bills were not rewritten. They were my bills, and I hit the ceiling.

In a closed session of the subcommittee, I questioned Miller about his action: "I am rather embarrassed to bring this matter up. I have no pride of authorship, but I do have pride of sponsorship. I didn't know the chairman of the committee had reintroduced my bill until I read about it in the papers, which has caused me to wonder if he is fully acquainted with the procedure in committee in which an individual sponsors legislation."

"It is the right of the chairman of the majority party to introduce all good legislation," Miller replied, and then admitted, "The leadership told me to introduce this bill in my name. I personally hesitated about doing this but I was told to do it. We are the majority party and we're going to be responsible for all good legislation."

"Then am I to understand that a Democrat or a member of the present minority party has no right to introduce and sponsor progressive and constructive legislation in his own name?" I asked.

"If it is a good bill we will reintroduce it in our name," Miller said. "We are going to take the cream. You fellows have had your way long enough."

"Then," I asked, "the present majority party is of the opinion that the minority party has no rights at all?"

"I said I was instructed to introduce the bill in my own name," Miller replied, evading the question.

"I guess I'm in the position of a fullback who has bucked the ball down the field for 99 yards," I said, "only to find the quarterback calling his own signal to take the ball over for the touchdown."

I was so put out with the unfairness of the matter that I issued a public statement to the effect that "the principle involved strikes at the very heart of our Constitution, which while acknowledging the responsibility of the majority, at the same time recognizes the duty of the minority and the protection of its rights.

"If the minority in this nation is to have no voice in the affairs of this country, then we are not far removed from a complete totalitarian form of government."

For some time it looked as if the Republicans had the upper hand, but I was not left impotent.

I reintroduced my bill, and when it came before the committee as a whole Everett Dirksen was the chairman, and he looked over at me and said, "Eddie, you don't want a count of hands, do you?"

There were nine Republicans and only four Democrats present, but I said, "I not only want a count of hands, I want a roll call." Well, he had me whipped, nine to four, but I pulled out six proxies. I had hit every damn Democrat on the subcommittee for a proxy, including Jack Kennedy, who was on the committee at that time, and I beat Dirksen by one vote.

It couldn't happen again. The Republicans didn't think I was going to pull that kind of stunt on them. They could have beaten me with a little know-how. But by catching them off balance, that is how I put the damn thing over. After that they changed the rules, making it mandatory that members be physically present.

Jack Kennedy's proxy was the last one I got. His vote decided the issue. But actually he was nothing as a congressman, and little as a senator. He grew to stature and came of age when he became President.

Hale Boggs and I had a television program, "Dateline Washington," and Kennedy came on it once when he was senator. It turned out to be one of the lousiest programs in the series. Kennedy couldn't talk. He just couldn't express himself. Uncertain, and with nothing to say. I was the most amazed guy in the world when he ran for the vice-presidential nomination against Estes Kefauver, for he certainly didn't do a thing in the House.

I would put Presidents Nixon and Johnson in my best Jesuit Latin as *exaequo*. I consider them both consummate politicians. Both great opportunists, an opportunist, not in a degrading way, but in the way the game is played. The pitcher throws the ball down the middle. The batter sees his chance and he hits it. That's what I mean by an opportunist. But for the man of stature, the man of depth, I would take Kennedy.

My opinion of Jack Kennedy, however, is deprecated by the influence his brother Bobby had over him. Bobby's influence was a very damning and dangerous thing. It was, in my book, an evil influence, for Bobby was driven by ambition. When he toured the country, was his reception spontaneous? It was Hollywood. It was Madison Avenue. It was all prearranged.

I once sponsored a bill for retarded children. When it went over to the Senate, Bobby did his best to get that bill put in his name. I sent word to him there would be no bill except my bill. When it came back to the House, I said, "I don't give a damn what's in the bill. Anything Bobby Kennedy put in it is out." And it was out! The President signed my bill. I wasn't about to let Bobby come along and make political hay out of my bill. I know how sensitive the family is on account of the retarded sister, and I can understand that, but don't politically capitalize on that kind of thing.

I'll never forget when Governor George Wallace stood in the door at the University of Alabama. Bobby Kennedy did a disgraceful thing. The attorney general of the United States put a television camera in his office while he was telling the President of the United States everything was going well, and for the President to do this and do that. For him to do that was a disgrace, an utter disgrace. Of course, being a Southerner, I'm always suspect whenever I say something like this, but history will answer whether or not it was right.

I think Jack had more of the milk of human kindness in him. I think he would listen to reason. I personally liked Jack. I thought he was charming. He was a terrific fellow. I disagreed with a lot of things he did. I may have disagreed with his philosophy, but I think he was honest. Certainly, he used politics, but those who are in a system, go along with the system. When a person plays baseball he doesn't use a cricket paddle, he uses a bat. Jack played the game according to the rules, but I think Bobby was vicious, heartless, and cruel. He had a great capacity for evil.

Again, I think Jack made a fine President. He was a most charming person, an understanding person. When Secretary of Defense Robert McNamara started closing bases all over the country, the only one he did not close was the Eighth Naval District because Kennedy told him not to.

Jack had a coffee over at the White House one day and, as I've said, I don't usually go to those things because all you do is bow and bend the truth to one another. This particular time, however, I happened to go. I told Jack, "Do you know what they're trying to do to that Eighth Naval District in New Orleans? They're trying to haul down the flag. Why don't you make those fellows leave me alone?"

Kennedy knew what I meant when I said they were trying to "haul down the flag," and he said, "The hell they are? Why don't you talk to John Connally?" Connally was then secretary of the navy.

"Who in the hell do you think I've been talking to?" I asked him.

He said, "Well, I'll call McNamara."

The next morning the telephone rang—Mr. McNamara was on the line. He said, "The President told me he had a little chat with you about the Eighth."

We worked out a deal to save face for everybody and keep my district open. It was the only one that was kept open. Later on I had to get Lyndon to keep it open when they were shooting at it again. By remaining open, the naval district grew significantly, becoming what former Secretary of the Navy John Warner called "the Naval Reserve capital of the United States." All Naval and Marine Reserve activities are directed from the Eighth Naval District, and its operations in 1975 represented a $35 million annual payroll.

Kennedy didn't have to keep that base open, but it just shows that he was open to reasonable talk. If I hadn't gone to that coffee, the Eighth Naval District would have been history instead of the Naval Reserve capital.

Kennedy had a good sense of humor, too. Jack liked to kid. The first time I saw him after he was elected President I was heading the Armed Services Committee's special investigations. He said, "How much money did you save today?"

The last time I saw him I was standing in a doorway at the White House. I said, "Listen, I have a message for you. I'm Judge Perez' personal representative to the White House and I'm going to try and get you back in the party."

He laughed and said, "It's about time." He was a very human man.

But back in 1947, when I was first becoming acquainted with Kennedy, there was a personal crisis developing, and try as I would to ignore it, it wouldn't go away. I had to face the moment of truth: I was going blind.

Since that childhood accident which took the sight in my left eye, I had been living and functioning almost unhindered by the loss. As I grew older, I was affected with nearsightedness, but now I had a real problem. A cataract was forming in my one sighted eye. I had tried not to let it interfere with my work, just as I had refused to let the loss of the other eye hinder me. Many people, most in fact, didn't realize I was blind in my left eye. But now, with the cataract, I felt an obligation to reveal the handicap.

Washington *Times-Herald* national columnist George Dixon told his readers about my plight several days after I had made a radio braodcast on the subject to my constituents in Louisiana. Dixon wrote:

> It used to take him the best part of an hour to traverse a couple of downtown New Orleans blocks because he was always stopping and shaking hands. The same thing became true in Washington following his original election to the 77th Congress. Even the most casual acquaintance was sure to get a big "hello" from him on the street.
>
> Then, about six months ago, a strange change in the man began to be noticed. He started snubbing people!
>
> He began passing old friends without even a nod. He'd stride past them, staring straight ahead, completely ignoring their friendly waves of greeting.
>
> I became concerned about it myself, particularly after he cut me cold at Joe Nunan's farewell party. Then, a couple of days ago, I discovered the reason.
>
> Eddie A-Bear isn't snubbing friends because he has gone high hat. The terrible truth is Eddie A-Bear is going blind.

Dixon told of the cataract growing on my eye, and wrote that

> it has rapidly gotten worse, until today he can hardly distinguish anything, even within a few inches of his face. He still manages to walk around, but it is becoming hazardous.
>
> He plans to undergo an operation this fall, after Congress has adjourned. The eye doctor has warned him it's a tough spot. The surgeon reminded him that people with two eyes have a second chance if the operation in one eye fails.

There will be no second chance for Eddie A-Bear. However, I do not think I have ever seen a man so philosophical. He has predicated all his future plans on the possibility of walking in darkness. He has studied deeply the lives of those who carried on in blindness—Liszt, Milton, Helen Keller, and even Alec Templeton.

He has also studied the careers of the only three blind men who ever sat in Congress—Senators Thomas P. Gore of Oklahoma and Thomas D. Schall of Minnesota, and Representative Matthew A. Dunn of Pennsylvania.

Dixon had learned of my eye condition as the result of my radio broadcast. I really didn't want to make the admission that I was suffering a physical disability, but once I arrived at the decision that it was obligatory, I did it straightaway.

Congress was drawing to a close, and the broadcast was to be my last of that session. I thanked Jimmy Noe for providing me with the air time to speak over WNOE, and I thanked my audience for listening. Then I brought up the problem I had been wrestling with for some time.

Under no circumstances do I want you, even for a moment, to associate this revelation with a plea for sympathy on my part or a desire on my part to become maudlin because of any circumstances over which I have no control.

I believe it only just and fair that you should know of an existing physical condition which is affecting me at the moment and which may affect the future health and well being of the individual who acts as your representative in the national Congress.

I cannot reemphasize too emphatically and too sincerely my eagerness to have you accept the statement which I am about to make in the spirit which I desire it to be accepted. I am only making a factual statement in as simple a factual manner as I can.

I have become afflicted with a cataract on my right and only good eye which will make it necessary for me to undergo a serious and delicate operation at sometime in the near future.

I want to bring you into my full confidence and I want you to know my condition from myself, from my lips, which is the sole reason for me making this most unusual and undoubtedly unexpected report to you tonight. . . .

I have a cataract. I can't help it. A quirk of nature and an act of God has placed it there. That's all there is to it. Others have had cataracts. What have I done or who am I that I should be an exception or immune?

You should know of the condition and should be informed of what effect it will have on my future as an individual and as your representative and spokesman in the halls of Congress. You should expect and will receive no less from me.

I do not want you to believe that I despair for the future. I do not. I want you to know the facts—that is all.

I hope to continue to represent you in Congress for many years to come. I have no intention of giving up, come what may. I will not quit, no matter what happens.

I fully intended to undergo the operation when that session of Congress ended. But the fact of the matter is that I delayed it twenty-two years. I put it off as long as I could function, as long as allowing the cataract to remain did not pose the danger of permanently damaging the eye. In 1968, less than a year before I finally had the cataract removed, I discussed my feelings about the affliction, which imposed upon me restrictions normally experienced only by the blind. And while I easily could have been classified legally blind, I treasured the meager vision left to me, and feared its loss. At the time, I said: "I have a terrific horror of going totally blind, groping in the dark. Black. That's the only horror I've got. If and when I get this operation, and if it's a failure, and I can still see light and dark, I'll be happy. I mean I'll be satisfied if I can tell when it's light and dark."

That was just about all I could distinguish during the last years before my cataract operation, and while I would settle for that much, I certainly hoped for more. In response to a question about my reaction to the problem, I said:

I miss my sight more than anything I can think of, and I have missed it for a long time. Lucky I'm not maudlin. I know damn well I'm not maudlin about it. I have complete acceptance of my condition.

When I first began to lose my sight, well, the first big dramatic thing which occurred was that I couldn't drive an automobile. I'd driven an automobile since I was in college. All right. Can't drive. So I haven't driven. That hasn't affected me emotionally. Then next came giving up this, giving up that. Now, I'm practically at the point of giving up everything. You see the difficulty I have trying to read around here.

And that annoys the hell out of me, too. I'd love to be able to read and quote from a book. Well, all this is gone. It's something in the past. Finished. I don't have it anymore. And I'm failing fast.

I just accept it. I think partially it's my temperament.

I've had to give up going down stairs until somebody is near me, or go down like a blind man. It seems like I'm feeble. But I know damn well if I go down alone I'd fall flat and break my head or something, so I just take it easy. These are things that I have had to give up. It just makes me live within a more limited world. If something falls on the floor, and I can't find it by the feel of my hand, then I can't find it.

And I'm color blind. You put red ink on that paper and it's just the same as if you hadn't written on it at all. I can see red in that picture, and the highlights and all, but . . .

Funniest thing—downstairs in the Federal Building here, there's this blind sandwich vendor. I let the blind man pick change out of my hand. I can't see it.

On March 3, 1969, under orders from Dr. George M. Haik, I entered Hotel Dieu Hospital in New Orleans. The operation was a success. Then came a three-month period of convalescence. Virginea Burguières, my executive secretary who runs the district office, best described that period in a biographical sketch of me she wrote for *Creed of a Congressman*, a study of my political philosophy by Glenn R. Conrad, Director of USL's Center for Louisiana Studies.

There followed long, slow weeks of light and darkness and shadowy outlines. To a man of Hébert's temperament—not distinguished for his patience—the hoped for vision at the end of the road tempered his wait.

I stood by with Mrs. Hébert in anxious anticipation the day they put the first pair of "practice" glasses on the congressman. He stood in the middle of the room and slowly moved his head from side to side, uttering not a sound. He suddenly stalked from the room with an entourage in anxious pursuit. We followed him from room to room. Perhaps for the first time in his life, the debator, orator, ad-libber and skilled extemperaneous speaker was at a loss for words. For the first time he was seeing in detail the interior of his home with a clarity of color perception unknown to him for twenty years. He then went from person to person to see the details of faces—blurred and clouded to his vision for so many years. Indeed it was an experience that challenged the adequacy of words to describe and express.

When I returned to my duties in Washington, I was greeted with a surprise party hosted by my staff. Friends gathered under a huge "Welcome Back" poster dangling in the center of my suite of offices in the Rayburn Building. Jazz blarred from stereo, ice tinkled in glasses, and Phillip Kelleher, an attorney for the House Services Committee and a clever versifier, had written a poem for the occasion. It was entitled "The Return of the Great Hébert." It ended thusly:

> Now Hébert's back upon the scene,
> The music lilts, the grass in green,
> Boys chase girls, as they were taught,
> And girls now manage to get caught,
> Martinis have got back their bite
> And whispers fill the summer night,
> Mini-skirts are maxi-fun,
> The dreariness of life is done,
> Thank you, Eddie, for what you've brought,
> Now Washington's the "Town that Care Forgot."

In the midst of all the hoopla, the telephone rang, and for one of the few times in my life, I failed to recognize a familiar voice. "Hello yourself, and who in the hell is this?" I shouted into the receiver.

"This is Dick Nixon."

"Uh, good evening, Mr. President."

"Welcome back, Eddie."

But just when everything seemed bright, I had to face another fight to save my sight. Another problem developed, and less than a year after the removal of the cataract, I was threatened with a detached retina. There was no option, and I underwent surgery again. Again the operation was successful, and my sight was restored.

In appreciation of Dr. Haik's splendid work, I became honorary chairman of a fund-raising campaign for the ophthalmologist's Eye Foundation of America. The organization, which has its headquarters in New Orleans, sponsors symposia on eye disease and treatment for the education of physicians, and is seeking to establish a research center.

After 1970 my vision, while imperfect—there were problems with depth perception, peripheral and night vision—was nevertheless a greatly appreciated gift. But during those intervening years, the time in which I said I had "the longest cataract in history," I continued my congressional career unabated. I walked the streets of Washington and my district while the people I saw were grey outlines, and I strained to read the necessary material through thick lens, cocking my head in order to see through the tiny part of the retina which wasn't blocked by the cataract. Very few people realized what I was going through, and that was the way I wanted it.

The growth of the cataract didn't effect my instincts at all, and when 1948 rolled around, I was right in the middle of the political wars.

The 1948 Louisiana gubernatorial race was a rematch of the 1940 donneybrook between Earl Long and Sam Jones, minus the candidacy of Jimmy Noe. But this time it looked as if Long had the heaviest armaments. It was a clear case of picking winners; otherwise, I could be out the next time. At the time I was recognized as one of the big shots in the Old Regulars. I was still a bad boy then. The Old Regulars were supporting Long, but I held out, and Judge Perez held out. He didn't particularly like Earl, but ultimately Perez and I both agreed to support him. One of the conditions of Perez' support was that he would get to name the adjutant general of the state National Guard, and that adjutant general was going to be Ray Hufft. Ray did not know Perez well at that time. They were not that close. Ray was my boy, but Perez remembered the incident in which Sam Jones, as governor, sent the Guard into Plaquemines Parish to install and maintain in office the man he had appointed sheriff.

When the Guard went in there, the officer in charge telephoned Ray Flemming, who was the adjutant general at that time. They had party lines in Plaquemines and Mrs. Perez was listening in. The first thing Flemming asked was, "Did you get Perez?"

When he said that, Louisiana had a new adjutant general. That was the end of Ray Flemming. I told him later to come out to the house and talk to me. I said, "I'll tell you Ray, you're finished, and I'll tell you why you're finished: You have to be pretty agile to stay adjutant general under six governors."

For his part, Earl Long quipped that he got Leander Perez' support by promising to rename the state flower after him—to change it from magnolia to oleander.

Anyway, I agreed to support Earl Long. Of all the people in the world for me to support, Earl Long. But being in the system, and being of the political system, I made the sign of the cross, said an act of contrition, and asked God to understand my weakness, and my necessity.

One of my first acts as a supporter of Earl Long was to defend him on the floor of the House against charges of income-tax evasion. The charges were lodged by my good friend and fellow congressman, James Domengeaux, a colorful representative from Louisiana's Cajun country. Shortly before the gubernatorial primary in Louisiana Domengeaux asserted that the Internal Revenue Service was pursuing an investigation into Long's taxes, including allegations of fraud. Instead of hurting, the charges seemed to help Long. The election was, after all, in Louisiana. Long won the first primary by a large majority, but the tax controversy spilled over into the Democratic runoff between Long and Jones.

When Domengeaux, who had aligned himself with the Jones forces, made the original charges, I was in New Orleans. The story of Domengeaux's allegations on the floor of the House hit the front pages of the afternoon papers, and the next morning, about four or five o'clock, when the overnight plane from Washington got in, I got a telephone call at my house. Domengeaux had just landed. He said, "Hébert, I got that son of a bitch."

I told him I had read the papers, and I asked him, "Have you lost your cotton-pickin' mind? You say you got Earl, well, I say you haven't got him. I know."

He said, "I will lay my political future right on the line."

"You do," I said, "and you will get it erased."

The upshot of it all was that I came riding to Long's rescue. I took the floor and defended Earl on his taxes, and if I do say so myself, it was one hell of a speech. Eventually Everett Dirksen, who was still in the House at the time, got involved. It looked like he was Jimmy's ace in the hole. He called for an investigation and made a lot of slurring remarks about things going on down in Louisiana and so forth.

When I was preparing to make my speech defending Earl, Jimmy asked me to give him a copy ahead of time. I said, "You little Cajun, you don't think you're going to trick me, do you? Get my speech the night before and eat me up when you get a chance to rebut me." I told him I would give it to him in the morning before I delivered it. Before I went on the floor I gave it to him. He read it and was so cute and cunning. He said nothing.

But the parliamentarian of the House, Lew Deschler, was a friend of mine and a friend of Jimmy's. He had a copy of my speech and he called me over as I walked onto the floor. He said, "You better look at that speech you have. Jimmy will sit you down if you use it as is."

I was calling Jimmy an unwitting tool and a few choice remarks like that, saying that he was a nice boy but had unwittingly got involved in this terrible thing. Well, Lew told me if I spoke those remarks on the floor, I was subject to what they called "taking down the words." That is, when a member impugnes a colleague and the affronted member demands that his accuser's words be taken down, and all debate immediately stops. The reporter transcribes the words and the Speaker decides whether the member has transgressed the laws of the House. If he decides affirmatively, the member is silenced for the rest of the day and the member who was charged is given one hour to talk about his accuser.

Well, Domengeaux was playing cute. The minute I uttered those words he was going to have them taken down and I couldn't have made my speech. Well, I cut the remarks and I made my speech. And I made a good case for Earl.

As the case was eventually resolved, it turned out that Long had to pay some back taxes, but he refused to pay a fine for fraud, which was never proved, and no formal charges were ever lodged against him.

In addition to this action in the House, I also campaigned for Long within the state. I made what was considered *the* speech of the campaign, a one-night stand on statewide radio hookup. I pitched it on this: Sam Jones and his people at that time were saying all the decent people and all the good people were supporting him. That meant that all the people supporting Earl Long were terrible.

For my oration I resurrected the story of the Pharisees.

You God-fearing people know the story. It is not necessary for me to repeat it to you, but I believe it is necessary for me to repeat it at this time in order that Mr. Jones and his followers can take a lesson from the very Bible to which they refer and perhaps redeem themselves in the eyes of God and their fellowmen. You remember the parable. . . .

I submit to Mr. Jones and his followers the parable of the publican and the Pharisee for their guidance in their conduct and their attitude to their fellowman, even though their fellowmen and fellow citizens in Louisiana, in great majority, do not subscribe to their political views and their political aspirations. . . .

Ladies and gentlemen, I have come to the end of my story. I have given you only part of the picture. I hope that those political Pharisees who are insisting upon Mr. Jones making this futile race at the expense of the taxpayers of Louisiana will see the error of their ways and be big enough, strong enough, courageous enough, to adhere to the will of the people of Louisiana in their expression that they want Earl K. Long for their governor.

That speech was one of the major factors in Earl's victory. Old Uncle Earl got on the platform with me and said, "Eddie, anything that you want from me you can have. By God, you were terrific."

Earl Long impressed me with his successes and amused me with his antics. Once when he was governor, he came to Washington and wanted to see me. I went over to the Congressional Hotel. There was Earl in his underwear, wearing a shirt in which he had undoubtedly slept, and his teeth were out. He was giving T. A. Thompson, a congressman from Louisiana, hell. He wanted to oppose Thompson because Thompson had misplaced a bet for him. He was eating breakfast and he took a coffee cup from the table, spat in it and put it back. That was Earl.

He was a good governor, a good administrator. He just wasn't socially acceptable. When Charles de Gaulle came to New Orleans it was a "high-falutin' " affair with the old Creoles and old French all involved in the thing. They were scared to death of what Uncle Earl was going to do, and he was not invited to participate in the ceremonies for de Gaulle.

The day before de Gaulle arrived, Colonel Pete Miller, who was in charge of the parade, got a telephone call from Dave McGuire at City

Hall. Dave said, "My God, get us off the hook. The governor is calling down here and wants to ride in that parade. What are we going to do?" Miller said that he would call Earl and he did.

When Earl got the call he said, "I have been expecting you to call me. I want my automobile in that parade and I want a big sign on it—Fifty Million Frenchmen Can't Be Wrong."

Miller said, "Well, governor, you know this is a military parade," and he sold him off the idea of the sign. Miller told the governor to meet him at Canal and Claiborne where the parade was going to start. When Miller got there the governor was already there and he wanted to ride with de Gaulle, but they wouldn't let him. Mayor Morrison was the one who was to ride with de Gaulle. The security people turned Earl away.

Pete said Earl was just as calm and cool, perfectly all right. So Pete put him in the car with the grand marshall, and congratulated him on the way he handled himself. Earl said, "I'll get that little son-of-a-bitch Morrison in due time. Don't worry about that."

Earl sat in the front seat of the grand marshall's car and was waving his big hat and everybody was hollering, "Hey, Uncle Earl," and Uncle Earl was having a hell of a time and nobody ever saw de Gaulle or Morrison.

When they got to the St. Louis Cathedral, where there was going to be a Mass, the band struck up the "Marseillaise" and Earl was smoking a cigarette and he spat over across de Gaulle.

Then Earl asked Miller how long the Mass was going to last, and Miller told him about forty-five minutes. Earl said, "I missed two races already. Let's get out of here." Miller drove him to the Roosevelt Hotel, to the Baronne Street entrance, and there was nobody there to meet him, so he took him around to the University Street side. There was a big crowd milling around.

Two Frenchmen came up to the car. Two French reporters had been arrested when they broke police lines, and these two fellows asked Miller if Earl was the governor. He said he was, and they asked if they could speak to him. Miller said, "Why not, everybody else does." They told Earl that two of their colleagues from a French newspaper had been arrested and they wanted to spring them. Uncle

Earl looked at Miller and said, "Miller, get me a piece of paper. Let me show them how we operate in this state." Miller took out one of those trip sheets the Army carries in its cars and Uncle Earl wrote on the back, "To Whom It May Concern: Release. . ." and he left the space blank and told Miller to fill in the names. With that blank piece of paper he could have released every prisoner in the state. I have a copy of that gubernatorial order.

Later at the de Gaulle banquet, Earl wandered around the hotel by himself, not sure where the banquet was going to be held. He went up to the head table, and of course, nobody was in that big hall before the thing started. Earl walked up and down back of the head table, looking at all the name cards, and drinking everybody's water as he went along. Someone finally found him and he got into the act. He made one of the finest speeches he ever made in his life, a very fine speech. Then he picked up his hat and walked right down the middle of the aisle and left the banquet.

Earl was the master. I used to get a big kick out of him. When Hale Boggs was campaigning for Morrison, who was running for governor, Hale had the communist tag hung on him unjustly from the time he was involved with some leftist organizations at Tulane. Uncle Earl went up in North Louisiana country, with those hard-shelled Baptists, where they think all Catholics have horns and are monsters, and he said, "They talkin' bout this fine young man, Boggs. That is a dirty shame what they are saying about that fine young man. Saying that he is a Communist. How can that man be a Communist when he has a brother who's a Jesuit priest and he is a Knight of Columbus? You know he can't be a Communist." Earl told those people that Hale was a Communist and a Catholic. He could destroy you in two seconds. He would say anything that came to his mind.

At the time Morrison was running for governor, he was making a big pitch to the South American countries to use the Port of New Orleans and to establish economic ties with the city. He visited with Juan Peron, who was in power in Argentina, and Evita, his wife, gave Morrison's wife beautiful rings and jewelry.

Well, when Earl campaigned in South Louisiana, which is Catholic and entirely different than the northern section of the state, he

The headline on the front page of the Times-Picayune *on Monday, September 9, 1935, threw Louisiana and the nation into turmoil.*

The only picture of Huey Long lying in state at the Capitol he built was made by my photographer, Oscar Valeton of the New Orleans States.

A reproduction of a Time magazine account of the "Scandals" story.

A tip I received as city editor of the States led to this photo by Wilfred d'Aquin and the accompanying article which broke a story of official corruption unparalleled in the history of this country. It became known as the "Louisiana Scandals."

In the midst of the Scandals, this colorful character became governor of Louisiana, and Ear! Long always made life interesting.

Governor Richard Leche and me in pre-Scandals camaraderie.

Covering the trial of Abe Shushan during the Scandals. From left: William Fitzpatrick, Meigs O. Frost and me, all of the States; *Leon Trice,* States *photographer; next two unidentified; Amos W. W. Woodcock, prosecuting attorney in the case; Herman Deutsch of the* Item; *and Edmond Lebreton of the Associated Press.*

Delta Sigma Phi convention in New Orleans. From left: Leslie Belnap, me, Fritz Chrysler, the great football coach, Salvador Roccaforte, Arthur W. Defenderfer, the mayor of Chevy Chase, Md., all of whom received the fraternity's Harvey Hebert Medal.

With Gov. Sam Jones and former Gov. James Noe before opening my first Congressional campaign, 1940.

With Jimmie Noe at the St. Charles Hotel on the opening night of my campaign.

Campaigning in shirt sleeves.

At a campaign rally in St. Bernard with Sheriff "Dutch" Rowley (first arrow) in attendance.

Campaign tactics. My daughter Dawn (seated between my knees) and I throw an ice cream party for the kids in my district.

Assured of at least two votes, Gladys and I cast our ballots at my first election.

My mother, Gladys, Dawn and I celebrate my first election victory in my suite at the St. Charles Hotel on election night when the early returns indicated I would win by a margin of better than two to one.

Major James Evans Crown was a happy man when two of his proteges were elected to Congress. Hale Boggs (left) had worked for the States *as a campus correspondent.*

House speaker Sam Rayburn, wearing his famous cutaway for the occasion, swears in Louisiana's five reform congressmen in January, 1941. From left, James Domengeaux, Boggs, Vance Plauche, me, and J. Y. Sanders, Jr.

Col. Thomas C. Campbell, the manager of the Tulane and Crescent theaters, and I pay our last respects to the playhouses during their demoliton.

Pascal Radosta, the owner of Manale's Restaurant in New Orleans, and I visit on one of my trips home from Washington. I always referred to Manale's as "my uptown headquarters."

"Smile, damnit," I said, as Mayor Robert S. Maestri (center), Robert Elliott, Maestri's co-campaign manager, and I left City Hall in 1946 after it had become obvious the city was going to get a new mayor.

John Courtney (left), Armed Services Investigating Subcommittee counsel, and Rep. Jack Anderson help me check part of my exhibit on military waste displayed in the committee's hearing room. The room became known as the "Chamber of Horrors."

Alger Hiss (standing left) confronts Whittaker Chambers (standing far right) before the House Un-American Activities Committee in 1948. The arrow indicates me. Then-Congressman Richard Nixon is obscured by Hiss. Committee Counsel Robert Stripling is the man standing in the center of the room. The woman seated to the right of Chambers with the white trimmed hat is Elizabeth Bentley who "blew the whistle" that opened the sensational case.

President Nixon speaks at ceremonies in 1971 honoring three former Tulanians, Sen. Allen J. Ellender, Rep. Hale Boggs, and me. Besides the President, those pictured (from left) are: Roque J. Avila, ambassador from Paraguay; Howard K. Smith, ABC-TV anchorman; Harold Timken, president of Quanta Systems Corp.; all Tulane graduates; then-Secretary of Defense Melvin Laird; and me.

In 1974, I was honored at Colorado Springs by the Air Force Academy during its football game with Tulane. My alma mater didn't forget me either.

Crozet Duplantier, the director of university relations at Tulane, looks over the entrance to the school's F. Edward Hébert Center.

Making sure Secretary of Defense Robert S. McNamara gets the facts straight during a news conference I suggested he call.

The Jesuit High School Class of 1920 at its golden anniversary dinner at Antoine's. Seated, from left: Monsignor Armand Kerlec; Father J. J. McCarthy, S. J., Father Edward Doyle, S. J., George Palermo, Fred Korndorffer, and Fred Andry. Standing, from left: Judge W. Blair Lancaster, Father Michael Majoli, S. J., Eugene Chalin, Gibbons Burke, John A. Bastian, Albert Sidney Cain, Lawrence D. Nicholls, George Schoenberger, me, Harold Oriol, John A. Schwarzenback, Pratt Martin, Father Cornellus Thensted, S. J., Edmund Crane, Jack Barker, and Howe Fuselier.

The president of the Congressional Medal of Honor Society, Charles MacGillivary (left) presents me with its Patriot's Award in 1975 as Gen. Louis H. Wilson, Jr., commandant of the U. S. Marines and himself a holder of the Medal of Honor, looks on.

Fritz Harsdorff, the associate editor of the Times-Picayune, *presents me with the Headliner of the Year Award of the Press Club of New Orleans in 1973.*

Gladys and I congratulate our granddaugher, Jeanne Duhe, after she unveiled my portrait at the F. Edward Hebert Defense Complex in New Orleans in 1975.

said, "Now that 'Della Soups' Morrison, you know who old 'Della Soups' is foolin' around with. That man Peron. You know who Peron is. He is the man the Pope kicked out of the church. Excommunicated him! That's 'Della Soups' pal." Earl ruined Morrison.

Two years after I supported Earl for governor, he wouldn't let Russell Long sit on the same platform with me, and I had not done a thing to him. He emancipated me, he really did. Up to that time I wasn't calling all the shots. I was just going along because I had to, never wanting to participate. All the time I wanted to be free.

Then, two years after I supported him, he didn't oppose me, but I knew that he tried to get some politicians to run against me, and I hadn't done a thing to him. You see, he hadn't forgotten those years when I fought him. He tried, but he couldn't get anybody to run against me. That's the way Earl would operate.

The next time Earl ran for governor, he came by my office with Blanche, his wife. Before he came in I put on an "Earl Long for Governor" button. He walked in the door and said, "You know you are not for me. What do you have that button on for?"

I looked at Blanche, and said, "Do you know his name?"

"No, Eddie, who is he?" Blanche said.

I said, "Earl 'Abraham Lincoln' Long. He emancipated Hébert. I am free. My shackles are cut, and the Great Emancipator has done it."

And from that day onward I never took part in another political election except my own. I discharged all political obligations. I owed nothing to anybody, and since that time I haven't endorsed anybody at all.

CHAPTER XVI

THE HISS-CHAMBERS CASE

BESIDES GETTING MYSELF reelected to Congress and greasing Earl Long's slide into the governor's chair, I had additional business in the tumultuous year of 1948, the first day of which I spent in the Sugar Bowl at New Orleans watching the great University of Texas quarterback, Bobby Layne, pass his Longhorns to a 27-7 victory over outclassed Alabama. Sprinkled throughout the stands, adventuresome women of fashion were wearing cuffed slacks tailored in a masculine pattern. Come summer they would appear on the New Orleans lakefront and around country club pools in "risqué" two-piece bathing suits with the bottom half held together by laces criss-crossed at the sides. While I enjoyed the sights and sounds of the games, I would have more important scenes to view that year.

The setting was to be in the hearing room of a congressional committee, a committee which had sprung from the ambitions and xenophobic prejudices of Texan Martin Dies. From the old Dies committee had emerged the House Committee on Un-American Activities where in 1948 "two irreconcilable faiths of our time, communism and freedom, came to grips in the persons of two conscientious and resolute men."

That is exactly what happened if you believe the man who wrote that statement, Whittaker Chambers, a writer and translator. He also called the drama which unfolded in that congressional-formed crucible "a tragedy of history." Or, if you are of another persuasion, then that swirling maelstrom which engulfed the last half of 1948 is the period when the United States shamed itself by making "an

American Dreyfus'' of Alger Hiss, a brilliant shaper of world policy, who, as a member of the State Department, played a prominent role in carving out the treaty Franklin Roosevelt signed with Josef Stalin at Yalta, and was a prime mover in drafting the United Nations charter in San Francisco.

Whether by fate, predestination or circumstance—call it what you will—my inevitable facility for being at the center of controversy guided me into one of the most sensational domestic news events of the twentieth century, the Hiss-Chambers case, or more simply, the Hiss case. To some, this story, like most melodramas of the press, to paraphrase Shakespeare, strutted and fretted its hour upon the stage, and then was heard no more. But did it? Is the Hiss case simply a footnote of history? If it were only that it involved intriguing men of intelligence set apart by personality and temperament and philosophy and training, then perhaps it would still be an asterisk. But it did more than that. It defined America as much as dropouts and demonstrations encompassed the sixties and Watergate occupied the early seventies. It also helped make a President of the United States out of one of its participants, a freshman congressman from California, barely thirty-five years old.

In 1948 the Un-American Activities Committee was looked upon with disdain by intellectuals, liberals and others who feared and abhorred the unfounded charges and violations of civil rights—the guilt by association smears—that characterized that body. I, too, felt that there was little dignity and much danger in a committee which could arbitrarily hang the epithet of ''Communist'' on a citizen and then offer him no recourse to reply. But I also felt that there was a need for the committee, if it would but operate under democratic trappings and not employ methods similar to those practiced by a totalitarian regime whose pawns it was trying to ferret out of the United States government.

I went on the Un-American Activities Committee because I did not like its flamboyancy. I thought it ruined itself through its own fault. It was a maligning committee. I could see this flamboyancy, this wildness, this throwing names around and charging things. I didn't believe in it. I thought they could make cases without all those monkeyshines. They'd throw names around, say so and so's a communist and then he couldn't come before the committee to defend himself unless he was invited; and even if he were invited, there apparently would be something going on, some reason that they never got around to giving him a hearing.

I had wanted to be on that committee for a long time. One day I walked into the chamber when the clerk was reading the resignation of Representative Herbert Bonner of North Carolina from the committee. I said, "Oh, hell, I'm going on that committee." If I hadn't walked in at that particular time I wouldn't have known that Bonner had resigned, and I would never have gotten on it. As it was, I had a hard time with Sam Rayburn about going on that committee. He did not want me on that committee. He said it would ruin anybody politically. I said I could take care of myself. Yet, he delayed it a long time.

Finally, on December 8, 1947, I was named to the Un-American Activities Committee. The first thing I did when I got on the committee was to insist on the one reform I thought was the most important. The committee had a lot of guys dangling in the air whose names had been mentioned in public testimony. They would never give these characters a chance to testify. They always had an excuse, and those people wanted to testify. But the committee would not let them talk. This was wrong, so I got them to adopt the rule that any time any individual was named at a public hearing, that individual had the right to come before the committee immediately—not next week or next year—but right now, and defend himself from the same forum in which he was charged.

Now, if that rule had not been in effect, Alger Hiss would have died in history. Just another name. But in all those names dropped before the committee, the one that stands out is the name of the man who came in to talk, to defend himself. The world would have never known of Alger Hiss except for my insistence upon the rule. It just shows how little things can alter history.

At that time the United States' uneasy covenant established during the war years with Russia was developing an ever-widening schism as Winston Churchill's "Iron Curtain" descended on Eastern Europe and the blockade of Berlin began. However, everyone in the United States was not anti-Russia. Intellectuals who had been appalled at the rise of Nazism sought to put as much political distance as possible between themselves and that aberration. Given that stimulus, plus their natural wont to see an end to the inequities and deprivations which they saw about them, there developed in some a sympathy for communism as the answer. Unfortunately they were ignorant of, or chose to ignore, the absurdist paranoia turning Mother Russia into an insane asylum, choosing instead to view the Soviet system as finally having given birth to Utopia. Some of those whose sympathies lay with communism could not separate that kinship from an affinity for Russia. This led many communists down a treasonous path. For them the line between support of the principles of communism and support of Russia was blurry, and naturally, for those who opposed them and their goals, it was ill-defined also. Frequently, too, liberals were confused with communists. This led to some of those fighting communism to be portrayed, and not entirely without reason, as tramplers of the Constitution who, in their eagerness to protect the country, were destroying the principles upon which it was founded. It was often another case of means perverting ends. Many sophisticated and cultured people—tagged as "commie dupes" and "fellow travelers"—in turn denigrated the Un-American Activities Committee members as "Red baiters" and "witch hunters." And much of the abuse heaped upon the committee, as I pointed out, was through its own fault.

In 1947, the Un-American Committee, as its detractors liked to call it, had heard testimony from more than fifty Hollywood directors, writers, producers, and actors. From that group came the then-famous "Hollywood Ten," who were cited for contempt of Congress. Many suffered "black listing" and, as Charlie Chaplin said, "If you step off the curb with your left foot they accuse you of being a Red." It was in the midst of this that I began to demonstrate a certain independence regarding the Red Menace. While I believed that communism threatened the United States, I did not seek to capitalize on the easy publicity which attacking it brought. A story which was carried in most of the film industry's trade papers in 1947 showed a dicotomy between me, not yet a member of the Un-American Activities Committee, and Richard Nixon, who was a member. "Defense of the [film] industry was echoed in—from all places—Washington, where six-foot booming voiced Rep. F. Edward Hébert (Dem., La.) took the floor to praise *The Best Years of Our Lives* and suggest that it be 'required seeing' for all Americans.

"Yet lest this pretty picture of people saying nice things about the movies be too good to be believed, Representative Richard Nixon (R., Calif.), a member of the House Un-American Activities Committee, charged that 'veiled' pro-Communist sequences and dialogue are being 'maneuvered' into some American films."

I was sincerely impressed with that film which has become an American classic, but I also was moved to cite the accomplishments of the entertainment community which I knew so well and admired so much. Few, however, had reason to believe that I, a fourth-term, conservative congressman from Louisiana, could serve as the conscience of the Un-American Activities Committee whose actions were to occupy so much newsprint when espionage hearings began on July 31, 1948. I also sought to serve as its common sense, slicing through the "legalese" of the lawyers on the panel to get to the essence.

In truth, my performance on that committee was compatible with some other of my undertakings—not as good as it could have been, but better than it had to be. I'm no saint, but I'm a pretty fair altar boy.

The espionage hearings opened in an atmosphere heavy with political overtones. At opposite ends of the political spectrum new parties had sprung up. At one pole were the Dixiecrats in the South, whose pride was hurt by attacks made on their basic decency and who were outraged by Truman's "gimme government." In New York, Henry Wallace's Progressive party, which become a haven and a hope for leftists of many degrees, was at the other pole. The Republicans, out of power for sixteen long years, sensed the opportunity to regain the presidency as the Democrats were split between civil and states' rights. And, indeed, if it could be proved that subversion, treason, and espionage had been rife in the administrations of Roosevelt and Truman, then the GOP would sink the Democrats into a quagmire from which they could not wade out unsoiled.

It is important to remember the political atmosphere of the times. The atmosphere we were operating in, an atmosphere of extremes, neither of which I agreed with. The Republicans were all gung-ho to smear everybody, particularly if they were Democrats. The Democrats were all gung-ho to get reelected and to make the hearings a "red herring."

J. Parnell Thomas, the New Jersey Republican and chairman of the committee, opened the first session on a hot, sultry Saturday. Committee members attending were Republicans Richard M. Nixon of California, Karl E. Mundt of South Dakota, and John McDowell of Pennsylvania; and Democrats were John Rankin of Mississippi, J. Hardin Peterson of Florida, and F. Edward Hébert of Louisiana. Robert E. Stripling, a Texan who had risen to the position of chief investigator after joining the old Dies committee ten years previously, also was present. Republican Richard Vail of Illinois and Democrat John Wood of Georgia did not attend. Interest in the hearings was modest as Thomas gaveled the meeting to order. Only a few spectators sat in the committee room and several reporters whose "beat" included the committee were there to hear Stripling call the first witness, Elizabeth Bentley.

When the newspapers hit the streets with her story, the 40-year-old, upper-middle-class spinster, whose education included a bachelor's degree from Vassar, a master's from Columbia, and study abroad at the Italian universities of Florence and Perugia, had become the "blonde spy queen." She had named thirty-two government officials, a high State Department employee, and a host of other strategically placed government employees—all of whom she said she had known as Communists during her seven-year reign as an espionage agent. The impact of her statements staggered the committee members. She dropped names like she was reading them out of a telephone book.

I had listened silently all morning to her testimony as Stripling and Mundt questioned her, interrupted occasionally by outbursts from Rankin, one of the men who was primarily responsible for bringing derision on the committee by his willingness to ignore democratic principles in his eagerness to suppress communism. He was often overruled by the level-headed members of the committee or simply ignored. If one wasn't the object of his attacks, Rankin's comments were occasionally comic relief. "Let's get something on that last man she named. Let's get the facts on him."

Among the names she dropped was the leader of a Communist ring, Nathan Gregory Silvermaster, a spymaster who had converted the basement of his home into a photographic studio in order to copy government documents. He also had been an official in several New Deal agencies. In the afternoon session, Stripling prepared to go into the testimony Silvermaster had given during an executive session of the committee. This was the first opportunity I had to push for a witness' rights. It occurred when Stripling said he intended to read Silvermaster's previous testimony in the presence of Miss Bentley "and call your attention to the answers he gave when we asked him if he knows certain people. I will read from Mr. Silvermaster's testimony."

> HÉBERT: May I before Mr. Stripling does that, and for the sake of orderly procedure, inquire if you do not think that these parts of the testimony that a man has given before—that he should be confronted with that testimony in open hearing?
>
> STRIPLING: As a witness?
>
> HÉBERT: As a witness.
>
> STRIPLING: This is testimony before our committee that I am reading.
>
> HÉBERT: I recognize that, but if you go into what Mr. Silvermaster testified in executive session here, would that have any bearing on what the witness testified about Silvermaster?
>
> STRIPLING: That ties right in.
>
> HÉBERT: I am sure Mr. Stripling knows what I have in mind, and I want to avoid that if it is going to be brought into it.

At that point Rankin interjected: "We are not supposed to bring all these men who are charged with treason or conspiring to overthrow this government before this committee. This is a form of grand jury by a committee of the House of Representatives. No grand jury ever calls a defendant. . . . Now, we don't have to bring them in here. If this witness has information that this man . . . is a Communist, we have a right to ask those questions now."

HÉBERT: I want to make this observation. I want to disagree with my colleague from Mississippi that this is a grand jury investigation. If anybody puts in jeopardy an individual who is charged with being a Communist, I think, in fairness, that this individual should be allowed his day in court here in public hearing as well. Now, if you were in secret session or in executive session, and these names were used, then we owe them no obligation, but the minute we allow a witness on the stand to mention any individual, that individual has a right to come before this committee and have his day in court, and every man or woman mentioned here has a right to be subpoenaed to come here.

THE CHAIRMAN: Mr. Hebert, I will promise you that they will have their day in court.

Later in the session, I questioned Bentley closely about the origins of her involvement in the Communist party. I couldn't understand how someone who had been thoroughly grounded in democracy could become a communist. "I think the mistake you make," she told me, "when you look at communism is that you take it as an intellectual process. It is not. It is almost a religion and it gets you so strongly that you take orders blindly. You believe it blindly. That accounts for the fact that no real communist is religious, or has any religion. . . . Your intellectual faculties cease to function in a critical way. . . .The mentality has been dulled by this emotional process."

After Bentley's testimony, the committee next met in open session at 11 a.m. on August 3 in the hearing room of the Ways and Means Committee in the New House Office Building. Reporters gathered in numbers, stimulated by the testimony of the "blonde spy queen." While her role in the communist espionage ring had been relatively minor (a courier) and her devotion to communism partially the result of her romantic involvement with one of the party's top functionaries, the next witness had been a man of stature in the party and had become a successful journalist since his defection.

"The first witness, Mr. Chairman," Stripling said, "is Whittaker Chambers."

His appearance belied the role he was to play in this emotion-charged episode destined to change the lives of many men touched by it. For nine years this short, dumpy, rumpled, basically nondescript man had been an employee of *Time* magazine, having risen to the post of senior editor. (The fact that he joined *Time* magazine after leaving the Communist party didn't improve Chambers' standing in Rankin's eyes, however. ''After all the smear attacks against this committee and individual members of this committee in *Time* magazine, I am not surprised at anything that comes out of anybody connected with it.'') From 1924 until 1937 Chambers had served as a Communist party functionary, and, as it developed, an agent of the Soviet Union. Disillusionment and/or realization led him to leave the party and go to the FBI with his tale of subversion and espionage.

Following his break with the Communists, and after having failed in an attempt to report to President Roosevelt personally about the Communist agents who had infiltrated high government positions, Chambers related his tale to Adolf A. Berle, Jr., an assistant secretary of state. A few half-hearted inquiries were made, but nothing came of the information Chambers passed along to Berle and the FBI, nothing until he appeared before the House Un-American Activities Committee where he expressed no doubts about the role of the Communist party in the United States. ''I think you could only say that in the extreme sense the American [Communist] party is an agency which serves the purpose of the Soviet government,'' he told the committee. And then suddenly—but without any fanfare—he opened the door for what would become the Hiss-Chambers Case.

''Who comprised this cell or apparatus to which you referred?'' he was asked about his contacts.

> CHAMBERS: The apparatus was organized with a leading group of seven men, each of whom was a leader of a cell.
> STRIPLING: Could you name the seven individuals?
> CHAMBERS: The head of the group, as I have said, was at first, Nathan Witt. Other members of the group were Lee Pressman, Alger Hiss, Donald Hiss, Victor Perlo, Charles Kramer.
> MUNDT: What was Charles Kramer's correct name?
> CHAMBERS: I think his original name was Krevitsky, and John Abt—I don't know if I mentioned him before or not—and Henry Collins.

Chambers had named names, and he would add others, but the name which ultimately was to cause the biggest sensation caused little stir initially. Alger Hiss was then president of the Carnegie Endowment for International Peace, having left the employ of the United States government. Chambers said that he had been intimate with Hiss when Hiss was with the State Department. He said that he had stayed at Hiss' Washington home on numerous occasions and that when he left the Communist party, he had tried to persuade Hiss to leave, also, but to no avail.

After hearing Chambers cite names in open session, I felt it was necessary to reiterate my position that those named be given an opportunity to defend themselves.

> What I am most interested in is that this committee is not witch hunting or Red baiting, but is trying to get the facts of what is going on. Since this is a public hearing, I think all these matters should be brought out in full public gaze and for full public interpretation and appreciation of what we are trying to do; and for that reason I think every individual mentioned should be brought before the committee to either corroborate the testimony or impeach it.

Alger Hiss wasted no time in letting the committee know that he definitely wanted to appear and testify. The next day we received a telegram from him.

> My attention has been called by representatives of the press to statements made about me before your committee this morning by one Whittaker Chambers. I do not know Mr. Chambers and insofar as I am aware have never laid eyes on him. There is no basis for the statements made about me to your committee. I would appreciate it if you would make this telegram a part of your committee's records, and I would further appreciate the opportunity to appear before your committee to make these statements formally and under oath. I shall be in Washington on Thursday and hope that that will be a convenient time from the committee's point of view for me to appear.

The committee scheduled Hiss to appear the following day, Thursday, and then proceeded with its next witness, Nathan Gregory Silvermaster, the man named by Miss Bentley as one of the top Soviet spies in America. In his opening statement Silvermaster called Miss Bentley's charges against him "false and fantastic," and characterized her as a "neurotic liar." As for himself, Silvermaster refused time and again to say whether he was a member of the Communist party, because to do so, he said, might incriminate him. He further relied on the provisions of the Fifth Amendment in declining to say whether he knew numerous persons identified by Miss Bentley and Chambers as being Communists. His evasions were only a preview of the course many future witnesses would take.

In an effort to elicit the true feelings Silvermaster was hiding behind the mask of slandered innocence, I began quizzing him about his Russian origin and his attitude toward the Marxist regime there.

HÉBERT: Yes or no—do you like the communist form of government?

SILVERMASTER: I don't.

HÉBERT: You don't?

SILVERMASTER: That is right.

HÉBERT: Why don't you?

SILVERMASTER: It is a pretty long story, I suppose.

HÉBERT: Let's hear it.

SILVERMASTER: I haven't had an opportunity to live under a communist form of government, and it is very difficult for any individual to say whether or not he would like a particular government if he hasn't had any experience with it.

HÉBERT: Do you like what it stands for? You know what it stands for. You are an educated man.

SILVERMASTER: It all depends on what you mean by "what it stands for." Every government stands for many things.

HÉBERT: I will tell you my appreciation of them and see if you agree. My appreciation of what the communists stand for is the destruction of the free enterprise system of government, the destruction of capitalism, the capitalistic system, and the destruction of all religion and churches and the establishment of a complete totalitarian form of government in which the dignity of the individual is violated and under which no man has an opportunity to advance himself on his own and in which everything is repulsive and indignant to what we in America believe.

That is my conception and appreciation of communism and I think it is the general conception of the communist form of government. Do you believe it?

SILVERMASTER: No, I don't. My whole attitude toward the question would be somewhat different from yours. . . .

During the Silvermaster testimony the politics of the hearings became more involved. Silvermaster testified that during the wartime administration Naval Intelligence recommended he be removed from his position on the Board of Economic Warfare because he was a Communist. However, Silvermaster got Lauchlin Currie, an economic adviser to Roosevelt, and later to Truman, to intercede in his behalf and he was retained. Elizabeth Bentley had testified that Currie, while not a Communist, was a traitor, having given information regarding the government's China policy to Russian agents.

Truman, needless to say, didn't rejoice over those allegations, especially when they came during his campaign against Thomas Dewey, "the little man on the wedding cake." As part of Truman's campaign to "mow 'em down and give 'em hell," the President called the HUAC hearings a "red herring." What he was really afraid of was that they would, instead, become his albatross.

On August 5, the hearings took on an even brighter political hue when Alger Hiss swore to tell the truth, the whole truth and nothing but the truth, so help him God. The tall, slim and boyishly good-looking former State Department official presented a sharp contrast to his accuser. His attitude, demeanor and appearance before the committee demanded respect, which he initially received. He was barely sworn in before he made his position plain: "I am here at my own request to deny unqualifiedly various statements about me which were made before this committee by one Whittaker Chambers the day before yesterday."

Hiss' opening statement was impressive and direct, denying any communistic affiliations, yet confirming that he knew a number of persons cited by Bentley and Chambers as being Communists. However, he said, he knew them only as a result of having attended the same schools or through official contacts in the line of governmental duties. He said he had no knowledge they were Communists, or that any of his other acquaintances were.

Hiss had no sooner finished listing the positions he had held in his impressive career when I introduced politics into the hearing. Although I was critical of the political aspects of the entire hearings, I felt compelled to acquiesce to the Democratic party's direct request that I ask a political question. It came as Hiss concluded his resumé by saying "I resigned [from the government service] in January, 1947, to accept the appointment to my present position in private life to which I had been elected the preceding December."

RANKIN: What is that?

HISS: I am president of the Carnegie Endowment for International Peace.

HÉBERT: May I ask the witness a question in connection with his past association?

MUNDT (acting chairman): Proceed.

HÉBERT: Do you know Mr. John Foster Dulles?

HISS: I do. He is the chairman of my board of trustees.

HÉBERT: Then you are in your present position through the urging of Mr. John Foster Dulles?

HISS: Mr. Dulles and others.

HÉBERT: But in particular Mr. Dulles?

HISS: I am afraid I cannot answer it exactly in those terms.

HÉBERT: Was he the leading urgency?

HISS: He was chairman of the board of trustees. I don't think he was more urgent for my services than some of the other trustees.

HÉBERT: But he first approached you?

HISS: He first approached me.

Now, as far as I was concerned, I didn't give a damn about politics. That's why I eventually got thrown off the committee, but there was an extreme example of politics.

Sitting in that big caucus room one day when these hearings were going on, Francis Eugene "Tad" Walter, who later replaced me on the committee, and later became chairman, and one of the most vigorous Red-baiters, if you please, asked me to ask a certain question of Hiss. They were attempting to show that Dulles put Hiss on the Carnegie Endowment for International Peace. The Democratic partisanship had me ask the question. We knew who named him, and everybody else knew who named him, and his answer had to be John

Foster Dulles. So what was the effect of that? John Foster Dulles was a Republican. They wanted to throw John Foster Dulles' name into the hat, the implication being that maybe something was wrong with him too. He just might have a little communistic tendency.

I felt it was my duty to do it because the party I represented insisted I ask the question. I had to ask the question, and let the question stand on its own. And I did ask the question, and I ended it there. But I knew the intent. I knew what the leadership was trying to do.

The rest of the questioning of Hiss proceeded smoothly. He denied that he knew Chambers and said he could not recognize Chambers from an Associated Press photo shown to him. "I would much rather see the individual," Hiss said. "I have looked at all the pictures I was able to get hold of in, I think it was, yesterday's paper which had the pictures. If this is a picture of Mr. Chambers, he is not particularly unusual looking. He looks like a lot of people. I might even mistake him for the [acting] chairman of this committee." When the laughter died down, Mundt replied: "I hope you are wrong in that."

Because Hiss acquitted himself admirably during his testimony, making a favorable impression on the committee, an executive session later that afternoon was held in an atmosphere of consternation. In his book *Six Crises*, Nixon writes that the committee "was in a virtual state of shock." Several members berated the staff for not checking Chambers' veracity before putting him on the stand.

> One Republican member lamented, "We've been had. We're ruined." Ed Hébert, a Louisiana Democrat, suggested that the only way the committee could get "off the hook" would be to turn the whole file over to the Department of Justice and hold no more hearings in the case. "Let's wash our hands of the whole mess," he said. That appeared to be the majority view, and if Hébert had put his suggestion in the form of a motion, it would have carried overwhelmingly.

I was the only member of the committee who expressed a contrary view, and Bob Stripling backed me up strongly and effectively.

Finally, Nixon's views prevailed, and he was appointed to head a subcommittee composed of McDowell and myself which would probe more deeply into the matter and question Chambers further. A subpoena was prepared, calling for Chambers to appear on Saturday,

August 7. On the night of the fifth, the subcommittee slipped quietly into New York in preparation to question "a highly important" mystery witness, according to what Nixon told reporters. He was Alexander Koral, a London-born Communist courier who had signed a sworn statement for the FBI that he was a Communist agent. Nixon told reporters, "All I can say is that Koral is as important a witness as any ever questioned by the Un-American Activities Committee." Conversely, I stated, "We have no mystery witness. All of them are important." Koral proved a disappointment. He refused to cooperate with the subcommittee.

News of the Communists began dominating the daily papers. Truman was calling the hearings a "red herring" designed to distract public attention from the fact that the Republican-dominated Congress had failed to deal with inflation. Truman's attorney general, Tom Clark, attacked the probe in concert with his boss. The press was carrying stories that Rankin wanted to call Henry Wallace, the Progressive party candidate and former vice-president, as a witness. And sensationally, two Russian schoolteachers were in the United States to tutor children of the Russian diplomatic corps, fled from their duties and sought refuge. One of them, Mrs. Oksana Kasenkina, was kidnapped by Russian officials from her sanctuary at a White Russian enclave at Valley Cottage, New York. The Russian consulate said she was rescued, not kidnapped, from the White Russians who were holding her prisoner. Several days later she leaped from a third-story window in the consulate, seriously injuring herself. The Soviet diplomats were hard-pressed to maintain their fiction, especially when she recovered enough to tell government officials and reporters that she had been taken from Valley Cottage against her will, and had leaped from the window in her desperation to escape.

In this atmosphere our subcommittee questioned Chambers in executive session. It was then that Chambers said Hiss knew him under the "party name" of Carl, not as Chambers. He said he had visited Hiss' home often, once for as long as a week. He also told us he collected Communist party dues from Hiss and gave details of Hiss' family, named various places of residence, and cited other personal information, such as that as a child Hiss had engaged in the business of selling spring water obtained from Druid Hill Park in Baltimore; that as an amateur ornithologist, he had seen a very rare prothonotary warbler; and additionally, Chambers described two of Hiss' automobiles and told of the manner in which he disposed of one of them.

There was a minor detail or two which Chambers didn't get exactly right about Hiss' life (the cost of his child's schooling, for example). But by questioning him during that subcommittee hearing in New York, I did establish beyond a doubt that Chambers either knew Hiss very well or knew a great deal about him. "I am interested in the houses he lived in," I told Chambers. "You said several houses. How many houses? Start from the beginning."

CHAMBERS: As well as I can remember when I first knew him he was living on Twenty-eighth Street and when I went to see Mr. Berle it struck me as strange because Mr. Berle was living in Stimson's house on Woodley Road near Twenty-eighth Street. From there I am not absolutely certain the order of the houses, but it seems to me he moved to a house in Georgetown—but it seems it was on the corner of P Street, but again I can't be absolutely certain of the streets.

HÉBERT: It was on a corner?

CHAMBERS: Yes, and I recall, you had to go up steps to get to it.

MANDEL (director of research for the committee): How many rooms were there in that house?

CHAMBERS: I don't know offhand, but I have the impression it was a three story house. I also think it had a kind of porch in the back where people sat.

Then if I have got the order of the houses right, he moved to a house on an up-and-down street, a street that would cross the lettered streets, probably just around the corner from the other houses and very near to his brother, Donald.

HÉBERT: Still in Georgetown?

CHAMBERS: Still in Georgetown. I have forgotten the reason for his moving. That was a smaller house and, as I recall, the dining room was below the level of the ground, one of those basement dining rooms; that it had a small yard in back.

I think he was there when I broke with the Communist Party.

HÉBERT: Three houses?

CHAMBERS: But I went to see him in the house he later moved to, which was on the other side of Wisconsin Avenue.

HÉBERT: Three houses in Georgetown?

CHAMBERS: One on Twenty-eighth Street.

HÉBERT: The last time you saw him when you attempted to persuade him to break away from the party—

CHAMBERS: That was beyond Wisconsin Avenue.

HÉBERT: Did you ever see their bedroom, the furniture?

CHAMBERS: Yes, but I don't remember the furniture.

HÉBERT: Did they have twin beds or single beds?

CHAMBERS: I am almost certain they did not have twin beds.

HÉBERT: In any of the four houses?

CHAMBERS: I can't be sure about the last one, but I am reasonably sure they did not have twin beds before that.

HÉBERT: The little boy, Timmie—can you recall the name of the school he went to?

CHAMBERS: No.

HÉBERT: But you do recall that he changed schools?

CHAMBERS: Yes, as nearly as I can remember, they told me they had shifted him from one school to another because there was a savings, and they could contribute it to the party.

HÉBERT: What year?

CHAMBERS: Probably 1936.

HÉBERT: Or 1937, but probably 1936.

CHAMBERS: It is possible.

HÉBERT: We can check the year.

CHAMBERS: The school was somewhere in Georgetown. He came back and forth every day.

Our committee now had the testimony from Chambers which it needed to determine to a degree of certainty whether he had actually known Hiss, and which of the men was guilty of perjury, a charge which was prosecutable by the Justice Department.

On August 9, the full committee questioned in open session the mystery witness, Alexander Koral, whom the subcommittee had interviewed in New York. He became another in the long list of witnesses to invoke the Fifth Amendment, refusing to answer questions as to whether he had ever visited either the nation's capital,

Washington, D.C., or its honeymoon capital, Niagara Falls. After other members of the committee failed to elicit informative answers from him, I took a crack at Koral. But the witness' attorney kept interrupting the questioning and the committee chairman, Parnell Thomas, became very abrupt with him, prompting me to say, "I may say, Mr. Chairman, that I appreciate counsel's attempt to protect his client, but at the same time, the chair is in this instance, and the committee's attitude at all times, has been that counsel could confer with his witness and not answer for his witness."

PRAEGER: [Koral's attorney] I appreciate that.

HÉBERT: Because there is no attempt here at any time to cut off the witnesses from having the advice of counsel. That is clearly understood and the chairman has so ruled in each instance in order to keep it within the lines of our accepted manner of testimony.

Now, Mr. Koral, I again ask you: Did you ever make a statement to the government in connection with your activities as a member of an espionage ring, as related to the Soviet or Russian government?

KORAL: I decline to answer that question on the grounds that it might incriminate me.

HÉBERT: You do not deny, it, then, that you may have signed such a statement, to anybody, government or otherwise—any statement?

KORAL: Is that a question, Mr. Hébert?

HÉBERT: I asked you that as a question.

KORAL: The same answer, Mr. Hébert.

HÉBERT: You do not deny it, then, on the grounds that it might incriminate you?

KORAL: I do deny on the grounds that it might incriminate me.

HÉBERT: Then you deny that you ever signed such a statement?

KORAL: I neither deny nor affirm; I simply am not answering the question.

HÉBERT: You neither deny nor affirm that you have signed a confession about your activities on the grounds that it might tend to incriminate you.

KORAL: I am not a lawyer, and I cannot unravel the intricacy of that question.

At this point it was becoming apparent that Koral was feeling the same exasperation as the attorneys who had questioned me years before in the suit over baseball owner A. J. Heinemann's codicil to his will. I continued, ''I am not a lawyer either; and I am not trying to involve you, I am trying to ask you a simple question, because if I told you, Mr. Koral, that I know you signed a confession, what would you say to that?''

> KORAL: I would not say anything to that.
> HÉBERT: You would keep quiet on that. You would not deny nor affirm it. Then, I say to you, Mr. Koral, that I have every reason to know that you did sign a confession. Do you still want to stand on your constitutional rights and not have this opportunity of denying it and proving that you did not sign such a confession?
> KORAL: I stand on my constitutional rights.
> HÉBERT: Then I will leave it this way, that I know from good authority that you did sign a confession.

Koral didn't provide any ''sensational'' new information to the committee, and while he could hardly be classified as being ''as important a witness'' as the committee had heard, he did have use as an instrument of public relations, to show that there was something to allegations of espionage rings operating within the United States. To reenforce the point, the committee immediately received testimony from one of its investigators who told of Koral's involvement in such a ring.

Then on August 10, the committee heard testimony from Duncan Chaplin Lee, a former OSS (Office of Strategic Services) colonel, whom Elizabeth Bentley charged with passing on governmental secrets to her. I conducted most of the questioning, and, in a personal analysis, pointed out for the first time that which would ultimately be the focal point of the committee's work.

> In connection with what has been said . . . let me make this point, which I think is most important at this time. That forgetting whatever else has been developed at these hearings, forgetting the implications of this far-flung espionage ring which exists, there is no doubt in anybody's mind. . .that a crime or a violation, a criminal violation of the law has been committed before this committee. These hearings are filled with perjured testimony. There can be no doubt about it.
> Witnesses have made diametrically opposed statements under oath

which, of necessity, makes one a perjured witness, and . . . there is one fact that the Department of Justice cannot escape, that is, that perjury has been committed here, and it is entirely their responsibility, and they cannot evade it, that when their attention is called to this matter, there must be prosecution for perjury on the part of the Department of Justice as to these witnesses.

Mundt expressed a desire to associate himself with my statement, calling for ''cooperation instead of stubborn, obstinate concealment by the executive agency. . . .'' And again, I made the point:

I will hold no brief for either side except in the integrity of this committee, and in the integrity of any congressional committee, and forgetting any excuse or lack of desire on the part of government officials to prosecute, they cannot escape the fact that perjury has been committed before this committee; and I, for one, insist and demand that the Department of Justice take steps to prosecute the guilty individual or individuals who have committed perjury before a congressional committee.

It was that kind of forthright statement which pointed out the duties of Tom Clark's Justice Department, which, of course, was in reality President Truman's Justice Department. It was not the type of statement the executive branch wanted to hear because it left it with the option of either fulfilling what was an obvious duty, or of admitting by inaction that it had no intention of meeting its obligations. Truman tried to convey the idea that a hostile Congress was attempting to embarrass the President—and some members were. But I pointed out the clear and unavoidable truth: If no action were taken regarding perjury, then the executive branch was simply saying it did not care whether the Congress was dishonored.

I was being pragmatic; also, I was interested in and puzzled by the human condition. While Nixon was more direct and legalistic, I approached the matter in the plain fashion of a good reporter. I sometimes conversed with the witnesses on a personal basis and often questioned them not as if I had already formed an opinion, but in the manner of a reporter interviewing a subject in an effort to get his facts straight. I also could jump on witnesses with all the ferocity, or disgust, used on reporters by a city editor who had been handed a story full of holes. I felt I had a keen eye for inconsistencies developed in twenty-three years of scratching out a living under the demands of deadline journalism.

My ability to quickly analyze a situation was put to use in the questioning of the committee's next witness, another enlistee in the Roosevelt Administration's New Deal agencies, Henry Collins, a former Army officer who bragged of his *Mayflower* origins. He was currently director of the American-Russia Institute, cited by the U.S. Attorney General's office as subversive. Additionally, Chambers had said Collins was a member of the same Communist ring as Alger Hiss.

Collins testified that he did not know Whittaker Chambers, but when he was asked whether he knew an individual named "Carl," which was Chambers' party name, he cited the constitutional protections of the Fifth Amendment. I pounced on this.

> I direct the committee's attention to the fact that the witness unhesitatingly says he does not know a man by the name of Whittaker Chambers as a name under suspicion in the Communist apparatus; but the witness then refuses to testify as to the name of Carl, which is admittedly the code name of Mr. Chambers, and it was not made public knowledge until Mr. Stripling just made it. So the witness did know why he would not answer to the name of Carl, and he would have no other way of knowing it except that it was a code name.

Collins was permitted to read a statement claiming his innocence, praising his own liberal political efforts and attacking the committee's methods and purposes. He closed by saying he would not answer the accusations against him. His attitude irritated me.

> HÉBERT: You made the statement that you did not want to answer the questions because they may tend to incriminate you. You did not want to answer questions of the chairman relative to your organizations. Is that your same attitude relative to individuals?
> COLLINS: Yes.
> HÉBERT: Why then did you readily say you never knew a man named Whittaker Chambers?
> COLLINS: Because that was a name that was used in the accusations in the newspapers. I never knew a man named Whittaker Chambers, so I thought I was entitled to say so.

HÉBERT: Well, it is in the record that you knew a man named Carl. Why do you not answer that question?

THE CHAIRMAN: Are you consulting with counsel now for advice?

COLLINS: Not now, sir.

THE CHAIRMAN: But you just were?

COLLINS: Yes.

THE CHAIRMAN: I want the record to show that he consulted with counsel.

HÉBERT: Why won't you say whether you know Carl or not? That is on the record.

COLLINS: For the same reason, sir, that I refuse to answer any questions about knowing any individuals at this time in connection with these accusations.

HÉBERT: But you just said you did not know Whittaker Chambers. You are blowing hot and cold. Which way do you want to blow, hot or cold? We have heard a lot of talking out of both sides of the mouth on this, so we may as well give you a chance to do it. It is a great acrobatic feat.

How do you justify, then, saying you do not know Whittaker Chambers? You did answer that question.

COLLINS: I go back to my previous statements, sir, in connection with that.

HÉBERT: Then you cannot justify it. You said you did not want to identify individuals who were in the record because it may tend to incriminate you. The name of Whittaker Chambers is in the record, and you unhesitatingly said that you did not know an individual by the name of Whittaker Chambers. And in the next breath you were asked if you knew a man by the name of Carl and you refused to answer on the grounds that it might tend to incriminate you. Now, which attitude do you want to take?

COLLINS: I do not remember ever having met any man ·named Whittaker Chambers. I have never engaged in espionage or—

HÉBERT: Never mind; that is enough. Now why do you refuse to say whether you know Alger Hiss or not? He has made no accusations against you.

COLLINS: I refuse to answer that question, sir, on the grounds that my answer might tend to incriminate me.

HÉBERT: All right, Mr. Chairman; the record is made and it speaks for itself.

The next witness was Charles Kramer, another New Dealer who had also worked for two important Senate subcommittees, War Mobilization and Wartime Health and Education. He had been named by Miss Bentley and Chambers as being a member of a Communist espionage ring. Kramer began his testimony in the same manner as had most of the others similarly accused, refusing to answer the questions. I listened for some time and then decided that the committee simply was not going to get straight answers to direct questions. I decided to use another means to reveal the true nature of Kramer's evasions, leaving no doubt about the truth of the allegations against Kramer except in the minds of the irrational.

I began by asking Kramer about a form he signed when he accepted employment with the federal government.

HÉBERT: In Form 57, which you know you did sign, it asks: "Are you a member of the Communist Party?" What was your reply to that direct question on Form 57, which you had to sign before you became a government employee?

KRAMER: I do not recall.

HÉBERT: Before you could become employed by the federal government you had to answer every question, and among the questions was a direct question: "Are you a member of the Communist Party?" Now, what did you sign to that direct question?

KRAMER: I do not recall my answer to that question.

HÉBERT: You do not remember what you signed?

KRAMER: That is right.

HÉBERT: Well, if you were a member of the Communist Party, you knew it, didn't you? Didn't you?

KRAMER: If I were, yes.

HÉBERT: If you were?

KRAMER: I said, if I were; yes.

HÉBERT: Then you would know it.

KRAMER: I would know it.

HÉBERT: Then, what did you sign?

KRAMER: I do not recall what I signed.

HÉBERT: Well, then, you did not know whether you were a member of the Communist Party or not? Of course you knew. I am merely paraphrasing your own reactions. Do you want this committee to believe that such an important question would escape your memory right now as to how you signed it?

KRAMER: I do not recall the answer to that question.

HÉBERT: If you were a member of the Communist Party, then you signed "Yes." Did you do that?

KRAMER: I don't recall the answer to that question.

HÉBERT: If you were a member of the Communist Party, then you would of necessity have had to sign "yes," would you not?

Kramer, beginning to resent being made a fool of, replied sharply, "I don't recall the answer to that question, I said."

Still I wouldn't let up. "If you were not a member of the Communist Party, then you would, of necessity, have had to answer 'No.'"

KRAMER: That is true.

HÉBERT: That is true. Why didn't you answer "that is true" when I asked you if the same question had been put to you as to whether you were a member of the Communist Party? The question was the same. I said if you were not a member of the Communist Party, you would answer "no." You said, "that is true." I asked you if you were a member of the Communist Party, you would have to answer "yes," and you said you don't remember. That is correct, is it not?

KRAMER: That is correct.

As my protracted wrestling with Kramer's pretensions and evasions continued, the tension in the room mounted, and we both became angry.

HÉBERT: We are trying to find out whether you are engaged in an espionage ring in the United States and you won't answer.

KRAMER: I have told you that I have answered to the best of my ability in these questions.

HÉBERT: The best of your ability is that you won't answer because if you will, you will incriminate yourself as well as your conferees.

KRAMER: You can draw any implication that you want from that, but that is a protection of the innocent, remember that.

HÉBERT: I am not drawing the implication.

KRAMER: You are drawing the implication.

I finally had my fill of Kramer's righteous indignation at being questioned by a congressional committee and knowing that Kramer had been a member of an espionage ring, I blurted out, "Yes, because we know you did, and you know it, and you know you sold your government down the river, and you know it will be proved if ever the proper authorities show the desire to prosecute."

I put the question to Kramer again.

> HÉBERT: Now, again I ask you, Mr. Kramer, and I ask you not to answer the question for me, but answer to the entire American public which is interested, and has a right to know who is telling the truth and who is not telling the truth. I ask you again, do you know that lady there? (Indicating Miss Bentley.)
>
> KRAMER: I have answered that question.
>
> HÉBERT: That is the question, then, that we go beyond the confines of this committee and tell the American people, and tell them that you will not identify the lady. . . . You don't answer to me. Now, answer to the American public. That is a good forum.

Kramer again refused to say whether he knew Miss Bentley, and Nixon told him, "Then it is pretty clear, I think, that you are not using the defense of the Fifth Amendment because you are innocent. You could answer that question very simply. You are either innocent or you are not innocent."

Such witnesses were making it more difficult for the Truman administration to classify the hearings as a "red herring," as it was becoming apparent that the witnesses obviously had something to hide. Following Kramer on the witness stand was Abraham George Silverman, who had had access to classified government information during wartime and who had been named as a communist. If possible, he was even more recalcitrant than his predecessors on the stand, refusing to say time and again whether he knew anyone in the world. Finally I asked: "Mr. Silverman, do you know Irving Russell?"

Silverman pondered the question and then replied, "On advice of counsel, I refuse to answer that question."

> HÉBERT: Do you know anything about Irving Russell that would make it self-incriminatory for you to know him?

Silverman, with a pensive and searching expression, hesitated, then whispered with his attorney before replying: "On advice of counsel, I refuse to answer that question."

HÉBERT: For your information, Irving Russell was just made up in my mind right now. I don't know any such man, either. I just wanted to find out how ridiculous you were going to become.

SILVERMAN. I would like to explain in terms of the context.

HÉBERT: You will have a chance to explain. In other words, you just don't talk.

SILVERMAN: On advice of counsel, I refuse to answer that question.

HÉBERT: Have you learned any other lines besides those? Will it incriminate you to admit whether you have learned any other lines?

SILVERMAN: I refuse to answer that question.

HÉBERT: On the grounds that it might tend to be self-incriminating?

SILVERMAN: Yes.

HÉBERT: That is just a mental test. I wanted to find out about your intellectual ability.

My treatment of witnesses depended upon the facts regarding them, and on their demeanor. If they answered questions, as Hiss had done, and if there was no positive proof of their subversive activities except another witness' testimony against them, I gave them every benefit of doubt and treated them accordingly. However, when known Communists showed disdain for the committee and perverted the high principles they cited in defense of their perfidy, I might not force them into committing perjury, but I was damn well going to make them pay the price of public embarrassment for their treason and mendacity.

"Dr. Silverman," I began when the questioning of Silverman started to lag,

I read a part of your prepared statement in which you mention—there is one paragraph before but I will pass it because you will get the context of what I am asking you, and I hope on advice of counsel you don't refuse to agree with what you have read already and say that it might incriminate you.

Speaking of the indictment, you say:

". . . and trial in open court where they would be afforded full opportunity to confront and cross-examine their accusers.''

Do you believe in that principle?

SILVERMAN: I do.

HÉBERT: Stand up, Dr. Silverman, please. Miss Bentley, please stand.

Dr. Silverman, you are now before the greatest open court in this country, I believe, beyond the confines of any limited courtroom in this country. You are now in the presence of probably 1,000 or more people in this committee meeting room. You are in the presence of an invisible audience of millions of American people who listen to the radio. You are in the presence of millions of American people who see moving pictures. You are in the presence of competent and able representatives of the American press, which is free.

I now tell you, Dr. Silverman, you are facing Miss Elizabeth T. Bentley, who may be known to you under the name of Elizabeth T. Bentley, or perhaps under the name of Mary or under the name of Helen. I tell you, Dr. Silverman, that this lady standing here, whom I have described by name, accuses you in open court before the American people of being an espionage agent, or rather of having given her secret documents, confidential documents, which you, Dr. Silverman, obtained through your government, and she tells you that you were untrue to your trust.

You face your accuser, Dr. Silverman. What is your answer? Is she telling the truth or isn't she telling the truth, and do you recognize her?

SILVERMAN: In my opinion she is telling a huge web of lies.

HÉBERT: You tell Miss Bentley here—that is contradictory now to the fact that you refused to answer because it might incriminate you. Are you waiving that now?

SILVERMAN: With respect to the charge of espionage and any other criminal conduct I waive.

HÉBERT: You waive any charges right now—(Silverman began to confer with his attorney)—wait a minute. You can answer by yourself. You are a doctor of philosophy and had access to all this. You don't need to have anybody tell you what to do. You didn't ask advice of counsel when you handed these documents to Miss Bentley, did you?

Miss Bentley has made these charges and you are familiar with them. Now, you have your opportunity in open court to tell this lady that you have never seen her before, that you have never received anything from her, that you never knew her as Helen, Mary, or Elizabeth Bentley, and tell her that she never gave you any documents that were confidential or in violation—rather, that she—you have got me confused—(laughter)—that you, Dr. Silverman, never handed to her any documents, and you further tell her that you never gave documents to any unauthorized persons. Now, you have got your chance.

SILVERMAN: That is too complex. I do not consider this to be a court.

HÉBERT: You are hedging. You asked for an open court. I am giving it to you.

THE CHAIRMAN: Let him go ahead.

SILVERMAN: I didn't ask for an open court. I asked for a court. On advice of counsel, I refuse to answer that question in the exercise of my constitutional privilege against self-incrimination under the Fifth Amendment.

HÉBERT: That is all, Mr. Chairman.

The intrigue continued to mount as Lauchlin Currie and Harry Dexter White, a former assistant secretary of the Treasury, were called to testify on August 13 about their connections with former government employees whom the committee said were known Communists. As interest in the hearings expanded, even the most superficial citizens in the country knew that something "big" was happening in Washington where "they" were investigating "a bunch of Communists." Not only were the hearings making the front pages, columnists often devoted space to behind-the-scenes activities. Peter Edson wrote in his *Washington Daily News* column that the executive sessions

are now said to be rip-snorting fights. Chairman Thomas and Committee Counsel Robert Stripling were at first all in favor of dragging in Bureau of Standards Director Edward U. Condon and trying to connect him with Miss Bentley's accusations.

Rep. Hebert, a former city editor of the *New Orleans States*, has fought this off and he also has fought for the right of every accused person to appear before the committee and answer charges against him.

The nature of the hearings, plus the publicity they received, made them SRO affairs with lines of the curious queuing up in the halls of the House office buildings and onto the streets outside. However, some of the more important hearings were in executive session in order that witnesses' testimony could not be used against them by their accusers. Such was the case in the second appearance before the committee by Alger Hiss. But the security of executive session was not satisfactory to Hiss. He told the committee:

> If what I testify to in this committee today, through no fault of any official of this committee or any member of its staff comes to his (Chambers') attention, as my public testimony, of course, came to his attention, he will again be able to testify ex post facto to my testimony today.

After being silent to this point in the executive session proceedings, I responded:

> Mr. Hiss, let me say this to you now—and this removed of all technicalities, it is just a man-to-man impression of the whole situation. I think it is pertinent.
>
> I don't surrender my place on this committee to any individual who has an open mind, particularly regarding you and Mr. Chambers. I am not interested in who is lying except to the extent that it will only give us an insight to further the case and that we are about to find out whether espionage was in effect in this country to the detriment of the security of this country.
>
> I do not take the stand and never have taken the stand in this committee that anything is invovled other than to get to the facts. I have tried just as hard in public hearings to impeach those witnesses who are assumed to be so-called committee witnesses as I have tried to impeach the other witnesses. I think the record will speak for that.
>
> We did not know anything Mr. Chambers was going to say. I did not hear your name mentioned until it was mentioned in open hearing.
>
> HISS: I didn't know that.
>
> HÉBERT: As I say, I am not trying to be cagey or anything, but trying to put it on the line as certainly one member of this committee who has an open mind and up to this point [I] don't know which one of the two is lying, but I will tell you exactly what I told Mr. Chambers so that will be a matter of record too: Either you or Mr. Chambers is lying.
>
> HISS: That is certainly true.
>
> HÉBERT: And whichever one of you is lying is the greatest actor that

America has ever produced. Now, I have not come to the conclusion yet which one of you is lying and I am trying to find the facts. Up to a few minutes ago you have been very open, very cooperative. Now, you have hedged. You may be standing on what you consider your right and I am not objecting to that. I am not pressing you to identify a picture when you should be faced with the man. That is your right.

Now, as to this inquiry which you make much over, and not without cause, perhaps, we met Mr. Chambers forty-eight hours after you testified in open session. Mr. Chambers did not know or have any indication as to the questions that we were going to ask him, and we probed him, the four of us—Mr. Nixon, Mr. McDowell, Mr. Stripling and myself—and we literally ran out of questions. There wasn't a thing that came to our minds that we didn't ask him about, these little details, to probe his own testimony or rather to test his own credibility.

There couldn't have been a possible inkling as to what we were going to say about minor details, and he could not have possibly by the fartherest stretch of the imagination prepared himself to answer because he didn't know where the questions were coming from and neither did we because we questioned him progressively; so how he could have prepared himself to answer these details which we now, and Mr. Nixon has indicated, we are now checking and for the sake of corroboration—for my own part I can well appreciate the position you are in, but if I were in your position, I would do everything I humanly could to prove that Chambers is a liar instead of me.

HISS: I intend to.

HÉBERT: And that is all we are trying to do here. Further than that, I recognize the fact that this is not an inquisitorial body to the extent of determining where the crime lies. We are not setting forth to determine ourselves as to which one of you two has perjured yourself. That is the duty of the United States attorney for the District of Columbia. He is confronted with the fact that perjury has been committed before this congressional committee, which is a crime. It is up to the United States attorney and the Department of Justice to prosecute that crime and that is all we are trying to do.

Now, if we can get the help from you and, as I say, if I were in your position I certainly would give all the help I could because it is the most fantastic story of unfounded—what motive could Chambers have or what motive—one of you has to have a motive. You say you are in a bad position, but don't you think Chambers destroys himself if he is proved a liar? What motive would he have to pitch a $25,000 position as the respected senior editor of *Time* magazine out the window?

HISS: Apparently for Chambers to be a confessed former Communist and traitor to his country did not seem to him to be a blot on his record. He got his present job after he had told various agencies exactly that. I am sorry but I cannot but feel to such an extent that it is difficult for me to control myself that you can sit there, Mr. Hébert, and say to me casually that you have heard that man and you have heard me, and you just have no basis for judging which one is telling the truth. I don't think a judge determines the credibility of witnesses on that basis.

HÉBERT: I am trying to tell you that I absolutely have an open mind and am trying to give you as fair a hearing as I could possibly give Mr. Chambers or yourself. The fact that Mr. Chambers is a self-confessed traitor—and I admit he is—the fact that he is a self-confessed former member of the Communist Party—which I admit he is—has no bearing at all on whether the facts that he told—or, rather the alleged facts that he told. . .

HISS (interjecting): Has no bearing on his credibility?

HÉBERT: No, because, Mr. Hiss, I recognize the fact that maybe my background is a little different from yours, but I do know police methods and I know crime a great deal, and you show me a good police force and I will show you the stool pigeon who turned them (the criminals) in. Show me a police force with a poor record, and I will show you a police force without a stool pigeon. We have to have people like Chambers or Miss Bentley to come in and tell us. I am not giving Mr. Chambers any great credit for his previous life. I am trying to find out if he has reformed. Some of our greatest saints in history were pretty bad before they became saints. Are you going to take away their sainthood because of their previous lives? Are you not going to believe them after they have reformed?

I don't care who gives the facts to me, whether a confessed liar, thief, or murderer, if it is facts. That is all I'm interested in.

HISS: You have made your position clear. I would like to raise a separate point. Today as I came down on the train I read a statement—I think it was in the *New York News*—that a member of this committee, an unidentified member of this committee believed or had reason to believe from talking to Chambers that Chambers had personally known Hiss, not that Chambers had been in Hiss' house. That is not the issue before this committee. You are asking me to tell you all the facts that I know of people who have been in my house or who have known me whom I would not feel absolutely confident are people I know all about, personal friends, people I feel I know through and through. I am not prepared to say on the basis of the photograph. . .

HÉBERT: We understand.

HISS: That the man, that he is not the man whose name I have written down here. [Hiss had jotted down the name of a man whom he said might be Chambers.] Were I to testify to that, what assurance have I that some member of the committee would say to the press that Hiss confessed knowing Chambers.

HÉBERT: You have said that.

Then Hiss was again asked whether he could identify a picture of Chambers, and he said he could not.

"For the record," I said, "the issue is whether Chambers did have the conversation [about leaving the Communist party] with you, that is admitted, but the only way we can establish the fact that Chambers had the occasion to have the conversation with you is we have to establish the fact that Hiss knew Chambers and Chambers knew Hiss, and this is very important."

In his book, *The Witness*, Chambers wrote of my dialogue with Hiss:

Congressman Hébert, a blunt man, could stand the shifts and thrusts no longer. He burst forth, and in his outburst can be heard the rumblings of the nation itself, a little entangled in its own language, a little foiled, but with a rough grip on reality, a bludgeoning instinct for the truth. It is the sincere outburst of a man who knows that he is being tricked, but does not quite know how the trick works.

After my exchange with Hiss, the committee took a brief recess to discuss the case. Hiss was left alone in the hearing room to consider what I had told him. When the committee and staff returned, Hiss had decided to tell us that perhaps he had known Chambers after all, known him as George Crosley. Crosley, Hiss said, was a free-lance writer who had stayed at his home in 1936.

Then, the next day, in executive session, Hiss acknowledged that Chambers was the man he said he knew as George Crosley. His testimony had now changed from not being able to identify

Chambers—never having "laid eyes" on him—to saying that he was a man who had sublet his apartment, a man to whom he had given an automobile, and who had been a guest in his home for as long as a week.

In his arrogance, Hiss also made a challenge which ultimately led to his downfall. He dared Chambers to repeat the charges against him outside the confines of the committee hearings—which were privileged—in order that he might sue him for slander. Chambers would later comply on a nationwide radio program. Hiss would sue, and the term "Pumpkin Papers" would become part of the nation's vocabulary.

But now the stage was set for the dramatic public confrontation between Chambers and Hiss. Into the caucus room of the Old House Office Building reporters and photographers came in droves on August 25. Newsreel and early television cameras lined the walls as their kleig lights heated the already tense atmosphere. The huge galleries were packed with the curious who wanted to witness a historic confrontation. Those who could not get inside waited in lines that winded into the streets. Republican Committee members present were J. Parnell Thomas, presiding, Karl E. Mundt, John McDowell, Richard B. Vail, and Richard M. Nixon. I was the only Democrat.

The session got underway with Nixon and Stripling grilling Hiss concerning the old automobile he said he had either sold or given to Chambers. Chambers had previously testified in executive session that Hiss had insisted on giving the car to a poor Communist organizer, which was against party rules because such action might be traceable. However, an exception was made in Hiss' case after he prevailed on a top-level Communist functionary, Chambers added, and Hiss turned the car over to an automobile agency whose owner was a Communist. (This would appear, based on empirical data, to be an ideal cover for a foreign agent, for very few car dealers exhibit communistic tendencies.) Committee investigators checked the auto agency named by Chambers and found that Hiss had indeed turned the car over to that agency. On the same day, the auto agency transferred ownership of the car to a William Rosen, but the evidence of the transaction was incomplete. Rosen, it turned out, had been a poor Communist.

Hiss has said he did not know the final disposition of the car, but he now became concerned with obfuscation. When confronted with a photostated copy of the transfer of his car, he refused to say whether the signature was his. "Well, if that were the original," Chairman Thomas asked, "would it look any more like your signature?"

HISS: I think if I saw the original document I would be able to see whether this photostat is an exact reproduction of the original document. I would just rather deal with originals than copies.

HÉBERT: Mr. Stripling, may I interrupt? In other words, in order to give Mr. Hiss every opportunity—if we recall what he did with the photograph, that he did not recognize Mr. Chambers for some time, and he finally recognized him. I suggest that the committee issue a subpoena *duces tecum* to the motor-vehicle people and let them come in here with the original and it will be just a matter of hours, and he will have to admit it is his signature.

After more wheedling, albeit intelligent wheedling, by Hiss, I again asked whether he could recall "the transaction whereby you disposed of that Ford that you could not remember this morning?"

HISS: No. I have no present recollection of the disposition of the Ford, Mr. Hébert.

HÉBERT: In view of refreshing your memory that has been presented here this morning?

HISS: In view of that, and in view of all the other developments.

Hiss was harder to pin down than a greased pig at a country fair. He was ducking and sidestepping like a child who was "it" in a game of dodge ball. With an observation, I summed up what many people were feeling about his performance: "You are a remarkable and agile young man, Mr. Hiss."

Then Mundt joined the fray asking when Hiss had first concluded "that instead of this Whittaker Chambers being a man about whom you knew nothing, whom you had never seen, that perhaps he was a George Crosley with whom you had a great many personal dealings? When did you first conclude that and why?"

HISS: That question is, to say the least, a slightly loaded question. You talked about a "great many personal dealings."

MUNDT: Yes. You loaned him a car or gave it to him, and you

loaned him your apartment or gave it to him, you loaned him money or gave it to him, you entertained him in you home, you took him out to lunch. I think that stands as "a great many personal associations."

After a few more exchanges between Mundt and Hiss, I said to Hiss: "When the picture of Mr. Chambers was first presented to you here when you first appeared, at that time you said you would rather see the man to positively identify him."

HISS: I did.

HÉBERT: Today you say you told the committee that you did recognize some familiarity in the photograph.

HISS: I did not testify today that I told the committee that on the 5th. It was in my mind. I do not find it in the record. I do recall having said that to a number of individuals on the 4th, the day before I testified. I did testify to it on the 16th.

The fact is, there was a certain familiarity in the features. I could not tell whether I was imagining it. There is still a certain familiarity.

HÉBERT: You told somebody before you appeared before the committee that there was a familiarity?

HISS: I told several people.

HÉBERT: But you didn't think it of importance to tell this committee that?

HISS: It did not at the moment that I was testifying on the particular subject of recognition. It didn't seem of sufficient importance for me to mention; that seems obvious.

HÉBERT: We were trying to establish an identity which is most important and very pertinent to this inquiry, and you left the committee with this impression, and I am sure everybody else that heard it, that you had never seen this man Chambers or anybody who even remotely looked like him.

HISS: Mr. Hébert, you are better able to testify as to the impression of the committee than I am.

NIXON: Now the impression that was left with me—and I must join Mr. Hébert in this—I think the [impression] left with the press and I have read most of the stories that appeared in the newspapers the following day—was that you testified you have never seen this man.

Nixon went on to quote Hiss as saying "As far as I know, I have never seen him." Nixon remarked, "I understand his testimony now is that he did recognize a certain familiarity and told friends the day before that he did recognize that familiarity.''

Hiss replied that if the press had received that impression, it was created by Stripling.

HÉBERT: Of course, Mr. Hiss, the record speaks for itself. Your replies were heard by the press and the people in this room and Mr. Stripling, as a matter of fact, had nothing to do to create any impression except by what you said.

HISS: Well, now. . .

HÉBERT: Let me finish. I might also say, Mr. Hiss, that you created a most favorable impression the first day you appeared.

HISS: Thank you, Mr. Hébert.

HÉBERT: And when anybody had an opportunity, however, to read the cold record, they didn't get the same impression from the record as they thought they had gotten when you were testifying orally because as I told you before, you are a very agile young man.

HISS: Mr. Hébert. . .

HÉBERT: Wait just a minute. I will let you make all the speeches you want. Let me get mine in now.

Now, that is the reason why I am trying to find out exactly where the truth lies. I can't understand and I can't reconcile and resolve the situation that an individual of your intellect and your ability, who gives to casual people his apartment, who tosses in an automobile, who doesn't know the law of liability, who lends money to an individual just casually, is so cautious another time.

It seems to me it is a demonstration of a very remarkable agility. Now, that is the reason why I want to be sure in repeatedly asking these questions that there can be no doubt in anybody's mind about what you mean to say as contrasted to what you say.

Now, the impression was definite that you had never seen that picture—and, incidentally, these pictures have been shown to several people, innumerable people, of Chambers taken in 1934 and the picture today. Without hesitancy every individual has remarked about the striking similarity between the two men, which are naturally the same man.

And yet, you, and you alone—you and you alone—sit here today and stand out as a lone individual who hedges and resorts to technicalities that you can't tell.

HISS: Mr. Hébert, that was a very loaded statement.

HÉBERT: I hope it was because I want you to get the full impact of it.

Hiss began to talk about the angle at which the photograph was taken and the length of time that had elapsed since he had seen Chambers. He concluded by saying, "You are privileged to have your own interpretation, Mr. Hébert, and, thank goodness, I am privileged to have mine."

HÉBERT: . . . I always respect your interpretation of anything the same as I think the committee wants its interpretation respected here, and we are only trying to get to the truth. As I told you the other day in executive session, I told you that either you or Mr. Chambers was the damndest liar that ever came on the American scene.
HISS: And I am just as anxious to get at the truth as you are.
HÉBERT: And whichever one of you is lying is the greatest actor we have ever seen in this country.

That statement, which is hard to argue with, made headlines around the country. Editorials sprang from it. It was a fact, they said, that needed resolving.

On the committee Nixon was the dogged investigator and relentless questioner on specifics; Mundt made copious and intelligent summaries of the testimony; but I turned out to be the phrase-maker. My reactions were only those of the average man.

After one of Mundt's summaries, Hiss cited a long list of high government officials and prominent Americans with whom he had been associated in one capacity or another and compared his record to that of Chambers. He also attacked some of Mundt's conclusions, and spotting flaws in the implication of Hiss' presentation, I joined the scrimmage.

HÉBERT: It is interesting to note that Mr. Chambers told us that himself in the conference in New York. He told us your stepson's education was paid for by the boy's father.
HISS: I do not know what Mr. Chambers said.
HÉBERT: I know; I know you don't. You will find out a lot that he said before these hearings are over, indicating that the man did know you at a time when you denied ever having known the man.
    We were trying to find out whether he knew you. That was a very intimate thing, that only a man who knew you could testify.

HISS: Unless he was checking carefully on me in the last 10 years.

HÉBERT: That is correct; unless he was checking on you in the last 10 years. That is the one thing I have not resolved in my own mind. What motive could the man have to go into such detail as to know all about your private life and to come before this committee and tell us these things? That is the unsolved riddle, as far as I am concerned at this time.

This man was confronted by us within 48 hours after you appeared, and, as I told you in executive session last Monday, the committee literally ran out of questions. He had no occasion to know, and he had no indication at all of knowing, what we were going to ask him. He did not have any indication at all as to what fields we would explore, and he unhesitatingly answered every question in the minutest of details which, as Mr. Mundt has indicated, comes back and checks, even down to the automobile sale.

HISS: Who would remember how would any man remember all those details about any other man after 14 years?

HÉBERT: Unless he knew him extremely well.

HISS: Unless he was studying up on it.

HÉBERT: Unless he knew him extremely well. You made mention here before that you are an ornithologist.

HISS: Amateur.

HÉBERT: Amateur. And that information could be obtained in *Who's Who*. Now, to anybody reading that or hearing that, why, that is a very plausible statement.

HISS: It is a factual statement.

HÉBERT: I am not saying it is not a factual statement, but the implication that you leave, as I tried to indicate before, Mr. Hiss—and we understand each other; you know we do—the implication that you leave is, why, anybody could look in *Who's Who* and see that you are an orinthologist.

HISS: That is certainly the case.

HÉBERT: But nobody could read in *Who's Who* that you found a rare bird, which I will ask Mr. McDowell to describe.

STRIPLING: A prothonotary warbler.

HÉBERT: A warbler, and the other day, in executive session, we asked you about that particular bird, and you said, "yes." Now, that is not from *Who's Who*.

HISS: I have told many, many people that I have seen a prothonotary warbler, and I am very, very proud. If Mr. McDowell has seen it, he has told very, very many people about it.

HÉBERT: Now, the question has been asked: "Do you recall certain individuals with whom you were friendly?" I will recall them from memory and ask you a question about each.

I then asked Hiss whether he knew four persons whose names had been mentioned in testimony as being Communists: Henry Collins, John Abt, Lee Pressman, and Harold Ware. Hiss said that he knew them all, but did not know whether they were Communists.

HÉBERT: Now, the reason I ask those questions, Mr. Hiss, is to bring you up to date on your letter, which you just read, and recited a long list of persons who would know you and know what you were about, and know who you are and what you are.

HISS: That is right.

HÉBERT: And it was an imposing array of fine American people. How would they know whether you are a Communist or not, when you don't know about intimate people that you know whether they are Communists or not.

HISS: Mr. Hébert, I did not cite their names on that issue. I cited their names on my record, because I think my record is relevant to this inquiry.

HÉBERT: You cited that list of names to leave the impression that these people could testify that you are not a Communist.

HISS: I said, and I say now, that those people can testify as to whether they noticed in my demeanor over sometimes prolonged periods any indication of any departure from the highest rectitude.

HÉBERT: Well, none of these people could testify as to whether or not you are a Communist, could they?

HISS: Have they testified?

HÉBERT: I did not ask that.

HISS: Whether I departed from rectitude, in their opinion?

HÉBERT: I asked a question: Can any of them testify whether or not you are or are not a Communist?

HISS: That is for them to say.

HÉBERT: Can they testify? You have injected their names in the hearing. I did not.

HISS: I did not cite them for that purpose, to you, Mr. Hébert. If you wish to ask them that question, that is your privilege. If you do not wish to ask them, I shall attempt to obtain affidavits from them for the committee's information.

HÉBERT: Well, their testimony would not be worth any more than your testimony will be against Ware, Collins, Abt, Pressman.

HISS: That is your opinion. I have told you why I think their testimony as to my character would be relevant.

HÉBERT: But they could not testify whether or not you are a Communist.

Despite pointing out the obvious irrelevance of Hiss' list of names, I was determined to be as objective as I could be, and later that afternoon when Chambers took the stand, I grilled him extensively, asking questions of him which had been propounded by Hiss. Before the questioning began, I told Chambers:

Mr. Chambers, let me make myself perfectly clear before I ask you any questions.

You look to me just like anybody else before this committee, and if I can impeach your testimony, I will do it, because I am only seeking the truth, and what I am trying to tell you is this, that as far as I am concerned, there is no such thing as a committee witness. By that I mean there are no witnesses, so far as I am concerned, who are going to be put on the stand to prove what some members of the committee think or might think. I am only interested in finding out the facts and the truth in the case.

I told Mr. Hiss that also in executive session last Monday, and I will try just as hard to impeach you to find out whether you are lying or not, as I will Mr. Hiss or anybody else.

I just want to make myself perfectly clear before I start asking you these questions.

I then took Chambers on a chronological trip from his birth down to that moment. Near the end I said,

Now, there is one additional charge which Mr. Hiss makes in his written letter which he gave to the press last evening, and which appeared in the paper today, and which we again heard read before the committee, and that was the fact that you are a confessed liar, a confessed traitor, whose word cannot be taken. By "confessed liar" I presume he means your activity in the Communist Party. By "con-

fessed traitor'' I think he refers to the fact that as a member of the
Communist Party you were a traitor to your country.

CHAMBERS: Perhaps he means that as a renegade from the Communist Party I was a traitor to the Communist Party.

HÉBERT: You are almost as quick on your feet as Mr. Hiss. . . .

Following Chambers' testimony, in which he refuted Hiss' story
about their relationship, the committee became involved in internal
bickering. In executive session I demanded immediate prosecution,
but Mundt and Nixon were angrily insisting on further public hearings. I told them,

> I'm getting sick of this messing around. Either Hiss or Chambers is
> lying, but it's not for us to decide who is guilty. We have presented the
> evidence and it's now up to the Justice Department to determine who
> committed perjury and to prosecute. I am strongly in favor of the
> committee continuing its investigation, but the Hiss-Chambers phase is
> finished. It's time we went on to other things.

I pointed out that the hearings were obviously becoming political.

> The Democratic Administration wants to shut off the probe entirely,
> while you Republicans want to keep this Hiss-Chambers pot boiling.
> Both sides are playing politics. I'm a Thurmond man [the Dixiecrat
> presidential candidate] myself, and I say you are both trying to drag this
> matter out until after the November election.

Mundt replied, ''We're laying the facts on a very important matter
concerning the loyalty of government officials before the American
people. Do you call that playing politics?''

''It's the way you're doing it,'' I said. ''You are obviously dragging this thing out in an effort to affect the election. We have already
established the fact that perjury was committed. What more is needed
for the Justice Department to act? It's got the evidence, let it step in
and take over. That's what the department is for.''

''That's your opinion,'' Nixon snapped. ''We don't think the
committee has uncovered all the evidence. Until we do, we should
not waive our rights. . . .''

Chairman Thomas said he was inclined to agree with me but
compromised on a motion to hear several more witnesses.

Meanwhile, prompted by remarks of President Truman and Attorney General Clark, which I considered insulting to the committee, I told reporters,

> It is naive to think this is not a far-flung espionage ring. Everybody wants to know what's going to be done about this. What can you do about it when you have a Justice Department that doesn't want to prosecute? The only thing the committee can do is to focus the spotlight on these activities. Although the Justice Department may not prosecute anyone for espionage there's one thing the attorney general can't overlook and that is perjury. Obviously, someone has been lying. Now the attorney general has got to prosecute someone for perjury or just come out and say he doesn't want to.

I added that it was "foolish for President Truman to call it a red herring.

"The committee has not obtained one iota of cooperation from either the Executive Department or the Justice Department," I complained. I was also nonplussed by Truman's closing of the government's loyalty files to congressional inspection, an action which not only hindered the committee but insulted and diminished it, and all of Congress as well. However, I wasn't going to let the Republicans make points out of that action unless their presidential candidate would assure the people he would react differently. I therefore challenged Dewey to say publicly whether he would open the loyalty files. When Dewey didn't answer, I told reporters the GOP candidate had maintained an "ominous silence" on the matter.

> It's only fair and proper that those of us who have been so critical of President Truman on these matters should know what position he [Dewey] would take.
>
> It's a tragedy that politics has played such a large part in the committee's activities. Democrats and Republicans together have contributed. The Republicans want to keep the headlines. They lose sight of the fact that the security of this nation is threatened.

Surprising a great number of people, including the editors of the *Chicago Tribune*, Truman defeated Dewey in November and won himself a full term in the White House. In December another surprise was awaiting the nation. Chambers had reiterated his charges against Hiss publicly, and Hiss sued. To defend himself, Chambers needed documentary evidence. Fortunately for him, when he broke with the Communist party a decade before, he had given a package of papers to his brother-in-law to hide. Suffering an almost paranoid fear of Communist retaliation, Chambers had kept those papers to be used as bargaining material if he were endangered.

When challenged by the Hiss suit to provide documentation of his charges, Chambers retrieved the papers, which he said Hiss had stolen and copied for him. According to testimony the papers had been hidden for ten years in the home of his mother-in-law. After retrieving them, Chambers hid them temporarily in a hollowed-out pumpkin on his farm. That is where they were when he turned them over to committee investigators. The story was a reporter's dream, and the documents became known as the "Pumpkin Papers."

With this startling development, the committee went back into session. One purpose was to determine the importance of the documents from the standpoint of national security. (Some were important.) Another was to learn from Chambers' brother-in-law the circumstances in which he had received the papers, where he had hidden them (in an old dumb-waiter which had been converted into a pantry), and to hear other pertinent witnesses.

Primarily I still was concerned with the politics of the situation. I was concerned that additional names of innocent persons would be needlessly dragged into the hearings. When the committee reconvened, a friend of Chambers, Isaac Don Levine, the editor of an anti-communist and anti-fascist newspaper who had aided Chambers when he broke with the party, took the stand to tell of his activities on Chambers' behalf.

Before Levine gave his testimony, I said:

> I understand, Mr. Levine, you requested to appear here in public hearing in order to give in public hearing the testimony which you gave in executive session previously; is that correct?
>
> LEVINE: No, sir. I wanted to appear to amplify the testimony which I gave briefly in executive session.
>
> HÉBERT: In other words, I understand your appearance here tonight is for the purpose of amplifying what previously is in the record?

LEVINE: Yes, sir; and to add facts.

HÉBERT: New facts which would be of interest to the committee?

LEVINE: And to the country, yes, sir.

HÉBERT: May I ask, before you begin to testify, do you intend to name any new names tonight that have not heretofore been projected into these hearings?

There was some discussion, and Mundt, the acting chairman, agreed that no new names would be mentioned without "studying the situation." I replied:

And in furtherance of that Mr. Chairman, I would like to say this: I would like to know in which connection Mr. Levine intends to bring any new names in. The fact that he writes them on a piece of paper is not satisfactory to me. I want to know how he can connect those names up, and if he intends to bring any new names in as I expressed myself before, I will immediately move for an executive session.

I objected to the names of two persons cited by Chambers as having given him secret information being mentioned until "those individuals have been brought before the committee in a private hearing and we hear them."

Rankin jumped in with:

I want to say in this connection that this is one of the most vital questions that has come before the Congress in the last quarter of a century. Undoubtedly, there are other people involved, and it is the duty of this committee to find out who these people are, and to bring them to justice. So far as I am concerned, I am not willing to put any witness in a straight-jacket and try to tell him what to say.

If this witness knows of any other individual who engaged in this treasonable conspiracy to steal these records from the State Department and turn them over to a foreign power, he ought to tell us who those people are and I shall not join in any attempt to prevent him from naming them.

I responded:

Mr. Rankin, may I say this: I don't want to put the witness in a straight-jacket. You understand as well as anybody else how I feel about the matter.

I am merely trying to possibly protect individuals who are not able to protect themselves, and I want to get the facts as much as you, but I do not lend myself to bringing names up in public before the individual knows anything about it or before we know anything about it.

During the questioning of Levine, I made a summation of the situation which put the hearings in perspective, and pointed out the function of the Un-American Activities Committee's hearings, a function often overlooked by some members of that committee.

We to this day don't know who the individual or individuals were in the Department of State who had access to those files, who gave them to Chambers, who was merely the messenger boy carrying them from the traitor in the State Department to the enemy in the Kremlin in Russia.

I think that is one thing we have to keep in our minds, and [I] just wonder how expansive and how far-fetched this whole proposition is, and [I want to] direct attention also to the fact that this committee is not the Department of Justice, nor a detective agency. We are not charged with the responsibility of apprehending the criminal. We are charged with the responsibility of bringing to the attention of the proper authorities the fact that a crime has been committed. Then it becomes incumbent upon, and the responsibility of, the proper agency of the government to apprehend that criminal when they know a crime has been committed and to prosecute him to the fullest extent of the law.

In that connection, let me say this: The committee needs no defense of itself. The committee's work stands for itself, Mr. Chairman. The fact, and the cold fact still remains, that if it had not been for the activity of this committee with its errors of omission and commision which we all commit—but never an error of the heart or error of intent of purpose—if it had not been for the activities of this committee over a period of years, this country would not have been alerted to the danger of communism, nor would it have realized the infiltration of communism in this government.

Finally, the fact still remains that if the committee had not given attention to Mr. Chambers and if Mr. Chambers had not appeared before this committee and given the limited or the conservative amount of testimony which he originally gave, had not named one Alger Hiss, Hiss would not have sued Chambers for libel, and if Hiss had not sued Chambers for libel, the documentary evidence would not be before the public today.

It all turns back to the fact that this committee insisted upon and gave attention to the fact, and now it is in the hands of the proper agents of this government to prosecute to the fullest extent of the law, or else acknowledge their guilt and their dereliction.

After the hearings, and as the committee was preparing its final report, some members continued to leak information to the press, which I have always found most irritating. In an executive session I announced, "It's getting so I have to read the papers every morning to learn what this committee plans to do. If these leaks don't stop I'll quit complaining in private and start raising hell publicly."

Rankin took offense. "The way you're talking you're placing everybody under suspicion. Not all of us are talking out of turn."

"Well," I said, "somebody is and it's putting the committee in a bad light. This irresponsible leaking of confidential information plays right into the hands of our critics and Lord knows, we have enough critics as it is."

"I think you yourself are doing a disservice to the committee by this sort of criticism," barked Rankin.

"That's your opinion," I replied, "you can act according to your conscience and I'll act according to mine."

This chiding of the committee had little effect. As the final report neared completion, the leaking of information increased. The last straw, as far as I was concerned, fell when Mundt told reporters that the name of Laurence Duggan, a former State Department expert, had come up during an executive session of the committee. What so outraged me was that Mundt made the statement to the press after Duggan had plunged to his death from a sixteen-floor window in New York.

I therefore called the reference to Duggan by Mundt "a blunder and a breach of confidence. I don't know whether Duggan is guilty or innocent [of espionage]. The important thing is Duggan cannot face his accusers. Duggan is dead. Not having been given a chance to defend himself while living, it is shocking that he should be branded as guilty after he is unable to defend himself."

I said I was disgusted with congressmen "conducting the committee's business with one eye on today's evidence and the other on tomorrow's headline." And, I added, there was no positive proof that Duggan was guilty of any criminal activity.

Despite that tongue lashing, more information continued to pour out of the committee and on December 30, the day the report was issued, I told reporters the committee had by and large

accomplished too much and succeeded too well in alerting the American people to the presence of the Trojan horse of communism within their walls, to allow it to be clouded by these indefensible practices. A silent tongue is far less dangerous than a wagging one. In making this statement I do so on my own responsibility as an individual member of the committee and speak for no one except for myself. I do not point the finger of accusation at any one individual. At the same time I do not indict every member of the committee because there are those, who have not given comfort to the enemies of the committee by such activities. They are blameless and it's about time that somebody comes forward in their defense and makes it clear that all members of the committee are not responsible for the activities of some.

Although I didn't specify who I had in mind, reporters and analysts said it was Nixon and Mundt.

With the issuance of its final report, the committee's work was complete. The result of these months of espionage hearings was greater security for the United States. Agents of foreign nations had been routed from sensitive positions in government and the need for more awareness had been made clear. Tighter security was enforced. Tougher legislation was passed regarding subversive activities.

Alger Hiss, steadfastly denying his guilt, despite the enormous weight of evidence against him, including confidential documents in his handwriting and others typed on his typewriter, was sentenced to five years in a federal penitentiary for perjury. He served time but was not penitent. He is still on the public platform proclaiming his innocence.

There are many who have never accepted the guilt of Hiss. For one thing, many liberals abhorred the House Un-American Activities Committee intrinsically, and felt so akin to the liberal credentials of Hiss that they would not accept his guilt. They grasped at each and every straw in an effort to prove that he was not engaged in espionage. They ignored evidence in favor of phantoms. But Hiss, of course, was never prosecuted for espionage; perjury was his sin.

I still find the case curious, and aspects of it puzzling. Chambers did strange and weird things like when he came up with the "Pumpkin Papers." Why didn't he give them to us earlier? Chambers said, "Nobody asked me." Now, a man of his competence would know damn well that we would want those files. As for Chambers' statement that he had been very fond of Hiss, and therefore withheld the incriminating evidence until forced to expose Hiss to save himself, I believe those are real reasons. But they are not in keeping with telling the truth, the whole truth and nothing but the truth.

Still, the proof is there. A person has got to accept it whether he believes it or not. The whole matter must be judged according to law, and according to the evidence. And the evidence is irrefutable.

As for me, I was kicked off the committee at the instigation of Truman and Clark when Congress and its new Democratic majority convened in January 1949. Almost as an added insult, Rankin, too, was put off at the same time, for ostensibly a different reason. But I took the advice of a contemporary poet, Dylan Thomas, and did not go gently. I followed the poet's counsel and my own instincts, and raged.

CHAPTER XVII

GIVING HARRY HELL

THE HOUSE DEMOCRATIC leadership in an unprecedented move ousted Rankin and me from the Un-American Activities Committee in January 1949. It was a maneuver somewhat similar to the action which occurred in January 1975 when I was stripped of my Armed Services Committee chairmanship by a group of freshmen legislators who stormed through Congress like Visigoths sacking Rome.

In 1949, however, the move was more covert. Ostensibly, I was evicted from the Un-American Activities Committee because I wasn't an attorney, a requirement enacted by the Democratic Ways and Means Committee as a prerequisite for membership on HUAC. There were, of course, some tissue-thin (and constitutionally questionable) reasons cited for the necessity of having passed a bar exam in order to sit on the committee, but it was obvious that the move was aimed solely at me. In Rankin's case another rule was trumped up to evict him. That piece of artifice stated that a congressman could not sit on HUAC while holding the chairmanship of another committee, and Rankin was in line to become chairman of the Veterans' Affairs Committee.

In its January 16 edition, the *New York Times* reported that I had declined to comment on the move, but quoted "friends" as saying the decision to remove me from the committee was prompted by my active fight as a States' Rights Democrat against President Truman, and by my frequent criticism of Attorney General Tom Clark.

To compound matters, just a few days before my removal, I had attacked Truman's message to the joint session of Congress. I acknowledged that the President deserved the initial ovation he received from the congressmen for the "great victory" won last November "in the gallant fight which Mr. Truman had made against overwhelming odds." Then I got down to basics.

> I disagree, however, that Mr. Truman's personal victory was a mandate from the people of America to abandon the system which has been the inspiration and the incentive for the building of the greatest nation which has ever existed.
>
> I cannot agree with the President that the majority of people who voted last November wanted to make permanent in this country a government by directive instead of a government by law. I cannot believe that the people who voted for Mr. Truman last November intended by that vote to abandon all rights of local self-government and to surrender to the central government here in Washington the inviolate rights of the sovereign states.
>
> The full impact and essence of the President's message to the Congress was an appeal for centralized government—for a government that will get bigger and bigger as it takes over more and more new functions.
>
> Perhaps a continued expansion of government is not a bad thing, although I personally do not agree.
>
> The people should understand that the area of individual initiative and responsibility diminishes as that of government expands.

Those sentiments did not get me any invitations to Margaret Truman's recitals, nor had my attacks upon Truman and Clark during the Hiss probe. I recognized that in being booted off the committee I was being punished for being a "disloyal" Democrat. "I displeased some individuals when I refused to play politics as a member of the committee," I acknowledged to the press, and quoted Shakespeare to the House Democratic leadership following my eviction: "The villany you teach me I will execute; and it shall go hard, but I will better the instruction."

In a formal statement on my dismissal, I said,

> There is a political axiom that you can do anything you want when you have the votes. That axiom has been obviously applied to me because I have exercised political independence in Washington and Louisiana, and as a result, I have failed to be reassigned (or if you care to use the

word, "purged") to the committee on Un-American Activities for the
81st Congress.

It would have been far more commendable and courageous of those
responsible for this move if they had not resorted to subterfuge in the
best Machiavellian technique to attain their end. Their position is
directly in contrast to mine which has always been straightforward,
forthright and to the point. My political integrity is not on the auction
block. I am immune to political police thought control and action
through fear of reprisal.

I cited the main reason for my removal.

In Louisiana I supported and participated actively and openly in the
States' Rights movement in which I believed and still believe. Apparently, this was a mortal sin in the eyes of some individuals who would
now have me seek forgiveness and absolution. I have no inclination nor
desire to do either. I have nothing to apologize for. Election results do
not change my principles.

I told one reporter:

They could not find a legitimate reason so they confected a flimsy
excuse. First thing you know they will be letting only generals and
admirals serve on the House Armed Services Committee. And I'd
better tell Representative [A. Leonard] Allen [of Winnfield, La.] to
watch out. He is vice-chairman of the Veterans' committee—and he's
not a veteran.

Reacting to my ouster, the *New Orleans States* said editorially,

Hébert has been in the forefront of those calling for reforms in
committee conduct. Hébert had asked the former committee members
to agree to a system which would allow each witness to retain a lawyer
and stenographer while he was being questioned; to a committee rule to
protect the names and reputations of innocent persons from being
connected with any probe until they had a chance to be heard from in
their own defense. All of these proposals the Republican leaders,
Representatives Mundt and Nixon, made public and claimed for their
own. . . .

Hébert has time and again protested against "headline grabbing" on
the part of committee members. He stood for a proper method of
interrogation and investigation, and with giving every witness a chance

to defend himself. Now, in a belated effort to arrive at the same conclusion Hébert himself arrived at a year ago, the Democrats on the committee set up rules which exclude the one man who fought for committee reforms. And whether it is because he isn't a lawyer or because he was a Dixiecrat may never be publicly known.

The more liberal *New Orleans Item* was equally aware of my role on the committee and said that apparently Truman wanted to kill the committee's effectiveness. As for me personally, the *Item* wrote,

It should surprise no one, least of all his fellow members in the House, if he manages to hold his own, and perhaps a bit more in any war of political reprisal. Hence it will remain for time to tell whether the House majority leaders and the administration in general have really played smart in dismissing him from a committee where he has rendered his nation such commendable service.

David Lawrence wrote in his syndicated column that while some may view the 80th Congress as the "worst," the 81st was shaping up as the "most intolerant." He continued,

The most amazing example of a denial of the rights of the people is the capricious way the leadership of the Democratic Party in the House has decided on certain committee assignments.

Only lawyers, for instance, are to be permitted to serve as members of the Democratic majority on the House subcommittee investigation of un-American activities. This is but a subterfuge to be rid of Representative Hébert of Louisiana, who did not support Truman in the last election but voted for Governor Thurmond.

The specious argument that only lawyers can serve on the Un-American Activities Committee can rise to plague the Democrats. For it can lead to demands for discrimination in choosing the members of other committees. Perhaps the Democratic chiefs will be asked to decide next that only members who once held cards in labor unions are eligible for membership on the House Labor Committee or that only persons who have been farmers can serve on the agriculture committee.

To say that Hébert, who already has had experience on the committee and is generally regarded as fair and impartial in his handling of witnesses, is now to be unseated because he doesn't happen to be a lawyer is to give an example of arbitrariness and intolerance which certainly doesn't come under the heading of "fair deal" or "liberalism."

In a radio address to my constituents, I laid bare the facts of my removal.

I can reveal to you now that it was suggested to me by Speaker Sam Rayburn of the House that I issue a statement saying that I desired to be removed from the committee because I could not devote the proper attention to it because of my ranking position on the committee on Armed Services which I have attained. Speaker Rayburn made this suggestion to me before the action removing me from the committee was made official and before it had been publicly announced. I refused to follow the suggestion because it was not the truth and because such a statement from me would not have been in accordance with the facts. To have done such a thing would have made me party to the type of insincerity and scheming which I condemn.

I then quoted a statement from Truman's inaugural address—"We believe that all men have the right of freedom of thought and expression"—and then I asked, "In view of what has happened and is happening what does the President really mean? Does he mean that everybody has the right of freedom of thought and expression only if that thought and expression concurs with his thoughts and expressions? It would seem so."

Throughout my political career I have fought ceaselessly against enforced regimentation by big government seeking an unobtainable Utopia through federal regulation. I sought to maintain what I believed to be the best form of government—not a perfect government, but the best of all possible governments—Jeffersonian democracy. This belief sometimes caused my motives to be erroneously interpreted. As a Dixiecrat I was not motivated by the lure of segregation, but by the magnetic appeal of its individualism, and by its insistence on the rights of the states. I viewed it not as "a Southern or sectional fight, but a fight involving a principle and an ideal of government which affects the East as much as the South, which affects the West as much as the South, and which affects the North as much as the South."

Not surprisingly, some intelligent persons refuse to grant me my philosophical beliefs; they prefer instead to attribute my actions to racism. Even though born into a Southern heritage, which in 1901 still had many raw scars of Reconstruction that could be rubbed the wrong way, I never descended into the cellar of race baiting. That has never been my style; it does not reflect my temperament. The worst anyone can accuse me of in retrospect is a certain paternalism, and a refusal to join patronizing movements. And if one refuses to grant dispensations for the environmental effects of the early twentieth-century South, then one should not seek them for the late twentieth-century urban North, South, East or West.

But, I need not apologize. In 1949 I saw politicians pitting the whites against the Negroes, and on the lowest level possible—a level of prejudice and hatred. My opposition to "civil rights" legislation stems not from my desire to deny opportunities to black citizens—I have consistently maintained that the Negro should have equal opportunities for education, advancement and development—but because it is impossible to legislate people to be good as well as it is to legislate them to be bad.

In 1964 the Civil Rights Bill was one of the big issues of Congress, and I opposed it. In doing so I alienated a certain segment of society which would not grant me the right to oppose the bill on the grounds of a life-long abhorrence to Big Brotherism, but chose instead to accuse me of racism. "The Bill of Rights," I pointed out in opposing the unnecessary Civil Rights Bill, "is not a white man's bill of rights, it applies to the Negro, too." At the time I wrote to a constituent: "I am opposed to all civil rights proposals, and I voted against the Civil Rights Law because I do not believe it is equitable. I do not believe it is valid. Now, if you find any sophistry or semantics in that, make the most of it."

"I am a deep, strong constitutionalist," I pointed out during a television program in 1967. "I believe strongly, firmly, and with feeling, in the full expression of the Constitution of the United States as it is written. Now, let us understand that clearly. I believe that every individual in this country should have the equal opportunity to earn a living. I do not believe that the government owes anybody a living. I do believe firmly and strongly that the government owes everybody the opportunity to earn a living and I do believe that everybody in the country should be equally represented and equally given the justice that is to be handed out by the courts regardless of race, color or creed. Now, I hope I make that clear. I cannot make it any clearer.''

I accept the fact that not everyone subscribes to my point of view, but I object when my motives are impugned. I object to the narrow mind which refuses to grant me the right to dissent when so-called liberal measures are proposed.

Take, for example, the Americans for Democratic Action, or the Liberal Party of New York. They don't accord those who disagree with them the same rights that they demand for themselves. For instance, Franklin Roosevelt, Jr., didn't hesitate to support a candidate under the Liberal banner in New York City. Yet, when I supported Thurmond, certain members of the party thought that was horrible. Why couldn't they accord me the same right they accorded Roosevelt. These horror-struck members didn't run Roosevelt out of the Democratic party. They didn't run those people out of the New York Democratic party who supported the Liberal candidate under a party name. That was perfectly all right for Roosevelt, and, in their eyes a most reasonable thing to do.

But any Southerner, and I use the term Southerner advisedly, who exercises the same right must be punished for supporting anyone but the party's nominee. As far as I'm concerned the States' Rights party was not a party, it was a democratic rebellion within the Democratic party. It was a plain case of a minority expressing itself. The States' Rights people never left the Democrats.

There was an exchange between John McCormack and myself in 1949 on the floor of the House which illustrates my position very clearly. Truman had sent word down the line that if we didn't vote for the administration's Taft-Hartley repeal bill, there wouldn't be any patronage. Poor Sam Rayburn's neck was about to burst, therefore, when I got up to speak on the floor. At a press conference earlier that day President Truman had made it plain that the vote on the labor-management bill would be a test of party loyalty. Truman said loyal Democrats are those who support the party platform, which is the law of the party and should be supported both before and after elections. Thus, when I rose to speak, Rayburn, knowing how I felt about coercion, was understandably uncomfortable. I said, "The President of the United States has officially placed a patronage purchase tag on votes," and Rayburn's worst fears had come true. "The position is very clear that the vote is for sale for a job or jobs."

McCormack, the majority leader, wasn't too pleased with my remarks either. He came screaming down to me. McCormack charged that if I had my way "we would not have a Democratic majority today in the House, and we would not have a Democrat elected President of the United States. I am very sorry the gentleman took the floor. He should have remained silent because he actively and openly supported a splinter party of the Democratic Party," and McCormack added, I was sitting as a Democratic member of Congress only through the "tolerance" of the Democratic party.

I retorted, "I was elected a Democrat and sit as a Democrat through the votes of the people of my district of the sovereign state of Louisiana. . . . I will vote according to their wishes and not under the compulsion of a leadership which would destroy the sovereignty of the state, and establish a welfare state, nor will I be subjected to the threats and intimidation of a chief executive who resorts to such practices."

McCormack and I really had it out, but I was determined he was not going to drive me out of the party because I am a Democrat, for whatever it's worth, in my conception.

When I first went to Congress I was naturally a conservative. I believed in the Democratic party as I knew the party, but I never would accept party dictation. Party dictation is a violation of the very basic concept of the Constitution. It is a very basic violation of the freedom of expression. If we are going to go to Washington as Democrats and Republicans and follow party lines we need no Congress. All we need do is elect a Democratic President and a Democratic committee and we'll save a lot of money that way. We can run the country by committee the way it's done in Russia.

Every time I turn around in Congress someone is spouting out that if you don't adhere to the party line, you are a defector. I don't buy that nonsense. I'm in Congress to pass my own judgment, whether it's Democrat or Republican. Suppose the Democratic party is going to support Al Capone for President. Am I supposed to support him because he is the party's nominee?

Shortly after my run-in with McCormack over party discipline, I introduced newly elected Representative Edwin Willis of Louisiana's Third Congressional District to the Democratic leader. McCormack then proceeded to make a speech to Willis about party loyalty. He was looking at Willis but he was talking to me.

The charge of party disloyalty has haunted me throughout my career, and it began with my removal from the Un-American Activities Committee, which was engineered by the Democratic leadership, even though not every member of it liked doing it. I think Rayburn personally hated and regretted having thrown me off the committee. I think he was forced to do it by Tom Clark and Truman, because Tom Clark was carrying a grudge. That is where the pressure came from. One of Rayburn's aides told me after Sam died that the Speaker certainly regretted having done it. I know our friendship never died.

Maybe they did me the biggest favor in the world. They probably did, because I would have been tied up in all that business, and who knows what effect continued service on the Un-American Activities Committee would have had on my career.

Despite my relationship with Truman in 1948, I had been on good terms with the chief executive early in his administration. I had spoken highly of Truman and backed him on controversial issues. In a 1946 address to my constituents, I argued forcefully that they should applaud the President's effort to have Palestine declared a homeland for Jews. I cited a long list of promises that had been made to the Jewish people, each of which had been repudiated. I noted:

> How can we as Americans deny to the Jews the right of liberty which we demand for ourselves? We do not have a monopoly on liberty and freedom. It is the God-given right, not only of Americans, not only of Christians, or Protestants and Catholics, but of every man and woman, Jew or Gentile.

I continued my appeal by citing Truman's work at Potsdam on behalf of a Jewish commonwealth in Palestine, and then concluded:

It is thus obvious to even the most politically naive that Palestine is to be used as the pawn for international bargaining.

The military triumph over Germany and anti-semitic Nazism does not end the matter. If we felt an obligation to engage in the war against persecution of the minorities we have just as great an obligation to concern ourselves with solutions to the problems of permanency.

Cries for food from starving countries throughout the world ring in our ears. The Jews of the world cry for more than food; they cry for the right to eat that food in freedom; they cry for the right to settle in the land of their forefathers; they cry for the right to be free in deed as well as in word; they cry for the right to have a land and a home of their own.

Could they ask for less of a nation and a people which professes its belief and existence in the premise that all men are created equal?

Open Palestine to the Jews. Give to the Jews of the world that which we demand and receive for ourselves as Americans, as Louisianians, as New Orleanians.

This was one of the few times that I actually spoke out in support of a Truman position. After 1948 my addresses regarding the President took on a somewhat different tone, as the titles of some radio talks indicate: "Truman the Bully," "Truman's Threats on Legislation," "Truman and Double Talk." I was conducting a one-man war against the President. There were any number of things which I didn't approve of in the chief executive's methods, but perhaps the President's most irksome trait was his intolerance of congressional dissent.

"President Truman, still suffering from the intoxication of his reelection spree, isn't kidding when he says he has inherent rights or when he says he has a mandate from the people," I said after Truman's inauguration. "When I say he isn't kidding, I mean as far as he is concerned he isn't kidding. He actually believes it. Never has a winner been so flushed with victory as Harry S Truman. From a docile, affable, friendly little man from Missouri, the average Mr. America type, President Truman today, apparently in his own mind at least, stands Colossus-like, astride the Rhodes of American politics, ready to take on all comers and do battle with any individual who dares have the temerity not to agree with him."

Yet, I knew that there was a time for opposition, and a time for reconciliation. When American forces were suffering reversals in Korea in 1950, I sent a letter to the President by General Robert Landry, a New Orleanian who was a member of Truman's White House staff. In it I urged the President to set aside a national day of prayer in an effort to unite the country behind its troops.

Dear Mr. President:

The present crisis in which we are living is naturally of great concern to every American and it is in that connection that I respectfully submit a suggestion to which I hope you will agree.

In these times of indecision and unrest it is most imperative that our people become united and solidified in the common cause of the preservation of our accepted way of life.

I believe and suggest that the spiritual leaders of our nation be called upon to set aside a Sunday on which the respective pastors shall urge the people of this country to join in prayer to the God of their belief to give to our responsible officials, political and military, the wisdom and the courage to arrive at the right and proper decisions. At the same time, I believe that our religious leaders should explain to their flock the ideals and principles for which we are fighting and for which many are offering up the supreme sacrifice.

I do hope I have your concurrence.

The answer came back on what proved to be a bad day for recipients of presidential correspondence. Truman was apparently in a feisty mood, for the same day Paul Hume, the *Washington Post's* music critic, got a letter from the chief executive in which he was threatened with a presidential horsewhipping if he ever had the audacity to find fault again with Margaret Truman's musical ability.

To me, the President wrote:

My Dear Congressman Hébert:

I appreciated very much your letter of the fifth, and I am enclosing you a copy of my Thanksgiving Proclamation, inviting your attention to the wind-up of the proclamation beginning, "Now, therefore." I think that effectively answers your suggestion.

I am extremely sorry that the sentiments expressed in your letter were not thought of before November seventh, when the campaign in your state, Utah, North Carolina, Illinois and Indiana was carried on in a manner that was as low as I've ever seen and I've been in this game since 1906.

That bit of plain speaking did not silence me. As usual I was determined to have the last word:

> I am stunned by the contents of your letter of December 7th in reply to my letter of December 5th.
>
> It is indeed exceedingly regrettable that you failed to grasp the real purpose and intent of my suggestion, but it is even more regrettable that you saw fit to gratuitously inject political distemper in your reply.

Part of this correspondence became a chapter in the now great play called *Give 'em Hell, Harry*. Although the text of the letters was changed on the basis of poetic license it did make the stage and screen as well as television. James Whitmore created the role and was succeeded by Ed Nelson who in his college days was a Tulane cheerleader.

Fortunately, I had had my political vaccination, and when it came time to defend Truman, although this was unpopular, I stepped forward. I chose not to make political hay over the firing of General Douglas MacArthur, which was then viewed as one of Truman's most unwise decisions. "I don't believe anybody will seriously disagree with my right to view with a critical eye anything that Mr. Truman has done," I told my constituents in mid-April 1951, but "the office of President is the highest in our country. The President is commander-in-chief of our armed forces, whether his name is Truman, Taft or Lincoln. The sanctity of the office is to be preserved to our people and in the eyes of the world, at the cost of even disposing the world's greatest general. . . .

"No matter how great in stature an American general becomes, he is still subordinate to the President of the United States no matter who that President is. . . ."

Despite my support of Truman in the MacArthur matter, the President still earned another shot from me. When Truman left office, I reported to my district that

> anybody seeing or hearing the Truman of radio and television saying,

"The time has now come for me to say goodnight and God bless you all," would not have recognized the defiant, vindictive Truman of a few hours earlier who had brazenly told a press conference that he intended to defy the twice repeated instructions of the Congress and the mandate of an overwhelming majority of the American people by issuing a proclamation placing the tidelands of the sovereign states under the jurisdiction of the Navy.

If ever an action on the part of Harry Truman clearly demonstrated the spite and the venom of the man, this action did. Even those who sincerely believe that the tidelands should be under federal cognizance rejected this action on the part of this Pendergast beneficiary who, through the strange workings of American politics, had become President of the United States.

It was politics at its crudest.

I think the most unusual aspect of my opinion of Truman is the extent to which it has changed. With an overview provided by the passage of time, it has rotated 180 degrees. During an informal chat in 1967, a friend remarked, "Eisenhower was a lucky president."

"Well," I replied,

I'll grant you that. But what qualified a haberdasher to become the President of the United States, or to become a senator? And he's going to go down in history as one of the greatest presidents we ever had.

Truman's going to go down as one of our greatest presidents, and that's coming from me.

He was handed. . . .

I don't care what he was handed. I disagreed with him, and I fought him, and I did everything in the world against him, and I look back in history and he's a great president. He just applied that old fundamental right and wrong, and he made decisions. He made them. And he's going to go down as a great president. He never backed off from an issue, he never backed off, and he made that decision. Now, what would be better: for him to make a decision and be strong and firm, or to have a man with the training in government and the training in this and the training in that but who won't make a decision?

Of all the presidents under whom I have served, I must place at the top of the list—Harry S Truman.

THE GATES OF HELL

THAT LONG WINTER of discontent between the United States and Russia was still in full freeze. Our troops were engaged in a bitter struggle in Korea. The country was living under the threat, real or imagined, of a nuclear holocaust. American superiority in military might, demonstrated effectively, if brutally, when Truman ended the war with Japan, was being challenged by the technologically advancing Soviet Union.

To meet this challenge, the United States was employing its (and Germany's) best scientific minds to maintain preeminence in nuclear weaponry in an effort to keep the Russian bear at bay. The scientists were successful on both counts. Whether one was responsible for the other is conjecture, but a convincing argument can be made for the effectiveness of military power as a deterrent, and an occurrence on a Pacific atoll in May 1951 spoke loudly of the military prowess of the United States.

American scientists believed they had surpassed the "ultimate weapon," the atomic bomb, believed they had rendered it obsolete by creating a new and more devastating device "several times more powerful" than the larger of the bombs dropped on Japan, as it was cautiously but pointedly described in news releases calculated to let the Russians know a new weapon was at the disposal of the United States. Theoretically, the new weapon would perform, but from a practical standpoint it was necessary to see it explode. Such demonstrations give presidents and generals confidence and provide a satisfying climax to the efforts of scientists. The first test of the new bomb was to be made on Eniwetok atoll which had been wrested from the Japanese during furious fighting in the Pacific theater of World War II. There the United States would detonate the greatest man-made explosion since creation. Although security allowed no names, the world would later learn that it was a hydrogen bomb which was responsible for the prodigious power.

As a member of the House Armed Services Committee, I was selected to view the test, along with fellow members Melvin Price and Sterling Cole, who were also members of the Joint Congressional Committee on Atomic Energy. All newsmen were banned from the test site and the world was hungry for reports of this awesome event which was awaited with fear and curiosity. Man *was* toying with the unknown and more than a few doomsayers harbored feelings that humanity was going to blast itself into Kingdom Come.

I fed that hunger for news in June with a three-part series on the blast which was copyrighted by the *New Orleans States*. The *States* in turn made it available to the Associated Press, the International News Service and the Newspaper Enterprise Association, all of which sent the articles to newspapers throughout the world. In two of the articles, I chronicled the easy life on the islands enjoyed by U.S. military personnel—thirty-five cent drinks and juicy steaks amid balmy surroundings—and related human-interest anecdotes which would have made good copy for my old front-page column. But it was the description of the blast itself which became the focal point of my journalistic effort. In its "Press" section *Time* magazine wrote:

> As former city editor of the *New Orleans States* and a Democratic congressman since 1941, Louisiana's F. (for Felix) Edward Hebert (pronounced A-bear) knows what makes a news story. This spring he got his hands on a natural. . . . Before he left, Hebert agreed to do an exclusive series on the tests for his old paper.
>
> Last week, when Hebert's pieces came out, the *States* offered the series free to others. The Associated Press and International News Service picked up the congressman's irradiated prose. Sample quote: "I had the feeling I was standing at the gates of hell looking into eternity. . . . Space was annihilated. . . . You feel so pitifully help-less."

I guess my prose was melodramatic, but more dramatic than mellow, and I consider it a vivid and explicit account of the event. In my account I feed the reader facts and make analogies which through a little imagination became exciting and easily comprehended data. *Newsweek* called the account "most moving;" "an exciting story you'll never forget," said the Philadelphia *Daily News*; "a graphic account," advertised the Associated Press; the Washington *Evening Star* called it a "thrilling account;" and on and on.

It netted me a nomination for the Pulitzer Prize, for which I was most appreciative, but perhaps the most singular praise I received came from United States Supreme Court Justice Robert H. Jackson, who wrote: "Your account of the Eniwetok atomic experiment is one of the most effective uses of the mother tongue that it has ever been my privilege to read. It made me feel that I was sitting beside you, and I cannot refrain from expressing appreciation of your craftsmanship."

Comments such as these are music to a writer's ears, and may have played a large part in my acceptance of an invitation to do a thirty-minute reading of the story for Mutual Radio Network. Needless to say, I really hammed that thing up. I had sound effects, the countdown, everything. It was all ham, but it was the only effective way to tell the story. Reenforcing the dramatics was, of course, the listener's imagination, which has become recognized as a prime ingredient in the attraction of radio drama. Exquisite tension was the result. Tape recordings of the program are kept in the Library of Congress, Michigan State University Library, and the libraries of Loyola and Tulane universities.

The copy I prepared for radio was altered only slightly from the written version which follows:

. . . I have seen . . . and I have heard . . . the greatest explosion in the history of civilization . . .

I had the feeling that I was standing at the Gates of Hell . . . looking into Eternity . . .

I was at Eniwetok . . .

It was an unforgettable experience which defies description. There, space was annihilated. There, time was measured by the millionth of a second, and heat multiplied by a million times a degree Fahrenheit. The sensation, the emotion, the reaction to witnessing an atomic bomb explosion for the first time is something which cannot be reduced to paper, nor translated into words. It is something far beyond written or oral description. It is something which challenges the imagination, and confuses the realization of what has really happened. There is an empty feeling in the pit of your stomach, and you are bewildered, when out of the blackness a great ball of fire plunges into your vision, and a wave of heat simultaneously sweeps across your face.

"What am I doing here?" is about the only question that comes into your mind . . . and it is a question which has no answer, because everything else is forgotten. You feel so pitifully helpless.

I have walked the streets of destroyed Hiroshima, and I have seen the first victims of the first atomic blast ever dropped on a people. I have flown over Nagasaki, where the second atomic bomb was dropped. I have heard first-hand the details of the dropping of the first bomb by the man who dropped the bomb. And I have been thoroughly saturated with the scientific explanation of the splitting of the atom. But all of that means nothing when you are brought face to face with the experience of actually being present when the atomic bomb is exploded.

Of course every precaution is taken for the safety of yourself and those involved in the explosion; but the cold, brutal fact that you are about to witness an experiment cannot be erased from your mind, no matter how hard you try. You keep asking yourself the question! Suppose something goes wrong? What then?

Theoretically and scientifically you have been placed in a position which is safe from harm, according to the calculations of human beings. But suppose those human beings have miscalculated? Suppose those human beings have made a mistake? What then?

This Eniwetok experiment was something more powerful and more devastating than anything else which man had ever attempted. This bomb was several times the power of the bomb dropped on Hiroshima. Now in order to better understand the power involved in the Hiroshima bomb, as an example, that bomb detonated approximately 200,000 tons of TNT, as measured by atomic energy. By the same yardstick, and in comparison, the explosion of nitrate at Texas City, Texas, several years ago, which killed thousands of persons and practically destroyed the city, detonated approximately 1500 tons comparable power. Thus by comparison, Hiroshima's bomb was approximately ten times greater than the Texas City blast. And the bomb which was detonated in connection with the affect on structures at Eniwetok was several times greater than Hiroshima. And here this bomb which I was to witness was to be greater even than that bomb!

Now here's another way to explain the power: Suppose an ordinary stick of dynamite, as used in a hand grenade, was stacked one on top of the other. It would encase the outside of a 17 story office building on a city square of ground. By arithmetical deduction, a bomb, for example, 2 ½ times 20 kilotons would mean 100,000,000 pounds of dynamite or TNT. And measured according to the building yardstick which I have just described it would represent approximately a 60 story building on four squares of ground! And again the blast which I witnessed at Eniwetok was greater than this!

It certainly must now become apparent how difficult it is to fully grasp the potential of such an explosion, and to fully comprehend its destructive capacity. This particular test was calculated to generate heat greater than that which man believes to be in the center of the sun!

Whether or not it was to be a success was strictly a matter of conjecture and hope perhaps to the scientific mind the atom bomb can be understood, and its full meaning of millionth of a second measurement grasped, but certainly not by a lay mind like myself! It was all beyond my comprehension.

I kept recalling a story which I'd heard when I was a student at Jesuit. It was told during the course of a retreat by a learned Jesuit priest who was attemping to make our young minds realize and grasp the significance and the understanding of what eternity really means.

"Suppose a tiny sparrow would take one drop of water from the Atlantic Ocean," the priest had explained, "and cross the continent with that drop of water and again fly across the continent, and deposit that drop of water in the Pacific Ocean, and repeat this performance time and again, until the Atlantic Ocean had been emptied into the Pacific Ocean. Then eternity would be just beginning."

As eternity defies full understanding and comprehension, so does the full import and significance of an atom bomb defy understanding and comprehension.

The moment of detonation of an atom bomb is a result of cooperation and physical endeavor and output of thousands of men, multiplying that many more man hours. Today the shot came only after months and months of preparation. The experiment of the atom bomb started many years ago, when the mind of man first conceived the idea of splitting the atom. "Eniwetok" itself started a long, long time ago in scientific minds. It was then translated to the laboratory and now brought into full scale experimental force.

I frankly didn't know what to expect when I arrived at Eniwetok. I had no idea or conception of what it would be like. Those in the official party of observers, and they were very limited, departed from Washington early one morning. We were in California approximately ten hours later. The next morning we left for Hawaii and were there just before the sun went down. Next morning we winged out over the Pacific, and landed in Eniwetok shortly before dusk after flying over Bikini, the site of the first postwar atomic experiment after Nagasaki.

Lieutenant General Pete Quesada and his staff met us upon arrival and escorted us to the LST which was to take us from Eniwetok to the island where General Quesada's headquarters as commander of Joint Task Force Three are located.

To grasp the magnitude and expanse of Operation Greenhouse, which is the official title for these atomic experiments, it is necessary to visualize its location. Contrary to popular conception, except to those veterans who captured the atoll from the Japanese, Eniwetok atoll does not consist of one little island in the Pacific, but of countless small islands completely enclosing an oval shaped lagoon approximately 25 miles long and 20 miles wide. On the larger islands are located the major portion of the operation; the huge landing strip, the commanding general's headquarters, and the biomedical station and laboratories. At the extreme end of the atoll, in the direction of Eniwetok, is another of the larger islands called Anjibi. In between Anjibi and Eniwetok are such islands as Amasabacu, Kurujan, Bononaraparu, Jamanatsu, Ebaruru, Omapolaso, oh and so many other unpronounceable names. The actual explosion, or tests, occurred on several islands in the atoll which are called "shot islands" or else could be described as target islands.

The day before the "bang" was one of tension and apprehension. The weather was atrocious. The rains came in almost continual torrents, and periodical weather conferences were held. Not until the early hours was it definitely decided to conduct the experiment, and even then a three hour delay was agreed upon. Then Shot Day arrived.

Long before light appeared on the horizon we were aroused from our bunks. In the darkness we gathered on the shore of Eniwetok to witness the last preparations for this great experiment. I had a sensation and a feeling which was perhaps experienced by every GI who had huddled in a landing craft before a beach landing. This was my first experience with an atomic bomb experiment and I, too, didn't know what to expect.

In the cold chill of the morning we stood alongside the runway at Eniwetok and watched the aircraft which were to participate in the experiment take off without mishap. The day before we had examined the crewless aircraft, and the entire operation had been explained as to how the airplanes would be controlled, without a human hand touching the instruments or riding the pilot's seat.

There was something weird and eerie about the huge B-17's resting on the runways. Each motor was operated separately and tested separately just as though a pilot sat in the cockpit. These pilotless aircraft are controlled on the take off by a portable ground board. Shortly after they become airborne they are taken over by a "mother aircraft" which in turn is contact for the second control aircraft known as a "master mother." These pilotless airplanes are sent directly into the area of the "bang" and into the cloud or mushroom caused by the blast. The purpose is to obtain samples of the cloud, and to take motion pictures by automatically controlled cameras.

Everything went according to schedule. The hour of the "bang" was fast approaching. All official observers were then taken to the Officer's Beach Club and given coffee and sandwiches. Chairs were arranged in front of the Club along the beach, facing the direction of the "shot" or target island. A voice from a loudspeaker kept us informed of the progress being made. Each new action was explained. Each progressive step of the operation was detailed. We were again warned to protect our eyes against the fireball. Dark glasses, which completely blacked out all light, were distributed among us. Those who preferred not to look at the fireball were warned to turn their heads and count "1,001, 1,002, 1,003" before turning in the direction of the "shot island." Those who elected to look into the fireball were warned not to remove their glasses following the bang until they had counted off three slow seconds. That apprehension of what might happen if all did not go as planned was ever present. It just couldn't be helped. I couldn't shake it off! Half an hour before the bang I was seated in the front row of chairs on the beach in front of the Club. Except for the knowledge of what was to take place in a few minutes the scene could well have been any exclusive beach club on any exclusive beach, from France's Riviera to California's Palm Springs.

We were told that a ten-second warning would be given before the explosion. I examined my glasses. I kept on my own personal sunglasses under the thick, black lens which had been given me. I was taking no chances. In test, I looked at the sun. It was a tiny, red speck, hardly discernible. That's how thick these dark glasses were. With eyes covered I was in a pit of darkness, and the sound of conversation among the other observers took on an eerie tone, which added to the uneasiness and the apprehension of the moment. You could not see anything, or anybody, but yet you could hear voices. All around was the repeated warning, "Be sure your glasses are adjusted properly!"

Then came those last ten seconds which I shall never forget! The ten seconds before the explosion, when anything could happen if something went wrong. Without feeling and without emotion, the voice in the loudspeaker began, and echoed . . .

". . .Ten. .seconds." I felt and adjusted my glasses, I pressed them closer to my eyes. I became more tense.

". . .Nine. .seconds." There was an ominous silence over the group—an inarticulate mumble in the back of me was all I could hear.

". . .Eight. .seconds." The observer next to me remarked in a rather hollow voice that I still remember, "Well, we will know if it works in a few seconds. How do you feel? Do you think it'll go off?"

". . .Seven. .seconds." I wondered what the others were thinking. What emotions were they experiencing? It was old stuff to many of them; it was new to all of us, because this was to be the greatest, and the mightiest explosion ever set off or witnessed by man.

". . .Six. .seconds." I gritted my teeth. And the panorama of the horrors of Hiroshima, and what I had seen there, and the ruins among which I had walked, became more vivid to me once again.

". . .Five. .seconds." Suppose the scientists had miscalculated, and this theoretically safe distance, miles from the "shot island," had been miscalculated, too? What would happen? Will it happen?

". . .Four. .seconds." Seconds are fleeting, but the count between those seconds seem hours apart. It sounded like the count of Doom. Men I have seen hanged must have wondered, just as I now wondered. They didn't know what would be found at the end of a rope a few seconds away. I didn't know what was to be found after this explosion had occurred—only a few seconds away!

". . .Three. .seconds." I was beyond the state of apprehension. I was scared, and I was afraid that we might be the real guinea pigs of this experiment if something went wrong—if there had been a miscalculation!

". . .Two. .seconds." I couldn't stop repeating the question to myself—what am I doing here? It's too late to turn back now! But what am I doing here?

". . .One. .second." My muscles were taut! My fists were clenched! I tightened the vise of my teeth on my jaws! Only a second now remained! But it seemed like Eternity! That one remaining second! Then it came. . .

". . .B hour!" At least that is what I think the voice on the loudspeaker said. But now it didn't matter—B hour, Zero hour, any hour—this was it!

Silence. Blackness. Suddenly all was bright!

Through the glasses in which I had seen the sun only as a tiny speck a few minutes before there was now a brilliance the like of which I had never seen! The sky was all lighted. There was a gigantic ball of fire on the horizon, and, simultaneously, there was a gush of heat across my face! The fire and the heat seemed to come at the same time. There was no sound. It was just the sense of sight and touch. No hearing. Oh, I lived a thousand lives in that one split second! Or was it one-millionth of a second?

I counted to myself "1,001, 1,002, 1,003, 1,004." I took no chances, and then removed the glasses. I was choked with emotion. I wasn't shaking, but I was unsteady. I didn't cry, but I could have cried. What a peculiar and funny effect and empty feeling! Perhaps the knowledge that nothing had gone wrong caused the sensation. Perhaps the knowledge that we were still there. I looked in the sky, as the now-familiar pattern of the gigantic mushroom of Bikini formed, and soared heavenward. The fireball resembled a human brain, just removed from a human body. The fireball could well have been the colored picture of cerebrum lifted from any medical book. It was a sight I shall never forget! Under the broad, table-like top of the mushroom was a slender stem, and on the edges of cloud were many colors of the rainbow, with a deep dusk the prevailing hue. The scientists calmly discussed the formation. The lay observers expressed admiration and wonderment at that which they now beheld.

It was only a minute later, but it seemed much longer than that, when there came a terrific rumble through the loudspeaker—the sound of the bang as it was just passing Parry Island. A few seconds later we got the full shock of the sound on Eniwetok—it was like a great thunderclap caused by countless clouds following a flash of lightning.

Did you ever notice the start of a sprint race on a cinder path at a collegiate track meet? First you see the smoke from the starter's gun, and then runners spring from their starting crouch, and then, in the infinitesimal part of a second you hear the sound of the pistol, following the sight of the smoke. Then picture this and grasp the significance, and you can better understand the sensation which accompanies the delayed sound, miles away from the center of an atomic blast. More than a minute after you see the light of the bang and feel the impact of the heat, you hear the sound. You are that far away, and yet you are so close!

In that great ball of fire was more energy than has ever been assembled in one place by man since the beginning of the world! Can you comprehend fully what that means?

For many minutes we stood there on the beach and looked at the phenomena. That cloud would go around the world several times before it was completely dissipated. In it were many of the secrets of this thermonuclear experiment. In the multitudinous, highly sensitive instruments placed in the surrounding islands were many other secrets.

Within two and a half hours, a party of radiological scientists had landed on the "shot island," and had safely approached to within 850 yards of the center of the bang, and had come out to report their findings.

Late that afternoon, when the sun was setting behind the horizon, we flew over the target island and I looked down from the sky. There was nothing on the island left standing except the charred remains of a few palm tree stumps. The huge steel tower, equal in height to a multistoried office building, from which the bomb had been detonated, was nowhere to be seen. The thousands of tons of steel had been vaporized by the terrific heat of this explosion. Only the day before I had stood at the base of the tower; today it was gone.

Today everything above the ground was gone, except the coral sands of the tiny island, lapped by the lazy waters of the ocean. As I gazed down on the utter destruction and hopeless desolation below, I heard once again in my ears what that morning a two-star major general, a hero of World War II, had said to me as we leaned over the rail of the crashboat while returning to our billet island and were gazing pensively into the waters of the lagoon:

"It looks as though we are playing with things which belong only to God!" he had said.

I didn't answer him. I just looked up, and slowly shook my head in approbation.

Oh! I wonder, God, are we playing with things which belong only to you? Did I see a preview of the destruction of civilization? Have I, God, seen the end of the world?

The general whose remarks so impressed me was General Maxwell Taylor, though I felt constrained at the time not to use his name. General Taylor was talking to me not as a reporter but just as a companion who had gone through a moving experience with him.

When my account of the explosion was published, there were some cries that I had violated security and furnished eargerly sought information to the Russians. Former Atomic Energy boss David E. Lilienthal, told a reporter that "for the life of me I can't see why we need to tell the Russians . . . how we are doing, what our priorities are in atomic weapons. To spill our guts . . . constitutes, I must say in my opinion, a terrible danger to the security of this country and everyone in it."

William L. Laurence, in the *New York Times*, charged that

scientists in the inner circles of the atomic-bomb program are expressing great concern over the violations of security and abuse of their privileged positions by trusted members of Congress who in interviews or syndicated articles, have, without being aware of the implications of their statements, given away information about our atomic weapons development of considerable interest to atomic scientists in Russia.

Part of this attitude was sour grapes because newsmen had been denied access to the blast site. They could not be asked and would not agree, as I had, to have their copy censored by the Atomic Energy Commission. Also, some of the doubts expressed by Laurence were obviously planted by Lilienthal, whose anti-Hébert remarks had come unsolicited during a radio interview over the American Broadcasting Company network. Dr. Lilienthal had a motive for slandering me. In 1949 I had charged in Congress that Lilienthal, then head of the AEC, had supplied a number of atomic secrets to Dr. Frank Graham, president of the University of North Carolina, who was listed in the files of the House Un-American Activities Committee as a member of seventeen Communist-front organizations. I was not being reckless with my charges. I simply felt it was my duty to bring such information to light. Anyone might accidentally belong to one or two radical groups innocently enough, but seventeen? I had also revealed that Lilienthal opened the secrets to Graham despite objections from the AEC's security board and Rear Admiral John Gingrich, the commission's chief security officer.

Despite accusations of security violations against me, it should have been obvious to anyone who knew me that I was not about to commit such a breach of confidence. I had, in fact, signed a pledge not to discuss anything I observed without Atomic Energy Commission clearance, and had declined to answer reporters' queries about the blast because I did not want to say anything which might violate security. My written account of the explosion was cleared for publication by AEC security. It told enough to increase respect for U. S. military might without providing details which would aid an enemy in the construction of a similar device.

A sidelight to the hydrogen bomb blast story was soon to appear. For twenty-three years, while I was struggling to earn my living as a writer, I tried to turn out pieces for magazines and collected nothing but rejection slips. But now, after I had been out of the writing business for eleven years, I was being swamped by magazines with offers to accept anything I cared to write.

CHAPTER XIX

THE CHAMBER OF HORRORS

So as not to miss a thing, a facial movement, a drop of perspiration, a lowering of the eyes, a flush, I had attached a moveable microscopic eyepiece to the right side of my glasses. I flipped the bulky black appurtenance over my cataract-damaged eye and gave Deputy Secretary of Defense William C. Foster what had become known as the "evil eye." "Now that is a fact. That is not fancy. It would be something for you to look into," I said, referring to the strange and almost unbelievable impasses whereby regulations prevented the Army from ordering new trucks until they were approved, and withheld approval until they were ordered.

Secretary Foster was the first witness to appear before a special subcommittee named by Armed Services Committee Chairman Carl Vinson to investigate massive waste in the military, waste which resulted from confusion, disorder, resistance to change, mindless systems, redundant procedures, and obsolete practices. There were many culprits, but primarily the responsibility could be placed squarely on the Department of Defense for failure to adopt a uniform standardization policy and cataloging system.

Congress had first become aware of the need for a single commodity catalog in 1929 when the *Federal Standard Stock Catalog* was authorized. The wheels of government, like justice and good conservatives, move slowly, and in 1945 President Roosevelt created the Standard Commodity Catalog Board to study and develop cataloging plans. By 1946 President Truman had seen a need to direct further study, and the National Security Act of 1947 established the Munitions Board Cataloging Agency, which itself got additional aid in 1949 from National Security Act amendments.

The result of all this activity was zilch. California Republican Jack Z. Anderson had fought long for a single catalog and noted that there could be only two beneficiaries from the confusing and chaotic system under which the military was operating: "empire builders" and "unscrupulous manufacturers." But despite his efforts, Anderson had been defeated by the bureaucratic intransigence of the military. He had not had the ammunition to take on the well-fortified armed services alone, though some thought he should have been given a purple heart for the headaches suffered by repeatedly ramming his head against the brick wall thrown up against his efforts.

In 1951 the long suffering Anderson got some help, me. We both picked up an invaluable asset in Colonel William A. "Spike" Kelley, who assisted us greatly and who continues to carry on the fight until this day. I was a street fighter who knew how to attack an opponent's vital organs and had an instinct for the juglar. I had no hesitancy to fix a top-ranking admiral with my "evil eye" and tell him straight out:

> This committee is not going to stand idly by and see the press conferences conducted, press statements issued, by an army of propagandists and alibi artists from the Pentagon whose job is to do just that. I am talking about the public-relations men down there. . . . When a challenging statement comes out . . . that the Pentagon has offered to take the gloves off and fight back, why I say to the Pentagon, my gloves are off and we will fight not under the Marquis of Queensbury rules. No holds barred and protect yourselves at all times. If that is the way they want it, we will have it that way. That is all, admiral.

When I was selected by Carl Vinson, the old Georgia Democrat who eventually served fifty-two years in the House, to head the investigating subcommittee, newspaper reporters wrote that Vinson must mean business. What they didn't know was that with the connivance of Bryce Harlow, who was chief counsel of the Armed Services Committee, I had wrangled my way into the subcommittee chairmanship. I wanted to make sure that an investigation, which Vinson wasn't too anxious for, would get the proper attention.

Once I got the assignment, I went straight to work. With a tip from a constituent, I was able to quickly save the government $455,000. John E. Pottharst, the head of the Meco Company in New Orleans, told me that he had made a bid on a Navy contract to provide water-distilling machines at a lower price than that of the firm which was awarded the contract. Armed with this information I looked into the situation and found that a third firm had bid even lower than Pottharst's company. I applied pressure on the Navy, and by insisting that it simply follow good business practices by accepting the lowest bid, saved almost a half million dollars of taxpayers' money.

Next the committee revealed that the Air Force had spent $200,000 more than normally expended on typist chairs to purchase some "super deluxe" models. "Imagine this even in Washington, D. C., which has the legal title of the seat of government, and where many think there is a whole lot of plain and fancy sitting done, we have only 130 of these chairs," I said. The Air Force had ordered 20,156 of them.

"If these procurement officials at Wright Field [where the purchases were made] were given a suitable reward for this plan to waste money, they might need a small contingent of super deluxe upholstered chairs—with compliments of the taxpayers," I concluded. And before I was finished kicking them in the tail, they would indeed need the soft cushions.

The committee also discovered the Air Force had wasted $10 million on lathes in a farcical contractual maneuver which appeared to have been directed by Mack Sennett. When such slapstick was real rather than satire, it wasn't funny. It simply left the committee nonplussed. In yet another burlesque of business practices, the committee found incompetence which left it flabbergasted. "It taxes one's credulity to accept at face value the story of representatives of the Detroit Ordinance District that a company could drop out of the sky and walk out with $3 million in contracts having neither money, plants, nor experience with which to perform them," the committee reported after investigating a contract in which a firm without assets was to supply the Air Force with 6,000 tow targets.

With some of those absurdities out of the way, the committee was able to turn its attention to the matter of cataloging. It hoped to cut costs by eliminating the duplication of purchases among the three services. Looking into what the military had accomplished along this line, the committee discovered another area for reform: the Army used five pages in its catalog to cite the specifications for a flyswatter, or in "armyese," "swatter, fly, olive drab." Four pages plus two pictures were needed to describe toenail clippers for dogs, of which the Army had purchased nineteen pair in the past four years. (Noting the revelations of the committee, the *Times-Picayune* epigramist, Pete Baird, wrote: "Old soldiers never die, they just waste away.")

After recoiling from such preposterous nonsense, I knew it was time to move into action. I set up an exhibit entitled "The Chamber of Horrors," and quipped that a sign reading "Abandon Hope, All Ye Who Enter Here" should be affixed above the door. The exhibit featured racks and tables displaying various products used by the military. On one rack were six apparently identical carpenter's steel squares. Each had a different specification and price, which ranged from sixty-five cents to $2.19. Identical light bulbs were displayed which cost various branches of the service from six and one-half to sixteen cents; cereal bowls which cost the Infantry twenty-three cents were displayed beside the Medical Corps' bowls which cost twice as much because they had a purple stripe painted on them (apparently for the recuperative powers inherent in purple stripes); practically identical shoes for which the Air Force paid $7.29 a pair cost the Navy $6.08 and the Marines $5.31; boots from the same manufacturer cost the Marines $16.80 a pair while the Army paid $24.65; the Army bought blankets for $8.65, the Marines for $9.89, the Air Force $14.15, the Navy $19.57, and the Medical Corps $21.75.

Selfsame common nails were purchased by different branches of the military at different prices. The Army listed them as "galvanized" nails while the Air Force described them as "zinc coated," which would be equivalent to one of the services calling its members men while the other designated them as male human beings. The Army gave the nail dimensions in guage sizes, the Navy in decimals of an inch. Galvanized (or zinc coated) metal sheets were procured under different specifications and issued by the pound in the Navy, the square foot in the Air Force, and the sheet in the Army.

For twenty years a particular manufacturer had been supplying sugar bowls to the Army. Then he made a slight change in the design of the bowl cover. Despite submitting the lowest bid when the Army needed new bowls, he didn't get the contract. The reason: The cover didn't slope enough and the knob was of "improper shape and not of proper balance." One supposes soldiers might desert in the heat of battle because they were disspirited over the slope of their sugar bowl covers.

Naturally, such display got wide and prominent coverage in the press, and the hearings which I scheduled in the Armed Services Committee hearing room of the Old House (Cannon) Office Building were well attended. As they opened on February 11, 1952, I noted, "By direction of the chairman of the House Armed Services Committee, this committee is charged with the responsibility and cognizance of every dollar, every penny expended by the several branches of the armed services with the exception of real estate. . . ." Making reference to the display in the room, I said,

As of now there has been no logical or acceptable explanation as to the wide divergence of cost in articles common to all the services. A shoe is a shoe, a blanket a blanket, a bowl a bowl. Shoes are worn by soldiers, sailors, and airmen; they are covered with the same blankets and eat out of the same bowls. They are common items for the same type of men; why should their purchase price be at different and uncommon levels?

Congressman Anderson, who knew the situation well, told the committee that one single item had been assigned 1,108 different listings and different numbers.

What does it mean? It means that for a single item of supply there will be at each depot storing such items 1,108 different listings and different bins, with 1,108 different locator cards, with 1,108 different stock cards; and it means that orders must be placed on production facilities for quantities necessary to fill the 1,108 duplicate bins. These duplicate quantities result in the freezing of critical materials in huge unnecessary stocks of items. Stocks of such items running up to 240 years' supply have been found.

With that the committee got down to the business of trying to find out why in twenty-three years the military had been unable to develop a standardized catalog and procurement procedure, and for its first witness called Deputy Defense Secretary Foster. The type of reaction the committee would grow to expect from most of its witnesses was signaled by the deputy secretary of defense.

> I came not to bury the Defense Department but to praise it. We welcome these hearings for several reasons. In recent weeks a number of charges of waste and inefficiency have been leveled at the Defense Department. A hearing such as this provides an opportunity to examine these criticisms in an orderly way so that you and the public can judge what kind of a job is being done at the Pentagon. . . . Criticism can be both useful and destructive. . . , however, irresponsible criticism, based largely on rumor and exaggeration, tends to destroy confidence in the whole defense effort, which is certainly a serious matter.

Foster hastily assured me, however, that he knew the committee had accomplished much good by its investigation. "I appreciate that," I replied, "because you realize that this committee doesn't have the facilities that your department has nor do we have the army of expert public-relations officers who are very expert in spreading propaganda. We have just a small staff, as you see. Only three investigators and eleven members of the committee. I wish we could indulge in public relations experts."

I was particularly irritated by press releases put out by the Pentagon rapping the committee for its exhibit, charging that it misrepresented purchasing practices and failed to note the difference in price as a result of different purchasing dates. Behind much of that criticism was a voice out of my past, Clayton Fritchey, a former editor of the *New Orleans Item*. Before being relieved of his duties at the newspaper, he had fomented an editorial campaign against me for which his paper later apologized. Since leaving New Orleans, Fritchey had become head of the Defense Department's public relations staff. His presence provided me with added incentive to expose the waste and inefficiency in the military and the propaganda efforts to explain it away.

Having got the public relations activities of the Pentagon temporarily off my chest, I turned to Secretary Foster's opening statement which had defended the military's efficiency and praised its money saving efforts, and had concluded with the remark, "and the Army's Operation Red Tape program is now under way to reduce and eliminate unnecessary paper work."

"Now," I said, jarred by the remark on the elimination of paper work,

> I suggest that the Army go over to the Pentagon and visit with the Air Force and explain how only just last week a memorandum sent from the secretary of defense to the secretary of the army in turn was given to a colonel to prepare for signature, which is understandable, and it was returned for repreparation because the original document contained the word "memo" instead of the word "letter." So it took eight different people to handle that one operation.
>
> I had a note here about the Material Command saving $45,000 at Dayton. I was going to be facetious and wonder if they save it on soft chairs or deluxe chairs, but I will skip that.

"You didn't say that," Congressman Anderson said jocularly.

"No, I didn't say that," I agreed.

During its preliminary investigations, the committee had been unable to find anyone in the Defense Department who was responsible for standardization of cataloging and procurement procedures, or anything else for that matter. I had dubbed the elusive figure "the Phantom of the Pentagon." "You know the Phantom," I said, "he's the little man who's responsible for military purchases, but he always seems to be gone. Whenever I try to get him before the committee he has either just retired or left on a trip to the Far East."

Now it appeared that the Pentagon had appointed a responsible official who had authority. Secretary Foster announced that Rear Admiral Joseph W. Fowler had come out of retirement to assume a supervisory position with the Munitions Board, the Department of Defense agency responsible for the military's cataloging efforts.

"Is he the responsible individual now who makes the decision for the attempted unification of procurement? Do I make myself clear?" I asked the deputy secretary of defense.

FOSTER: No, sir, not the unification of procurement. He is the director of the cataloging agency. It is one of the agencies within the Munitions Board.

HÉBERT: Now, is he in the Munitions Board or in the department? Let's find out where he is.

FOSTER: Well, the Munitions Board. . . .

HÉBERT: He merely represents the Defense Department? Does he have any power of direction in the Defense Department—let's talk in simple language—to tell the Army, the Navy, and the Air Force, "Now, you three men get together and let's get this unified or I will make my decision after you present your situation?"

FOSTER: Perhaps this is oversimplification, but if all the services come in with the eighteen different names for the same item, he had the power to name the final name for that item and to make that binding on the entire department.

HÉBERT: He has that power?

FOSTER: Yes, sir.

HÉBERT: I congratulate you. We finally found a responsible official. Now, he carries that authority in the Defense Department and there he represents the Defense Department on the Munitions Board?

FOSTER: No, sir. He is a component part of the Munitions Board, this activity being one of the responsibilities in the procurement and productions field.

HÉBERT: Then he wears two hats?

FOSTER: Of the office of the secretary.

HÉBERT: Then he wears two hats, in effect. Certainly he does.

FOSTER: No, I don't think so, sir.

HÉBERT: And then he also sits on the Munitions Board.

FOSTER: The Munitions Board is a statutory agency which is. . . .

It was getting so that one couldn't tell the players even with a program. Determined to try, the committee called its next witness, Rear Admiral Morton L. Ring, who was acting as vice chairman for Supply Management of the Munitions Board. He told the committee that one of the problems in getting out a master catalog was that it would contain approximately four million items used by the Defense Department and almost 500,000 items used by the civil agencies of the government, which were not used by the military. (The Munitions Board was assigned jurisdiction over the entire project.)

Congressman Anderson asked Admiral Ring whether he could

name one item out of 500,000 which was used by civil agencies and not by the military. He could not.

"Don't you know one, admiral?" I asked. "You have been in this business a long time."

"I can think of items which the Department of Agriculture might use which the military do not and will not use," he said.

"Name one out of 500,000," I said.

The admiral hemmed and hawed and concluded "there must be scores of items which are unique to that."

"Why, of course, admiral, there must be scores of items. But here you are an individual who has been exposed to this cataloging by your own admission over these many years and when a member. . . .

ADMIRAL RING: Working, Mr. Chairman, only in military supply. I am still not an expert in agriculture, sir.

HÉBERT: We are not confining ourselves to agriculture. Mr. Larson says—and you are not responsible for his statement—that there are 500,000, one-half million, items procured by the federal government that are not usable by the armed forces. Now certainly you, in all your many years of experience in cataloging, out of 500,000, could just almost out of the sky name one. You can't do it?

RING: Well, . . .

ANDERSON: Let me help the admiral out.

RING: I am sorry, I did not come prepared. I will certainly. . .

HÉBERT: You shouldn't have to be prepared. Certainly in your experience and your exposure to this program, somewhere along the line somebody, somewhere, sometime, came along and offered you at least one of these 500,000 items and said, "Does the armed services need this?" and you said, "No," or contrariwise, you said, "We do need this in the military. You must need it in the civilian procurement." Just one out of a half million items. You can't mention one, after your experience?

"I might be able to help the admiral out," Anderson offered again. "I asked another admiral in the Navy that same question the other day. He thought for a minute and then said, 'It might be wampum that they use on the Indian reservations.' That is the only one he could think of."

RING: Thank you, Mr. Anderson. Wampum is one item, Mr. Chairman.

HÉBERT: I think this is very, I would say, electrifyingly productive of exactly what we are trying to find out, admiral, as to how this whole operation exists.

RING: Yes, sir.

Questioning Ring, the committee found out little about how the uniform-purchasing system was being handled, except that a decision regarding the uniform purchasing of shoes had been under consideration for a year and a half, prompting me to ask, "Does it take that long for intelligent men to set up and have something before them, for a year and a half, and can't come up with an answer? No wonder the boys aren't able to make a decision in Korea if that is the kind of training they have had, and it hasn't come on the [Munitions Board] agenda yet." Caustically, I commented that the situation could be resolved "if the services would demonstrate the same zealousness . . . as they do in getting rid of the money before the fiscal year is ended. . . ." Instead, "the services come up here [to Congress] with an empty sack and ask for more money."

When reporters surrounded me following Admiral Ring's hours of testimony, I told them, "We're less satisfied and more baffled than ever. We were given the ridiculous summation that the ultimate authority is the President of the United States—even on a nail."

The next morning I opened the third day of the hearings by announcing, "Now, we will continue, gentlemen of the committee, with Admiral Ring, and continue our efforts to find the elusive phantom of the Pentagon, a man who could make decisions over there, yes or no."

In the previous day's testimony Ring had rubbed a sore spot when at one point he had sought to belittle the significance of the differences in cataloging of nails by the various services. Addressing Ring, I said, "We are not only interested in the small items of nails. I will tell you exactly what we want to do: We want to follow the origination of this order for clothing which involves, as I understand, some $2 billion. Now that certainly is an item of concern." In response, Ring read an order entitled "Interdepartmental Procurement Coordination of Clothing, Clothing Textiles and Footwear."

HÉBERT: That is the document that came to the attention of the Munitions Board as of January. . . .

RING: Twenty-third.

HÉBERT: It was originally formalized on August 28? . . . Now, can you tell me, admiral, what happened between August 28 and January 23? Did it take that long to carry that piece of paper to the Munitions Board?

RING: It did not, Mr. Chairman.

HÉBERT: Well, where was the paper between August 28 and January 23?

RING: The paper was somewhere in the Army or in the Navy or in the Air Force.

HÉBERT: That is an illuminating statement.

Despite the frustrations, I persisted. I intended to extract the obvious, uncomfortable truth of the military's obstinance and negligence. This, as the *Saturday Evening Post* pointed out, made "the brass see red."

"No one individual had any responsibility," I said summing up Ring's testimony. "They just went hither and yon and [the order] just floated around in the Pentagon until somebody came up six months later with the formal report. Now somebody had to be responsible, admiral. I don't want to seem piqued at your answers and I appreciate your position, but somebody has to be responsible and that is the phantom of the Pentagon we are trying to find. That paper just didn't walk away. Let's be practical. Who was supposed to carry through that responsibility? That is the man we want."

"I can't answer your question," Ring said, and suggested I look elsewhere for the answer. However, the admiral didn't disappoint the committee when I asked him whether he had "come up with that one example out of that 500,000 yet?"

RING: I have an item, yes, sir. I have one, if you want it.

HÉBERT: Oh, yes; give it to us. We want to know.

RING: Smoke jumpers' parachutes.

HÉBERT: Those smoke jumpers' parachutes are different from those used by the military.

RING: Quite different.

HÉBERT: Thank you for getting one out of 500,000. I won't grade you, then, percentagewise, on that one.

RING: Mr. Hébert, I think you ought to give me a mark of 100 percent. You asked for only one. I gave it to you.

HÉBERT: That is right. I agree, and compliment you in coming up with it in twenty-four hours. If we can expedite all the other answers that quickly, I will give you a star.

The other answers weren't that forthcoming, however, and no stars were given. When the day's session ended, I told inquiring reporters that after three days "all we've got is that the Pentagon is against sin and for virtue but is doing nothing against living in sin and waste."

In an effort to find out more than that, the committee called for its next witness the newly appointed head of the Munitions Board cataloging efforts, Admiral Joseph W. Fowler. He began with a lengthy statement which concluded: "Gentlemen, the Munitions Board has granted me ample authority to do this job and I intend to do my best to accomplish it."

Coming on the heels of what the committee had previously heard, it was an almost unbelievable statement, and I was grateful if somewhat incredulous. "Well, admiral," I said,

> on behalf of the committee, I extend to you my deepest appreciation for the statement that you have just made. It comes like a fresh breeze in a smoke-filled room, after what we have been subjected to heretofore. I may further comment, if I am allowed to mix my metaphors a bit, that the document that you have just read will serve as a magna carta to the overburdened taxpayers who have been tragic victims of waste in government, in the field of procurement and buying and purchasing.
>
> To the committee, it is a fire that you build for the committee's use to which it will hold your feet. To you personally, I hope it is not a Banquo's ghost that will come back to haunt you. . . .

Unfortunately, the apparition was not slow in materializing. It appeared as soon as I asked Admiral Fowler about the clothing procurement policy formulated on August 28, but which had not been put into effect six months later. "Would you have taken until this time to make the decision or would you consider you had the power to make decisions? That is a specific case; that is what we want to deal with."

FOWLER: I want to give you a specific answer, but I have to be honest and say I would not have had the power to make the decision.

There was a chorus of "Oh, no!" from the committee members, and Fowler explained that he had the power to "make the catalog and to standardize the specifications . . .I have no power in the field of procurement. . . ."

HÉBERT: Well, that is the thing this committee is concerned about. The cataloging is one feature. The standardization is another feature. Price is a byproduct of that. And we are interested in the whole picture of procurement, to get the material at the cheapest cost to the taxpayer.

I want to know where do we go from here? In other words, we have the shell game, almost. First you see the pea, then you don't. It is jumping all around. When we think we have it, we haven't.

Although I clearly wasn't becoming a candidate for the Pentagon's choice as "Man of the Year," the admirals and generals now knew, nevertheless, how to pronounce my name. It was no longer "Hee burt," but "A-Bear," and in the labyrinth of the Pentagon it was preceded by what my father feared would happen in Cajun country if I had been named Gordon. In an attempt to score some points against my team, the Pentagon was preparing to send its star running back into the game, Vice Admiral Charles W. Fox, the chief of Navy material. He had been attending the hearings as an observer, and I knew he had been scouting the proceedings, looking for a weakness in our team. In one session, Fox had raised his hand to answer a question asked of the witness who was testifying, and I acknowledged his presence. "Admiral Fox lifted his hand. Admiral Fox will have his day before the committee. I understand Admiral Fox is designated as the Red Grange of the Pentagon to carry the ball. We will give him a clear field any time."

On February 15 the committee was scheduled to hear from Undersecretary of the Army Archibald S. Alexander, but I had more pressing business first. I had just read a story in the *New York Herald Tribune* in which Admiral Fox had charged that the "alleged waste" depicted in the "Chamber of Horrors" exhibit was "bunk" and said he could prove it.

The story went on to quote the admiral as saying that the interservice supply research and cataloging programming, which he created, had already saved the Navy alone "hundreds of millions of dollars." It said that when the admiral was informed by a reporter that the committee planned to recess for several days without calling him, Fox replied, "I could tell them one thing very quickly and that is that this whole [Chamber of Horrors] display is bunk. Maybe they don't want to give me the chance."

I focused on Fox with my "evil eye" apparatus which had been fashioned by Dr. Fred Ketchum, a New Orleans optometrist. "Admiral, did you say that?"

> FOX: No, sir. I think that is a little distorted, Mr. Chairman. If you will recall yesterday, after you adjourned, several of the newspaper reporters came up to you and I think with some humor asked you when you were going to put Red Grange in the game or words to that effect, and when I heard one of them say, "Are you afraid to put him on?" I turned my back and walked away. When I got down to the door, these gentlemen came down and said, "I don't think they want to put you on, Admiral."

> I shrugged my shoulders and I said, "I would like to go on because"—turning, and I apologize for this remark, I said, "I think I can debunk a lot of this chamber of horrors," and I conscientiously think I can.

> HÉBERT: Is there any question that this exhibit and this hearing is bunk?

> FOX: No, sir; I don't think it is bunk. I think it is a good thing. I would be less than frank if I didn't tell you that we are keenly hurt by what we consider the unwarranted criticism that has come to the Navy as a result of the publicity of this hearing.

> HÉBERT: Wait. Let's not go afield. I asked you a question, admiral. Are you criticizing this committee or any of the members in misleading the public in any statement that has been given?

The admiral complained that Congressman Anderson had stated "he found 1,108 bins and was quoted in the newspapers: 'multiply this by the number of activities that have 1,108 bins and you get some idea of waste.' "

"The story," Fox continued, "I believe had its genesis in me. It wasn't 1,108. It was 1,181. There were not 1,108 items. There were 1,181 numbers for the same identical item. . . ."

I leaned across the circular committee bench toward the Defense Department spokesman and said,

> We may as well know exactly how we stand on both sides of the table. This is one thing that you, the Pentagon, or anybody else in this government today had better get into its mind: That as long as this committee sits and as long as I am privileged to be the chairman of this committee, this committee is going to run its affairs in the manner in which it sees fit and proper. . . .
>
> Now, I think it would be very interesting to find out since the matter has been projected into the open as to why we are calling witnesses up here at this time in the manner in which we are calling them. You know as well as I know, admiral, that a conference, several conferences were held at the Pentagon in which you were present. I am sorry I have to go into this in the open but we may as well discuss it so we can find out where we stand; and the strategy, yes the strategy, was discussed on many levels and by many people over there as to how to "take the play away" from these horrible examples of waste that are being shown over here. The whole attempt over there has been to confuse the issue and to befuddle the American people as to what is going on. . . . I told you at the beginning—not you personally—that we intend to get responsive people and we intend to do that. And in this whole set-up the strategy decided upon by the Pentagon, or whoever, is to put you on the stand first so you could put the big act on and the big show and take it away and make everybody forget about those exhibits back there. . . .

Admiral Fox began a combination apology and filibuster, but I was having none of that. I knew that what the Washington *Times-Herald* had editorially pointed out was true: the Navy and the White House, with Truman running the show, were trying to pressure Carl Vinson, chairman of the full Armed Services Committee, "into calling off his dogs" and closing the hearings.

The editorial went on:

> The whole purpose of this little drama is to persuade the subcommittee that the single catalog system, or at least something just as good, can be set up without specific legislation. That it can be done "administratively," as the boys on the public payroll like to say.
>
> Ever since 1929 when the single cataloging system first was urged before Congress, the bureaucrats' strategy was to get specific legisla-

tion called off on the plea "we are making great progress toward a single catalog system; we have adequate legislation; there is a new administration with a new spirit." Every word was bunk.

This was in my mind when I warned Admiral Fox that "This committee is not going to stand idly by and see the press conferences conducted, press statements issued, by an army of propagandists and alibi artists from the Pentagon whose job is to do just that. . . ."

Fox admitted there were some needed changes but said, "it is most unfortunate" that the hearings have received such publicity. "This newspaper publicity is really eating into the innards of the American morale, and that I feel very deeply because we are in trouble. I think we all know it." Admiral Fox inadvertently lifted the lid on Pandora's box, and a couple of butterflies flitted out.

"Now, admiral," I responded ("roared" according to one reporter), "we are in trouble and we know it, and I thank God for the American press in this particular instance. I think the press has done a magnificent and a wonderful job, because the facts speak for themselves." And, I added, that until the committee was formed and its exhibits publicized, nothing had been done to correct the unorganized and wasteful procurement system of the military.

> Now, that is the record; and all this would not have come about if it hadn't been for the contribution that the American press made to this case, to arouse the people of this country as to what is going on. And I think that dragging—and [this] one time I will use "red herring" with deep apology. This is one time a red herring is attempted to be dragged across the trail, in the form of calling it a morale breaker. The morale was broken long ago by these practices in the armed services, because it had come to the attention and cognizance of the junior officers who were frightened of the braid that you wear on your sleeve; that they won't talk to you superior officers but carry in their hearts the things they see going on about them, and because of the military discipline, can't express themselves. That is where the morale is broken.

That straight-forward statement by a member of the Armed Services Committee who was not an anti-militarist, served to stimulate more attacks upon the committee from the Pentagon publicity mill. When the committee recessed for several days to further its investigative efforts, the "alibi artists" of the Pentagon took the opportunity to wine and dine their friends in the news media, particularly some friendly columnists, and plant their message. One of them, Robert Ruark, a talented novelist and syndicated columnist, speculated that the committee would uncover insignificant matters—like nails—but overlook major problems. Fritchey, of course, had been mining his sources in the media. He and Ruark had been friends when the *Item* ran his column.

When the hearings resumed, I recalled Admiral Ring to the stand, and he confirmed what the committee had learned during its investigative recess. There was a secret and unchartered organization known as the Armed Services Procurement Regulation Committee which made decisions on procurement policy and purchases. It operated under a ridiculous procedure. The group, known as "Asper," was composed of two representatives from each of the three services. They would reach decisions without the counsel of the man who was actually given the authority to make those decisions—the chairman of the Munitions Board.

In unusually candid testimony for the hearings, Admiral Ring admitted that the Asper group "has been responsive only to the three procurement [under or assistant] secretaries [of the Army, Navy, and Air Force]. It has not been responsible to the chairman of the Munitions Board."

Ring said the existence of Asper was responsible for delays because "there is no proper programming for scheduling of effort that has to be done to get on with the job." "The staff of the Munitions Board can't present to the chairman of the board, working through a group over which the staff of the board has no direction or control, a reasonable program for the discharge of the responsibility in that particular field."

"I want to compliment you on your forthrightness and frankness in revealing this to us," I told Ring.

> I am compelled to make this observation at this time. This is the most shocking revelation that has come before this committee since we started these hearings. I think it is also significant that during the whole time we have conducted these hearings and have attempted to probe as

much as we could as to the real cause of confusion, at no time has any witness from the Department of Defense come before us and informed us of the existence of this informal board. It only came to the committee's attention from a source outside of the Pentagon and if this source had not informed us and had not rendered the duty, the civic duty, of so informing us, we would still be pursuing the elusive Phantom of the Pentagon . . . I find myself at a loss to describe this particular instance. And I am wondering what the Potomac pitchmen will alibi on this one and say it is insignificant.

Following the disclosure of Asper's role in decisions affecting military procurement, Under Secretary of the Army Alexander was brought back to the witness stand for some explaining.

HÉBERT: Now, let's understand each other there, Mr. Secretary. The Asper board must submit its findings to the [Munitions] Board?
ALEXANDER: That is right.

***

HÉBERT: But it goes back to what I originally said. It is submitted—in effect through these other three people, I mean the two people from each division, are designated by the individual procurement secretary. That is correct, isn't it?
ALEXANDER: That is right.
HÉBERT: And compose the Asper conference or whatever you want to call it. But then when it is submitted, it is submitted to the same superiors.
ALEXANDER: No, sir. The conference actions are submitted directly to the board, not through me.
HÉBERT: Well, who is the board?
ALEXANDER: The Munitions Board.
HÉBERT: And who is on the Munitions Board?
ALEXANDER: The chairman and the three procurement secretaries.
HÉBERT: That is correct, and the three service procurement secretaries name the members of this conference.
ALEXANDER: They do not name the Munitions Board representative.
HÉBERT: Now, don't let's get confused. They are on the Munitions

Board already, but the three secretaries name the personnel of this informal board.

ALEXANDER: Except for the individuals whom the chairman names to attend the meetings.

HÉBERT: But that chairman—he has no power in there. He is merely an observer. That is all he is.

ALEXANDER: Well, he knows everything they do.

HÉBERT: All right. Everybody knows everything over there except the committee of Congress what is going on. But here is the proposition that I am trying to stress. It is this—well, let me put it in simple language so that the garden variety individual like myself can understand. Say we three members up here, Mr. Doyle, for instance, Mr. Elston, and myself, name the people who are going to represent us on this Asper board, but we are the responsible individuals. We are the ones who make the decision, theoretically, at least. Is that correct?

ALEXANDER: Sir, I think that that is not completely. . .

HÉBERT: Then when it comes up for decision, who does it come up to? It comes right back to us.

ALEXANDER: You are omitting the chairman of the Munitions Board.

HÉBERT: No. The Munitions Board chairman gets in after there is a decision. Politically speaking, this is like an intercaucus within the big caucus. The intercaucus brings it up after they have made the decision.

ALEXANDER: Mr. Chairman, when you are speaking about caucus, you confuse me as much as I do when I talk about an ad hoc committee, I am afraid.

HÉBERT: I am sure, Mr. Secretary, you wouldn't hold your position if you didn't know what a caucus meant.

It appeared that Asper was simply a way the three services joined together to oppose unification. Within a week of the committee learning about its existence, Asper had been deprived of its ability to "stymie" (as I put it) military purchases. It was given a charter and the chairman of the Munitions Board was appointed to head the group.

However, the Pentagon Publicity Department continued to issue press releases trying to indicate the congressional committee was misrepresenting purchasing practices of the Defense Department with its "Chamber of Horrors" exhibit. It was comparing apples and oranges, they said. This tactic entrenched my determination to find out how many "pitchmen" were being used by the Pentagon and at what cost to the taxpayer.

On March 6, I finally got a "purported list of the press agents, ghost writers, phrasemakers, alibi artists, propagandists, and whatnot from the mill of the Potomac pitchmen. A cursory examination indicates that the list is not complete by any means," I announced, then continued,

> I don't think it any secret that the committee has in its possession lists obtained from other sources which contain many names that I do not find on this list, names of individuals who are engaged in spreading this propaganda line, or rather the propaganda from the Pentagon line.
>
> I submit this list to the committee and place it in the record and make the observation that a hurried examination would indicate moneywise it runs in excess of $1,000,000 a year. I repeat, a million dollars a year for the Pentagon to spread its propaganda, with its habitual distortion—I would say, in truth, contortionists—and this long list of individuals, and direct the attention of the committee that this particular committee is the object of the present attack by the Potomac pitchmen in distorting and confusing and befuddling the American public as to the true intent and purposes of this committee.
>
> One million dollars, as compared to approximately $40,000 spent by this committee up to date, which has a staff of only three people. I think it's about time the American public finds out and learns for what purposes its tax dollar is being used in an effort to discredit and confuse the issues which involve the spending of that tax dollar.

The next day I continued hounding the P. R. men. I indicated that the list given to the committee contained only seventy-two names whereas I had a list "through unofficial channels" which contained the names of 283 persons engaged in public relations activities for the Department of Defense. The salaries paid these 283 persons would be well over $2 million, I concluded, since the seventy-two names I had received from the Pentagon represented more than $1 million in salaries.

By March 8 the committee was trying to wade through the series of *cul de sacs* thrown up by the military to guard its standardization and cataloging programs. The committee called Colonel Whitmell Rison, the director of procurement and production engineering, deputy chief of staff, Materiel, for answers. While it got some answers, the committee still found the military obstinate, evasive or ignorant.

The colonel was unable to answer satisfactorily my questions but said the Air Force would furnish a witness who knew more about the subject.

> HÉBERT: Do you tell me that every time a committee wants to know an answer to a question we have to give a specific question and then find out what specific individual is going to come before this committee to answer it?
> RISON: We want to give you the best answer we possibly can to any question that you ask.
> HÉBERT: You knew we were investigating. Why wasn't the responsible individual brought here today?
> RISON: That I can't answer.
> HÉBERT: Well, who can answer? Who can answer?
> RISON: We will just have to get you an answer.

I said I was disposed to adjourn the hearings until the Air Force provided someone who could answer the question, but I deferred, and soon the questioning got around to shoes.

> HÉBERT: Now, colonel, can you answer this question or is somebody here—we didn't write this down or request you and say we are going to talk about shoes this morning, so probably your shoe expert isn't here. Can any of your witnesses tell me something about the standardization of shoes?
> RISON: I would like to call on Colonel Lehrke, from our supply division at Wright Field.
> HÉBERT: Can he tell us about the chairs, too?
> RISON: He is not here this morning, sir.
> HÉBERT: Oh, he is the little man who isn't here. Now I want to get to the shoes and he is not here.

Stuck with what was available, I asked Rison, "Is there any reason why a flier can't wear the same shoe that a soldier wears when they are walking? Is there anything peculiar about the way a flier walks as compared to the way a sailor or soldier walks?"

RISON: No, sir.

HÉBERT: Why do you need different shoes?

RISON: We don't.

HÉBERT: There must be a weakness in the system somewhere if that prevails. What is your answer?

Rison paused.

HÉBERT: Silence?

RISON: No, sir; we can't speak for the Navy.

HÉBERT: I didn't ask you to speak for the Navy. I asked you: Couldn't a sailor wear the same shoes?

RISON: Absolutely.

HÉBERT: And if they don't wear the same, then there must be a weakness in the system somewhere, which procures those shoes?

RISON: They are certainly not coordinated together, that is right.

HÉBERT: Then there must be a weakness, if they are not coordinated?

RISON: Yes, sir.

HÉBERT: All right. If you had said that in the beginning we would have saved a lot of time. It is like pulling teeth to get answers. I might say, not to you personally, but the demonstration of what the Air Force has sent up here this morning is the most emphatic testimonial we have for the necessity of mandatory legislation. It seems like the services have to be told what to do and then policed after they are told what to do.

Colonel Jess Larson, the General Services administrator, was the next witness, and he brought good news. The standardization and cataloging process was proceeding absolutely fantastically in his organization. And, he added, "it is my belief that is the direction which the Department of Defense is traveling by centralization of increased responsibilities in the Munitions Board. However, that is only an assumption of mine."

I had heard too much about how well the programs were going and had seen too little proof of it. "It is a pious hope that everybody is going to heaven," I said, "but a lot end up in hell."

"I beg your pardon?" Larson said incredulously.

"I said it is the pious hope that everybody goes to heaven but a lot of people end in hell," I repeated, and then proceeded to question Larson on whether he thought Congress should enact a law requiring

Luncheon at Antoine's. Seated, from left: Elliott Roosevelt; Gov. Richard Leche; President Franklin D. Roosevelt; Mayor Robert S. Maestri; James M. Thompson, publisher of the New Orleans Item; *John O'Brien,* Philadelphia Inquirer *reporter; last two unidentified Standing, from left: Ray Alciatorie, owner of Antoine's; James Crutcher, WPA administrator of Louisiana; Police Capt. Joseph Cassard; Marvin McIntyre, presidential secretary; Leonard K. Nicholson, publisher of the* Times-Picayune; *Bascom Timmons, Washington correspondent for the* Times-Picayune; *and me, a* New Orleans States *reporter.*

At the "Little Red School House" in France. Members of the old Naval Affairs Committee toured war-torn Europe in 1945. They are, from left: Reps. William Hess, Michael Bradley, Lyndon Johnson, Sterling Cole, me, and Capt. Donald Ramsey.

This vile example of the Nazi's base mentality stunned our congressional party in 1945 when we toured Germany.

"I saw Dachau! Dachau, the concentration camp near Munich where every dignity of the human existence was violated and degraded."

President Harry Truman and I share a light moment in the Executive Office at the White House in 1946 over his characterization of Secretary of the Interior Harold Ickes.

Eniwetok. Rep. Sterling Cole, Senator Henry Jackson, myself, and Rep. Melvin Price were congressional observers selected to witness the first hydrogen bomb explosion.

In 1953 President Dwight D. Eisenhower participated in a re-enactment of the signing of the Louisiana Purchase in New Orleans. Numbered in the picture are: 1. Mayor deLesseps "Chep" Morrison; 2. French Ambassador Henri Bonnet; 3. me; 4. Rep. Hale Boggs; 5. Rep. Overton Brooks; 6. the President; 7. E. V. Richards; 8. J. B. Gasquet; and 9. James Wilkinson.

Mayor Morrison presents me with the City of New Orleans' Order of Merit in 1958. At the same time I received the Army Association Award and the Distinguished Service Medal from the State of Louisiana.

When President John F. Kennedy and I flew into New Orleans in 1963 we enjoyed a light moment at the airport with Times-Picayune *reporter Podine Schoenberger and a Secret Service Agent.*

President Johnson presented certificates of merit to four youths, one of whom was from New Orleans, in 1964. Numbered in the picture are: 1. Atty. Gen. Robert F. Kennedy; 2. the President, 3. Sen. George Smathers; 4. FBI Director J. Edgar Hoover; and 5. me.

In 1968 President Johnson gave former Armed Services Committee Chairman Carl Vinson an 86th birthday party at the White House. Pictured, from left: former Rep. William Hess, Vinson, me, the President, and former Rep. Sterling Cole.

Texas charm. Gladys and I are photographed with President and Lady Bird Johnson during a White House visit.

*During ceremonies in which my official portrait as chairman of the House Armed Services Commit-
tee was presented, President Nixon got a kick out of my imitation of his victory salute.*

*Two men I admired also attended the ceremonies: Admiral Hyman
Rickover and Admiral Thomas Moorer, former chairman of the Joint
Chiefs of Staff.*

When President Nixon returned from his history-making journey to China in 1972 he briefed congressional leaders in the Cabinet Room of the White House. Rep. Hale Boggs is in the foreground with his back to the camera. Others are, from left: Rep. Frank Bow; me; Sen. J. William Fulbright; Sen. Margaret Chase Smith; Rep. Leslie Arends; Sen. John Stennis; Sen. Gale McGee; Rep. George Aiken; Sen. Robert Byrd; Sen. Hugh Scott; Rep. Carl Albert; President Nixon; Sen. Mike Mansfield; Rep. Gerald Ford; Sen. Allen Ellender; Sen. Barry Goldwater; and unidentified.

President Nixon signed the lottery draft bill in 1969. From left: John "Russ" Blanford, chief counsel of the Armed Services Committee; me; Rep. L. Mendel Rivers; the President; and Rep. Leslie Arends. Assistant Secretary of Defense Roger T. Kelley is partially hidden by my shoulder, and Rep. Clark MacGregor is visible between Mendel and me.

In 1972 President Nixon signed the bill which provided for the establishment of the Uniformed Services University of Health Sciences. From left; Frank Slatinshek, chief counsel of the Armed Services Committee; Dr. Richard S. Wilbur, assistant secretary of defense; me; Rep. Charles Bennet; Secretary of Defense Melvin Laird; Rep. Leslie Arends; Rep. Durwood Hall, M. D.; and Dr. Louis Rousselot of the National Institute of Health.

Dedication ceremonies in 1972 for the 8th Marine District Headquarters Building in New Orleans, the F. Edward Hebert Building. From left: Adm. Robert Emmet Riera, commandant 8th Naval District; Capt. John Beaver, resident officer in charge of construction; Capt. H. H. Osborne, commanding officer, Naval Support Activity; Adm. John D. McCubbin, commandant, 8th Coast Guard District; Col. Haywood Smith; me; Gen. Robert E. Cushman, Jr., commandant, U. S. Marine Corps.

Three years after President Nixon signed into law the Military Medical Academy bill President Ford participated in the groundbreaking ceremonies for the university. From left: Dr. Anthony Curreri, president of the academy; the President; David Packard, president of the board of regents of the school; me; and Secretary of Defense James Schlesinger.

Having demonstrated he could handle a shovel, President Ford was invited to participate in the ground-breaking ceremonies of the F. Edward Hébert Library on the shores of Lake Pontchartrain in New Orleans. With the President are Ernest Carrere, president of the library's board of trustees, and me.

Platform guests for the library ceremonies were, from left: Rep. David Treen, Sen. J. Bennett Johnston, Secretary of the Navy J. William Middendorf II, Mayor Moon Landrieu, Lt. Gov. James Fitzmorris, Gov. Edwin Edwards, Levee Board President Guy LeMieux, the President, Mrs. Ernest Carrere, Mrs. Gladys Hébert, me, Mrs. Dawn Hébert Duhe, John Duhe, Ernest Carrere, Kim, Jeanne, Edward and Martin Duhe.

This was the scene at a breakfast meeting at the White House with congressional leaders. From left: me, Sen. John Stennis, Secretary of State Henry Kissinger, Sen. Strom Thurmond, Rep. Thomas "Tip" O'Neil, Rep. John Rhodes, Sen. Hugh Scott, House Speaker Carl Albert, President Gerald R. Ford, Sen. Mike Mansfield, and Rep. William Bray.

Sprucing up the image. After the breakfast meeting, I presented President Ford with a sports coat made by Haspel Bros. of New Orleans.

I attended the swearing-in ceremony for Rep. Lindy Boggs in 1973 when she was elected to fill the unexpired term of her husband, Hale Boggs, who was lost in an airplane crash in Alaska.

Secretary of Defense Melvin Laird and I enjoy a laugh following a meeting at the White House in 1972.

Mrs. Patricia Nixon stopped to chat with Gladys and me when she accompanied the President to New Orleans in August of 1970. The man in profile between Mrs. Nixon and myself is Rep. Joe D. Waggonner of Louisiana.

Pictured at the keel-laying ceremony of the U.S.S. Baton Rouge at Newport News, Va., in 1972 were, from left: Adm. Elmo Zumwalt, chief of naval operations; Mrs. Ruth Legendre of New Orleans, matron of honor; Secretary of the Navy John Warner, Mrs. Gladys Hébert, the sponsor of the ceremony, and me.

I was grand marshal of the Daytona Firecracker 400 under the direction of William France in 1971. It was run in honor of the winners of the Congressional Medal of Honor. With me are Donald O. Heumann of New Orleans, chairman of the Board of Visitors of the U. S. Naval Academy, and the reigning Miss Universe.

New Orleans' Pete Fountain, one of the world's best clarinetist, presents me with his portrait painted by Henrietta Lumetta (right).

My Washington office staff, from left: Nancy Fanning, Gina Bishop, Alice Huy, Lou Gehrig Burnett, press secretary, Alma Moore, receptionist, and Mary Swann, administrative assistant.

My district office staff, from left: Bonnie Nelson, who worked for me the summer of 1975; Virginea Burguieres, executive secretary; Susan Wetzel, secretary; and John McMillan, press secretary.

standardization of procurement and cataloging procedures. Larson said it was up to the committee to decide that question but personally he considered the same purpose could be accomplished by directive.

"As far as I'm personally concerned," I said, "long ago I decided that taking chances with government was very hazardous under our present setup; that we have gotten away from the basic concept of this government and that is that it is a government of law and not of men. And that is the reason we find ourselves so confused today. I think it is about time that Congress enunciates by law its policies and sees that they are carried out."

With that, the committee concluded the hearings and immediately began preparing legislation which ordered the irrational purchasing and cataloging systems used by the military replaced by a sane, sensible uniform system. It noted that the Munitions Board had expended $100 million from 1945 to 1952 in its efforts to develop a single catalog system and that an additional $87 million had been spent on separate catalog systems by the three services during that same period.

It was a conservative estimate that a law requiring mandatory standardization and cataloging would result in an annual savings of $5 billion based on the military budget in 1952. The savings, of course, would increase at a level corresponding to the increase in the military budget.

The Armed Services Committee took its proposals to the floor of the House of Representatives, and despite vehement protests from the Pentagon, it won the fight for new legislation by a vote of 224 to 48. The measure passed on a voice vote in the Senate and was signed into law in June 1952. It became known as the Defense Supply Standardization Act.

I immediately acknowledged that the legislation was not a panacea to cure all Pentagon purchasing practices, but it certainly was a step in the right direction. Constant vigilance would be necessary to insure that the secretary of defense did not forget the importance of the single standard catalog as he spent the Pentagon's gargantuan budget.

It was, nevertheless, a victory for my subcommittee over the "phantom of the Pentagon" and the "Potomac pitchmen" who tried to misconstrue issues and draw attention away from the clear examples of waste and inefficiency. As an ancillary reaction to the changes taking place, my old rival from New Orleans, Clayton Fritchey, the head "pitchman," left his job shortly before the new legislation was passed. He landed in the arms of President Truman and served as one of his secretaries.

I guess I had every right to feel satisfied with the job I had done, saving the government $5 billion a year, but I set my sights on other goals. Much to the military's chagrin, one of those goals included investigating the practice of retired officers taking jobs paying top dollar in the defense industry. Spurred by President Eisenhower's charge that the "munitions lobby" had interests other than what was militarily best for the United States, my subcommittee began looking into the hiring of high-ranking officers by defense contractors.

My investigation established that large numbers of retired officers had taken big-salaried positions in the defense industry; that senior officers were entertained lavishly at weekends in the Bahamas; that large advertising campaigns were conducted by the defense industry seeking to influence decisions of the top brass who decided what weapons to purchase.

In 1961 I compiled a list of 726 retired officers above the rank of colonel who were then employed by the one hundred biggest defense contractors. I did not contend that it was improper for retired officers to go to work for those contractors, but I did point out there was a danger these admirals and generals might use intimate knowledge gained via their former positions and their connections to obtain favorable treatment for their firms.

"The 'coincidence' of contractors and personal contracts with firms represented by retired officers and retired civilian officials sometimes raises serious doubts as to the complete objectivity of some of these decisions," the subcommittee reported.

The report noted that the problem of "conflict of interest" did not stop with military officers. It also included civilian employees of the Defense Department and political appointees, and it pointed out problems created when men hold political or military jobs one day and represent companies with government contracts the next.

As a result Congress passed a law prohibiting retired officers from becoming contract salesmen for a two-year period following retirement, and government agencies became more aware of possible areas of conflict of interest.

Asked how I felt about keeping retired generals and admirals out of defense-related work for two years, I said, "It'll give 'em a chance to work on their golf games."

CHAPTER XX

McNAMARA'S BAND, HÉBERT'S TUNE

Robert strange mc namara was blessed with high intelligence and he attempted to use it, for whatever psychological reason, to insulate himself emotionally from the battles of life. He seemed to see himself as having no personal axes to grind; he was simply doing the intelligent thing: One didn't become irritated over conflicts, one intellectualized them.

The secretary of defense, with his slicked-down hair parted in the middle and his rimless, owl-eyed spectacles, became known as "The Computer." The name wasn't solely derived from his manner and appearance; McNamara had a special affection for, and trust in, those mechanical servants for whom he was nicknamed.

I am the antithesis of such an approach. For me life means work rewarded by one hell of a good time. Even without conscious effort, I attempt to turn the driest, most mundane duties into pleasurable activities. Moreover, I have always loved to tease, to "needle."

This characteristic didn't always sit well with the secretary of defense, who wanted to keep personalities out of his business. After one of those "needling" sessions, McNamara stormed into his Pentagon office and, uncharacteristically, flung his briefcase onto an overstuffed leather chair. "Well," McNamara fumed, "I kissed his ass in public. I hope he's satisfied."

The incident about which McNamara was steaming arose from his plan to "streamline" the auxiliary military forces of the United States by combining the Army Reserve with the National Guard forces. I opposed it the instant I heard of it. To McNamara the merger was just another way to make the military more efficient. Everything was "cost effectiveness," and the merger simply meant the ruination of the Reserves and an unconstitutional means of depriving the states of a militia.

The first word I heard of the plan came from Cyrus Vance, the deputy secretary of defense. He had flown down to New Orleans with Steve Ailes, secretary of the Army, to break the news. It was common knowledge among Pentagonian and congressional observers that while I was only third in seniority on the Armed Services Committee at the time, for all practical purposes I had a big hand in running it. L. Mendel Rivers of South Carolina was the chairman. Still, I would sit up there next to Mendel, and anytime anybody wanted to do something, Mendel would tell them to "go see Eddie." Mendel always leaned on me.

Vance was aware he would have to get my approval if he wanted McNamara's planned merger to succeed. I headed the critical sub-committees on Armed Services, including the one which had jurisdiction over the Reserves.

Cy Vance sat in my New Orleans office, and I told him, "You can't do it."

Cy said, "We can do it."

I said, "You can't do it." And they didn't do it. I was able to block it.

But I didn't just wave a magic wand and make McNamara's plans disappear. McNamara was resourceful, and the battle was joined in 1964. By 1965 my determination was finally paying dividends. I got him to come around and admit that he needed legislation to make the proposed merger legal.

With that admission, McNamara was acknowledging defeat for his streamlined, cost-effective, computerized brain child. He had admitted to me that he needed legislation, and now the only thing which remained was public acknowledgement (groveling?). For that, I arranged a full-dress news conference in the ornate Armed Services Committee room on the first floor of the Rayburn Building.

The gist of McNamara's statement to the press was that he was postponing the merger. The idea in principle was sound, he said, but he had decided to postpone the matter in view, . . . etc. I was sitting by his side, grinning like a schoolboy who had just put a dead rat in the teacher's desk drawer. Each time I felt McNamara was misrepresenting the facts, I would lean over, shake my finger, and say, "Now, Mr. Secretary, that's not quite accurate." He could have murdered me.

It was following that news conference that McNamara roared into his office at the Pentagon and complained that I had made him "kiss his ass in public." McNamara ranted, "That's what he wanted, and I did it."

One of McNamara's staff members told me the story, but I dismissed it at the time, thinking that the fellow was just trying to curry a little favor.

Later, however, McNamara himself confirmed the story's authenticity. One day I was down in the office of Frank Slatinshek (then assistant counsel for the Armed Services Committee) and Gladys called me. She was working as my receptionist and appointments secretary. She said, "Is Mr. Vance down there, Secretary Vance?" I said, "No."

Gladys said, "Well, Secretary McNamara is here looking for him."

About fifteen minutes later—I was still in the office with Frank—and who comes walking in the front door but Cy Vance. I said, "Oh, Cy, you'd better get back to the Pentagon. Teacher's looking for you."

And who's right behind him but McNamara. They came in and sat down. McNamara looked at me and said, "Eddie, you know we're in a hell of a fix. We're in trouble."

I looked at him and said, "What do you mean we? You're in trouble. I'm not in trouble. I'm doing all right." He was talking about some Pentagon project.

He said, "Goddamn it, didn't I kiss your ass in public? Aren't you satisfied?"

That convinced me he had said it before. Later, when I was maneuvering to get the Reserve Bill of Rights passed, I was talking to him and he said, "What's the matter with you? You know what I did for you."

I said, "No, you bit me and it still hurts."

Recognizing McNamara's reputation for having a long memory and great tenacity, I decided that despite the postponement of the merger, I had better find a way to halt permanently the possibility of combining the Reserves and the Guard. The answer, I concluded, was legislation, and I set about preparing it.

Overcoming strong lobbying efforts by some of the Pentagon's ablest executives, I produced a bill in 1966 which established manpower floors for both the Reserves and the Guard, and established a Selected Reserve, which was composed of separate contingents from each of the Reserve branches. It took me a considerable amount of time to present this bill because I intended to leave nothing to chance. Parliamentary procedure was my forte, and I wanted all my checkers to be kings before I struck. When I moved, the bill passed the House by a vote of 333 to 6. However, my efforts to insure passage had taken time. It was late in the 89th Congress and the bill died in the Senate.

When the 90th Congress opened, my bill was reintroduced as House of Representatives-2, which is, of course, a prominent number. Number one is the best number, but John McCormack had promised it to John Rooney of New York. So he gave me Number 2, which is a very captive number. John said, "Remember this: I'm giving you this on friendship, and not on political philosophy. I'd give you number 10,000 on political philosophy."

With the spadework out of the way, this time I pushed the bill through the House by a vote of 324 to 13. It then went to the Senate where some minor changes were inserted, but the crucial Selected Reserve concept, which established a law against merger, was retained. The differences between the House and Senate versions were quickly resolved in conference and the bill was signed into law by President Johnson on December 1, 1967, only a few days after McNamara had resigned his post as secretary of defense.

The autonomy and integrity of the Reserves and the National Guard were insured by this bill. The organizational chances provided by the bill should enable the Reserve to more effectively fulfill its role as part of our national defense force. It will contribute significantly toward providing a combat-ready reserve force.

Before McNamara left office I had won still another victory. It involved the Junior ROTC program for high school students. McNamara announced one day that the program would be dismantled, and correlatively, Senior ROTC programs in colleges would be severely reduced. The next thing McNamara knew, I had established 970 more Junior ROTC units and had strengthened the senior program. I sponsored and pushed through Congress the ROTC Revitalization Act, known at the Hébert Bill, which gave the ROTC programs a statutory basis throughout the country, increased the number of units, and expanded the once Army-dominated program to include the Air Force, Navy and Marines.

To Jesuit High School, my alma mater, I brought General Wallace M. Greene, Jr., commandant of the U. S. Marine Corps, to review the first Marine Junior ROTC unit in the nation as it was activated. Fifty years before, when I was a student at Jesuit, I had won the title of best debater, arguing the affirmative side of the question: "Resolved: That Military Instruction in High School Be a Compulsory Part of Education." McNamara hadn't known that.

No sooner had McNamara resigned—or had been told to resign by Johnson because he had become a "political liability," as I saw it—than Drew Pearson charged in his syndicated column that the downfall of the secretary of defense was the result of a plot by me. He said that three years before I

> called in one of the authors of this column and asked cooperation in a plan to "get" Secretary of Defense McNamara.
>
> The plan included keeping the new chairman of the Armed Services Committee, Mendel Rivers of South Carolina, sober, and using him to battle against the civilian boss of the Pentagon, whom the generals, the admirals, and the hawks on Capitol Hill hated. Hebert expressed the hope that this column would not report on Rivers' alcoholic binges.

Rivers' drinking problem was well known on Capitol Hill, and beyond. And I admit that I did call my old friend, Drew Pearson, to ask him not to report on Rivers' drinking because he had been abstemious since assuming the chairmanship. The conversation had absolutely nothing to do with McNamara. I was perplexed by Pearson's accusations, and issued a press release in response to the Pearson column:

> It reads like one of Grimm's Fairy tales.
>
> No such conversation ever took place as described by Mr. Pearson.
>
> At no time have I ever plotted, connived, urged or solicited the aid of Drew Pearson or anybody else to get rid of Secretary McNamara. Any suggestion to the contrary is imaginary and emphatically untrue. . . .
>
> My disagreements with Secretary McNamara on numerous occasions have been lively and publicly stated. Our areas of difference are well known. Nor is it any secret that I have always expressed admiration for his intellect and tenacity for doing what he thought was right but what I thought was wrong. However, I think the secretary of defense and I share a mutual respect for each other. This is all I ask of anyone with whom I disagree. How could I connive to get rid of Mr. McNamara when I will miss him so much? Where now will I go for excitement?

If the story by Pearson was accurate, it is curious that a good newsman would wait more than three years to reveal it. The fact that an overture was made to a newsman to help "get" someone would surely have more impact and credibility when it occurred than after the fact.

In the news columns of papers, I was magnanimous in my praise of McNamara, saying, "No one could suggest his actions were anything other than what he felt in good conscience was best for his country." It was also noted in several news items that McNamara resigned, never having been able to claim a victory for his position over an opposite one espoused by me.

McNamara was a very smart individual. I never did dislike him personally. I respected his brains, but I liked to needle him a great deal because I knew I could needle him. I did needle him.

Although the needling wasn't limited to McNamara's appearances before my subcommittee, those appearances did provide prime opportunities, such as the time McNamara testified about the closing of military bases. "Now, Mr. Secretary," I said, "this makes 673 bases you've closed. In retrospect, looking back, did you make any mistakes?"

McNamara said that he had not.

"Mr. Secretary, out of 673 decisions or judgments that you made, you didn't make one mistake?"

"No," McNamara repeated.

"You're better than Christ," I grinned. "He blew one out of twelve."

McNamara was just a typical accountant. That's what he was, a CPA, and he had a remarkable memory, a remarkable brain. He could remember everything—a typical CPA.

When we had only 25,000 troops in Vietnam, McNamara made a statement twice on television that we could not defend an air base there. I said, "Now, Mr. Secretary, maybe you won't *successfully* defend an air base, but you can defend it."

He said, "Well, we don't have enough people over there."

I said, "How many you need?"

He said, "250,000."

I said, "Well, put the 250,000 in or get out," or a statement to that effect.

He said, "If we put them in, more people will get killed."

I said, "You have to win or get out, one or the other."

That was his philosophy—the whole destructive thing of the entire Vietnamese operation—the idea that we're not supposed to win. We merely were supposed to defend some given position.

Those boys went to Vietnam with their hands tied behind their backs. Mendel Rivers and I fought for a long time to mine Haiphong and to bomb Hanoi, and if we would have done it, in six months we would have been out of there. We were there to win, but McNamara wouldn't go in. Win or get out! If you're going to pull a gun, be ready to shoot; don't pull it if you're not.

History can't be erased, it just can't be rubbed out. History was repeating itself and we weren't learning. Korea and Vietnam were the only two wars this country lost; we won every other war not because we were smart, but because the enemy pulled boners in judgment and action.

We lost Korea. We had North Korea and couldn't hold it because we weren't prepared. We lost in Vietnam because of a lack of will—not on the part of the men who were shooting, but on the part of the government.

In Vietnam the big move came with the Gulf of Tonkin Resolution by Lyndon Johnson. I voted for the Gulf of Tonkin Resolution. As far as I was concerned it was a declaration of war. I thought we were going in to fight. That's why I voted for it. I thought we would go in there and clean them out and then get out. I thought that's what Johnson was going to do, but he didn't do it.

I readily acknowledged that a fear of intervention by Russia or China made the United States hesitant to use massive force against North Vietnam. Certainly, the government was afraid of that, but there are times (*i.e.* Cuban Missile Crisis) when a government must gamble, when it must have guts. If a government does not have the stomach to fight, then don't get involved in one. On the other hand, a government cannot always be afraid of another government all the time. History has clearly demonstrated that everytime our government has called the Russian hand, the Soviets have backed down. They never call the pot.

The bombing of Hanoi is a good example. As soon as we began that the communists rushed to the peace table. If we had bombed the city long before that, the headlong rush to the peace table would have occurred a lot sooner. In all likelihood we wouldn't have had 200,000 casualties.

In 1967 I told Jimmy Noe:

McNamara has caused the death of more boys over there than you can count. Everytime he makes more mistakes, and wastes more money, he claims to be saving money. Nine times he went to Vietnam. He made nine different statements and made nine different mistakes.

And yet, I admired McNamara, realizing that while I thought McNamara was making mistakes, he was doing so with the best motives in mind.

On one of our last occasions together, we were at the White House one evening. With a scotch and water in hand, I told the austere McNamara the story of how, as the result of breaking the Louisiana Scandals, I had helped put three of my friends in jail—a former governor and two prominent New Orleans businessmen, but never lost their friendship. I tried to make him understand what human beings are, which is hard for him to understand. But, in the end, I don't think I got through to him.

Then I said, "Bob, there's one thing I want from you, an autographed picture." He looked at me as though I was nuts.

I said, "No, I mean it. I wouldn't ask you for a picture if I didn't want it, and I don't ask for pictures of people I don't like."

The next morning when I got to the office there was a beautiful autographed picture. The autograph was, "To Eddie, the greatest swordsman I have ever known. With respect and affection, Bob McNamara."

I think that demonstrated McNamara's character more than anything else. How meticulous and definite he is. When he said swordsman, he meant the way I talked and fought—darted in and out in a verbal duel. I called him and told him that flattery would get him nowhere.

Looking back, I realize that I would tell him the damndest, most outrageous things. One day he was sitting in my office and I told him, "Robert, you know, you're just a transient here." I said, "I've seen 'em come and I've seen 'em go, and I'll be here when you're gone."

And I am.

CHAPTER XXI

MY LAI:
A TRAGEDY OF MAJOR PROPORTIONS

THE STORY STUNNED the nation when it broke in the spring of 1969: a group of American soldiers had waded into a South Vietnamese village on March 16 the year before and slaughtered old men, women, young girls, toddlers, and babies in their mothers' arms. They also had taken a page from war immemorial and burned homes, destroyed food supplies, and killed livestock. A few days later "not even a bird was singing."

The American public recoiled in shock. When it recovered, a schism developed; opinion immediately polarized. Anti-war factions were almost jubilant over the news, using it as a raison d'être of their cause, citing it as an example of how the unjust Vietnamese War corrupted and crippled morals. Many Americans backing the war effort, on the other hand, rushed to the defense of the soldiers accused of participating in the incident. Innocent civilians by day became Viet Cong killers at night, they argued; the children whom American soldiers treated to candy one day would set booby traps for their benefactors the next, they reasoned. Then, too, soldiers must follow orders.

Yet, between those two extremes, a third opinion circulated. Those who held it were anguished, appalled, and demoralized by the incident. They knew it could not be justified, but they were aware that extenuating circumstances might—at least partially—explain the motivation. It was difficult for these Americans to condemn this horrible incident when anti-war fanatics, who ignored or justified

Communist atrocities of far greater magnitude, would seize it for their propaganda. Still it was wrong, and unlike the communists' modus operandi, American Democracy and decency demanded the truth.

To the United States Congress fell the duty to investigate. The branch of Congress which would do the job was the House Armed Services Committee. The chairman of that committee was L. Mendel Rivers, a man who totally backed the war in Vietnam and venerated the military. Rivers was one of thirty officials who was informed of the incident by Ron Ridenhour, a twenty-two-year-old former soldier from Phoenix, Arizona. He had returned home from Vietnam to enter college and put the war behind him. However, he couldn't forget the stories he had heard of the incident in the South Vietnamese village and agonized over them for months. Many of his friends had urged him to keep quiet about the incident, but his conscience would not acquiesce.

On April 4, 1969, Rivers received his copy of Ridenhour's letter. In it the young man was careful to point out that the story he related was only what he had heard, not what he had witnessed. But the letter detailed conversations he had had with individuals assigned to the 11th Infantry Brigade, and they indicated a large number of Vietnamese civilians had been killed in an area known as Pinkville. He included map coordinates of the area and the names of individuals alleged to be involved, plus names of witnesses. These witnesses, he wrote, told him that troops from "C" Company, 1st Battalion, 20th Infantry, had murdered a large segment of the population of Pinkville, so named by GIs because the area was shaded pink on maps to indicate a heavily populated region. The largest populated area in Pinkville was Son My village, which was composed of four hamlets; My Lai, Co Luy, My Khe, and Tun Cong. A subhamlet known as My Lai 4 or Thuan Yen was located in the Tun Cong hamlet area. Because of Pinkville's strategic location, bounded on one side by the Song Diem Diem River and on another by the South China Sea, the area had been a Viet Cong redoubt for years. It was purportedly the headquarters of the Viet Cong's 48th Battalion, which carried the reputation of being the best communist fighting force in South Vietnam.

On April 7, just three days after receiving Ridenhour's letter, Rivers forwarded it to the Department of the Army with a request that the matter be investigated. The Armed Services Committee received a similar letter from Congressman Morris K. Udall of Arizona. By April 10 the Army had received six congressional referrals enclosing the Ridenhour letter, and it was clear some action would have to be taken.

On April 24 the Army advised the Armed Services Committee that the Inspector General, the Army's chief investigatory agency, was undertaking an investigation of the alleged My Lai incident. By September 5 the Army announced that charges would be filed against Lieutenant William L. Calley, the commander of a "C" Company platoon, the unit to which Ridenhour had alluded in his letters. Calley was charged with the premeditated murder of more than one hundred men, women, and children, all noncombatants living in the subhamlet of My Lai 4. On November 4 another name was added to Calley's as being responsible for the killings, Sergeant David Mitchell, the platoon sergeant who accompanied Calley on the assault of the area.

News coverage of the events escalated—to use a popular term of the day—and public interest became intense. The incident became known colloquially as My Lai. Mendel Rivers realized that as chairman of the House Armed Services Committee he had to act independently of the Army in the matter, and on November 24 he announced from the floor of the House that the Armed Services Investigating Subcommittee had requested all information the Department of the Army had on the incident at Pinkville. He said the subcommittee would study the information and determine whether further inquiry was warranted.

On the same day, the Army, sensing increased public and congressional concern, announced a special inquiry of its own, one to be headed by Lieutenant General William R. Peers. Its purpose was to "explore the nature and scope of the original Army investigation of the so-called My Lai incident." The Army, already under severe attack by many anti-war factions, had been grievously wounded by reports of the My Lai affair and it had to respond. The public wanted to know, and had a right to know, whether charges that American soldiers had conducted a massive slaughter of Vietnamese civilians were true, and if so, why nothing had been done or said about it in the year and a half since it occurred.

After studying the information passed to it by the Army, the Armed Services Committee decided that it had an obligation to investigate the incident itself. On November 26, the committee called its first witness, Secretary of the Army Stanley Resor. Members of the news media—television reporters, camera men, sound men, light men, newspaper reporters and photographers, radio reporters—were wedged into the wide first-floor hall outside the Armed Services Committee room in the Rayburn Office Building. Inside, Secretary Resor testified behind closed doors. When Resor appeared from behind those doors the reporters fell on him seeking information. They received precious little, which gave them something in common with the Investigating Subcommittee. Resor had not cooperated, and further hearings were delayed.

The Army would not supply the information requested by Rivers and also threw a roadblock in the committee's path by encouraging prospective witnesses not to testify before the committee until they had appeared before the Army's Peers' inquiry. It was becoming obvious that the Army wanted Congress to keep its nose out of the My Lai incident, but this attitude only served to convince us that we had to press forward with the investigation.

When the hearings resumed several days later, the subcommittee heard testimony from General Peers, Captain Ernest Medina, who was the commander of "C" Company, and Lieutenant Hugh Thompson. Thompson, a helicopter pilot, had been awarded a Distinguished Flying Cross for allegedly rescuing a number of Vietnamese caught in a cross fire between American and Viet Cong troops at My Lai. Following Thompson's testimony, word leaked to the press that he said he had trained his helicopter's guns on murderous American troops in order to rescue the Vietnamese civilians.

There were countless leaks coming out of the committee. I immediately realized that the news value of the story about Lieutenant Thompson would bring a posse of reporters riding down on Rivers. I told Mendel they would swarm all over him. They wanted to get a confirmation or denial on the Thompson testimony. I advised him not to answer any questions and to simply respond with "No comment." As we walked down the hall to the elevators (heading for a vote on the House floor), he kept saying "No comment, no comment." I was whispering in his ear, "That's right, you going good, Mendel." But reporters kept vigorously baiting Rivers, repeatedly asking him questions about the Thompson testimony. Rivers, who didn't like the press under any circumstances, was turning blood red. "No comment" did not satisfy his desire to strike out.

When we got to the elevator, the doors were closing as we turned around, and Mendel yelled, "It's a damn lie."

I said, "Well, you gave them the story."

The next day the papers played it big. He couldn't understand how he gave them the story by denying it. Mendel could never understand reporters. He wanted to dictate the story, the lead, and the headline; and if it wasn't the way he wanted it, he would say the reporter was no damn good. A lot of people in public office don't understand reporters.

But I don't blame Mendel. He was one of the most dedicated men I have ever known, and he was trying to do a good job in a difficult situation. His staunch support of the fighting forces made him a natural target for the liberal press.

The four days of hearings the Investigating Subcommittee held under Rivers' chairmanship—complete with reporters vying to see who could get the biggest leak from the subcommittee—resulted in a Barnum and Bailey atmosphere. The goings-on of the subcommittee made headlines each day. The carnival had to end, and suddenly on December 12, Rivers announced that I had been named to head a special subcommittee to conduct an "in-depth" probe of the My Lai incident. Rivers called me "the most experienced and hardest hitting investigator in Congress." He went on to say that I would brook no foolishness and was not in the business of whitewash. "He will call a spade a spade and let the chips fall where they may."

Despite Rivers' assurances, the announcement of the formation of a special subcommittee to investigate My Lai brought immediate speculation that a whitewash of the Army was in the works. The Washington *Daily News* wrote that "Defense Secretary Melvin R.

Laird's personal intervention has prompted Chairman L. Mendel Rivers to call off his House Armed Services Committee's turbulent hearings into the alleged My Lai massacre in favor of a smaller, quieter probe.'' The story said that Laird, ''in a hush-hush meeting'' with Rivers, ''registered the Army's and the Defense Department's grave concern over the way the closed-door My Lai hearings were being conducted.'' It further said Rivers promised that the subcommittee which I headed ''would proceed quietly and slowly, to give the Army a chance to finish its own work.''

The Washington *Evening Star* reported that the Army and Laird had prevailed upon Rivers to call off his hearings because the investigation ''had gotten completely out of hand.'' The *Star* said there was concern that the atmosphere of the hearings ''might make it virtually impossible to try any of those involved in the incident or to obtain a conviction that would not be reversed on appeal.'' The purpose of the Hébert subcommittee, the story asserted, was to merely create ''a graceful way of getting out of a difficult situation.''

To round out the consensus of Washington newspaper opinion, the *Post* said editorially that there was ''nothing in the record of events so far to suggest that what follows will have any more dignity than the escapades we have already witnessed.''

Obviously, in some press corners, little was expected from my subcommittee. Yesterday's headlines in these same papers trumpeting my record as an investigator were forgotten or ignored. I was a known hawk and they presumed that ''whitewash'' was the name of the game. I had other ideas. When Rivers asked me to take over the investigation, I told him I would accept it on the premise and the promise that I would be the full boss of the committee, and that I would run the committee. I also handpicked the men I wanted on the special panel. They were the people I thought could best serve the purpose, who could investigate. For the difficult job ahead I selected Samuel S. Stratton, a Democrat from New York, and two Republicans, Charles S. Gubser of California and William L. Dickinson of Alabama. I also called on former Congressmen Porter Hardy, Jr., who had previously headed the Armed Services Investigating Subcommittee, and Charles Halleck, who had been the Republican leader in the House. Both served as consultants. John Reddan and John Lally were the counsel and assistant counsel to the subcommittee.

I made it plain to members of the news media that they could expect no leaks from this panel. In language they would understand, I told the reporters, "I intend to do the job of searching facts from fantasy and printing the story after the facts are in. Until then I have nothing to say." I added, "Don't call me. I'll call you."

Stories about the subcommittee dropped off after that, but the investigation did not lie dormant. Quietly going about its work, the subcommittee began building up knowledge of the events of March 16, 1968, as they prepared themselves to question witnesses. By April the subcommittee and its staff were ready. On April 15 six witnesses were called, including Captain Ernest Medina, the "C" Company commander who had admitted killing a woman whom he mistook for a Viet Cong soldier. He was charged with the responsibility for the actions of his company at My Lai.

In concomitance with the calling of witnesses, trouble with Secretary of the Army Resor resumed. I was forced to subpoena Medina and other witnesses because Resor refused to allow them to testify voluntarily. Flamboyant defense attorney, F. Lee Bailey, who represented Medina, said Resor had issued six countermanding orders attempting to halt Medina's testifying before the subcommittee, and at one point, had Medina listed as absent without leave.

The subcommittee was hampered in its investigation in every conceivable way. It got to be such an impasse that I refused to discuss the matter with the secretary of the army at any time. The only communication we engaged in was through the written word. At one point Resor wanted to bring General Westmoreland to Louisiana to discuss the situation, but I told the caller who inquired about the possible meeting, "We don't talk. We write."

Nevertheless, the hearings got underway, and the news media was back in the halls of the Rayburn Building in full force. In an effort to bring some dignity to the proceedings, I met with the newsmen. Despite some philosophical differences, most capital correspondents and I exhibit mutual respect so that they now agreed to my guidelines. I asked them not to flock around the door to the subcommittee hearing rooms; instead, to wait in the large foyer of my office, about fifty feet down the hall. They were given *carte-blanche* use of my office telephones and the Louisiana coffee we serve. In return only one designated member of the media would approach each witness as he emerged from testifying and inquire whether he would consent to be interviewed.

I explained to the press what the subcommittee was about. "We are trying to find out what happened, and if it did happen, what course was taken to investigate it and what conclusions were arrived at." I pointed out the subcommittee was conducting an inquiry and not a trial. I assured them we were making a sincere effort to find out the facts in the case.

At about the same time, Mendel Rivers, who had become emotionally involved in the controversy over My Lai, gave a speech before the Chamber of Commerce in Altus, Oklahoma, saying he was going to try and stop the courts-martial of those charged with killing the civilians at My Lai. "We bring them home from the Army and let some idiots try them like this. I had something to do in the Green Beret fiasco [the case in which members of that Army unit were freed from charges of murdering a Vietnamese double agent], and I will have something to do in this other thing also. You just wait and see. They're not going to get away with this."

While Rivers' comments were not specifically directed at the subcommittee's investigation, but at the pending trials of the accused, it once again raised the specter of whitewash. I ignored his remarks—with the exception of telling an inquiring press: "I'm not a whitewash man"—and proceeded with the hearings.

I explained to the witnesses that their testimony would be held in strict confidence, that the sanctity of congressional executive session would not be violated. Witnesses were advised that if they themselves chose to disclose the nature of their testimony, they were free to do so. And I also explained to them my arrangements with the news media regarding their rights.

The investigation proceeded despite the interference of the Army, the fulminations of an emotionally distraught chairman of the Armed Services Committee, and a cynical press. I pushed the committee through the mammoth task which included interviews with 152 witnesses, 1,812 pages of sworn testimony, 3,045 pages of statements and an extended field investigation in Vietnam.

On July 15, 1970, the committee issued its startling report: "A tragedy of major proportions" occurred at My Lai which "was so wrong and so foreign to the normal character and actions of our military forces as to immediately raise a question as to the legal sanity at the time of those men involved."

These hawkish, pro-military congressmen, headed by a Southern conservative, reported: "It can reasonably be concluded that the My Lai matter was 'covered up' by the Army and the State Department."

While such findings were amazing to the committee's detractors, equally amazing was Mendel Rivers' statement on the report: "I agree with everything in it. They have done a masterful job." That statement had not come easily, however. I had to prevail on Rivers' basic sense of right, and there was some speculation that I had to "con" him into approving it. I wouldn't say that I "conned" Rivers, I simply convinced him it was the type of report to make. Rivers wanted to come out with a—I don't want to use the term "whitewash"—more of a vindication, and we wouldn't go along with that. In the end Rivers did what he eventually recognized as being the right thing to do.

I had a direct hand in drafting the report. I wanted specific information included and I wanted it handled in such a way that it would be absolutely clear to the reader. My sense of history told me I was responsible for a report on a major incident in the annals of the armed services of the United States, and I was determined the public would get the facts, plain and simple. The report was not myopically prejudiced against the Army, but neither was it in any way a "whitewash."

> There is no question but that a tragedy of major proportions involving unarmed Vietnamese, not in uniform, occurred at My Lai 4 on March 16, 1968, as a result of military operations of units of the Americal Division. . . .
>
> Precisely how each of these persons was killed cannot be determined. However, there is convincing evidence that some were killed by

artillery, some by gunships, and the remainder by small arms fire. Some were killed inadvertently under circumstances which would preclude the assignment of blame. Some were deliberately killed, and that cannot be condoned. The evidence indicates that a relatively few U. S. troops actually committed any of these acts, all pertinent factors must be considered. The acts themselves should not be viewed in isolation.

In trying to view the incident with the requisite perspective, the report noted that the inhabitants of the area had been removed only to return; that they had been warned to leave again and refused; that it was a hardcore Viet Cong area used as a base and supply camp; that many soldiers had been maimed or killed by booby traps and attacks emanating from the area.

This then was the political and military climate in the area when [the soldiers] were conducting operations early in 1968. And at this late date, who can judge the cumulative effects of the horrors, fears, and frustrations which the men of "C" Company had been forced to endure just prior to their action at My Lai on March 16 of that year? The orders and objectives for that day were apparently far from clear, and such confusion could only compound the problem.

The subcommittee is well aware of that line of cases which holds, in effect, that an unlawful order must be resisted. This presupposes that the accused has the requisite judgment capability under the circumstances obtaining at the particular moment. Undoubtedly, the correctness of a man's decision can be measured with academic precision in the quiet comfort and safety of the Pentagon, or a courtroom. But such decisions on the battlefield must be made in haste and woe betide the man who wrongly refuses to carry out an order. Under these latter conditions, a man could reasonably be expected to place more reliance on his commander than on his conscience, and from the reported actions of some of the men at My Lai, one might conclude that this is exactly what happened.

What obviously happened at My Lai was wrong. It was contrary to the Geneva Conventions, the Rules of Engagement, the MACV (Military Assistance Command, Vietnam) directives.

Those men who stand accused for their actions at My Lai, have, in the minds of many, already been "convicted" without trial. By the same token, the U. S. also stands convicted in the eyes of many around the world. Those two tragic consequences might have been avoided had the My Lai incident been promptly and adequately investigated by the Army.

Getting down to specifics, the subcommittee said that following the rampage by Calley's platoon through the area, an order was given "by radio to the commander of 'C' Company to return to My Lai 4 . . . to determine the sex, age, and cause of death of those civilians killed." That order was immediately countermanded by the commander of the American Division, Major General Samuel Koster, who was monitoring the frequency on which the order was transmitted. He testified he did so for tactical reasons.

That action in itself was enough to conclude that "responsible officers of the American Division and the 11th Brigade failed to make adequate, timely investigation and report of the My Lai allegations," the report stated. As a result, "It can reasonably be concluded that the My Lai matter was 'covered up' within the American Division and by the district and province advisory teams. To keep the My Lai matter bottled up . . . required the concerted action or inaction on the part of so many individuals that it would be unreasonable to conclude that this dereliction of duty was without plan or direction."

My subcommittee noted that except for statements by the commanders of the 11th Brigade and the American Division, Colonel Oran Henderson and General Koster, "there is not a shred of evidence to support the claim that an investigation was conducted" by the commander of Task Force Barker. "Each witness identified by Koster and Henderson as having furnished signed statements, which they claimed were attached to the report, has denied that he was ever interviewed by Lieutenant Colonel Barker, or that he supplied a sworn statement to any person."

The only report of the incident which could be found was a two-page summary of the occurrence at My Lai prepared by Colonel Henderson. It said twenty noncombatants were killed, and concluded that they were accidentally caught "in preparatory cross fires." The Henderson report also said that no civilians were assembled and shot by U.S. troops. Written on April 24, 1968, more than a month after the My Lai incident, the report was placed in a double envelope and addressed: ''For Eyes of Commanding General Only.'' The 11th Brigade intelligence sergeant who handled the report had been instructed to treat it as sensitive correspondence. ''There is some question whether he was told to conceal the copy or whether he did so voluntarily,'' the subcommittee said. In any event he kept the copy in a folder in his desk drawer rather than in the classified files of the brigade because, he said, 'I wanted to keep it out of the files where anybody could see it.''' When a search was instituted for the report, the only copy known to exist was found in the desk.

The subcommittee noted that Army regulations regarding Vietnam specifically required all military personnel to report any ''incident or act thought to be a war crime'' to his commander. In turn, the commander was to notify the proper authorities of any report received. In addition to those directives, General Westmoreland had frequently voiced his concern about civilian casualties and insisted that ''all known, suspected, or alleged war crimes or atrocities committed . . . will be investigated.'' The general testified before the subcommittee that military personnel were allowed no discretion in reporting suspected war crimes. Unfortunately, the committee stated, ''the testimony disclosed an incredible breakdown in the reporting of the allegation of a possible war crime in this situation.''

In an effort to obtain an explanation of the failure of a report being made in any of the various channels available, I questioned General Westmoreland about the reporting procedures.

HÉBERT: Thank you very much, general. There are four areas I would like to ask you about before we proceed with the questions by the other members of the committee.

Number one, of course, is a very obvious question. You were in Vietnam in command of our troops there, wearing three hats as you have testified here, and you never heard anything untoward at My Lai 4 during your time in-country?

WESTMORELAND: I heard nothing suggesting any irregularities. The only report that I received was the operations report that I made reference to in my prepared statement. . . .

HÉBERT: Now, when is the first time you heard about these allegations?

WESTMORELAND: After the Ridenhour letter, which is in my

prepared statement—the date of his letter was 29 March, and I received a verbal report that such a letter had been received several weeks later from a member of my staff, General Milton, my secretary of the general staff.

He told me that a letter had come in referring to Pinkville. I had never heard of Pinkville. And we finally discovered that Pinkville was the nickname that soldiers had given because of the color on the map of the My Lai village, or I think it was specifically My Lai 4.

That was the first I heard of it, which was almost a year later.

HÉBERT: Again it becomes the concern of the committee and it is hard for us to realize that something of this nature did not surface itself, when so many people apparently knew so much about it, but yet nobody knew anything about it.

WESTMORELAND: Well, this is absolutely unexplainable to me.

HÉBERT: It is fantastic, I will say that much.

With no niceties reserved because of his rank, the subcommittee concluded: "While General Westmoreland might find it impossible to explain the failure of his chain of command to surface the report of the alleged atrocity, the subcommittee believes that the explanation lies in a concerted action among military and State Department officers to suppress all evidence of the allegation and its investigation."

The testimony clearly established, the report said, that James May, a State Department foreign service officer,

was apprised of atrocity allegations by Vietnamese government sources. It further established that members of his staff had discussed the allegation and its investigation with representatives of Americal Division, and with others from the advisory team attached to a (South Vietnamese) division. It further demonstrated that he had personally been informed of the allegation at several times during the investigation. Despite the evidence that his unit had demonstrated concern over the admittedly unusual allegation and its investigation, Mr. May claimed to have no recollection of the incident.

The committee also said that the same conspiracy of silence applied to Army intelligence. Numerous members of the intelligence community, both civilian and military, were stationed near My Lai 4 during 1968 and 1969. Yet they consistently denied having heard anything in that period which would have caused them to suspect any untoward action had occurred in the area on March 16, 1968. "This is unbelievable," I said.

> We have documentary evidence which establishes clearly that one organization attached to an intelligence agency had a report as early as March 18—two days following the incident—alleging the killing of civilians at Son My.
>
> The intelligence personnel apparently saw fit to dismiss all allegations concerning it as merely Communist propaganda. Yet most of the allegations, which came to them through South Vietnamese officials, were specific as to time, place and units involved.
>
> As far as I'm concerned, failure to fully investigate and report these allegations to higher authorities raises a very serious question as to the reliability and usefulness of our intelligence activities in Vietnam.

Besides the derelictions of the State Department and Army intelligence, there were several other spin-offs from the My Lai affair which were upsetting to my subcommittee. One involved an Army photographer, Ron Haeberle. Another involved the Distinguished Flying Cross awarded to the helicopter pilot, Lieutenant Thompson. The third was the overreaction by the Army in recommending charges against soldiers where there was insufficient evidence to convict.

Haeberle was one of the most perplexing witnesses to testify before the subcommittee. He had been assigned by the Public Information Office of the 11th Brigade to accompany "C" Company on its mission. Haeberle testified he had carried three cameras with him that day. Two cameras were issued by the Army and contained black and white film. The third camera was his personal property and contained color film. His purpose on the mission was to obtain action pictures to accompany news releases to "hometown" newspapers.

He testified he took as many as fifty black and white pictures and eighteen color photos, the latter which he kept for his personal use. He turned the black and white pictures in to the public information office. "All but one of these," the subcommittee said, "could be called routine pictures of GIs or My Lai residents . . ." The one exception showed the feet of what appeared to be two dead adults. It could not be determined whether they were civilians, or, if they were dead, how they had been killed. It could have happened at Son My, or any place up and down the road. There were pictures of bodies. But where those bodies were, nobody knew. They could have been on a Hollywood lot. They could have been a city dump for all we knew.

The benign black and white Army pictures were in sharp contrast to the sensational color photos Haeberle claimed to have taken with his personal camera and film, and later sold to news organizations in America and abroad. These pictures have since become part of the Vietnam legacy. As for Haeberle, I'll never understand why he failed to report his observations and his photographs. He testified he was disgusted by what he had seen and photographed that day. Yet he never made any complaint about the conduct of the troops. And he never advised any military superior that he had photographs of the victims of an atrocity. In fact, he later testified before me he didn't even know the village was named My Lai.

Haeberle had been discharged eleven days after the incident at My Lai. Still he made no effort to report the incident to military authorities. Instead he used the color photographs—which were graphic evidence that a number of Vietnamese had been killed somewhere at some time—in a series of lectures he gave to civic groups. When Army investigators finally located him in the summer of 1969, Haeberle concluded that the pictures had been taken at My Lai 4 on March 16, 1968. He refused the Army's request for the pictures, but he did make copies for them. He was asked not to publish the pictures while the investigation was in progress, but he released them to the *Cleveland Plain Dealer*. Following that he began big-time negotiations with at least ten different publications, including *Life* magazine, and grossed more than $35,000. The photographer's activities caused me to comment: "It appears that Haeberle was more concerned with profit than he was in aiding the disclosure of an atrocity." But this conclusion stemmed from testimony I elicited from Haeberle.

HÉBERT: All right, then. Let's find out how it ended up. You sold the pictures to *Life*, did you?
HAEBERLE: That is right.
HÉBERT: How much did you receive from *Life* for those pictures?
HAEBERLE: *Life*, $17,500.

HÉBERT: They gave you $17,500.

HAEBERLE: Yes.

HÉBERT: Did you ask for more, and was that a compromise price?

HAEBERLE: I could have had more. I could have had a hundred. . .

HÉBERT: I didn't ask you what you could have had. I asked did you ask for more?

HAEBERLE: I settled for that. I was satisfied with that.

HÉBERT: Did you ask for more and compromise at $17,500?

HAEBERLE: At first, yes.

HÉBERT: What did you ask for?

HAEBERLE: We asked for $125,000.

Haeberle's financial records disclosed he eventually received a total of $19,500 from Time-Life, Inc., for publication rights; foreign rights to the pictures brought his profit to $35,099, and his testimony indicated Haeberle was not entirely disinterested in financial gain.

HÉBERT: You have never taken the time to total the amount of money you got from these pictures?

HAEBERLE: No, because it was split between two years, '69 and '70.

HÉBERT: What do you mean split?

HAEBERLE: I received some in '69 and some in '70.

HÉBERT: Why did you make a split of it?

HAEBERLE: Income tax purposes.

HÉBERT: Income tax purposes. Who was advising you?

HAEBERLE: I have a person figuring my income tax.

While Haeberle contended that the pictures he profited from were his personal property since they were taken with his own camera, the sergeant in charge of the brigade public information office stated that the standing operating procedure required all pictures taken by brigade photographers while on official assignment—even those taken with privately owned cameras—to be turned in to the office. Haeberle said he had never heard of such a requirement. Although less extreme, Haeberle's position was comparable to an infantryman contending that any area he captured with his government-issued rifle was the Army's, but anything captured while using his privately owned weapon and ammunition was his personal spoils.

Haeberle was very vague about not having heard about the orders. It was an impossible situation. He didn't seem to know until My Lai was internationally publicized that his pictures were of My Lai.

Besides my disgust for Haeberle's profiteering, I had another purpose in the intensive grilling of Haeberle and his superiors. The questioning brought out the fact that the Army's supervision of information specialists was very informal, or casual. If Haeberle had been properly supervised, the Army would have known if he took photographs at My Lai 4 on March 16, 1968. Then the pictures, of course, would have been evidence in determining the truth or falsity of the allegations arising from the incident. Photographers assigned to cover a combat operation should be acting for the benefit of the United States rather than for their personal enrichment.

As a result of Haeberle's deeds, the subcommittee recommended all military departments review their policies governing information specialists and include in their training the necessity to report any wrongdoing, with emphasis on their duty to report possible atrocities or war crimes. I believed that it should include clear directives that their work product is the property of the United States and is not for sale to the highest bidder.

Regarding Lieutenant Thompson, the controversial helicopter pilot, the subcommittee concluded that he and his two crew members were given military decorations for actions "on the basis of statements which were at substantial variance with the truth." It had been reported in the news media that Thompson landed near My Lai 4 and had his crewmen train their guns on American troops to prevent them from killing Vietnamese civilians, whom he evacuated to a safer location. The military citation said Thompson was awarded the Distinguished Flying Cross and his crew members were awarded Bronze Stars for action in which they risked their lives. It said they landed between American and Viet Cong forces engaged in a battle and rescued a number of civilians trapped in a bunker.

In actuality, the subcommittee determined that Thompson did indeed evacuate the civilians from a dangerous area and that he reported seeing a number of dead Vietnamese in the My Lai area. These actions were meritorious and admirable; they did not need elaboration and embellishment.

In contrast to the stories circulating in the news media, Thompson testified before the committee that he did not order his crew members to cover him in case he was fired upon by American troops, but rather in case enemy soldiers should attack while he was removing the civilians from the bunker. He also admitted he had seen no enemy that day, much less landed between the Viet Cong and American troops who were engaged in a fire fight. Additionally, one of his crew members, Lawrence Colburn, who had been the door gunner on the helicopter, testified Thompson never indicated he wanted him to cover him in case the Americans assaulted him. The decorations the three men received were based on recommendations supported by a statement from Thompson. It contradicted his testimony before the subcommittee.

> REDDAN (committee counsel): Where did you get that? Did you dictate it, write it out in longhand and get somebody to type it for you?
> THOMPSON: Yes, sir, I guess it was typed in the orderly room.
> REDDAN: Well, I have a copy here that I would just like to read to you a moment, telling of this incident. I won't read the whole thing.
> ''While flying over the village of My Lai, Sp/4 Andreotta spotted fifteen children hiding in a bunker located between friendly forces and hostile forces engaged in a heavy fire fight.''
> Is that correct?
> THOMPSON: Fifth Amendment, sir.
> HÉBERT: What is that? What did you reply?
> CAPTAIN JOHNSON (Thompson's appointed attorney): He respectfully declines to answer questions about the citation. . . .
> REDDAN: Is the part I read to him correct with respect to ''heavy fire fight?'' It said, ''The bunker was located between friendly forces and hostile forces engaged in a heavy fire fight,'' and I said, is that correct?
> THOMPSON: I will just stay with that.
> HÉBERT: You will stay with the Fifth?
> THOMPSON: Yes.

Under further questioning, Thompson admitted he didn't ''recall any heavy fire fight,'' and the subcommittee noted that

> it may be significant that recommendations for the awards were made during that period of time during which complaints were being received

through Vietnamese government channels concerning the My Lai operation of March 16. It was also during that period that the commanding general of the Second (South Vietnamese) Division directed that the district chief's allegation of widespread killing of civilians be checked out with the Americal Division. Those factors suggested that the awards might have been part of an effort to cast the best light upon an operation of Americal Division which has resulted in serious criticism of the actions of its troops.

If medals are to retain their significance as a reward for heroic action, they should not be dispensed under such questionable circumstances.

Concerning the overreaction of the Army in filing charges, the subcommittee said it was part of an effort by the military to redeem itself for its earlier failings. In general, the subcommittee found the inquiry conducted by General Peers for the Army was praiseworthy, but in the preference of charges against certain officers the Peers Inquiry "overreacted." By so doing, the Army filed charges which were unsupported by evidence and resulted only in tainting the officers' reputations. "If the investigators had acted in accordance with the advice of the professional legal officers, several officers could have been spared the agony of a public announcement of charges which were subsequently dismissed," the subcommittee report stated.

To prevent further such occurrences, the subcommittee recommended that the Uniform Code of Military Justice be amended to provide for secrecy during investigations—modeled on civilian grand juries—to guarantee that suspects be protected from the dangers of premature disclosure.

The report also noted that soldiers who had been discharged since their participation in the My Lai incident could not be tried. They were immune from courts-martial; there was no jurisdiction to try them in a state or federal court; and no treaty existed with the South Vietnamese under which they could be extradited for trial there. "Those individuals appear to be free from prosecution in any jurisdiction, while their associates who remained in the military service may be brought to trial by courts-martial. This is manifestly unjust," the subcommittee concluded.

To correct the situation, the subcommittee proposed that the jurisdiction of United States district courts be enlarged to provide for prosecution of discharged servicemen for crimes committed while on active duty.

When the wide-ranging report—which not only pointed the finger of blame, but suggested solutions to ancillary problems arising from the incident—was issued, it put some of the subcommittee's congressional critics "in shock." But this was only because they held opinions which said that those who disagreed with their point of view regarding the Vietnamese War and the armed services in general could not possibly conduct an impartial investigation.

There had been no whitewash. The rights of individuals were not compromised. There was no interference with any criminal cases stemming from the incident. And while the report did severely criticize the Army's role in covering up the tragedy at My Lai, it did not hysterically assume that there were no provocations or extenuating circumstances involved in the incident itself.

One newspaper called the investigation "one of Congress' finest hours, albeit a sad one." As for me, I was proud that the investigation had been conducted in a dignified manner without one leak to the news media, a rarity comparable to Congress agreeing unanimously on anything. I could take no excessive pride in the fact that I had done what was necessary and that the evidence indicated the Army was culpable. Some perceptive people realized my personal discomfort with the entire matter. "We can't avoid the thought of how heavily his investigation and its gut-wrenching findings must have weighed on subcommittee Chairman F. Edward Hébert, long a champion of the Armed Services," one paper noted.

My own opinion of the experience was that I had simply taken the Army behind the woodshed.

But the final curtain on this tragedy did not drop with the release of the report. There was still much to come. I had continuously refused to honor the subpoenas issued against me and the subcommittee to produce the secret testimony taken in executive session. As was noted in the report, I said I would release the testimony only after all legal matters in connection with Calley had been resolved.

The military took the position, and properly so, that its findings were not subject to a review by the civilian courts, and its verdict on Calley was rendered before his appeal in the civilian courts reached the United States Supreme Court.

During this entire procedure, Calley remained the only individual tried and convicted for his part in the My Lai tragedy. All others charged were found not guilty. In almost each case, the testimony taken in executive session was demanded, and in each case, I refused to honor the subpoena. The House of Representatives sustained my position.

Finally, on April 5, 1976, the Supreme Court refused to hear the Calley case, years after the episode began, and the end of the legal road had been reached. This decision by the Supreme Court indicated that my position of refusing to release the secret testimony was correct. The Calley case was finally closed.

Within a few days of the Supreme Court ruling, former Colonel Reid Kennedy, who was the military judge at the court martial of Calley, talked for the first time. He is now a practicing attorney in Marietta, Georgia, and he expressed the opinion that others knew of and took part in the killings at My Lai and should have also been convicted.

"I don't believe that Calley should have been the only one convicted," Kennedy said in an interview with Kathryn Johnson of the Associated Press in Atlanta. Of course, this comment was very interesting, but more important was the fact that Kennedy spoke publicly about his refusing to review the case and said that my position of not honoring the subpoenas was right. This was no surprise to me. I knew privately he shared my position, but neither he nor I would talk as long as the matter was in litigation.

The curtain had fallen, and now he was free to speak. "There were others involved in the shootings with Calley, but some refused to obey his order (to kill)," he said. He further stated in the interview: "Calley thought what he was doing was right. That's not the issue."

Refusal by the House Armed Services Committee to release its confidential testimony was the major issue on which Calley's conviction might have been overturned, Kennedy told the AP. As I have noted, Calley requested the testimony and Kennedy twice directed the prosecution to ask for it. I refused both times.

Kennedy explained in the interview: "The law in that area is that the executive and judiciary branch must disclose any secret testimony, but that Congress does not have to since they have excluded themselves. If Congress was forced to disclose testimony, then any single congressman could make any sort of investigation and then thwart a trial later."

Kennedy said that is the reason why he ruled the way he did in refusing Calley's request to strike the testimony of any witness who had testified before the subcommittee.

I ordered the release of this secret testimony after the Supreme Court action with the approval of the members who served with me—William L. Dickinson, R–Alabama and Samuel S. Stratton, D–New York; both still active House members. The other member of the subcommittee, Charles Gubser, R–California, is retired. I also obtained the approval of Melvin R. Price, chairman of the full House Armed Services Committee. What was said behind those closed doors and guarded so jealously, and about which not a leak of a single paragraph, a single sentence, or a single word occurred, is now in the public's hands. The testimony is available to any writer or individual who cares to examine it. Nothing in the testimony has been altered or changed, only highly sensitive secret passages have been deleted.

Important to me is that the secret testimony which is now available will substantiate the statements made in the subcommittee's report. Anyone analyzing the report and the testimony will determine beyond a doubt that everything said in the subcommittee report was fully documented.

Through it all, however, My Lai remains a horrible nightmare and a terrible tragedy of major proportions.

CHAPTER XXII

SOLDIER, HEAL THYSELF

THE PRECISE MOMENT when the thought first flitted across my mind cannot be pinpointed, but I had been mulling over the idea during idle moments for several years before I gave vent to it vocally during an Armed Services subcommittee hearing in 1947. Why, I asked, has the government "spent billions of dollars to train men to kill and has spent nothing to train men to save lives? It doesn't make sense to me."

The subcommittee was considering possible inducements which would lure more physicians into the armed services. Secretary of War Robert P. Patterson had testified that with World War II duty behind them, thousands of doctors were leaving the armed services to take up civilian practice and resume their lives which had been interrupted by warfare. The situation was draining the military of medical personnel and it was becoming difficult to recruit more doctors. "There is," Secretary Patterson told the committee, "no West Point for doctors."

It was easy to understand why young physicians would want to return to private practice, but, if the armed services had a "West Point for doctors," perhaps that would solve the problem of the continuing critical shortage of medical men in the military. "So wouldn't it be more practical, more economical, and more desirable to let the armed services set up a school for the individual who wants to go into the school and become a doctor, being willing to exchange his talents over a longer period of years, so that the government could get its investment back?" I asked.

Yes, Patterson agreed, the idea had merit.

James Forrestal, the secretary of the Navy, testified that same day and called my suggestion "interesting and provocative," and added, "I agree that it is something that we should give serious study to." The Army's surgeon general, Norman T. Kirk, admitted that a new military medical school could be the answer to the doctor dilemma but estimated it would take ten or fifteen years before the school could become "a going concern."

Three days later General Dwight D. Eisenhower, the Army's chief of staff, told the subcommittee,

> We must get doctors. That is the problem we have. We must get good doctors. They have got to be capable of dealing in every field of medicine, including that of preventive medicine in which our own doctors have been so successful. On top of that, they have got to be of the quality, Mr. Chairman, to produce what you might call a medical general staff. Otherwise, how are we going to organize this country in war, particularly if we face the kind of war that so many of us fear, one of great destructiveness and terror throughout the country. No longer will it be merely a problem of taking care of the wounded on the battlefield. It is going to be equally the problem to take care of the sick and wounded of great cities, in order that the country can operate at all.

I then brought up the idea of a "West Point for doctors."

Eisenhower replied that doctors were needed immediately and that it would take "fifteen years, or certainly at the minimum, eleven, before you would begin to get returns from this investment in your school. We have got a problem now."

"Certainly, general," I said, "you have got a problem that is going to take fifteen years, but if we wait, it will be fifteen years, and then fifteen more years, and we still won't have any."

"I agree," Eisenhower responded.

Other prominent military men also thought the idea was worth pursuing, but none of the witnesses rushed to the stand with wholehearted endorsement, demanding that we get busy on the school right away. In fairness to the whole idea, I must note that rarely does anyone endorse anything wholeheartedly in front of a congressional committee, especially the military. They have learned by experience that it is far more prudent to play it safe, sit on the fence and get the drift of the wind. This attitude does not apply to such controversial areas as the American flag or motherhood. It does apply to almost anything else and that is why no one said, "Certainly, Mr. Hébert! A wonderful solution, let's get going on it in the morning."

Despite tacit agreement that such a school was a "good idea" in 1947, nothing had been done toward establishing it by 1961. In fourteen years, no studies had been made, no action had been taken, no medical school was on the horizon. Realizing that my idea was going nowhere, I introduced a bill calling for the establishment of a military medical school. The Department of Defense indicated that it was not enraptured by the idea, and Armed Services Committee Chairman Carl Vinson saw no point in pushing for something the Pentagon did not particularly want. Later Mendel Rivers would feel the same way.

But I persisted, and like a congressional Sisyphus I kept pushing the medical school legislation up Capitol Hill. My detractors maintained that if more doctors were needed, then existing medical facilities should be funded to do the job. The American Medical Association and the Association of American Medical Colleges opposed the idea, ostensibly because it might result in a lowering of standards. I saw a different reason for the opposition by the medical colleges. They wanted the government to give them money, but they weren't turning out more doctors, they just wanted the money.

Liberals and conservatives were about equally divided in opposition to the proposed medical school. Liberals were not inclined to give the armed services funds under many circumstances, and especially not when the Pentagon did not seem to want the money. Conservatives thought the federal government had no business intruding into the medical business to the degree of running a medical school.

I did not, however, have trouble with my conservative conscience on that point. To my mind, if the government could fund academies to train soldiers, sailors and airmen, why could not it also train doctors to tend these soldiers, sailors and airmen. Few conservatives advocated abolishing the Military, Naval, and Air Force academies and having private universities train officers exclusively. At the time I asked: "We have three academies where we teach people how to kill; why can't we have an academy where we teach them how to live?"

I also pointed out, "A medical education is so expensive. There are a lot of boys who could have become good doctors but they didn't have the wherewithal, and they ended up driving trucks or something because they could not afford medical school. But you take a young man with talent who is willing to trade his time by serving in the military in exchange for his education and we'd get a good doctor."

Further, I felt that many of these doctors would specialize in military-connected problems such as battlefield wounds and tropical diseases, two areas in which American medical science had not advanced to the extent that there was no room for improvement.

Between 1961 and 1971 I continued to push the military medical school idea. But it was an exercise in futility. Then, in 1971, my proposal suddenly became more palatable to the Pentagon. It was the same proposal I had been pushing since 1947. But there had been a change which affected thinking on the medical school: I had become chairman of the Armed Services Committee. They had fought the hell out of me, but when I became chairman, everybody was suddenly for me.

Secretary of Defense Melvin Laird developed a new-found enthusiasm for the project and allowed me to merge the medical school bill with a piece of legislation calling for the establishment of a military medical scholarship program, which was held in high regard by many influential congressional leaders.

Once Laird had acknowledged the need for a medical school, I called hearings. This time military men and members of the Armed Services Committee vied with one another in heaping praise on the medical school proposal, and the American Medical Association and the Association of American Medical Colleges caught their lumps for obstinacy in opposing the idea.

Few were surprised when the Armed Services Committee put its stamp of approval on the legislation and sent it on to the floor of the House. There it received only token opposition, passing by a vote of 352 to 31.

Still, a major hurdle lay in the path of the medical school

legislation—the United States Senate. Early in 1972, the Senate Armed Services Committee held hearings on the proposed legislation and found that not everyone supported it. The Office of Management and Budget opposed it on the grounds of fiscal outlay, and the Department of Health, Education and Welfare felt that the military would be usurping its powers by running a medical school. By the time the Senate hearings were over, I sensed that my patented "parliamentary procedures" would be necessary to save the school. I met with my Mississippi friend, John Stennis, the chairman of the Senate Armed Services Committee. Stennis supported the medical school legislation, and we concocted a plan, or as some would term it, a scheme.

The Senate Armed Services Committee removed the medical school authorization from the legislation but approved the scholarship plan. It appeared that I had sustained a defeat on the congressional battlefield. Actually it was a tactical retreat which fit right into the strategy of Generals Hébert and Stennis. The "parliamentary procedure" scenario was following the script.

From the Senate Armed Services Committee, the bill went into conference in an attempt to resolve the differences between the Senate and the House renditions of the legislation. The difference was the Senate had cut out the medical school. After the meeting, Stennis told his colleagues that the house members were adamant, insisting that the medical school legislation be retained. He said they felt that procrastination and study had delayed the program excessively, and now was the time for it to be implemented. The senators, practicing the art of politics, compromised in order to keep alive the scholarship program which they wanted. Only a few senators objected to the legislation publicly, and the measure was passed by a voice vote.

All that remained was for Richard Nixon to sign it into law. Elliot Richardson, the secretary of HEW, and Casper Weinberger, who was running the Office of Management and Budget, sent separate drafts to the White House calling for a veto of the bill. White House staff members were opposed to it also, calling it inflationary at a time when the President was vetoing everything he could get his hands on in an effort to cut federal spending.

Nevertheless, I received a call requesting my presence at the White House on September 21, 1972. "Is it a good bill?" the President asked me, pointing at the legislation which lay on his desk.

"Of course, it's a good bill," I said.

"It had better be," Nixon replied, and showed me the veto drafts, which he then shoved aside. Picking up a pen, he signed the bill into law.

I was beaming, but I told the President I wanted one more favor.

"What is it now?" Nixon asked, feigning exasperation.

I told him I wanted Dr. Ashton Thomas, a good friend of mine from New Orleans and a fine doctor, to be appointed to the medical school's board of regents.

"Can he read and write?" Nixon teased.

"I don't know," I retorted, "he went to Whittier."

The President got a kick out of the bantering. "I knew I shouldn't have asked you," he said as I left the Oval Office, having gotten everything I had come for. The Uniformed Services University of Health Sciences, as it was called, was legally in existence and Dr. Thomas would be appointed to the board.

Unfortunately I was not able to bask in the sun and enjoy this hard-won victory. After the signing of the bill came the real action. Weeks went into months and no board of regents had been named. This was singularly important because without the regents there was no one "to conduct the business of the university," which was called for in the legislation. Nothing could be done to make the university a reality until they were sworn in.

By January 1973 Elliot Richardson had been appointed secretary of defense. He paid a call on me, in my capacity as chairman of the Armed Services Committee, to present his credentials. This gave me the opportunity to complain that the regents had not been appointed. Richardson, who had opposed the school as HEW secretary, replied that for Nixon to appoint the regents would imply "tacit approval" of the school.

"Tacit approval!" I exclaimed. "It's the law! There's no 'tacit approval' about it."

I then asked Richardson whether he had read *The Godfather* or seen the movie. The secretary of defense—a Renaissance man—said he had done both.

"Okay," I responded, "I'll make you an offer you can't refuse: You don't appoint a board and there's no procurement bill."

The only importance of the annual procurement bill is that it determines which major defense program will survive. In other words it is generally the lifeblood of the Pentagon. I told him that if the regents were not appointed I would not put in the procurement bill. He said he'd carry the message, but nothing happened. Now, I hadn't seen the President or talked to him. But it didn't take long for me to figure out what was going on over there with Ehrlichman and Haldeman. It was getting blocked.

I realized that I had to get Nixon's attention if I wanted to save the medical school. I understood the machinations of Haldeman and Ehrlichman well, and knew that a call or a letter to the White House would be screened.

Fortunately, I had other means of access. Nixon was planning a reception near the end of February for the supporters of his Vietnam policy, which I called a little party for the Vietnam white hats. Just before the gathering, I received another thank-you-for-your-support letter from Nixon which I normally read and filed. This time, however, I answered it, thanking the President for his kind words. I also mentioned the medical school situation, and included that I had heard that members of the White House staff were considering impounding funds authorized for the school through the ploy of failing to nominate regents. I further hinted that if that be the case, the procurement bill might never see the light of day.

I did not mail the letter; I carried it with me to the party and handed it to Nixon in the reception line. The next morning at ten o'clock Ehrlichman called me with the message that "the tracks were all clear" on appointing the regents. At midafternoon the President called to inquire whether everything was satisfactory. It certainly was, and I congratulated Nixon on being "a man of action."

Within a short time Nixon had sent his nominations for the regents to the Senate. By June 15, 1973, they were confirmed. By June 18, the House Armed Services Committee had approved the defense procurement bill. Planning on the medical school began immediately.

On July 10, 1975, the groundbreaking took place with President Gerald R. Ford turning the first spadeful of earth. The dais was filled with dignitaries who had come for the long-awaited event. In addition to the President and myself, there were these other notables: David Packard, chairman of the Board of Regents; Secretary of Defense James R. Schlesinger; Senator Strom Thurmond; Dr. Anthony R. Curreri, president of the university; and the Surgeons General of the three military services.

Also present were the distinguished members of the Board of Regents: Vice Chairman Lieutenant General Leonard D. Heaton, former surgeon general of the Army, retired; Dr. Alfred A. Marquez of San Francisco; Dr. H. Ashton Thomas, a good friend who is vice president of the Louisiana State Medical Society; Dr. Philip O'Bryan Montgomery, Jr. of the Southwestern Medical School, University of Texas; Dr. Durward G. Hall, a former member of Congress from Missouri; Joseph D. Matarazzo, Ph.D., of the University of Oregon Health Sciences Center; Charles E. Odegaard, Ph.D., President Emeritus of the University of Washington; and Dr. Malcolm C. Todd, past president of the American Medical Association.

The Surgeons General—Lieutenant General Richard R. Taylor, Army; Lieutenant General George E. Schafer, Air Force; and Vice Admiral D. L. Curtis, Navy—are ex-officio members of the Board.

The stage was set, and I was excited that this dream of mine would finally become a reality.

Dr. Curreri, in his welcoming remarks, set forth the mission of the university as I had envisioned it. "The mission of this university will be to train a cadre of motivated, dedicated young men who will be serving global medicine in terms of cure and control. Moreover, they will be able to mobilize and deploy rapidly, as teams, to meet military and civilian crises . . . and provide humanistic, as well as scientific, health care to the sick and injured. In addition, this university will provide opportunities for aspiring young military officers to attain academic recognition and support continuing education of health providers. Finally, it will be one of the main sources in the United

States in developing optimum models for the study of health care and health education.''

Secretary Schlesinger, after recognizing me by name and mentioning my efforts in connection with the university, set forth his philosophy for the institution. He told the large crowd gathered for the occasion on the grounds of Bethesda Naval Hospital, ''It was Robert Louis Stevenson who said, 'There are men and classes of men that stand above the common herd; the soldier, and the sailor, the shepherd not infrequently, and the physician almost as a rule.' I do not know what he meant by that equivocal word 'almost,' but it is certainly the case that the military physician earns all of the approval that Robert Louis Stevenson suggested. The military physician has been the pioneer in emergency medicine, tropical diseases, parasitology, and the adverse effects of hostile environments, be they high altitude, deep sea, or the tropics.''

He concluded, ''To insure a continuation of the great contributions that can be forthcoming from military medicine to our society, there should be given to military medicine the opportunity to develop its fullest potential and its public prestige. That potential and prestige will be greatly enhanced through the developments of the Uniformed Services University of the Health Sciences.''

Packard, the chairman of the Board of Regents and a former Under Secretary of Defense, had the task of introducing me. He said: ''I have already alluded to the fact that the Congress, particularly the members of the Armed Services Committee, had a very important role in the development of the policies and the approaches to the all volunteer forces and to the special problem relating to providing future men and women for our military service in the armed services. When I was here, the Chairman of the House Armed Services Committee was the Honorable Edward Hébert and if there is one man who deserves credit for initiating the legislation which made this program possible, for having the vision to see the importance of such a program, it was this great man who was a wonderful friend to me during the time I was at the Pentagon. So it is a special privilege for me today to present to you the Honorable Edward Hébert, a good friend and really the father of this medical school.''

The remarks and attributions by Packard were most gracious, and I recounted to the audience the battle I had in getting the legislation passed. The fight lasted many years, but as we shall see, it was not over.

We saved the big gun for last. The President of the United States. I was pleased he decided to come and lend his presence and prestige to the undertaking.

The President knew what I had gone through, and he alluded to it in his remarks. "I feel greatly honored to have the opportunity of being here on this very historic day when the hopes of so many for so many years are finally coming to fruition. I know from firsthand experience how long and how hard Eddie Hébert worked on this legislation in the House of Representatives. As he left the podium he observed that the first year I introduced it he was a freshman in the House of Representatives. And that's a long time ago," the President said.

He related his support of and commitment to the university as he told us, "Now by bringing together the men and women from the Army, Navy, and the Air Force, I think this new facility will perform another vital function. It will give members of the three services, three proud, and yes, independent services, the opportunity to work together for a common goal without forsaking their separate traditions . . . It's a bold innovation, and true in my judgment to the best traditions of the Armed Forces."

He closed out his dedicatory remarks by saying that the ground-breaking for the university "will prove to be true; a great American undertaking, one that we can all be proud of, and one that will pay great human dividends in the form of outstanding health care for the men in our uniformed services as well as humanity on a global basis."

The President added, "This is a proud day for the Army, the Navy, and the Air Force, and I think equally important, a proud day for the American people that they serve so well."

I know it was a proud day for me, one that I will never forget and an accomplishment I regard as one of my greatest contributions during my Congressional career. It had been a thrilling and satisfying day.

Then, when everything appeared to be going smoothly, Representative Jack Edwards, an Alabama Republican, proposed an amendment to scuttle the school on the same old grounds I had been fighting for years: It is a waste of money because civilian medical schools could graduate physicians for less money than it would cost the government to do the job.

The proposed amendment shook me. I could see my dream failing for lack of support in the liberal-dominated 94th Congress which had ousted me from my chairmanship the preceding January. Fighting for the life of this long-suffering project, I took the floor of the House of Representatives. After refuting objections to the school, I said,

> Nobody has mentioned here today the great expansion of the school. It will have 1,680 students by 1984, and they will not all be medical students. There will be nurses, there will be technicians, there will be corpsmen being trained, there will be administrators—the whole vast field of medical care specialists will be there.
>
> This institution is not going to be a parochial or provincial institution. By the time it is fully expanded, by the time it has grown out to its great, global institution, one will find doctors and scientists from all over the world coming to visit this great institution, which is surrounded by Bethesda Naval Hospital, Walter Reed Hospital, the National Institutes of Health, and other great hospitals in this area.

When the roll was called, the medical school had triumphed by a vote of 221 to 190.

Even this victory was not the end of the fight. When the appropriations bill including money for the school reached the floor of the Senate, the fight was renewed by Senator William Proxmire, a Democrat from Wisconsin.

I had suffered a broken right arm and was confined to Walter Reed Army Hospital. I left the hospital and went to the Senate floor to talk with Senate friends, such as Barry Goldwater, Mike Mansfield, and John Stennis. It was touch and go, but ''go'' won in conference and I had won my fight.

I was immensely pleased, for I truly believed in the necessity of the school, and would enjoy watching it grow on 150 grassy acres near the Naval Medical Center at Bethesda, Maryland. Of course, if it had started 24 years ago when I first wanted it, the military would now have 3,000 doctors. Now we have to wait until 1979 before the first doctor is graduated.

Still, there is a deep satisfaction for me in the fact that the medical school is now a reality. The surgeon general of the Navy, Admiral Curtis, has said that I will be known as the "father of military medicine," and that, too, gives me great satisfaction.

When my service is ended and I look back over the milestones of my career, I want most of all to be remembered for the military medical school.

It will live long after those of us who read this are dead.

CHAPTER XXIII

SLINGS AND ARROWS

Party politics exert much more influence over national and international affairs than the casual observer notices. It is far from an intramural sport. Its effects, however, are not always immediately obvious: a vote against a bill in 1941, for example, kept me from becoming Armed Services Committee chairman until 1971.

When I came to Congress, the ordinary thing for a young man to do was to follow the leadership, to follow whatever line the party laid down. But I led five members of the Louisiana delegation and beat a party motion. I led them to vote for the Dirksen Amendment. It was an amendment keeping within the Congress the power to revoke the Lend-Lease deal. I was against the liberalization of the discretionary powers of the chief executive.

That amendment was to HR 1776, and the number of the bill was there by design. John McCormack wanted 1776 because we were helping the British. It was a good P. R. idea.

My vote for the amendment kept me off the Naval Affairs Committee. Sam Rayburn even told me that. Jere Cooper of Tennessee, who was on the Ways and Means Committee at the time, was sitting in the chairman's chair. It was during a hearing of the Committee of the Whole, and when I tried to get on the Naval Affairs Committee, Sam Rayburn told me, "Eddie, Jere saw you walk through that aisle [to vote with the Republicans]. I can't budge him."

I got beat eight to seven. Mendel won it. Mendel had Jimmy Byrnes backing him, who was then secretary of state, and old Bob

Doughton, who was chairman of the committee, from North Carolina. Mendel had a lot of good horses going for him.

I got on next, when Mr. Maloney came back to Congress. After Mendel became chairman, I would tease him with "There but for the grace of Jimmy Byrnes goes Hébert."

I had a great deal of respect for Rivers' ability as a legislator, too; we were almost parallel in our defense postures. When I took over the committee chairmanship in 1971, following Rivers' death, and the defeat of Congressman Philip J. Philbin of Massachusetts who was in line for the chairmanship, I said, "I loved Mendel Rivers, and my goal is the same as his. The goal is that the United States have an uncontestable military defense and overwhelming offensive power."

However, to love someone is not necessarily to be blind to that person's faults and limitations. It was certainly no secret that Rivers suffered occasional drinking bouts. I don't think you could keep a secret in Washington if you told it to your mirror. The trouble with Mendel was he would sit there and tell me he hadn't had a drink in six months, and I would know he was just coming off a jag. I got so damned mad at him one day, I said, "Mendel, let's get this thing straight. You know I'll do anything in the world for you that I can possibly do. But damn it, you can't lie to me now." He tried to take my drinking capacity and apply it to himself. "The way you drink," he said, "I wish I could drink that way."

Well, he should have been honest with himself, but he couldn't understand that approach.

Drew Pearson wrote a column about Rivers' drinking, charging that it held up an $18 billion military authorization bill because he was drying out at Bethesda Naval Hospital. (This actually was one of the rare occasions he fell off the wagon after becoming chairman because he had, as I told Pearson earlier, been abstemious since assuming the responsibility of the chairmanship two years previous to that 1967 incident.) The column sent Rivers into a rage. He wanted to strike back at Pearson from the floor of the House, but I knew that would just bring more detrimental publicity. I always had problems with Mendel on that point. He wanted to get up on the floor and knock Pearson. If he knocked him the wire services would have had to repeat it and that would have just spread the story. He didn't understand that.

I prevailed, and arranged a welcome-back reception for Rivers with the leadership of the House paying tribute to him upon his recovery from his "illness." I joined in the speeches, saying Rivers "is just as much a human being as anybody in the House, with all the faults and frailties and all the sterling qualities, whatever you want to call them, which we all, to some degree, may possess. That is what makes him the real man he is and the real leader that he has demonstrated himself to be."

As I finished with this tribute to Rivers, I prepared to fulfill an obligation Rivers had performed the year before: grand marshall of the Armed Forces Day parade in Torrance, California, a city noted for its patriotic fervor. I commented to a friend, "I'll make a real hair-raising speech. That's what they want. I'm going to give 'em what they want. They want the roof to be raised. They want flags to fly. They want a Rivers' speech. I won't drop the bomb on Hanoi though." When Rivers was the grand marshall out there the previous year he made a real humdinger. He would drop the bomb every time he talked. He bombed new places every day.

That same year the Armed Services Committee was conducting hearings on draft law revision. The committee was opposed to the lottery plan of draft selection being pushed by President Johnson, a plan dubbed FAIR, an acronym for Fair and Impartial Random Selection. Strongly opposed to the idea of selection by lottery, I said during one committee hearing, "This FAIR ought to be called Futile and Irresponsible Roulette." U. S. Senator Edward M. Kennedy, ever taking up that which he senses to be the liberal cause of the moment, appeared before the committee with a lottery plan of his own. I summed up the difference between our plans: "I would pick them by divine providence. You would pick them by human error."

As the hearings on the draft continued, the committee began questioning Justice Department officials as to why they were not prosecuting persons who advocated that young men evade the draft and refuse to fight in Vietnam. This led to one of the most painful events in my political life.

I was involved in a lengthy colloquy with Fred Vinson, an assistant attorney general, about this failure on the part of the Justice Department to prosecute those who encouraged draft evasion. In response to a statement by Rivers, Vinson had said the department's batting average in prosecuting actual draft evaders was .975. "But your batting average in prosecuting people for violating this law obstructing recruiting is .000," I retorted.

Vinson began to defend the Justice Department's lack of prosecution by saying that persons who advocated draft evasion were protected under the First Amendment's guarantee of freedom of speech. I countered by saying that there were laws already enacted under which the Department of Justice could prosecute on grounds of treason. I said the department was using the First Amendment as a cloak for not prosecuting persons who were committing "disloyal acts."

So it went, back and forth. Each time he was pressured, Vinson retreated into the First Amendment. Finally, becoming irritated at the evasions, I said, "Let's forget the First Amendment." Well, I couldn't have stirred a bigger storm of controversy had I stood on the steps of the Capitol advocating draft evasion and burning the American flag.

I had, of course, meant that Vinson should ignore the First Amendment excuse for the purpose of discussion and concentrate on the laws under which those encouraging draft resistance could be prosecuted. If such prosecution did violate the First Amendment, which I did not believe it did, I said the courts were the proper body to decide that issue, not the Justice Department. I did not, *under any circumstances*, mean that the First Amendment should be done away with or bypassed. Considering my past performance and journalistic career, Job would have denied God before I would have advocated abridging the Constitution.

I think it was perfectly obvious from the beginning what I had meant, but *New York Times* reporter John Herbers had a story. It was headlined: "Forget Free Talk, Congressman Says." It began:

> Members of the House Armed Services Committee demanded yesterday that the Justice Department disregard the First Amendment right

of free speech and prosecute those who urge young men to defy the draft law.

"Let's forget the First Amendment," Rep. F. Edward Hébert, Jr., D-La., told Asst. Gen. Fred M. Vinson, Jr., in a loud voice during hearings on the draft.

Two sentences had been written by *New York Times* reporter Herbers and each contained an error of fact, sending Herbert Bayard Swope's dictim of "accuracy, accuracy, accuracy" begging. In the first place it was not members who had uttered the statement, it was me; and in the second place, I am not a junior.

The story also contained an idiotic statement by Rivers from the previous day's hearings. He had told a witness, Everett R. Jones, a representative of the Methodist Board of Christian Social Concerns, "There are only two ideologies in the world. One is represented by Jesus Christ and the other by a hammer and sickle. Which do you prefer?" This, coupled with my statement, taken out of context, had the effect of making the committee members appear to be a reincarnation of the leaders of the Inquisition.

The next day Herblock of the *Washington Post* impaled Rivers and me with one of his cartoon thrusts. The drawing depicted "L. Mendel Rivers" burning the U.S. Constitution, and "E. Hébert, Jr." carrying a sign saying, "Let's Forget the First Amendment." An unnamed committee member was carrying in one hand a sign saying, "Hell with the U.S. Courts," and in the other, a Confederate flag. Two young men with long hair were burning a copy of the "Draft Act" and carrying a sign reading, "To Hell With the Draft Act." The line over the cartoon which was obviously to be attributed to the committee members said, "We'll Teach You Patriotism and Respect for the Law."

Practically every newspaper in the country ground out an editorial attacking me for my statement on the First Amendment which I had either "snorted," "shouted," "said in a testy outburst," "advocated," "suggested," or "demanded," depending on which paper one read.

The coverage tormented me. I felt more hurt than angry at having my remarks taken out of context, repeated, and given the status of being accurate by perpetuation of the error. In a conversation with a friend a few days later, I agonized over the original report and the ultimate damage it caused.

> I didn't say "Let's forget the First Amendment, period." I was having a discussion with an assistant attorney general of the United States, who was then telling me, and telling the whole committee, and telling the world, that despite the fact that there is a law on the statute books of the United States in the Criminal Code which spells out that any individual during war or an emergency, who attempts to violate the law, who urges—or attempts, it says—to violate the law, is guilty of a crime, he was not going to prosecute.
>
> They've never said those laws were not valid before—the Department of Justice didn't recommend that those laws be vetoed by the President when we passed them because they were in violation of the First Amendment. One way or the other the Justice Department failed to do its duty: by not calling attention to the probability that the law that I wanted them to enforce was unconstitutional when it was enacted, or by not enforcing the law after it is on the books.
>
> We were discussing this point and the attorney general was saying, "Well, they come under the umbrella of the First Amendment."
>
> I said, "Let's forget the First Amendment." And the implication was, for the purpose of this discussion *only*! That's obvious. Do I have to say, "Now, Mr. Attorney General, understand me well, when I say let's forget the First Amendment, I don't mean that I'm denying anyone the right of free speech, I don't mean that I don't believe in the Bill of Rights and the Constitution. I do. It is just for the purpose of considering this law that I ask you not to keep bringing up the First Amendment, because there is not a law on the books which could not be interpreted as violating the First Amendment."

Referring to Herblock's cartoon, I continued:

> See where the cartoonist has a third member carrying the Confederate flag. This is totally irrelevant to the discussion, but it raises the race issue. Immediately! The race issue was never injected into the conversation. I recognize the fact that since I'm from Louisiana I'm not supposed to have any objective ideas; I'm supposed to be prejudiced. I'm supposed to be bigoted. These are things we are indicted for. We are charged with. Of course the bigotry in the North is perfectly all right; it doesn't count. That's fine; that's their right.

In this particular case the South or race was never injected into it, but this cartoonist puts that Confederate flag into the cartoon, indicating Mr. Rivers and myself and members of the committee were motivated by the race issue, which couldn't be further from the truth. Or he's indicating that we're from the South and, of course, no one from the South has any respect for the First Amendment.

I realized, nevertheless, that I should have been more careful, recognizing the fact that my words could be easily lifted out of context. That was the most unfortunate phrase I have ever uttered. I don't know one major newspaper in the country which didn't criticize me with violence by quoting me out of context. No one is more in favor of the First Amendment than me.

I only received one apology for being quoted out of context, and was somewhat surprised where that came from: *Time* magazine. The editor wrote me and said, "We apologize. We quoted you out of context." So I wrote the editor back, "That's very fine of you, my dear man, but I don't want apologies, not interested in apologies. I'm interested in the correction of the record for your readers. That's all I'm looking for."

As a result I got a call from Miss Virginia Adams, who was in charge of the letters to the editor. She told me that she'd be happy to print whatever I wanted printed within the limitations of space—two paragraphs, and I could say that I was quoted out of context.

I said, "What? That's a self-serving statement. Unless you admit that you did it, my statement that I was quoted out of context means absolutely nothing to me."

"Well," she said, "Write us a letter." So I wrote the letter.

Dear Sir: I desire to publicly acknowledge and express my gratitude to *Time* magazine and its editor-in-chief, Mr. Hedley Donovan, for their prompt and responsive reply to my letter of May 10, 1967. The letter which follows speaks for itself:

"Dear Mr. Hébert: The story in *Time* containing the quotation ascribed to you, 'Let's forget the First Amendment,' was in no way intended, as you imply, to be a 'slant' on the news. However, as we now realize from scanning the full testimony, *Time* did take your remark out of context and for that we apologize. Our only

defense is that the *Congressional Record* was not available to us at
the time that the story was written.''

I then got a call from *Time* saying, ''We can't print this.''

Hell, they didn't want to print it, but they admitted it to me. I wrote
the editor of every paper which came to my attention. I didn't write a
letter to the editor; I merely said, this is the record. I sent them the
complete record, and I said, ''Now, after you've read the record I'd
appreciate your reaction.''

Any honest newspaper reporter, who was sincere and wanted the
record to be correct, would have corrected the record. Everyone of
them wrote back and said I was not quoted out of context. All of this
started with a reporter's story in the *New York Times*, and all of these
other people picked it up without checking it, without knowing
whether it was right or not.

Eventually, two writers did acknowledge in print that I had been
given short shrift by the media. David Lawrence, the respected
conservative columnist and publisher wrote in his column:

> F. Edward Hébert of Louisiana, Democrat, got into an argument
> with Fred S. Vinson, Jr., assistant attorney general, when the latter
> testified on May 6 before the House Armed Services Committee con-
> cerning laws that would cover such demonstrations. When Mr. Vinson
> seemed to be stressing possible restriction by the First Amendment,
> Mr. Hébert told him to ''forget the First Amendment'' for the time
> being on the proposed law, while he concentrated on the obligation of
> the Department of Justice to enforce a law when it has been passed.

Roscoe Drummond, whose column was syndicated by the Publishers Newspaper syndicate, said,

> I want to report on Hebert's plight as a case study on how a phrase out
> of context can lead to inaccuracy in the news and quickly generate such
> a thunderstorm of editorials that there is probably not one in a hundred
> persons who have read about the controversy who doubts that Hebert
> called for the end of the Bill of Rights.
>
> For the purpose of inviting Vinson to discuss the proposed change in
> the law, Hebert suggested, ''Let's forget the First Amendment.''
> . . . But it is clear that he did not advocate abandoning the First
> Amendment.

Hebert must be blamed for speaking so loosely, but his critics accepted reports of his words without checking for accuracy.

The people who know me well recognized the unfairness of the First Amendment publicity. Frank Slatinshek, the chief counsel of the Armed Services Committee, commented to a reporter, "Hébert is probably the most principled man I know in Congress as far as adherence to certain ideas and forthrightness. Really. He kids and all this, but when it comes down to the hard shell of the thing, you can predict what he's going to do and he makes no bones about it. And if there's anybody in Congress who believes in free speech, it's Eddie."

Additionally, the generally accepted idea that I am in awe of the armed services was completely discounted by Slatinshek.

Hebert doesn't have any particular preference or great love for generals, or any particular love for civilians [in the Department of Defense] either, that is, in those capacities. He calls them as he sees them.

He's very direct. He wants to know what the problem is and he doesn't play one group against the other. It's a refreshing thing to work for him because I haven't had to compensate for—well, to take care of a personal desire of his. In other words, he wants legislation just the way it should be ideally, without regard to personal likes or dislikes on his part. Even if he didn't exactly agree with something personally, he's never said so if it was right.

But Eddie likes to give the impression that he's a conniving, scheming politician. The truth is though—and of course, he's operating, but the base or the objective is completely honest and worthwhile—if he could do it the direct way, by going through the door, he'd rather take the circuitous route because it's more fun. He loves it. It sort of appeals to his, well, mischievous, youthful zest for the game. He gets a big charge out of it. He really does, manipulating and talking. It's much more fun than doing it directly.

On the other hand, his maturity is evidenced by the fact that he doesn't get upset by what appears to be little personal affronts, or indignities. He doesn't need it to bolster his ego. He's mature. And, as a matter of fact, he likes to poke fun at himself, and people love him for it.

Slatinshek and others recognized that I am no syncophant of the military simply because I advocate a strong national defense. On another occasion Slatinshek commented to a newsman:

> I know there are a lot of people on this committee who distrust the civilians in the military and who tend to think the military is right almost all the time. Eddie isn't so committed to the military. He doesn't automatically assume they're right.
>
> I think he's one of those people who is basically suspicious of concentrations of power in any form. In the 40s and early 50s the military had a lot more control. Now the power's somewhere else [in the Defense Department] and Eddie recognizes this. But as long as you question this power you can keep it from getting too concentrated.
>
> Eddie's one of the people who helped shift it this way. He's one of the people who approved the merger of the services and went along approving the strengthening of the defense hierarchy, and he was always one who felt that civilians rather than the military should make the ultimate decisions. But now he feuds with the civilians because that's where the power is. Still, that doesn't mean that he automatically feels that the military is right. He's not a general worshipper at all. I don't know whether he would agree with this idea at all; I don't know if he's even thought of it, but I think the genesis of his tendency to beware of the concentrations of power is his newsman's training. I know it keeps him from being too wild or going off half cocked. He doesn't go off half cocked.

During my time on the Armed Services Committee, I have been able to get along well with most of my colleagues, regardless of their political philosophy. One member whom I've admired, despite often conflicting views, is Otis Pike. Once I went up to his district in Long Island and talked for him. Otis represents the eastern end of Long Island and the registration is two-thirds Republican, the Great Gatsby district of F. Scott Fitzgerald's novel. Otis is a Democrat, but he gets elected, he gets sixty percent of the vote.

And he's a character, has a wonderful sense of humor, very honest. Even when people disagree with him he says something with a little touch of humor in it and they accept it. They know he's being honest.

When I made the appearance for Pike, Art Bergmann, a writer for *Newsday*, the respected Long Island newspaper, called it "A Rare Moment."

Every so often, American politics produces a flashing, magical moment, that, for a brief instant, stops the clock of the trade, and then it is gone in the blink of an eye.

These moments, like falling stars, are rare. One occurred at San Francisco's Cow Palace in the summer of 1964 when Nelson A. Rockefeller defied the jeers of a pitiless mob at the Republican National Convention, and insisted on his right to talk.

Another occurred last Saturday night at a Patchogue restaurant when a white-haired, soft-spoken congressman from Louisiana lumbered to his feet and conversed with the three hundred and thirty persons who turned out to help pay for the campaign to reelect Representative Otis Pike (D-Riverhead).

The speaker was Representative Felix Edward Hébert (D-New Orleans), whose name is pronounced A-bear. His message was simple and clear. "Our government," he said, "is a government in which independent thinkers are in the minority. The essence and purity of the government in which we believe, that historic heritage that places the good of the people ahead of party labels and political expediency, is fast falling," Hébert said.

"To me, Republican and Democrats don't mean a damn. It's the people who count. We need people in public life who think for themselves. All we have today is a strong emphasis on the two parties. But don't let anybody kid you; all that means is we have the 'Ins' and the 'Outs' with the 'Ins' trying to stay in and the 'Outs' trying to get in," Hébert said.

"The only reason I'm a Democrat is that's the way to get elected in Louisiana," Hébert said, "but I don't think either party has any principles."

Hébert was there pinning his audience in their seats at Pike's request. He came to praise Pike, but in the praising, he offered a searing insight into a major failing of many of the representatives who are biennially elected by their constituents.

"We live in a world of do something for me and I will do something for you. We are facing today the greatest challenge in our history. I do not believe our democracy owes anybody anything except the opportunity to make of himself what he will," Hébert said.

It may be that men like Hébert and Pike are not above exploiting their individuality, their 'independence' of party label during election campaigns, or using pressure to their advantage, but while Hébert spoke words unmarred by cynicism to a hushed gathering of Republicans and

Democrats, the candles that lit the room seemed to grow a little brighter. And Hébert's gentle voice appeared to ring with truth.

My relationship with Democrats and Republicans had always depended upon my feelings regarding specific issues. While my registration card reads Democrat my mind thinks Independent.

One day Jerry Ford (when he was the Republican leader in the House) was having a breakfast "for the leadership," and I was invited. I said, "Well, if Jerry Ford wants it, it's okay with me." Jerry is a friend of mine, a real good friend of mine, but I couldn't understand why I was invited to the "leadership" breakfast. What leadership?

The letter I got said, "the Ranking Members." I wondered what the hell is this "Ranking Member?" So I went back to the office and got the letter. It was a form letter: "Dear Colleague." Well, I recognized immediately what it was. This was a breakfast the Republicans always have. They are all "Ranking Members." None of 'em are chairmen; they are all "Ranking Members."

I said, "Call up and see if this is a Republican or a Democratic breakfast." Of course it was Republican, so I didn't go.

In the meantime, however, Jerry was making mistakes. He was saying the Republicans didn't want the South, that he's going to drive us into the "hands of the Administration" and beat us, and all that kind of stuff.

So there was a vote on the Housing Bill, the rental subsidy, and the Cities of Demonstration. These were Republican motions. I voted with the Republicans both times. Housing was thrown out; the Cities of Demonstration was kept in.

I went over to the Republican table. Les Arends, who was the Republican whip, and Jerry were over there. I said, "All right, you two ungrateful guys, I voted for you—twice. No wonder you invited me to the breakfast, Jerry," and I told him what happened. He laughed and said, "Well, why didn't you come anyway."

But the point, which overrides the fun of it at that time, is, I don't care whether Jerry Ford or the Republicans wanted me, or didn't want me. They can't drive me out of any place; because if I think they're right, I'm going to vote with them. They can say, "we don't want your vote,'' but it is my vote! That's what I've been preaching all the time. There's too much of this other stuff—the idea that because a Republican offers a bill it's bad; because a Democrat offers it, it's good; or because a Democrat offers it, it's bad, and a Republican offers it, it's good.

That doesn't influence me a damn bit! I'm going to vote the way I want to vote. I enjoy the luxury of independence.

I've always maintained something of a little-boy sense of wonderment at the governmental system of the United States. It is something to know that in the great span of the United States there is not the smallest hut in which a person lives, that that person does not have a voice in Washington if he wants to take advantage of it. He is part of a congressional district. There's not a single inch of ground that is not represented in Washington. And the only way a person becomes a representative is through a direct vote.

In 1966 a reporter for the New Orleans *States-Item* called my district office, explaining the paper was conducting a survey on how congressmen felt about a four-year term for U. S. representatives, noting that he was sure I was in favor of such a move. When I came into the office, my executive secretary, Virginea Burguières, relayed the message, including the reporter's assumption that I would favor a four-year term.

"Is that so," I said as I hung my coat over a chair, rolled up my sleeves, loosened my tie, and perched myself in front of an old Remington typewriter which I've kept since newspaper days. In my two-fingered style of typing, I banged out this reply:

The last thin thread between the people and a voice in the government is the two-year term. Take away the two-year term and the people would have no way to express themselves as to the conduct of the government for four years. Under the present system the people have the opportunity at the end of two years to indicate whether they are satisfied with the manner in which the incumbent administration is reflecting the wishes and desires of the people. A four-year term would mean that a successful candidate for the presidency could carry into office many members of congress who would only be rubber stamps, as is vividly demonstrated by the present Congress.

Selfishly, I would like to be elected to Congress for life and never face any opposition, but this would not be in the interest of representative government. Every two years each member of the House of Representatives must come before his constituency to make a report and either get a renewed vote of confidence or be dismissed because he has failed to reflect the views of the people he is supposed to represent. This is as it should be.

When the Rayburn Office Building was under construction. I scouted the premises and discovered a location where the design would provide space for an office of extraordinary size and configuration. I staked my claim, and when congressmen began moving in, I decorated my office with expensive furnishings paid for out of my own pocket or presented to me as Christmas gifts from family and friends. It is not only the largest but the most striking office on the Hill. Passersby stop to browse in the large entrance foyer, complete with a fountain, and gaze at photographs of New Orleans scenes which decorate the walls. My staff occupies four rooms. There are also a small kitchen and two restrooms. Additionally, I have a small suite. The center of attention there is a huge, highly polished mahogany desk on which sits memorabilia of my career. Soft indirect lighting adds an elegant subdued atmosphere.

One of my favorite pastimes, before I went on a diet, was to entertain luncheon guests at my office. The staff served up typical New Orleans dishes—crab gumbo, shrimp remoulade, oyster jambalaya—after the guests had been plied with a Ramos gin fizz, unless they had insisted upon something more prosaic. During my States' Rights days, a concealed recording gave out with a few bars of "Dixie" at 12 sharp. Betty Harter would enter, fire a little brass cannon and announce: "Fort Sumter has been fired upon, sir," which was the Dixiecrat code meaning lunch was about to be served.

I considered inviting friends and colleagues to dine at my office not only good public relations for New Orleans, but good business. People relax when they walk into my office, just as they would at home.

Helping them relax is Mary Swann, who joined my staff as a clerical worker when she was eighteen years old. Shy by nature, she had to be encouraged to apply for the position by her mother. I recognized her potential, hired her on the spot and through dent of hard work, attention to duty and loyalty, added to her pleasant personality, Mary Swann became my administrative assistant.

I am often the butt-end of some good-natured teasing about my role in Congress and how I got where I am. Congressman Joe Waggonner of Louisiana, for example, jokes about how I reached the pinnacle of my power through the connivance of God. "The Lord works in many ways," Waggonner told me one day in a very serious tone of voice. "That Man upstairs wanted you. He wanted one of His boys to be chairman instead of that Baptist, Mendel Rivers. So what does He do? [Representative Philip J.] Philbin's in the way. He's blocking. So He goes over there to Boston, gets that Jesuit [the Reverend Robert F.] Drinan—another one of the boys—to beat Philbin. So that clears the way for you. Then He grabs Rivers and takes him off and a Jesuit-trained boy gets the job," and Waggonner walked off laughing.

Upon assuming the chairmanship, I learned firsthand how powerful the post could be. An admiral came into my office and said that there was a little "dilution" going to take place in the Eighth Naval District.

I looked at him and said, "Admiral, I don't know whether you heard or not, but Mendel Rivers is dead. Have you heard? He's dead."

He got the message.

"The image I'd like to have is that I'm fair," I told a reporter after becoming chairman, "that I'm not swayed by partisanship, and that I believe in giving every man his day in court. That I'm trustworthy and that when I say something I mean it. I think that's the image I want most."

Upon assuming the chairmanship, I instituted a rule whereby each member, regardless of seniority or party, was allowed five minutes to question witnesses and then wait his turn again. I clocked them with a cooking timer similar to the one Gladys uses in the kitchen. In fact that's where I got the idea. This approach was in sharp contrast to the committee under Rivers who did most of the questioning, and his friends did the rest. When so inclined, Rivers would arbitrarily shut off debate. Carl Vinson often didn't even know the names of the junior members of the committee.

Congresswoman Bella Abzug, of whom I am fond despite our often diametrically opposed political views, had tried unsuccessfully to get on the committee after her election to Congress. She later testified at length before the committee urging the repeal of the draft law. "When I finished," she wrote in her book, *Bella*, "Ed Hébert, who's really a very pleasant man, came over to me and said, 'Bella, you can appreciate how lucky you are not to have gotten on the committee. Had you been a member you would have been limited to only five minutes. This way you got forty-five.'"

The five-minute rule was to the disadvantage of the senior members and to the advantage of the junior members. I never stopped debate on the floor. I gave the junior members rights and I was criticized by Common Cause for not giving it to them. All these things I did which Mendel never did. As a matter of fact I thought I was the best chairman in the house. I took pride in the way I ran the committee. Took plenty pride in it. I used all the tricks I could to win my point. I don't deny that.

A good example is keeping the public health hospitals open in this country. President Nixon had vetoed keeping them open. The Senate put it into a rider on the procurement defense bill. It was non-vetoable. I held the provision in conference. That's one example of using the parliamentary situation.

Another example is a method by which I got $1 billion restored to a $2 billion weapons bill after the House had reduced it. I went into conference with Mississippi's John Stennis, the chairman of the Senate Armed Services Committee, and several of his colleagues on the committee. The bill came back to the House with the $1 billion restored and was passed. That was what I call a "conference triumph."

But I didn't always get the Senate's acquiescence or approval. On one occasion it rejected my demand that the Defense Department be prohibited from sending officers to study at universities which had canceled their ROTC programs. Seeing the door was closed to my legislative action, I took the direct route. I called the Pentagon and instructed its top echelon members to blacklist Harvard University, with or without congressional sanction. After listening to the chairman's logic, they thought it was a good idea. I was not reticent about my role in the blacklisting; indeed, I bragged about it: "I not only had a hand in it, I was the leader."

Several years later when the *New York Times* criticized me for the action, I responded:

> I was amused by your February 19 [1974] editorial, "Mr. Hébert Sees Crimson."
> At first blush, I thought you were talking about the Alabama Crimson Tide and the Sugar Bowl game. Then I realized you were talking about the elite—in its own estimation—Harvard. Knowing of your desire to be objective, I was amused at the statement, ". . . American universities are independent institutions and as such are entitled to determine their own policies and, on occasion, make their own mistakes." I never said they didn't have this right, and I will defend their right to make mistakes. But I want the same rights to make decisions and do what I feel is proper. It's all so simple.

As chairman, I was proudest of upholding the defense of the country despite all the efforts to beat down the national defense. They didn't beat it down during my tenure. I fought them off. I was in constant contact with the President [Nixon] and [Secretary of Defense] Mel Laird. I supported the bombing, and urged untying our hands. Now, again, it reacts against me. These liberals come in and they're pacifists. They hold that against me. Everything they used against me to throw me out of the chairmanship is easy to understand. I got this group mad and that group mad. You put them all together and everybody's mad. I can understand that, but I'd rather that come from within Congress than from some anti-defense, discredited group like Common Cause, the lobbying organization which worked against my chairmanship.

I had recognized long before the loss of Cambodia and South Vietnam to the communists what lay in store for Southeast Asia if the United States pursued its policy of folly there. In 1973 I told Dan Rapoport, a freelance writer who covered Congress, "And when it goes down the drain and the domino theory takes place, then look around and see whose face is going to be red.'' I was prophetic about the drain, but, unfortunately, those who fought hardest against my position didn't appear to be embarrassed.

When I became chairman, President Nixon knew he would need my strong support, and he readily got it. In appreciation, the President attended the unveiling of my portrait in the House Armed Services Committee Room. The President said during the course of the ceremony:

> When the great issue of national defense is concerned, you have voted for strong national defense so that we could build what we all want in the world, build a lasting peace. I think one of my favorite quotes from Eddie Hébert's many gems, and he has many—I'd love to sit in this committee and hear what he says sometimes—one of them that I recall went something like this: He said, ''I'm a hawk, but no dove could want peace more than I do.''

I appreciated President Nixon's attention and I worked hard for the President's position on defense and Vietnam. I was instrumental in blocking the Mansfield Amendment, passed by the Senate, which would have limited further the United States' participation in Indochina, and as Rapoport points out in his book, *Inside the House*, I protected Nixon's ''right flank by seeing to it that no criticism was heard from the conservative councils of the Armed Services Committee'' when the President initiated his moves toward détente with Russia and diplomatic contacts with China.

I provided the support because I believed in Nixon's goals. There was nothing complex about it. Ideologically, Nixon and I agreed.

I felt that Nixon had changed since the days of the Hiss-Chambers investigations. I had recognized Nixon's ability. My objection then had been to Nixon's means, not his ends. The years and the Presidency had matured Nixon and added depth and wisdom, I believed, and I felt a personal warmth toward the beleaguered man.

Nixon recognized that through my efforts and those of others, he was able to pursue the policy he believed would bring ''peace with honor'' to Vietnam. He acknowledged my help with small notes and letters, which trace the tragic history of this country's involvement in

Indochina. That tragedy can be specifically traced to the divisiveness in the country which prevented a unified course of action, one way or the other. We simply did not "win or get out," early enough, either way.

November 12, 1969.

Dear Eddie: The resolution which you and so many of your colleagues introduced in the House following my November 3 message to the nation should serve as ample evidence to the leaders of North Vietnam that the time has come to move forward at the conference table to end this tragic war. Your expression of confidence that our course will lead to peace is a source of deep encouragement.

May 12, 1970.

Dear Eddie: It is encouraging to know that you approve the decision I have made to ensure the protection of our men in Viet Nam and the continued success of our withdrawal and Vietnamization programs.

October 21, 1971.

Your vote on Tuesday of this week was a difficult one, I am sure. When the record is finally written in the Viet Nam War, however, I believe that your confidence in our policies will prove to have been well placed.

On June 24, 1971, after I had helped defeat the Nedzi-Whalen proposal for a deadline on the United States participation in Vietnam, Nixon wrote a lengthy letter which follows in part:

While we continue to reduce American forces in Indochina, various proposals may be advanced in Congress similar to Nedzi-Whalen. Their adoption would seriously jeopardize the progress we are making in ending American involvement in Viet Nam and in achieving a just peace.

I look forward to working with you in the months ahead so that together we might increase the chances not only of ending this war but also of ensuring that other Americans will not have to fight other wars in the future.

May 11, 1972.

It was most encouraging to learn of your forceful expression of support for the peace proposals I presented to the nation this past Monday evening. Acceptance of these proposals, I believe, will bring an end to the killing, a return of our prisoners of war, a withdrawal of all forces with honor, and continued progress toward peace for all countries that have suffered for so long in this conflict.

I want you to know that you have my deepest gratitude and warmest appreciation for your support of these objectives.

January 24, 1973.

Now that we have finally achieved peace with honor in Vietnam, I particularly want you to know how much I have appreciated the support you have given during these difficult years to the policies that made such achievements possible. Without those in the Congress who stood steadfast as you did, we could not have won the settlement that I announced last night.

I know how great pressures have been. I know the sort of attack to which you have been subjected, as a result of following your conscience. But I also am confident history will prove you have been right, and that in the years to come you can look back with pride on a stern test nobly met.

Although in the past I had been critical of Nixon's modus operandi, our joint efforts during the Vietnam War and the attacks leveled against our position, created a bond between us. The President also evidenced a resolve to follow what he believed to be the correct course of action despite almost continuous attacks. I interpreted Nixon's action as a profile in courage; to others it was obstinance. But whatever it was, it cast us in an allied role, and when Watergate broke, I refused to believe that a man of Nixon's stature could under any circumstances be remotely connected with such a petty, stupid and useless escapade.

Even before Watergate, I had developed a distrust for H. R. Haldeman and John Ehrlichman. I felt they were isolating the President from Congress and controlling too many of his activities. The tail didn't wag the dog in my office, and I didn't think it should in the Oval Office. On one occasion Ehrlichman called me to say that the President wanted a particular piece of legislation. I replied, "Which President, you or Haldeman?" In another exchange, I told the President's domestic advisor, "I don't talk to the apostles, I talk only to God."

But I found it so difficult to get through the screen which Haldeman and Ehrlichman had thrown around Nixon, so much so that I had to pass the President a note in a reception line about the military medical academy. And when Watergate progressed to the point where Haldeman and Ehrlichman were removed from office, I allowed that it was the best thing that had happened to the country in a long time.

I continued to believe, or hope, that Nixon was innocent of covering up the break-in at Democratic Headquarters in the Watergate Building. I would not comment upon the evidence as it unfolded. In February of 1974 I wrote in response to a constituent's inquiry, "Personally, I have not seen any evidence thus far which warrants impeachment. However, I want to study whatever facts the House Judiciary Committee turns up before making my decision. It is imperative, I believe, for the good of the country that the Judiciary Committee get on with its business and conclude it as soon as possible."

My position was that as a prospective member of a jury (the House of Representatives) which might be called upon to consider impeachment charges against Nixon, I would not make up my mind on guilt or innocence until the evidence was presented to the House. This position rankled more than a few people, some of whom wrote me unflattering letters about it. To one I replied:

> I am amazed that you are disturbed over my position on impeachment. I am a member of the jury, since the House of Representatives will vote on the issue, that has to hear the evidence. What kind of man do you think I would be to prejudge a case before having the evidence? When I have the evidence, however, I will make a decision, but until I have the evidence, I have nothing to say whatsoever. If this attitude is wrong then I am afraid you and I could never agree on anything. . . ."

I maintained that position right up until the end, when I said privately that Nixon had to be "crazy" to have become involved. Publicly, I said, "Boiled down to a few sentences, a bunch of stupid characters broke into the Democratic Headquarters and got caught.

Then more stupid people tried to cover up and got caught. That's about the story.''

Nixon's resignation was a traumatic experience for me, as it was for the rest of the nation. I was one of a select group of Nixon's congressional friends who were invited to meet with the chief executive during the hour before he would announce to the nation that he was resigning the office of the President of the United States. A few minutes before 8:00 p.m. those who had been invited to meet with Nixon during those last emotional minutes drove through the southwest gate of the White House, past a phalanx of television cameras and newsmen and entered the home of the First Family. We gathered in the Cabinet Room, next to the Oval Office, where momentous and historic decisions had been reached. But we had no decisions to make; we were simply offering our presence to a friend who had become a pariah, a modern-day protagonist in a Greek tragedy.

Anybody who was present will never forget it. I think I've experienced a cross section of life—maybe as much as anybody—murders, suicides, gone to the gallows with more men than I can remember. Nothing could compare with that tragedy in the Cabinet Room.

The people there were those whom Nixon considered his closest friends in Congress. There were three Louisianians present: Joe Waggonner, Otto Passman and myself. Mississippi had Senator John Stennis and Sonny Montgomery. Texas had Clark Fisher, Omar Burleson, Tiger Teague and George Mahon. Senators Carl Curtis and Roman Hruska from Nebraska were there. Harry Byrd of Virginia and George Aiken of Vermont, Bob Sikes of Florida, Bill Bray of Indiana. Those are the ones I remember. Alexander Haig and several people I did not recognize, who were not members of Congress, were there, and his legislative liaison staff was there too. We were all seated around the table. I was directly opposite Nixon's chair.

He came in at exactly eight o'clock. I felt almost like I was covering another hanging. Then everybody stood up and applauded, loudly and very long. He looked around and smiled at everybody. You could see that he was terribly haggard and drawn, obviously tired. When he sat down he said, ''This is the last time I'll sit in this chair as President of the United States.''

He then began to explain why he called us there. He said he wanted to thank us. If I can remember his words, he said, "You, who are in this room, made it possible for me to accomplish those things which I have done. Without you I couldn't have done anything. That is why I wanted you here at this moment." Then he began to talk about his days at Whittier. He laughed, talking about playing on the football team as a freshman. He said they only had eleven men and that's how he made the team. He talked about running a mile race, and having won in the last ten yards. He said, "You know I'm not a quitter, and I don't want to quit."

He talked about his family, Pat, Julie and Tricia. He said none of them wanted him to quit. They wanted him to stay and fight on, but, he said, there comes a time when a person has to bow out in the best interest of the nation. He told us—and he repeated it on television—that in the next six months he could not be a full-time President, because of the impeachment proceedings, which would not have been in the country's best interest. He said in Jerry Ford we were getting a good, vigorous, strong man.

By now, he was beginning to choke. He was trying to make it look like nothing was wrong with him. He would stop for maybe thirty seconds, and his jaws would clench and he would puff them out, and he covered up a sob. It was the most terrible thing to see this once strong man sitting in a slump, and then outwardly crying. When he did that, everybody was overcome, without exception. I don't think there was anybody who didn't cry, including me. When I say cried, I mean *cried*! Everybody just bawled. We all had handkerchiefs out.

He looked around the table, still choked, and said, "There's only one last thing I want to say to you all: I hope you don't think I let you down." And he just got up and walked out.

We remained behind. They had arranged for us to watch his television speech in the little theater room of the White House. During the half hour before he went on, he absolutely had recomposed himself—completely.

I was in a state of shock two hours later. There were drinks being served in the theater. The first thing I did was tell that waiter to fill a glass with ice and pour whiskey to the top.

After Nixon's television speech, I went home to Alexandria where several close friends from New Orleans were waiting to commiserate with me. Over several drinks, I recounted the evening for them, and then retired, the balm of drink and talk providing the catharsis which allowed me to sleep. About 1:30 a.m., I was awakened by the ringing of the telephone. It was Nixon, calling to thank me for having been present at the Cabinet Room farewell.

In the morning, I called my press secretary, Lou Gehrig Burnett, into the office and dictated a press release on the resignation, which said in part:

> There is no doubt the President has erred, but he has done so in a sea of complexities which one finds most difficult to unravel. There are many things which I personally could not understand and many things which I would have done differently.
>
> In this tragic moment, I hope that those who cry the loudest in damnation will remember that Richard Nixon brought our boys home from Vietnam and our POWs home from Hanoi, that he opened the doors of Red China, and he shook the hand of Russia in his quest for friendship.
>
> When the dust settles and emotion wanes and prejudices are diluted, I am sure the good will be balanced with the bad.
>
> I have consistently refused to comment on how I would vote if the matter had gone to the floor of the House, believing strongly in the judicial process which clearly has demonstrated the ability of our system of government to work. This now becomes a moot question.
>
> The resignation of the President is in the best national interest.

CHAPTER XXIV

UNBOUND

UNDONE BY HUBRIS, Nixon was gone from the scene. His most
vigorous opponents felt useless without a dragon to slay. While their
bloodlust was still up, they searched frantically for someone else to
drag from power. They had little difficulty selecting their target. It
was a natural, and they were already prepared for the hunt.

For several years the antagonists had been gathering their forces,
trying to gain the necessary strength to topple the strong men of
Congress who didn't pass their ideological litmus test. The chairmen
of the powerful committees in the House of Representatives were
their targets, and I was the bull's-eye. Most of these chairmen were
the last of the individualists, men who had grown to maturity pulling
on their own bootstraps and they would not be dominated by the
powerbrokers of the Eastern Establishment whose money had bought
and sold many a public officeholder, or at least frightened them into
line. As microcosms of their constituency, these rebels kept being
elected and rose to seats of power through seniority. They were the
people's choice, and a representative form of government kept them
in Washington.

To combat their power, the Eastern Establishment looked into its
suburbs and plucked out a man who could serve its needs. In John
Gardner they found the type of man who, because he had not been
spontaneously elevated into a position of unrestricted rule, had an
obsession to remove those who had risen by longevity to positions of
power. He was well prepared, having run the Carnegie Foundation
for ten years until President Johnson tapped him in 1965 to become

437

secretary of the Department of Health, Education, and Welfare, a powerful position, but one still subservient to Congress. He also served on the board of directors of several large corporations which found it advantageous to have a man of his caliber in their employ.

Gardner, however, gained his greatest fame as the founder and leader of Common Cause, the citizens' lobby which he billed as a non-partisan organization to correct the ills of society by making government "accountable." The ostensible purpose was not to grind any ideological axes, but to deal with the processes of government, on a sort of altruistic basis which shunned political bias. The late Stewart Alsop, an insightful and thoughtful pundit, caught on to Gardner early. "I'm not arguing whether the dove Democrats and Common Cause are right or wrong," he wrote. "My point is that a spade really does occasionally need to be called a spade. And John Gardner, who is undoubtedly an admirable fellow, is no more the head of a non-partisan citizens' lobby than I am. He is the head of a lobby for liberal Democrats—which, of course, he has every right to be."

In addition to making government "accountable," which after some study one concludes means accountable to Gardner, Common Cause wants to redistribute the wealth by taking it from the producers and passing it out to the phlegmatic; shift the decision making power from individuals to organized society; dismantle the defense establishment; and bring about other "reforms." To do this Gardner has assembled a cadre of true believers who push his programs and recruit a membership of dilettante joiners, those people who follow the fashion trends of liberal politics and have $15 for annual dues. They buy the non-partisan label and prepare to do good works in their respective states. However, if their goals offend Gardner, they are immediately hobbled and threatened with expulsion. "We just want people who will follow the party line," one Common Cause official explained to a reporter.

Kenneth Crawford, writing in the *Washington Post*, said,

> Judged by the positions it has taken, it is hard to detect any great differences right now between Common Cause and the Americans for Democratic Action, long the Democratic Party's ally on the liberal

flank. There the similarity ends, however. ADA is democratically run. Its membership decides its positions on the issues after lengthy and often hot debate, whereas Gardner seems to speak for Common Cause without let or hindrance. He has a board of advisors but is now, to all intents and purposes, Common Cause itself.

First term congressman (you can't call them freshmen anymore) Lawrence P. McDonald, a conservative from Georgia, who observed the machinations of the power brokers from the inside, said the purpose of Common Cause is "gross interference with the operations of the Congress of the United States. If Common Cause doesn't like the way congressmen are elected, or the way the committee system works, it simply spends money until it has bought off or terrorized enough members of Congress to change things."

Washington Post columnist David Broder pointed out that Common Cause was joined in its efforts by big labor lobbyists and the National Committee for an Effective Congress, an elite organization of liberal powerbrokers, to pull the strings which make the Democratic Study Group operate. In doing so, he said they took over most of the newly elected Democrats who took the oath of office in January of 1975, and then set out to remove the conservative chairmen from their committee posts.

The Democratic Study Group originated in 1957 under the direction of its founder, Eugene McCarthy, then a U.S. representative. Known variously as "McCarthy's Mavericks," the "Liberal Manifesto," and "The Young Turks" during its early days, it only gained strength and power following the death of the powerful Speaker of the House, Sam Rayburn. Although columnists Broder and James Reston of the *New York Times* speculated that I lost my chairmanship because I was unaware of the move to "democratize" the House, David Chandler, New Orleans author and political maverick, (he has consistently opposed me, once inducing a friend to challenge me for office) wrote I indicated in an interview in early 1974 that I was very much aware of the moves underway to strip Congress of the seniority system. "It was four years ago," I told Chandler, "when they set up the caucus system. They dictate to the committees, to the chairmen, and they will ruin Congress."

The five senior members of the House became targets of the attack, and only three of them were "strong," Mills, Mahon and myself. Wilbur Mills of Arkansas, who was chairman of the consequential Ways and Means Committee, removed himself, in effect, when under the influence of admitted alcoholism, he continued to pursue Annabel Battistella (a stripper known as Fanne Fox) from the Tidal Basin in Washington to the stage of a Boston burlesque house. George Mahon of Texas, the chairman of the Appropriations Committee, who was second in seniority in the House, kept his job, but only by allowing himself to be cut into a political eunuch to keep office. Mahon gave up the power to name his own subcommittee chairmen. I kept my integrity, but lost my chairmanship. So did W. R. Poage of Texas, who was third in seniority and chairman of the Agriculture Committee. So, too, did Wright Patman of Texas, who led the House in tenure and was chairman of the Banking and Currency Committee.

Patman was the only true liberal among the five men, more of a populist really, who rallied against big bankers and high interest rates, two causes which were not inclined to make him popular with the financiers of Common Cause. He also had the audacity to investigate the financing and funding of tax-exempt foundations, those angels who provide the wherewithall for myriad liberal projects, such as Common Cause. During this investigation, Patman's committee came across the fact that Peter Edleman, a top staff member of Common Cause, had used a $19,091 grant from the Ford Foundation to take his bride on an around-the-world honeymoon. Edleman had been a member of the late Senator Robert F. Kennedy's staff, and the purpose of the Ford grant was to "ease the transition from public to private life."

When the 94th Congress went into session in January of 1975, Common Cause had a full-time staff of paid lobbyists patrolling the halls of Congress daily, harassing, encouraging, managing, and seeing to it that those representatives in their fold toed the line. Sessions and seminars were held to make it plain to the malleable "representatives" exactly what was expected from them, what was the party line. They were told the seniority system was "the most shocking barrier to accountability in national government.'' To right this wrong, committee chairmen must be required ''to stand individually before their fellow party members for re-election.'' In other words, for government to operate on standards acceptable to Common Cause, caucus must be king. ''King Caucus,'' that discredited tool of party demagoguery designed to make congressmen vote the party line or pay dearly, was Common Cause's panacea which would cure the ills of government. A congressman would not be able to vote his conscience or the will of his constituents if either conflicted with the wishes of the party. Individualism was taboo.

I recognized early what Common Cause and its allies were about: ''The ruin of the seniority system and the destruction of the committee system. Those institutions were set up to guard against 'tyranny by the majority.' Now everything that happens in committee and in the House is dictated by a simple majority of the caucus. They want me to kow-tow to the Democratic Party label, and I'll never do it.''

As the 94th Congress approached, the attack on the seniority system was given much attention by the media. Stories of the projected uprising to unseat the powerful senior chairmen proliferated. In mid-December, I remarked, ''All they are saying is 'let's get rid of the Old Bastards.' They're upset because they can't run the show. They want to take the power from us and set up a power system of their own. They believed anybody over 30 years of age should be regarded with suspicion. Most of them weren't born when I first came to Congress. I was against seniority when I first arrived too, but I got to like it better with every passing year. What in the hell do they know?''

Because of my outspoken, no-punches-pulled, stand on Vietnam and my conservative, individualistic philosophy, I was the biggest of the ''Old Bastards'' whom the liberal wing of the party had set in its sights. It didn't matter that I had reformed the committee after taking over from Mendel Rivers. It was ideology, not autocracy, that made me a target, *Common Cause's protestations to the contrary*.

As the days moved toward the January 15 vote by the Democratic Steering Committee, whose twenty-four members would nominate chairmen on whom the caucus would vote, the ''Freshman Bloc'' conducted inquisition sessions with the chairmen being paraded before them, hoping to receive a thumbs up gesture, a signal they could continue to exist.

Some freshmen, who considered me arrogant and a patsy for the Pentagon, said I began my pitch to them by addressing them as "boys and girls." The freshmen had been transformed from individuals into a mob of crusading knights out to slay evil dragons. They were not noted for their sense of humor, particularly when it was insinuated there might possibly be something more important in the universe than a freshman congressman. At any rate, I did not refer to them as "boys and girls." "It's a damned lie," I said. I never said anything like that. And I repeat, "I did not say any such thing."

What I did do was defend the bombing of North Vietnam, citing the fact that Americans were no longer involved in the conflict and that American prisoners of war had been released. When questioned about party loyalty, I affirmed the fact that I had written a letter praising Maryland's Republican congresswoman, Marjorie Holt. It had been read at one of Mrs. Holt's reelection campaign rallies. I said I judged people individually and that Mrs. Holt was an intelligent woman who had contributed much during her service on the Armed Services Committee. "There are no Democrats or Republicans on my committee, just Americans," I explained. But my reasoning had little positive effect on the Democratic first termers. As one of their more reasonable members noted, "Hébert could have promised to tear down the Pentagon, brick by brick, and it wouldn't have made any difference."

On January 13, Common Cause, its propaganda mill working overtime, issued a "Report on House Committee Chairmen" to each member of the House of Representatives. It listed three standards by which it said the chairmen were judged: compliance with rules, personal and procedural fairness, and use of power. Three chairmen, the report said, "Madden, Patman, and Straggers—show significant shortcomings. Three chairmen—Mahon, Poage, and Hays—show a pattern of more serious abuses. And one chairman, F. Edward Hébert, flagrantly violates all three standards."

Quick to respond, I said, "The statements made about my conduct as chairman of the Armed Services Committee in the diatribe issued by Common Cause are so distorted and unfair as to make the conclusion inescapable that the distortions are deliberate." I immediately fashioned a rebuttal which was sent to all representatives the next day.

Charge: Hébert assigns members to subcommittees as he pleases without ascertaining their preferences.

Fact: At the start of the 93rd Congress most members retained the subcommittee assignments they had from the previous Congress. Assignments for new members were made as necessary to complete the various subcommittees. Preferences were considered and seniority taken into account. No member of the committee complained in writing about his subcommittee assignment or submitted a request for change. For this Congress, a memorandum was provided to all prospective members of the committee calling a caucus of the Democratic members on Friday, January 17. In that memorandum I asked members of the committee to notify me in writing regarding their preference as to subcommittee assignments. [The memorandum is dated January 9, prior to issuance of the Common Cause statement.]

Charge: Hébert refuses to refer to subcommittees certain bills opposed by the Pentagon.

Fact: In order to effectively conduct committee business, the committee rules provide that bills shall be referred to subcommittee by the chairman. However, in every instance in which a subcommittee chairman has requested assignment of a bill or matter within his subcommittee's jurisdiction, it has been assigned to him. The committee rules were adopted by the committee unanimously. Anyone who cares to study the committee calendar will find that I have refused to assign most of the legislation requested by the Pentagon. Of 74 legislative proposals submitted by the Pentagon, only 35 were introduced, 24 were acted on by the committee, and 17 were enacted into law (another four initiating in the Senate were enacted.)

Charge: Two Armed Service subcommittees do not have the required party ratio of the full committee.

Fact: The ratio on the full committee in the 93rd Congress was 46 percent Democrats and 44 percent Republicans, a determination made up by the House. Two legislative subcommittees had 55 percent Democrats and 45 percent Republicans. With the exception of these two subcommittees, which were a miniscule one percentage point off the desired ratio, all subcommittees had a higher ratio of Democrats to Republicans than the full committee.

Charge: Hébert has packed key subcommittee slots with senior members who agree with him philosophically.

Fact: Anyone who looks closely will find practically all subcommittees had senior members in key slots who very often did not agree with me philosophically.

Charge: Hébert unilaterally stripped members of their assignments to subcommittees. (One offending member had expressed dissenting views in a report of the subcommittee.)

Fact: I can find no instance where a member was removed from a subcommittee during a Congress against his wishes. When a new subcommittee on European commitments was appointed in 1974, a member who had been on the special NATO subcommittee in 1971 and 1972 was not reappointed to that subcommittee. The reason was that the member failed to make both European trips of the earlier subcommittee, during which the subcommittee held 17 hearings in 8 countries and, therefore, did not participate in a majority of the subcommittee's hearings. Therefore, the member was not appointed to the similar subcommittee a year later. I have never received written or oral objection from the member concerned.

Charge: Hébert fails to execute oversight of the Pentagon.

Fact: Oversight of the Pentagon is not the prerogative of the chairman. It is the responsibility of the entire committee. The committee takes its actions by majority vote. The committee's actions on the defense program reflect the views of the majority. Those actions are taken after extensive hearings and debate, and involved many, many changes in presidential proposals, both additions and reductions. If the actions taken by the majority of the committee do not agree with the position of Common Cause, that is hardly a reason for determining that I have not chaired the committee fairly or used my powers properly. Common Cause apparently assumes that the greater the reductions made, the better the job is done and that any additions are inherently wrong. The Congress, regardless of who is chairman of the Armed Services Committee, would be just as wrong in being the rubber stamp for Common Cause as it would be in being a rubber stamp for the Pentagon. . . .''

I concluded, ''Common Cause accused me of personal unfairness.

The Caucus rules state that any ten members of the committee can request a caucus in writing. No such request has ever been received from even one Democratic member of the Armed Services Committee. If I were personally unfair to members, surely some members would have requested a caucus to air the matter.

"I trust the caucus will make its decision on the record and not on the bias of any outside organization."

On January 15, the Democratic Steering Committee nominated me to retain my chairmanship by a vote of 14 to 10. I had had the pledges of 17 committee members, but three had lied. It's always a question of who is going to outscrew who. Still, I had cleared the first hurdle.

One hundred and forty-six votes represented a majority of the Democratic Caucus, which was to decide on the Steering Committee's nominations the next day. I had pledges of 207 votes based on the count of friends who were leaders of their respective state delegations. Knowing the nature of Washington politics, I was aware that not all 207 would vote for me; but with 146 representing a majority, 61 pledges could renege and I could still win. However, I was concerned about the secret ballot on which my fate rested. Common Cause maintained it was against secrecy in government but was highly pleased that the vote would be in secret. That way, the congressmen it controlled would not have to answer for their votes.

In an attempt to justify the secret ballot, some have tried to make it analogous to the secret ballot in which citizens elect their public officials. There is no analogy, for congressmen are sent to Washington to represent the interests of their constituents, and their open votes are one of the most important measuring sticks the constituents have. As feared the secret ballot proved to be my undoing. I was defeated 152-133.

But I was not through. I stalked from the caucus to the press gallery where I announced I was going to take my fight to the floor of the House in an unprecedented challenge to the majority party. Such a move would allow both Republicans and Democrats to decide on the chairmanship.

Meanwhile, David Treen, one of two Louisiana Republican congressmen and a friend of mine, called my ouster an outrage. He said it was "an act of political vindictiveness directed against a Southerner and a conservative." Treen said he planned to lead a drive to gain GOP support for a floor fight. Other powerful Democrats and Republicans also voiced support for me.

Unexpected support for my planned battle came from the Baton Rouge (La.) *Morning Advocate*, which said editorially,

> At the outset, let it be said that this newspaper is a member of Common Cause and long has backed a vast majority of its aims, including the abolition of the seniority system. The Democratic Caucus went behind closed doors to assail Hébert and Poage in a move that Common Cause called "the final healthy act of demolition that brings the seniority system crashing down."
>
> Was it so "healthy" an act?
>
> The desire of the majority of the members of the Democratic Caucus and of Common Cause, to oust Hébert, Poage, et al., may or may not be representative of the feelings of the majority of the entire body of representatives sent to Washington to speak for the people.
>
> If Hébert has not been good for the country as chairman of the Armed Services Committee, for such reasons as rewarding people who agree with his pro-military views, then let the full House say so. If Poage is to be ousted for following his constituency over the views of the Democratic Party, then let the House say so.
>
> If the majority views of the caucus and the House at large prove the same, then so be it.
>
> It does make sense, as said, to remove the seniority system and it is proper to broaden the base of decision on who are to be the leaders in Congress.
>
> But the manner in which these goals have just been approached does not.
>
> Hébert is correct in not accepting the decision of the caucus, secretly voted, as the final word in this matter.

I had my strategy planned. The Steering Committee would nominate Melvin Price, my long-time friend and second in seniority on the Armed Services Committee. When the Democratic Caucus met to vote, Price would say he didn't want the chairmanship and I would be nominated. If I then lost, the fight would be taken to the floor and all members of the House of Representatives would vote on the matter.

As I prepared to leave his office that evening, Lou Gehrig Burnett, my press secretary, read a statement by Poage. "He's throwing in the towel," Burnett said.

"Hébert's a different type," I said, and walked out of the door.

The next day, Tip O'Neill, the majority leader, and Carl Albert, the Speaker of the House, had issued statements saying Democrats who voted for me on the floor would be "out of order" and would be disciplined. They said a vote of the caucus was binding on all Democrats.

"Albert and O'Neill can't bind the caucus," I told Clarence Doucet, a free-lance writer I have known since he was a reporter and columnist for the *Times-Picayune*. "Only the caucus can bind itself by a two-thirds vote and only the caucus can strip members of seniority by two-thirds vote. I've read the rules and I understand them. There may be doors marked closed in some people's minds, but there are no locks that are locked." Later Albert modified his statement to "it would seem" to be "out of order," and O'Neill changed his statement to "in my opinion."

Congressman G. V. "Sonny" Montgomery of Mississippi, a close friend of mine and a member of the Armed Services Committee, stopped by my office. He said O'Neill had just told him that any Democrats who voted against the caucus' selection for chairman would be disciplined. Montgomery sensed that he had been given the message with the idea he would convey it to me. He also told me that on the way to my office he had run in to Representative Peter Rodino, the chairman of the House Judiciary Committee. Rodino told him he had delivered all the New Jersey delegation with the exception of one member to me in the caucus, but now he was unable to renew the pledge if it came to another caucus vote, and that it would be asking too much to deliver the vote if it came to the floor.

I began to realize that the deck was stacked against me. I discussed the situation with Melvin Price and Joe Waggonner of Louisiana, a power in the House and the head of the conservative Democratic Research Organization, a bloc formed to counter the Democratic Study Group. Waggonner was bitter about the developing situation. "These anti-defense groups have never been right," he said. "It was reform that brought the seniority system about. We're going from rule to ruin.''

I still had a great deal of loyal support, but my personal loyalty to friends was beginning to take precedence over my desire to retain the chairmanship at any cost. I decided to call off my war. "A situation has now come to my attention which would cause embarrassment to my many friends on both sides of the aisle as a result of intimidation, reprisals, and threats,'' I said in announcing my decision.

I am now informed that members of the Democratic Party in the House would be stripped of their seniority and committee assignments and expelled from the Democratic Caucus if they voted for me on the floor of the House in an open vote.

In spite of this, many have informed me that they would still vote for me in an open vote. So have many members of the Republican Party expressed that they would also vote for me despite retaliatory threats to them.

There is no doubt in my mind that a majority of the members of the House of Representatives desire me to be chairman of the House Armed Services Committee. However, under the circumstances just explained, I cannot in good conscience do anything that would embarrass or cause harm to my loyal friends who support me in my fight for a strong national defense.

Faced with the reality of the situation, I, therefore, will not take the matter to the floor of the House, but will accept the decision of the largely unidentified minority of 152 out of 435 members of the House of Representatives.

In the usual manner, I am next in seniority for the chairmanship of the House Ethics Committee. I have advised Speaker Albert, the chairman of the Democratic Steering Committee, not to consider me for that position.

I shall continue my fight for a strong national defense and the security of this nation in the future as I have in the past.

Following my decision, I noticed my staff members moping around the office with long faces. "The king isn't dead,'' I said in an effort to cheer them, "he just sleeps.'' My staff members were not the only ones saddened by the turn of events. Congressman Otis Pike, the liberal Democrat from conservative Long Island, had butted heads with me on the Armed Services Committee for 14 years, but we remained friends, for he, too, did not take philosophical and political differences personally. Pike, because of his liberal credentials and, perhaps because he was often mentioned as one of the most intelligent members of the House, was a darling of the freshmen, it was said that he could have had my chairmanship for the asking. Instead, he resigned from the committee, giving up 14 years of seniority in the process, for a seat on the Ways and Means Committee. He could have ingratiated himself with the freshmen and other liberals by firing a final blast at me. Instead, he showed his integrity.

"I have never been a great admirer of the seniority system," Pike began a message to his peers. "This year I gave up 14 years of it to switch committees (from Armed Services to Ways and Means). I voted against some of the old bulls. One, however, I voted for; he knows it and I want you to know it. His name is F. Edward Hébert . . . and I've probably had more fights with him than with any other member of Congress . . . and I disagreed with him on many issues. He won most of those fights but I had a few notches on my gun.

"He fought hard, and sometimes he'd get angry, and I fought hard and sometimes I got angry. Over it all, however, he remained fair. He could have been vindictive, but he wasn't. He made me a subcommittee chairman. He considered the issues which in my judgement needed considering. In my book he was a great chairman, and I grieve for his defeat." It was a kind and generous statement by a man who would not let ideology supplant principle. It warmed me to have the truth told even during a period when truth apparently stood for little among many.

Naturally, the loss of the chairmanship disappointed me, and I was stung by the vituperation and irrationality of the attacks upon my character. But I wasn't one to pine away the days sulking in the womb of my office. Immediately I set about salvaging what I could of my power and prestige. I was unanimously named to head the Armed Services Investigating Subcommittee, the one I had created when I conducted the Chamber of Horrors investigation, and which controlled all legislation in the committee. At meetings of the full committee, I sat to the immediate right of Price in order that the new chairman could consult quickly and privately with me on important issues. And Price began referring callers with tough inquiries to me. For all intents and purposes, I had the power I had before. Only the title was missing—some of the time.

Ironically, I was named permanent representative from my region of the country to the Democratic Steering Committee, the group which set caucus policy and nominates chairmen. Referring to my election to the steering committee, I said that my presence at the liberal-dominated committee meetings would be "like a bastard at the family reunion."

As I looked at the hourglass and saw the sands slip relentlessly from the top capsule to the bottom, I realized the time had come when I could no longer look back over my shoulder at the past, but instead I was compelled to keep my eyes glued on the future. I found myself in a position of being what I described as a statistical fatality. By this I mean that at seventy-four, I was in a bracket whereby my life span could come to an end at any time. This reality demanded that I make up my mind whether I would continue in Congress or retire at the end of my 18th term.

Throughout the years it has been said that the graveyards and old folks homes in my district were filled with those who kept waiting every two years for me to call it quits.

I was again in the enviable position of being assured of reelection. But I found myself in the unenviable position of being in a situation where I might be carried out instead of walking out and being able to see the last curtain fall on my two careers while I was still of sound mind and body.

I came to a conclusion. I discussed the entire matter with my old and dear friend, Ashton Phelps, who had succeeded the one man, who, if he had lived, would have guided me in any decision I would have made, Jack Tims, as president and publisher of the *Times-Picayune*. I went to New Orleans, and on the morning of March 29, 1976, in Phelps' office, at a conference attended by Ed Tunstall, editor of the *Times-Picayune*, a decision was reached that I would make the announcement on my future on March 31, 1976.

On that morning, the *Times-Picayune* carried the message—simple, direct, straightforward: "I will not seek reelection to the United States House of Representatives in the 95th Congress."

Writing that statement was one of the most difficult assignments I ever faced during my career as a newspaperman and a congressman.

The *Times-Picayune*, in a rare page one editorial entitled "Hébert: Hail, Farewell" said: "He was often the center of controversy—'Eddie' did not mince words or pull punches—but he was always a tower of strength, particularly in his special field, the armed services and national defense . . . But he was no captive of the services he went to bat for—the report of his energetic investigation of the My Lai massacre pilloried the Army for trying to cover it up and was timed by the wily former newspaperman for maximum headline impact."

Another old friend of mine, Phil Johnson, news director of WWL-TV in New Orleans, said in his own inimitable style in an editorial aired that night: "The retirement announcement of Congressman Eddie Hébert came complete with the Hébert stamp: It was dramatic, it was a complete surprise. And it will be making people talk for a long time. This is how Hébert does things . . . with an eye for effect and for maximum coverage, as befits an old newspaperman who became one of the greatest politicians in this state's history.

"Will he be missed? Of course. After 36 years, his seniority is awesome. He can pick up a phone and do in five minutes what it might take a new congressman five days to do. Or five weeks. He has been called a 'hawk' and 'superpatriot.' And he denies nothing. He made no bones about standing for a strong America. He still doesn't . . . And the best thing about this retirement . . . according to the man, himself, is that he can still be around to read all the nice things people will be saying about him. That sounds like Eddie Hébert. Congress will never be the same without him."

And on that March 31, I went to the floor of the House and stood in the Democratic well, where I had stood so many times before, and announced to my colleagues my decision to retire.

The words of my colleagues in reaction to my announcement still ring with gratitude in my ears.

Speaker of the House Carl Albert: "The departure of the gentleman from Louisiana is the departure not only of a friend, certainly a personal friend of mine, but the departure of an extraordinary man and an extraordinary legislator from these Halls, one of the strong men whose will is built of steel, whose determination is inflexible."

House Majority Leader Thomas P. "Tip" O'Neill, Jr.: "The armed forces of this great Nation owe a debt of gratitude to Eddie Hébert. He has been their champion and our defenses are strong today because of his dedication and fervor."

Chairman Melvin Price of the House Armed Services Committee: "I've had the pleasure of serving with Mr. Hébert for more than 30 years on the Armed Services Committee. I've never had a closer friend or wiser advisor."

Republican Leader John Rhodes: "The gentleman from Louisiana is a great American in every sense of the word and I am sorry he is leaving."

Representative Joe D. Waggonner, Jr., of Louisiana, a dear friend: "Eddie Hébert is beyond any shadow of a doubt one of the greatest Americans I have known. Eddie Hébert is beyond any shadow of a doubt one of the greatest public servants this Congress ever had."

Representative John Breaux of Lousisiana: "His contributions to the Nation's security are almost beyond measure and his work on behalf of Louisiana was untiring."

Representative David C. Treen of Louisiana: "I am grateful as an American citizen for his contribution towards maintaining this country's military strength. The chances for my children and grandchildren to enjoy their freedom as American citizens have been greatly enhanced by his service. Mr. Hébert is one of the great statesmen in the history of the House of Representatives."

The laudatory comments went on and on, and I am grateful to all the members of the House who saw fit to speak on that day. It was truly a heartwarming experience.

When I got back to my office I found on my desk a letter from the President of the United States. In it he said: "The strength and freedom of our country and its national security can be equated, in large measure, with your many years of devoted leadership of the Committee on Armed Services. I have never known you to fail to voice outspoken pride and faith in the principles upon which our great Nation was founded." It was signed, as he signs all of his personal notes, "Jerry."

How thankful I am that I can read the headlines, hear the applause, and smell the flowers.

As I conclude this chronicle of my life and times I am 74 years old, and despite the handicaps of the loss of one eye and partial blindness in the other, I can say that I have had not one but two successful careers: one as a newspaperman, the other as a congressman. I have put together what talent and intelligence, wit and charm, nature bestowed upon me to grab life's brass ring. I am guilty of vanity and, on occasion, autocracy. I am not beyond reproach. But I hope I have brought moments of enjoyment and entertainment to many through my personal pleasures at reporting sports, reviewing night club acts, and squiring beautiful ladies through the night. I had the pleasure of working on a newspaper with complex and colorful characters in a simpler more romantic time. This gave me the opportunity to play a role in freeing Louisiana from the corrupt grasp of the Long machine and Congress was part of my reward. There I exposed unscrupulous union officials who hindered the war effort against Hitler, and then I traveled to Europe to report on the ramifications of the holocaust. I chronicled waste in the military and brought about reforms which saved the American taxpayers billions annually. I decribed for the world the experience of witnessing the first hydrogen bomb explosion; I fought with and for seven Presidents; I exposed communist activities in government and the cover-up of My Lai by the Army. I am the father of a school to train physicians to serve the military. Most importantly, I believe I have played a major role in keeping America safe, and free. I have always sought to leave the world a better place than I found it.

All this I did while serving my district, my state, and my nation with an attitude and lifestyle which refuses to surrender individualism. And I have enjoyed it all so much.

To defy Power, which seems omnipotent;
To love, and bear; to hope til Hope creates
From its own wreck the thing it contemplates;
Neither to change, nor falter, nor repent;
This, like thy glory, Titan, is to be
Good, great and joyous, beautiful and free;
This is alone Life, Joy, Empire, and Victory.

Percy Bysshe Shelly
Prometheus Unbound

THE MEN OF THE FIRST

Here are the men who have represented the First Congressional District of Louisiana in the United States Congress.

1806–1809—Daniel Clark (territorial representative)

1809–1811—Julien de Lallande Poydras (territorial representative)

1811–1812—Vacant: Sens. Allan Bowie Magruder and Eligius Fromentin accorded privileges of House floor

1812–1818—Thomas Bolling Robertson

1818–1821—Thomas Butler

1821–1823—Josiah Stoddard Johnston

1823–1829—Edward Livingston

1829–1834—Edward Douglass White

1834–1839—Henry Johnson

1839–1843—Edward Douglass White

1843–1845—John Slidell

1846–1851—Emile La Sére

1851–1853—Louis St. Martin

1853–1855—William Dunbar

1855–1859—George Eustis, Jr.

1859–1861—John Edward Bouligny

1861–1863—Benjamin Franklin Flanders seated in 1863 by wartime resolution.

1863–1865—Vacant: credentials presented by M. F. Bonzano, A. P. Field, W. D. Mann, T. M. Welles and Robert W. Taliaferro, but their claims were not finally disposed of.

1865–1867—Vacant: credentials presented by Jacob Barker, Robert C. Wickliffe, Louis St. Martin, John E. King and John Ray and referred to the Committee on Reconstruction; no further action taken.

1868–1875—Jacob Hale Sypher

1875–   —Effingham Lawrence

1875–1883—Randall Lee Gibson

1883–1885—Carleton Hunt

1885–1887—Louis St. Martin

1887–1891—Theodore Stark Wilkinson

1891–1908—Adolph Meyer

1908–1919—Albert Estopinal

1919–1931—James O'Connor

1931–1941—Joachim Octave Fernandez

1941–1977—F. Edward Hébert

INDEX